MW01474744

Drivers of Global Business Success:
Lessons from Emerging Markets

Also by F. Zeynep Bilgin

BASICS FOR CONSUMER BEHAVIOR

YÜKSEK LISANS VE DOKTORA TEZLERI YAZIM EL KITABI (Handbook for Writing Theses and Dissertations)

Also by Gerhard Wührer

DER AUFBRUCH INS DRITTE JAHRTAUSEND: Die Jahre 1994–1999 aus Sicht des Instituts für Handel, Absatz und Marketing (The Setting-out for the Third Millennium: The Years 1994 to 1999 as Seen from the Department of Marketing at Johannes Kepler University) (*editor*)

INTERNATIONALE ALLIANZ- UND KOOPERATIONSFÄHIGKEIT ÖSTERREICHISCHER UNTERNEHMEN (The Capability of Austrian Enterprises for International Alliances and Cooperations) (*editor*)

TRENDS IM INTERNATIONALEN MANAGEMENT: STRATEGIEN, INSTRUMENTE UND METHODEN (Trends in International Management: Strategies, Instruments and Methods) (*co-editor*)

AUSWIRKUNGEN DES EU BEITRITTS FÜR ÖSTERREICHISCHE UNTERNEHMEN (Impact of EU accession for Austrian Companies) (*co-editor*)

```
HF1379  .D75 2004
```

0134110224356

```
Drivers of global
  business success :
     2004.
```

```
                              2007 09 10
```

Drivers of Global Business Success

Lessons from Emerging Markets

F. Zeynep Bilgin
Marmara University, Istanbul, Turkey

Ven Sriram
University of Baltimore, Baltimore, USA

and

Gerhard A. Wührer
Johannes Kepler University, Linz, Austria

With international contributions from experts in their fields

palgrave
macmillan

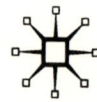

Editorial matter and selection © F. Zeynep Bilgin, Ven Sriram and Gerhard A. Wührer 2004

Individual chapters © contributors 2004

All rights reserved. No reproduction, copy or transmission of this publication may be made without written permission.

No paragraph of this publication may be reproduced, copied or transmitted save with written permission or in accordance with the provisions of the Copyright, Designs and Patents Act 1988, or under the terms of any licence permitting limited copying issued by the Copyright Licensing Agency, 90 Tottenham Court Road, London W1T 4LP.

Any person who does any unauthorized act in relation to this publication may be liable to criminal prosecution and civil claims for damages.

The authors have asserted their rights to be identified as the authors of this work in accordance with the Copyright, Designs and Patents Act 1988.

First published 2004 by
PALGRAVE MACMILLAN
Houndmills, Basingstoke, Hampshire RG21 6XS and
175 Fifth Avenue, New York, N.Y. 10010
Companies and representatives throughout the world

PALGRAVE MACMILLAN is the global academic imprint of the Palgrave Macmillan division of St. Martin's Press, LLC and of Palgrave Macmillan Ltd. Macmillan® is a registered trademark in the United States, United Kingdom and other countries. Palgrave is a registered trademark in the European Union and other countries.

ISBN 1-4039-1701-9

This book is printed on paper suitable for recycling and made from fully managed and sustained forest sources.

A catalogue record for this book is available from the British Library.

Library of Congress Cataloging-in-Publication Data
Drivers of global business success: lessons from emerging markets / edited by F. Zeynep Bilgin, Ven Sriram, Gerhard A. Wührer.
    p. cm.
Includes bibliographical references and index.
ISBN 1-4039-1701-9 (cloth)
1. International trade. 2. International business enterprises. 3. Globalization—Economic aspects.
I. Bilgin, F. Zeynep. II. Sriram, Ven. III. Wührer, Gerhard, A.
HF 1379.D75 2004
658.8'4—dc22   2004044688

10 9 8 7 6 5 4 3 2
13 12 11 10 09 08 07 06 05

Transferred to digital printing 2005

To my dad Fuat Bilgin and all my graduate students who inspired me with new ideas

                                                          Zeynep

To my wife, Angela, my mother, Seetha, and all my students from whom I have learned so much

                                                          Ven

To the children in emerging markets and their future societal competence

                                                          Gerhard

Contents

Preface	ix
Notes on the Contributors	xi

1 Introduction: Understanding Emerging Markets   1
    F. Zeynep Bilgin, Ven Sriram and Gerhard A. Wührer

Part I   Why Emerging Markets?

2 World Trade Trends   9
    F. Zeynep Bilgin, Ven Sriram and Gerhard A. Wührer

3 A General Look at Emerging Markets   26
    F. Zeynep Bilgin, Ven Sriram and Gerhard A. Wührer

Part II   Views on Emerging Markets: Management Thinking in Transition

4 Market Orientation from a Hungarian Perspective   41
    József Berács

5 Leadership in Central and Eastern European Countries   54
    Manfred Reichl, Gerhard A. Wührer and Ven Sriram

6 Market Entry Strategy of a Slovenian Jewellery Producer   61
    Vito Bobek

Part III   Views on Emerging Markets: Management in Practice

7 Give a 'FILIP' to Your Marketing Programme   73
    Rajan Chhibba

8 Export Success: Lessons from Award-Winning Pakistani Firms   85
    Farrah Arif and Irfan Amir

9 Gerdau: Multinational Steel Giant from Brazil   97
    Rusty Mae Moore

10 China Business: A Relationship-Based Market-Entry Approach   114
    Helena Chiu and Gerhard A. Wührer

Contents

11 The Attractiveness of the Azerbaijan Market: The Case of Betek 128
   Dilek Zamantılı-Nayır and F. Zeynep Bilgin

12 Expansion to International Markets by use of Product and Trade Name Franchising: The Case of Kompen 140
   Çağatay Ünüsan

13 Best Practices in Emerging Markets: Examples from the US Hotel Industry 152
   Michael A. Anikeeff

14 International Market Entry and Expansion Strategies of Anadolu Efes A.Ş. 168
   İrem Eren-Erdoğmuş, Hale Taşdemir-Çaloğlu and Muzaffer Bodur

15 Ashanti: Saving an African Mining Giant 182
   Mohamed H. Warsame and Franklyn Manu

16 From Obligation to Opportunity: A Case Study of Tasty Bite 193
   Ashok Vasudevan, Meera Vasudevan and Kartik Kilachand

Part IV Lessons Learned

17 From Classical to Neoglobal Perspectives 209
   F. Zeynep Bilgin, Ven Sriram and Gerhard A. Wührer

18 The Organization 218
   F. Zeynep Bilgin, Ven Sriram and Gerhard A. Wührer

19 The Markets 227
   F. Zeynep Bilgin, Ven Sriram and Gerhard A. Wührer

20 The People 235
   F. Zeynep Bilgin, Ven Sriram and Gerhard A. Wührer

21 The Operations 242
   F. Zeynep Bilgin, Ven Sriram and Gerhard A. Wührer

22 Concluding Thoughts 250
   F. Zeynep Bilgin, Ven Sriram and Gerhard A. Wührer

Appendix: Methodology for Networks – a Meta-Analysis 260

Bibliography 265

Index 267

Preface

What is really going on in emerging markets (EMs) from the point of view of international business operations? This question often intrigues executives from all over the world. In terms of a global vision, is this a question that is of interest only to the large multinational companies (MNCs) from advanced markets (AMs)? Do EM companies simply follow strategies developed in AMs or do they create their own unique strategies and global vision? Could their success be related to completely different and new approaches based on their cultural and business backgrounds, or is that possibility not a very realistic one? And if they do have a vision of their own, can it help other companies in other parts of the world and thereby contribute to management knowledge?

Without a doubt, the perspective of doing business in emerging markets can be unusual, novel and often astonishingly creative. With their growing economies and improvements in their infrastructure, the business environment in EMs has changed dramatically. Competition has become multifold, both among AM and EM firms. At this point, is it reasonable to speak of the global success of firms from EMs and, if so, on what is this success based? How do EM companies survive and succeed in a globally competitive environment?

These and other similar questions have motivated us and the contributing authors to identify the *drivers of global business success*, the hidden and sometimes overlooked success factors that have made many EM companies globally successful. Just as management theory and practice have been enriched by analysing the successful strategies of the better-known MNCs from economically developed countries, we try to present lessons learned from EMs and their companies, many of which may not be very familiar to readers from outside their home countries.

Our intention is to add to the understanding of business and address important developments in EMs for two audiences, academics and practitioners.

- *Academics*: As issues relating to success in EMs come to the fore, there is a need to understand the phenomena that drive this success. Institutions involved in educating and training future managers can use this book as a resource in understanding these markets from a fresh perspective and learn about the unique strategies applied. For academia, the book can be used at the graduate level (PhD, MBA, and certificate programmes) for courses such as 'International Perspectives in Emerging Markets', 'Trends in International Business' or 'Strategies for Newly-Developing Markets'.

- *Practitioners*: For many managers, success in EMs will hinge on being able to understand the strategies pursued by their competitors in these markets. This book will help identify these strategies. Also, EM managers may be able to adopt successful strategies employed by EM firms in other countries. Both private and public-sector executives of different countries can learn about successful new global strategies that may help them in their efforts to develop appropriate strategies in EMs.

The book is organized into four parts. Following our introductory Chapter 1, in Part I we provide an overview of global business trends and emerging markets. Parts II and III of the book comprise contributions from international experts in their field, followed in Part IV by our own detailed analysis of their contributions.

This book project began during the early startup phase of the collaboration between the Marmara University, Istanbul, and Johannes Kepler University, Linz. Ven Sriram was then teaching at Marmara University as a visiting Fulbright Scholar. During that important period, Professor Tunc Erem, Rector of Marmara University, helped create the environment where our collaboration could grow and flourish.

An undertaking like this could not have been completed without the help of several people who gave us ideas, motivation and encouragement. Our contributors very readily and enthusiastically shared their passion and knowledge about emerging markets. Their active cooperation and involvement has enriched the book, and their timely response enabled it to be completed on schedule. Stephen Rutt and Jacky Kippenberger, Publishing Director and Commissioning Editor respectively at Palgrave Macmillan, were extremely helpful and supportive throughout the entire demanding process. Our friend Daniel Yett in Istanbul was generous with his help in interpreting the contract and making it understandable. We also want to thank the 'Marketing Förderer Verein' Linz for financial support throughout the study. Dr Petra Kuchinka of Johannes Kepler University gave us the benefit of her insight and helped us improve parts of the manuscript. Asuman Atik, doctoral student at Marmara University spent countless hours helping us with the very important task of organizing and editing the manuscript. Elif Karaosmanoglu, doctoral student at Warwick Business School, and Dawn Taylor, Sarika Vaidya, Antonio Moore and Deborah Williams at the University of Baltimore were invaluable in helping us finalize everything. Fikri and Mustafa supplied us the tea and allowed us the extra time in the office we needed to finish our marathon discussion sessions at Marmara University. To all of them and our numerous other unnamed relatives, friends and colleagues, we are eternally grateful.

F. Zeynep Bilgin
Ven Sriram
Gerhard A. Wührer

Notes on the Contributors

Irfan Amir is Associate Professor of Marketing at Lahore University of Management Sciences (LUMS), Pakistan. Dr Amir joined LUMS in June 1994 after completing his PhD from Manchester Business School, UK. He has an MBA from the University of the Punjab, Lahore, Pakistan. He has written or supervised over a dozen case studies and thesis projects in the area of marketing, and has consulted widely with government and private organizations. His current research interests are in marketing services and global marketing.

Michael A. Anikeeff is Professor of Business, Chair of the Real Estate Department and Director of the Allan L. Berman Real Estate Institute at Johns Hopkins University. His research interests and publications are in the areas of seniors housing, urban development and strategic management. He has published in the *Journal of Real Estate Research*, *Journal of Real Estate Portfolio Management* and the *Journal of Managerial Issues*. Prior to joining Hopkins in 1991, Dr Anikeeff was a Senior Associate in Research and Education at the Urban Land Institute in Washington, DC. He also served as Assistant Professor in the Graduate Planning Programme in the School of Architecture, University of Arkansas, legislative assistant to Congressman Charles Bennett (D-FL), and Assistant Professor of Sociology at the University of North Florida. Dr Anikeeff received his AB from the University of California at Berkeley in social science, a Master's in city planning from the School of Architecture, Ohio State University and a PhD in sociology and planning also from Ohio State as well as an MBA in finance from American University.

Farrah Arif is on the Marketing Faculty at Imperial College, Lahore, Pakistan. She has an MBA from Imperial College and a BSc from Kinnaird College in Lahore. She started her career following her MBA in 1998. As a freelance marketing researcher she worked on consumer and industrial researches under the aegis of multinational organizations like Tetra Pak Pakistan Ltd. and Coopers & Lybrand Consulting, Pakistan. Her areas of interest and specialty are marketing simulation computer games and multivariate analyses. Currently, she teaches marketing at Imperial College.

József Berács has a Master's degree and a Doctorate in Economics from the Karl Marx University of Economic Sciences and is attached to the Department of Marketing at the Budapest University of Economic Sciences and Public Administration, where he has chaired the Department since 1992. He has earned a Candidate of Sciences degree from the Hungarian Academy of

Sciences, and been a Visiting Professor at the University of Texas (USA), Otago University (New Zealand), and Bordeaux Business School. He is a member of the Executive Board of the European Marketing Academy. He is the Deputy Chairman of the Marketing Committee of the Hungarian Academy of Sciences. Professor Berács has authored and coauthored more than 100 publications, issued in several languages. He is the editor of the series 'Transition, Competitiveness and Economic Growth', published by Akadémia Kiadó.

F. Zeynep Bilgin is Professor of Marketing at the Department of Business Administration in Marmara University in Istanbul, Turkey. Based on a DAAD scholarship, she worked on her PhD dissertation at the University of Hamburg, Germany for 16 months. She received her doctoral degree from the Boğaziçi University Istanbul, Turkey. She has been a Visiting Professor at the State University of West Georgia and at the University of Memphis in the USA. Her research interests are international marketing with a special emphasis on emerging markets, and service quality in marketing. She has published a book on consumer behaviour and also a handbook for thesis writing. She has book chapters and her research has appeared in international journals such as *Thunderbird International Business Review*, *The International Journal of Marketing*, *Journal of Business and Management*, *International Journal of Service Industry Management*, *Tourism Analysis* and *Case Research Journal* and many of her studies have been presented in several international conferences.

Vito Bobek is Professor of International Business in the University of Maribor, Slovenia. He holds BA, MSc and PhD degrees from the Faculty of Economics and Business, University of Maribor, and has worked for the Truck and Bus Factory of Maribor and the Economic Institute Maribor before joining the University of Maribor faculty. His teaching and research focus is on foreign trade policy and international trade. Besides his academic work he is involved in a variety of consultancy work for many companies and is also working with several institutions such as the European Commission Academic Expert Group (evaluation of projects within the Socrates/Erasmus programme), the Ministry of Economic Relations and Development of Slovenia (Strategy of International Economic Relations).

Muzaffer Bodur is Professor of Marketing in the Management Department of Boğaziçi University, Istanbul, Turkey. She received her DBA from Indiana University and worked as a Visiting Assistant Professor at George Mason University upon graduation. At Boğaziçi University she teaches global marketing management research and methods courses. She has organized training programmes and seminars for executives and served as the department head. She is a member of Academy of International Business (AIB) and Consortium for International Marketing Research (CIMAR). Currently, she is the editor of *Boğaziçi Journal: Review of Social, Economic and Administrative Studies* and serves on the editorial board of *Journal of International Marketing*. She had visited Uppsala University of Sweden and Odense University of Denmark to teach international marketing courses and conducted cross-cultural research on the implications of business culture for internationalization of firms. Her publications focus on marketing strategies of multinational firms in emerging markets, export-marketing management, expatriate managers and consumer satisfaction, dissatisfaction and complaining behaviour with services and intangible products.

Rajan Chhibba has a B. Tech (Electrical Engineering) from the Indian Institute of Technology, Delhi, and a MMS (Marketing) from J. Bajaj Institute of Management, Mumbai. He has several years' experience as a line manager, entrepreneur, professor and a consultant and has recently started his own management consulting company Intrim Business Associates after heading, as Managing Director South Asia, KSA Technopak – a specialized consumer-products retailing, fashion and healthcare consulting firm. Rajan was a global partner of the US-based firm. He also spent a year as Visiting Professor at the University of Rhode Island, USA. Rajan has handled large consulting projects for major clients including Indo Rama Thailand, Unilever India, Visa, Government of India, Indian Railways, La Poste, France, India Post, Philips, Godrej, Nokia, BPL, Mother Dairy, and ITC (BAT India). He also advised and helped implement the launch of two leading Indian food brands in the USA. He has written articles and is the author of *Starting a Successful Business* published by Penguin, and is an active member of many committees of the Confederation of Indian Industries.

Helena Chiu holds a PhD degree in business administration from Johannes Kepler University in Austria. Before Dr Chiu pursued an academic career, she worked for many years in the fields of project management and new business development for several large corporations in Europe, such as GE IT Solutions (branch in Austria), Hoedlmayr Logistics AG (Austria), and in Southeast Asia in Sahaviriya Public Co. (Bangkok, Thailand). Currently she is employed as an Assistant Professor of Marketing at National Kaohsiung First University of Science and Technology in Taiwan. Before she moved to Kaohsiung she was assistant professor at Chang Jung Christian University, Department of International Business in Tainan. Her principal areas of research and teaching are industrial marketing, international marketing, and relationship marketing.

İrem Eren-Erdoğmuş has a BA degree in political science and international relations from Boğaziçi University, Istanbul, and an MBA from Marmara University, Istanbul. She has been working as a Research Assistant in Marmara University since 1999, and is a PhD candidate in marketing at Boğaziçi

University, Istanbul. Her academic areas of research are international marketing, brand management, and customer-relationship management.

Kartik Kilachand is Executive Vice-President for Business Development at Preferred Brands Inc. Kartik started his career with GE and prior to co-founding Preferred Brands he spearheaded a global joint venture with PepsiCola International for marketing a range of specialty beverages in the USA, using India as a manufacturing base. As President of Parle International, India's largest beverage company, he set up and managed the manufacturing and franchising operations in the Middle East, Africa and the USA and created India's first global FMCG. Since 1990, he has been a consultant specializing in business development in the Asia/Pacific region, with particular focus on the Indian sub-continent. He was advisor to Tropicana Beverages' business development team in designing its entry strategy for India and then was designated project manager in setting up Tropicana India. An engineer by training (IIT, Mumbai), Kartik holds a Master of Science in electrical engineering from Cornell University and an MBA in international finance from the University of California at Berkeley. Kartik is currently a member of the Board of Directors of Tasty Bite Eatables Limited, India, and of Preferred Brands International LLC in Stamford CT.

Franklyn A. Manu is Professor in the Earl Graves School of Business and Management, Morgan State University, USA. He holds a BSc (administration) from the School of Administration, University of Ghana, Ghana, and MBA and PhD degrees from the Stern School, New York University, USA. His research interests are in the areas of foreign direct investment in African countries, social marketing programmes, and tourism. He is currently the Coordinator of the PhD programme in business administration at Morgan State University.

Rusty Mae Moore is Associate Professor of Marketing and International Business at Hofstra University, USA, where she has been on the faculty of the Frank G. Zarb School of Business for the past 26 years. Prior to coming to Hofstra, Dr Moore was on the faculties of New York University, the University of Texas at Austin, and the Thunderbird Graduate School of International Management. Dr Moore's doctorate is from the Fletcher School of Law and Diplomacy, Tufts University, and her undergraduate degree is from Northwestern University. Dr Moore held a Latin American Teaching Fellowship at the Escola de Administracao de Empresas de Sao Paulo da Fundacao Getulio Vargas in 1969–70, and a Fulbright Fellowship at COPPEAD, Universidade Federal do Rio de Janeiro, in 1986–87. She is a former Associate Dean of the Hofstra School of Business, and is the author of several monographs and papers dealing with international marketing focused on Latin America.

Manfred Reichl attended a high school in Salzburg, Austria, that specialized in music, then studied industrial engineering and management at the Technical University of Graz. He completed a Doctorate in Law at the University of Graz while continuing doctoral studies in industrial engineering at the Technical University of Graz, where he worked as an academic assistant at the Institute of Management and Organization. He then joined Hewlett Packard in Böblingen as European Marketing Programme Manager. He has been with Roland Berger Strategy Consultants since 1987, working in Munich and becoming Managing Partner of the company's Vienna office in 1992. He is today a Senior Partner of the Roland Berger Group, responsible for Austria and Central and Eastern European offices (CEE), and is a member of the Management Committee for Roland Berger's offices in Germany, Austria and Switzerland.

Ven Sriram is Professor of Marketing at the University of Baltimore, USA. A native of India, he holds a BA in Economics from Madras University, an MMS in Marketing from Bombay University and a PhD in Marketing from the University of Maryland, USA. He has been a Fulbright Scholar at Kathmandu University in Nepal and Marmara University in Istanbul, Turkey. He has also taught at Universidad Nacional de Lomas de Zamora in Buenos Aires, Argentina, and has been a Visiting Fellow at the Centre of International Studies at Cambridge University. His research interests are in the areas of marketing strategy, emerging markets, and global marketing. His work has been presented at several international conferences and has appeared in such journals as *International Marketing Review, Journal of Business Research, Journal of Retailing, Industrial Marketing Management, Omega* and *Case Research Journal*.

Hale Taşdemir-Çaloğlu has a BA in Business Administration from Boğaziçi University, Istanbul. Her MBA degree is from Pennsylvania State University, USA. Having worked in bank marketing in Turkey, she is currently a PhD candidate at (marketing) at Boğaziçi University, Istanbul. Her academic interests are in international marketing, entrepreneurship and relationship marketing.

Çağatay Ünüsan is a Professor of Marketing at Selçuk University, Konya, Turkey. He received his BA from Dokuz Eylul University, İzmir, his MBA from Selcuk University, and his PhD in marketing from Nottingham University, UK. His areas of expertise are in marketing channels, franchising, internet marketing, branding, and tourism marketing. His research has been published in journals such as *Journal of Marketing Management, Journal of Marketing Channels, Journal of Euromarketing,* and *Journal of Marketing World*. He is on the Editorial Review Board of the several business journals in Turkey and has participated in several marketing conferences nationally and internationally.

He was a president's advisor of the Konya Chamber of Industry, is a board of member of the Turkish Marketing Association and an honorary member of the Turkish Franchising Association and is currently president's advisor of the Association of Turkish Travel Agencies' Konya branch.

Ashok Vasudevan is a Chief Executive officer of Preferred Brands Inc. Ashok headed the India desk of Pepsi World Trade and prior to that was a member of Pepsi's start-up team in India as Vice President – Exports. During his tenure at Pepsi he helped set up India's international trading division in a wide range of businesses including commodity trading, food processing, and value-added exports. In the process, he has been involved in the design of several joint ventures in India and the USA and was awarded the Pepsi MVP award. Before joining Pepsi, Ashok spent 10 years with the Unilever group in India in various functions that included management development and sales and marketing, and during his last three years with Unilever was Operations Manager for Eastern Europe. Ashok regularly lectures at leading business schools in the USA and India. He has a Bachelors degree in agricultural economics and a Masters in business administration. Ashok is currently the Chairman of Tasty Bite Eatables Limited, India and of Preferred Brands International LLC in Stamford CT.

Meera Vasudevan is Executive Vice-President for Marketing at Preferred Brands Inc. Prior to co-founding Preferred Brands in 1994, Meera co-founded Quantum Market Research, India's first and largest specialist qualitative research company. She stared her marketing career with ORG-MARG, India's premier market research company. Meera has probably researched over 200 or more FMCG brands and conducted dozens of studies to track emerging trends, understand consumer motivation and predict behaviour and has done a lot of work in the area of product packaging and creative development. She has researched established brands with corporations like Unilever, Colgate, Cadburys, Johnson & Johnson, British American Tobacco, and done market entry research with PepsiCo, Gillette, Mars, Mattel, Nabisco, Citibank, and others. She has also worked closely with government departments and UNICEF on social research projects. Meera has lectured on qualitative research in various management institutions and has authored several research papers. She has a Bachelors degree in English with postgraduate qualifications in marketing and advertising. Meera is currently a member of the Board of Directors of Tasty Bite Eatables Limited India and of Preferred Brands International LLC in Stamford CT.

Mohamed H. Warsame is a doctoral student in the Earl Graves School of Business and Management, Morgan State University, USA. He holds a BSc (business administration) from the Stuart School of Business, Illinois Institute of Technology, USA and an MSc in finance from the University of

Strathclyde, Scotland. His research interests are in the areas of financial accounting and capital markets. Mr Warsame also has work experience as a financial analyst.

Gerhard A. Wührer is Professor and Head of Department of Marketing at the Johannes Kepler University, Linz, Austria. He studied management science and technology at the University of Stuttgart and became Assistant Professor in the Department of Management. He worked as a consultant and marketing researcher in Roland Berger Consultants, Munich. In 1988 he became Assistant/Associate Professor in the Department of Marketing and International Management at the University of Klagenfurt. He has been a Visiting Professor at the University of Northern Iowa, USA, the University of Trujilo, Peru, and Chang Jung Christian University, Taiwan. He is also permanent Visiting Professor at the University of Maribor, Slovenia. His areas of interest include international marketing, strategic marketing management, relationship and network marketing, marketing and network research and research methodology. He is also supervisor of several postgraduate/post-experience programmes at JKU and works as a consultant in several industries. In addition, he has edited a number of books and has contributed chapters to several books.

Dilek Zamantılı-Nayır is a Research Assistant in the area of organization and management in the Department of Business Administration and Business Informatics at Marmara University in Istanbul, Turkey. She studied business administration at Istanbul University and completed her MBA at Marmara University and is currently a PhD student there in the business administration department. She is a member of the Academy of Management and the Academy of International Business. Dilek Zamantılı-Nayır joined academia after 12 years, working experience in the multinational business environment in the fields of export, product management and PR. Along with her doctoral studies, she is currently involved in cross-cultural research jointly with the University of Manitoba (Canada) and Ohio State University (USA).

1
Introduction: Understanding Emerging Markets

F. Zeynep Bilgin, Ven Sriram and Gerhard A. Wührer

Introduction

Multinationals are changing life in big emerging markets (EMs) dramatically, but the opposite is also true.[1] For local companies, multinational company (MNC) entry can often appear to have the potential to be lethal. Accustomed to dominant positions in protected markets, they now face foreign rivals with a formidable array of advantages: financial resources, advanced technology, superior quality and products, powerful brands, and well-tested marketing and management techniques and skills.[2] How will they survive?

When EMs became attractive during the globalization process of business, it was initially the large MNCs (mostly headquartered in advanced markets, AMs) that tried to take advantage of the benefits of operating in these then unfamiliar overseas markets. Whether it was the search for cheap labour, outsourcing opportunities or foreign direct investments to expand the business from the saturated markets to new regions of trade, MNCs with their accumulated experience in marketing and management and their financial strengths felt that they were sure to succeed. However, recent evidence and research focusing on strategies of MNCs entering emerging markets shows that in some cases their initial successes have not been sustained and there has therefore been a reassessment of the early optimistic expectations, and their entry strategies have needed to be modified as a result. Lack of market knowledge and insufficient adaptations in marketing and management-related strategies have proven that standardized global strategies do not always work. For example, in the early 1980s many Japanese and US firms that invested in the Chinese automobile market limited their operations to licensing and stayed rather short-term-oriented, and missed the opportunities that were present in the growing passenger car market in China.[3] In Europe, while the Single Market programme aimed at an integrated marketplace by the end of 1992, many European companies have localized their operations in order to gain market share.[4] A good example is the Euro-oven of Electrolux, which has a special pizza setting for the Italian market and a special fish and shellfish compartment for the products sold in France. *Ad hoc* globalization efforts like in the case of Maytag's operations in China, or Whirlpool's efforts in selling a 'single world washer' in Europe just led to failure in these different markets.[5] And when MNCs from industrialized countries fail even in countries familiar to them, should companies from emerging markets try to adopt these inappropriate recipes?

Recent research on strategies of MNCs entering emerging markets sheds increasing doubt on the success stories once taken for granted. One of the voices[6] pinpoints the matter: '...marketing programmes are scarcely adopted for these markets. The result is low market penetration, disappointing market shares and poor profitability. These multinationals are trapped by their own devices in gilded cages, serving the affluent few but ignoring the potential of billions of new consumers that attracted them in first place.' The largest group of multinationals just transplanted the existing 'first-world' products with minimal investment into the new markets; but in reality, consumer goods companies in particular should not export their business models, products and marketing formulas when they seek a large and profitable presence in EMs.[7] McDonald's enjoyed early success when it opened in 1985 in Istanbul's city centre, however, during the economic crises of 1999–2002 many McDonald's outlets all over the country were closed and even localizing the menu did not help. Now the company is reorganizing and seeking a 'localizer' licensee.[8] Similarly, Nescafé, after many years of operations in Turkey, is now trying to create a new taste for Turkish consumers.[9] Rugman and Hodgetts[10] believe that there is no uniform spread of US-style market capitalism, nor are global markets becoming homogenized. Only in a few sectors, such as consumer electronics, is a global strategy of economic integration viable. Successful multinationals now design strategies on a regional basis while unsuccessful ones pursue global strategies. The examples of regionalization and strategic success are IKEA, Kingfisher, Nokia and Ericsson, Nortel Networks, Unilever, Procter & Gamble, and P&O.[11]

On the other hand, companies from EMs have also proven to be successful in world markets. In addition to the better-known South Korean success stories such as Hyundai, Daewoo and Kia in the automotive sector, and Samsung and LG in consumer electronics, there are other lesser-known examples such as the Malaysian car manufacturer Proton and Indian information technology companies Infosys and Wipro. In addition, Dawar and Frost[12] cite numerous examples of emerging markets companies that have successfully defended their home turf against strong multinational competition, and others that have even matched MNCs globally. Developing success strategies can sometimes take a decade or more, but they are positive examples for other new entrants to global marketing. Vestel, the Turkish electronics and white-goods manufacturer, has been operating since 1997 in the EU market with 1,300 different models and the company today exports 93 per cent of its production and develops and produces different models of TVs taking into account the detailed segmentation needs of the different European markets. For Vestel, size, industrial design, distribution networks and electronic specifications are some of the dimensions that have contributed to its success.[13] All these examples reflect the importance and necessity of local, tailormade strategy development in international markets, based on a deep understanding of the cultures and different types of mentalities prevailing in different market settings.

Philosophy, goals and objectives of the book

This book focuses on an EM perspective in global strategies and incorporates different examples from all over the world. The presentation and analyses of the different success factors in the selected countries will hopefully help firms from both EMs and AMs to reformulate and restructure strategy dimensions and to design new business strategies and concepts for the markets of the future. The book focuses on the major regions of the world where EMs are located. Hopefully, these lessons from a diversity of geographic areas, industry sectors and companies will facilitate a knowledge transfer from EM firms to other EM firms as well as AM firms.

The book's uniqueness relies on several factors. It is written from an emerging market perspective: all the material, specifically written for this book, focuses on the factors that contribute to success – whether in EMs or by EM companies. This makes it very different from the many books that cover mostly the AM perspective, describing strategies proven to be relevant in advanced markets or analysing these strategies' success and failure when applied in emerging markets. It tries to avoid typical business jargon and attempts to present material that is thought-provoking and different, but in a way that is interesting and readable. We present a highly diverse sample of emerging market studies from several countries all over the world in the hope that this research perspective offers a more universal view on business problems and solutions dealing with the topic of emerging markets. While some of the companies discussed here may be familiar to many readers, the intent is to also include the success stories of lesser-known, small and medium-sized enterprises from emerging markets. Clearly it is not feasible to represent all the emerging markets, however we try to merge the information provided in an attempt to create a new perspective for business knowledge.

Plan of the book

The book is organized in four parts: Parts I and IV are written by ourselves. Parts II and III comprise an anthology of contributions from a variety of experts from all over the world. They are a mix of conceptual pieces, empirical studies, and case study research.

Part I focuses on the key literature detailing the role of EMs in world trade, and provides an overview of the trends in international business and the importance of EMs in the future global world. Part II provides some insights into the current managerial thinking from emerging markets of Eastern and Central Europe, while Part III is composed of 10 studies from invited authors. Through these studies the contributors identify and discuss the global success drivers for EMs as well as EM companies, based on analyses of the business activities of real companies.

The earliest studies in the field of international business dealt with the examples of a company from an advanced market entering the market in another advanced economy. These studies are well-documented and are not within the scope of this book. The case of a company from an advanced market internationalizing into an emerging market is also common especially in the literature dealing with multinational companies.

Our research interest and the studies presented in Parts II and III cover EM to EM and EM to AM analyses, but also include one AM to EM analysis. Hence, this part of the book draws primarily on studies that detail an underrepresented situation, namely EM to EM. The evidence is then synthesized by ourselves in Part IV in order to determine whether any common points exist among the studies in terms of success factors, to identify the differences, to discuss the implications, and to draw important lessons. The framework used to analyse success factors revolves around a success diamond (Figure 1.1) composed of four basic dimensions for identifying and classifying the drivers of global success. These are: Organization, Markets, People, and Operations.

- The *organization* dimension focuses on the following factors: company organization and structure; company resources such as financial, technological, product and brand-based, skills and competencies; internal and external communication structure; enterprise culture-based vision and

Figure 1.1 Success diamond

mission; customer and market orientation; embeddedness of companies and actors and use of networks and networking.

- The *markets* dimension focuses on a list of factors: market screening, selection and expansion; market-entry mode and timing; and target marketing decisions.
- The *people* dimension relates to top management's commitment and management style; negotiation style employed by the executives; relationships with different parties such as partners, suppliers, distributors and customers (such as backward and forward linkages); employee skills, education, motivation, experience, qualification; social capital of actors and entrepreneurs for building and nurturing relations; as well as mind frames of actors (organizational culture).
- The *operations* dimension incorporates customer needs and expectations, trends in consumption; market stimulation strategy like preference-based strategies versus price focus; marketing-mix-related attempts (use or adapt 'traditional' marketing approaches as necessary such as marketing logistics, channel management); and focus on new trends (such as word-of-mouth focus, following new trends in distribution).

This approach is consistent with that advocated by Cavusgil, Ghauri and Agarwal[14] who recommend that firms investigate five basic areas before beginning internationalization attempts. These are: business background, motivations for going international, top management commitment, product strengths and market-specific strengths. The fit between the firm-specific capabilities and the internationalization process are very important. A close look at the dimensions stated earlier and the five basic areas recommended by Cavusgil, Ghauri and Agarwal reveal certain similarities:

- Business background: organization dimension
- Motivation to go international: organization/people dimension
- Top management commitment: organization/people dimension
- Product strengths: operations dimension
- Market-specific strengths: markets dimension

The framework itself is tentative and expresses a very general view on drivers of global success. It is merely a guide rather than a conceptual model from the outset. The different studies in Parts II and III, sequenced largely based on the commonality in their organization characteristics, concentrate on specific factors in this framework which should not be seen as a straitjacket or a rigid theoretical framework which might constrain innovative ideas or new concepts, but rather as a structure that provides a backdrop which fosters new and challenging approaches.

Part IV compiles and synthesizes the information generated in Part I and Parts II and III, and focuses on identifying differentiated, unique as well as common denominators of success in selected markets. It provides a detailed analysis of the 10 studies presented in Part III, using the conceptual mapping technique (see the Appendix for details of this methodology). This analysis should add to our knowledge of what drives the success of emerging market companies and what determines success in emerging markets.

Notes

1. C.K. Prahalad and K. Lieberthal, 'The End of Corporate Imperialism', *Harvard Business Review* (July–August 1998): 69–79; J. Stiglitz, *Die Schatten der Globalisierung* (Berlin: Siedler, 2002).
2. N. Dawar and T. Frost, 'Competing with Giants. Survival Strategies for Local Companies in Emerging Markets', *Harvard Business Review* (March–April 1999): 120–9.
3. Z. Hai-Yan and D. van den Bulcke, 'The Restructuring of the Chinese Automotive Industry: The Role of Foreign Direct Investment and the Impact of European Multinational Enterprises', in C.C.J.M. Millar, R.M. Grant and C.J. Choi (eds), *International Business – Emerging Issues and Emerging Markets* (Basingstoke: Macmillan – now Palgrave, 2000): 290–312.
4. M.E. Bleackley and P.J. Williamson, 'European Integration and the Restructuring of MNE Operations', in C.C.J.M. Millar, R.M. Grant and C.J. Choi (eds), *International Business – Emerging Issues and Emerging Markets* (Basingstoke: Macmillan – Palgrave, 2000): 176–99.
5. S. Samiee, 'Globalization of Firms: Strategies and Outcomes', in M. Kotabe and P. S. Aulakh (eds), *Emerging Issues in International Business* (Cheltenham: Edward Elgar, 2002): 201–22.
6. N. Dawar and A. Chattopadhyay, 'Rethinking Marketing Programs for Emerging Markets', *Long Range Planning*, 35 (2002): 457.
7. J.A. Gingrich, 'Five Rules for Winning Emerging Market Consumers', *Strategy – Management – Competition*, Second Quarter (1999), www.strategy-business.com/strategy/99204/page1.html (retrieved on 17 July 2001; 5 pages).
8. 'McDonald's Türkiye'de yeniden yerelleşiyor', Ekonomi, *Hürriyet Newspaper* (20 November 2002): 10.
9. 'Nescafe'den Türkiye'ye özel tat', Ekonomi, *Radikal Newspaper* (1 November 2003): 12.
10. A. Rugman and R. Hodgetts, 'The End of Global Strategy', *European Management Journal*, 19, 4 (2001): 333–43.
11. Ibid.
12. Dawar and Frost, 'Competing with Giants. Survival Strategies for Local Companies in Emerging Markets', op. cit.
13. 'Başarının Sırrı Farkı Yaratmak', Söyleşi, *Radikal* (26 August 2002): 12.
14. S.T. Cavusgil, P.N. Ghauri and M.R. Agarwal, *Doing Business in Emerging Markets: Entry and Negotiation Strategies* (Thousand Oaks: Sage, 2002): 51–5.

Part I
Why Emerging Markets?

2
World Trade Trends

F. Zeynep Bilgin, Ven Sriram and Gerhard A. Wührer

This chapter reviews the history of emerging markets, examining moves towards regionalism as well as the opposing forces of integration and disintegration, and the impact of globalization and the recent backlash against it. It captures key recent historical trends but recasts them from an EM perspective. Much of this is not new, although some of it is certainly still evolving. However, our desire is to understand the current condition of emerging market countries by examining their recent history which may provide useful insights since it may reveal the extent to which their present state is a function of their past.

Emerging market history

The events of the second half of the twentieth century gave rise to a variety of developments in economic and political terms, with many parts of the world going through a dynamic change from the Second World War to the Cold War period up to the collapse of the Soviet Union and the subsequent collaboration of efforts through integration such as the European Union (EU) and the North American Free Trade Agreement (NAFTA). What is happening now may be termed a 'paradigm shift' as the changes seem to be so fundamental and demand new approaches from the point of understanding and conducting international business.[1]

So far, the changes taking place can be grouped under three major waves: (1) from colonialism to political freedom, (2) from communism to capitalism and (3) from economic/political authoritarianism to a free market orientation.

For a long time now, the Western world has been deeply concerned with the impact of communism on society. While some of the political aspects of the way communism has been practised – repression of freedom, violation of human rights and so on – are not relevant to this book, communism's impact on the economy certainly is. Indeed, for many emerging markets of Eastern Europe, and others such as China and Vietnam elsewhere, communism has been arguably the most important historical backdrop against which to understand recent developments. However, it is worth remembering that for most other emerging markets, communism was never really the issue. Their present and future cannot be properly understood without recognizing the impact of another Western export – colonialism. Here again, the social dimension has to be separated from the economic one. When one realizes that most former colonies (outside the Americas) have been independent fewer than 50 years and some African countries barely 25, the significance of colonialism takes on even greater import.

The other significant item of note that has been a part of the recent history of emerging markets, particularly in Central and South America, the Middle East, but elsewhere as well, has been authoritarianism in its various forms. Some of it has been military and other civilian, but its impact on the local economy has been undeniable. It should be emphasized that we are not suggesting that the following categorizations are mutually exclusive; in fact it will be immediately apparent that there is some overlap between them. We merely use them as a framework within which to understand some of the key forces that have shaped the economies of many emerging markets in the last century. We now take a closer look at these three movements.

Colonialism

For much of Africa, Asia, the Caribbean and the Middle East, movements for independence from European powers have characterized the period since the 1950s. For most, the colonial and immediate post-colonial period meant a reliance on the export of agricultural and extractive products to the 'mother' country such as rubber from Malaysia, textiles from India, jute from Bangladesh, copper from the Democratic Republic of Congo, oil from the Middle East and cocoa from Ghana and the Ivory Coast; and the import of manufactured goods to the colonial territories. It was an exchange with special rates, often favouring foreign goods and ruining the domestic (non-) competitive industry. While many former colonies have been able to make successful transitions to manufacturing, tourism and other industries to drive their exports and economic development, others still remain dependent on these products for their survival. In addition, few of these countries are involved in the processing of these products, where most of the value is added, due to the lack of the specialized machinery and equipment that is often needed. As a result, much of their labour is engaged in low-end activities such as extracting and harvesting and the resulting export is processed, packaged and marketed elsewhere, where the majority of value is captured. In addition, even today, many of these post-colonial societies are blighted with civil unrest and political instability that have inhibited their ability to attract the necessary foreign investment to their industries.

Communism

For nearly a century, different parts of the world, particularly Russia and all the countries around, tried a system where the economic and social welfare of citizens was secured by the state alone. This created a closed economy behind walls where interaction with the rest of the world was highly limited. This method of self-sufficiency, however, was the big barrier in the development of international trade relations.

As mentioned earlier, for many European emerging markets, it is now the struggle to escape from the damaging vestiges of communism that has characterized their recent history. Some of these countries have a pre-communist history, such as Poland and the Czech Republic, which was entirely capitalistic, that makes them different from most post-colonial countries. Since the collapse of communism in the Soviet Union and Eastern Europe in the late 1980s, many of the former communist countries have created free market economies and have hence embraced different forms of market capitalism to varying degrees. In fact, people have argued that the ideological conflict between Marxism and capitalism is dead, with capitalism as the clear winner.[2] The future for many of these countries is now inextricably linked to Western Europe and the EU, with its promise of market access and new investment. Indeed, the eastward expansion of the EU in the twenty-first century is testament to that. While the overt consequences of communism may disappear swiftly, the deep-seated effects (such as the reliance on the state and the suppression of entrepreneurial initiatives) may take longer to erase. Besides, business knowledge is at its infancy in many of these markets, and because prior fundamental capitalist experience is lacking, these countries will enjoy the advantage of developing their own system on their way to becoming promising EMs, such as the case in Hungary.[3]

Interestingly, many formerly communist countries and other nominally communist countries such as China have now begun to privatize large swathes of their economies[4] and have turned to market socialism rather than communism in its more rigid and doctrinaire form.

Authoritarianism

Unfortunately in many cases, authoritarianism has not been just limited to civilian controls from the government but also military controls over societies. We use the term authoritarianism to refer to a wide variety of civilian and military controls over economic and political freedoms. Unlike, centrally planned socialism, these societies permitted some amount of private ownership and control over the factors of production. Here again, there is an overlap with the movements discussed above. For example, many of the authoritarian regimes of Latin America, Asia and the Middle East were once colonies. Some, such as Singapore are examples of economically successful, if authoritarian[5] post-colonial countries whereas others, mainly in South

America, are now making a transition to market capitalism. For many, such as Argentina,[6] this transition has been painful but they appear publicly committed to it. However, massive unemployment and a 21 per cent shrinkage in GDP in 2002[7] have put privatization and reform in doubt in Argentina, and possibly elsewhere.

Another area of overlap is the degree of state participation in the economy, as under communism. Here again, many of these countries have begun to privatize many hitherto state-owned industries. In Turkey until 1980, import-substitution-based protectionist policies dominated the mixed economy run by five-year plans. Although these plans still prevail, they have a more long-term goal-oriented role, and export promotion coupled with trade liberalization encouraged foreign trade and inward foreign direct investments (FDI), helping Turkey to become one of the leading EMs.

There is also some overlap between communism, colonialism and authoritarianism in economic policy in that many of the post-colonial societies such as India initially adopted many socialist principles in the way that they patterned their economies. Many such countries initially believed that the state should control the 'commanding heights' of the economy and thus either nationalized or tightly controlled several key industries (such as coal and steel production, broadcasting, banking, transportation). Similarly, many Arab countries that were colonies of European powers have been governed by authoritarian regimes in their post-independence period. While there is some private ownership, many sectors of the economy are owned, controlled or tightly regulated by the state.

The preceding discussion has tried to recap the recent past of many emerging markets in order to understand their present situation, which may offer some insight into their future. While it appears that free market economy in some form is the way ahead for most countries, in other words the basic 'hardware'[8] for their economies, emerging markets are at various points on that road. Some such as China and India appear to have decided to slowly combine private with state ownership, while others like Turkey have opted for a more rapid transition. In some cases the speed of change has been externally driven by, for example, the requirements for membership in the EU or mandates from international lending institutions as in the case of Argentina and Turkey, while in other situations internal considerations are the driver. In India, for example, fears of massive unemployment and social upheaval and resistance from trade unions and other groups have meant that governments have chosen to privatize gradually so as to minimize hardship to workers in state-owned enterprises. What appears beyond doubt, however, is that there is a high correlation between the degree of economic freedom and the extent of market orientation. In the Heritage Foundation's[9] 2003 Index of Economic Freedom, most emerging markets are ranked as less free than economically advanced countries (North Korea and Cuba are ranked as the least free respectively, while Singapore and

Hong Kong are the freest). While there are many other, arguably equally important, dimensions to consider in ranking countries, understanding the factors that have shaped their history is an important first step to appreciating what factors will shape the economic future of emerging markets (see Manrai and Manrai[10] for a summary of the key historic developments and their impact on emerging markets).

Integration and disintegration attempts

There appear to be two major, and opposing, trends emerging in world markets. On the one hand, countries are integrating to form economic and even, in the long run, political unions, that is a trend towards centralization; whereas on the other they are disintegrating to form independent new countries, a trend towards decentralization. It is surprising to note that while in both cases there is clearly an attempt to create a free market economy and encourage foreign direct investments, at the same time there is a desire to preserve cultural identity and value systems.

Regionalism

Economic cooperation among nations to achieve economies of scale, improvements in terms of trade, and increased economic growth has been a goal for many countries, particularly after the Second World War. The benefits of economic integration are seen as larger potential markets for members, lower prices and better quality products due to cross-border competition, and lower distribution costs of selling to neighbouring countries.[11] Economic cooperation and mutual dependence can also lead to closer political ties, thus minimizing the threat of conflict in many unstable parts of the world. In the absence of effective and quick multilateral solutions, countries may prefer regional integration in order to address their common concerns.[12] Much of the benefit from political stability will accrue from cross-border investment more than trade since the presence of investments in another country is more of a deterrent to conflict.[13] Regionalism and liberalization of trade through the World Trade Organization (WTO) could result in significant trade gains for the EMs.[14] On the other hand, the potential for stabilization of the economy as well as the political scene is one of the basic reasons why EM countries especially feel the pressure to join one of the regional agreements.

Perhaps one of the earliest examples of an attempt at multilateral cooperation was the Commonwealth, a loose and often unwieldy attempt by Britain and most of its former colonies to create a preferential trading system. The decision by the United Kingdom to join the EU (the European Economic Community as it was then) in 1973 diluted the influence of the Commonwealth as a trading bloc but it still exists, largely as a political and cultural entity. Many emerging markets of Africa, Asia, the Caribbean and the

Middle East (in addition to AMs like Australia, Canada and New Zealand) are Commonwealth members. The formation of new regional groups, and the revival of others, in the last 15 years appear to suggest that the benefits of regional integration outweigh the costs. These groups are often formed on the principle that since the 'first-best' option of non-discriminatory global free trade, such as that visualized by the WTO, is often not easily attainable, free trade among a smaller group of countries provides a reasonable 'second-best', more achievable, alternative.[15] These regional agreements are often seen as the first step toward a global non-discriminatory trade regime.[16]

Perhaps the most ambitious, multilateral initiative aimed at creating a global trading system is the WTO, the successor to the General Agreement on Tariffs and Trade (GATT). Formed in 1995, and headquartered in Geneva, with the goal of creating a freer trade world, the WTO has not been without controversy (see the section on Anti-Globalization). While its former Director General Renato Ruggiero claimed, 'Free trade is a process that cannot be stopped',[17] it remains to be seen whether the organization succeeds sufficiently to render other preferential trade agreements irrelevant. In the meantime, other, smaller, mainly trading regional blocs continue to exist, while new ones are formed with the aim of reducing barriers to trade between members (for a thorough and complete analysis of attempts by emerging markets to create preferential trading agreements, see Page[18]). It should be pointed out that, with rare exceptions, most emerging market attempts at creating regional trading blocs have failed to live up to their initial expectations. Some of the reasons for this include economic instability, political disagreement among members, and low intra-regional trade prospects, which in turn has led to a general lack of commitment to the association.

Emerging markets that have been able to gain membership into successful blocs (such as the Eastern and Central European countries joining the EU) may benefit from this membership. While this may be true for the EU, questions and suspicions have been raised about emerging markets joining regional agreements such as the Free Trade Area of the Americas (FTAA) and the Asia-Pacific Economic Cooperation (APEC) agreement. Some critics argue that 'the FTAA is a pawn of US supremacy...an imperialist, neocolonialist project for Latin America'.[19] Thus, while emerging markets will benefit from participation in international trade, they cannot rely entirely on this trade as the main force for their development. Ultimately, they will have to cooperate regionally with other emerging market countries in order to reduce their reliance on developed countries in order to become stronger and more self-reliant. While the WTO rules are intended to foster greater trade, there are those that argue that the 'most powerful nations in the WTO – the US and the EU – have, in key sensitive sectors such as agriculture and garments, exempted themselves from the very disciplines that they now expect to be rigidly applied by other parties'.[20] Economically advanced countries subsidize their farmers by around $1 billion a day, making it hard for farmers in developing countries to compete.[21] These subsidies escape WTO sanctions because they are considered 'non-trade distorting'. Situations such as this cast serious doubt on whether the world trade regime being pushed by the WTO will be fair to emerging market economies. However, given that emerging markets have only limited influence over WTO rules, stimulating intra-regional trade in their trading blocs will be in their own best interest.

Disintegration

Paradoxically, while many countries look to strengthen regional ties with neighbours and enhance trade between themselves, in many parts of the world there is another force trying to break countries up. The motivations for these two forces are frequently very different. Regionalism and integration are normally motivated by the economic argument of the benefits from trade and globalization in general – increased employment and investment, foreign exchange earning, cheap imports, enhanced productivity and so on.[22] Disintegration is usually an outcome of political and cultural differences within countries and inequities perceived by certain groups within those countries. Examples from the recent past are many. The collapse of the Soviet Union saw the breaking away of the many former Soviet republics and the creation of new countries, some of which are now EU members. In Europe, similar situations have arisen in the former Czechoslovakia and Yugoslavia. East Timor broke away from Indonesia and Eritrea from Ethiopia. Separatist and secessionist groups are active in India, Russia, Spain, Sri Lanka, Turkey and other parts of the world as well.

Globalization–antiglobalization trends

At this point it is important to look at another dimension of integration and disintegration. These are the attempts towards globalization and the anti-globalization-related views and actions that have a tremendous role in shaping the global shift of today.

Globalization

The last decades of the twentieth century were highly influenced by the trend towards globalization. The success and significance of globalization, however, is an open question as far as the applicability of uniform standardized strategies in different markets of the world is concerned. Standard strategies relevant for AMs of the world economy are not always successful in the newly emerging markets of the future. For example, multinational companies rushed into EMs with their own, domestically-used advertising strategies assuming that the same type of lifestyles existed in different markets. However in many cases the choice criteria of customers differed – convenience was less important than the price in EMs; besides, local competitors' knowledge of the culture was largely overlooked.[23] So, the hegemony of the

MNCs from AMs is threatened by the power of a variety of firms from EMs. Regardless of size, in the global world of today, the 'fittest' with a global cultural orientation will survive. A number of small and medium-sized firms from all over the world are now influential in international trade; enjoying the liberalization of international trade policies in their countries, domestic-market leaders from emerging economies now operate in international markets and keep up with foreign competition hence, 'the idea that the global marketplace is the sole domain of large multinationals must change'.[24] Hence, new visions have to be developed based on the lessons learned in the last decade of the twentieth century.

The benefits of globalization were anticipated to be greater mobility for companies, closer ties were expected to facilitate global standardization policies, and easier access to free flow of information and knowledge. Also, global mega-brands were expected to become more powerful; consumers would have more buying options in a healthy competitive environment; enjoying affordable prices and high-quality items and consumer consciousness and protection were expected to improve.[25] But, in many cases, these benefits are more easily realized by multinationals, which serve a small sliver of the global customers in EMs, and this is not sufficient for investors to cover the costs of operating in a new market setting; this necessitated a shift from globally-standardized to locally-adapted programmes for EMs[26] in order to generate success. Pure globalization where the world becomes a true single market for standard products is seen today as a utopian view, an illusion of an inevitable worldwide free market, a rather ideological fantasy[27] that is also strongly opposed by cultural and political factors.

Unfortunately, in most management books and articles about international business operations the focus is still from a Western perspective, and most of the theories and solutions suggested do not hold true and are not relevant for much of the rest of the world. In fact what is often neglected in these books and articles is that many of the world's organizations function based on rules other than those relevant for Western societies, such as family-like human relationships in business operations.[28] But, as long as a true understanding about what globalization of today represents is not developed, globalization will be subject to criticism for long into the future. The work of groups such as the International Forum on Globalization offers alternatives to globalization.[29]

The need to encourage and accelerate international capital movements as an important feature of globalization gave rise to two big organizations after the Second World War: the International Monetary Fund (IMF) and the World Bank (WB), both the result of the Bretton Woods system.[30] Without a doubt the IMF and the WB play a decisive role in the societal development of emerging market nations in general, and the debate concerning the role of these two institutions has been ongoing for a long time. Perhaps it has become much fiercer since an insider, the former chief economic advisor to the World Bank, Joseph Stiglitz wrote a critical review[31] of the practices of both of these institutions. Stiglitz says that globalization itself is neither good nor bad;[32] it has the potential to do good on a broad basis as long as the globalizing countries become global at their own pace.

Although the hope is that the support of the IMF and the World Bank will help them to stay competitive in the global economic environment, 'emerging market economies are suffering from capital outflows and higher borrowing costs'.[33] Being aware of this fact makes people in these countries more and more suspicious about the benefits tied to globalization.

The challenge to globalization: the power of culture

Societies often have different ways of perceiving business life based on their own cultural characteristics. As a result, it is not only cross-cultural negotiations but also the entire process of strategy development in international business that is affected. Difficulties in reconciling diverse cultural values all over the globe constitutes one of the major challenges of globalization.

Scholars of international business deal with the problem of understanding the reasons behind these differences based on a variety of concepts developed in the field. These include categorizing societies as low or high-context;[34] talking about the social values relevant in different societies that affect business life directly;[35] and focusing on individual characteristics, plus the attitudes towards time and to the environment as determinant factors affecting business relations in diverse cultures.[36] Hofstede, Hampden-Turner and Trompenaars are researchers who evaluate national culture as continuing to be critically important in the selection of organizational structures and methods, although transnational firms also create their own corporate culture applicable globally in form of convergent strategies.[37] National differences in cultural values mainly influence personal style, rewards desired, how people relate with others, and the degree of contextual structuring they seek.[38] Further, contingency studies reflect that the environment has a great impact on applicability and hence the effectiveness of business methods.[39]

Hofstede was criticized that the surveys used in his research were developed by AM scientists and cannot therefore be truly applicable to EM settings. Also, most of the theoretical perspectives used for cross-national organizational studies derive from Western scholarship, whereby an attempt is made to develop general social theories to trace the development of different societies.[40] But to what extent will these theories and applications match what is required by the social systems of EMs? In fact the diversity of the environmental factors may be one of the reasons for that criticism. For cultural studies, new dimensions need to be developed to more truly reflect value systems in EMs.

Culture is one of the basic dimensions to be considered when it comes to differences between EMs and AMs, and even within the group of EMs. Textbooks are full of examples of how successful managers of AM firms fail when they are in a different cultural setting. In many cases these examples reflect the problems experienced in EMs or other newly developing economies, whether based on language, non-verbal communication, or contrasting cultural values.[41] It is interesting to note that when cultural differences between AMs and EMs are significant, it is not surprising that global strategies applied by AM multinationals in EMs have not always proven to be very successful in the long run. On the other hand, when cultural differences between countries are insignificant, some lessons can be learned on how to cope with differences observed in the new market environments in which they want to operate.

Even a brief look at the unified Europe reveals that there are significant differences not just between Germanic and Latin Europe,[42] but even between the neighbouring Belgians and Dutch that directly affect management styles, and nowhere do cultures differ so much as inside Europe.[43] So when this is true, it is no wonder that managers experience perceptual differences when they move from AMs to EMs or vice versa.

In their study, Zivko, Zver and Bobek[44] compared countries within Europe, and the results on 25 countries in and around Europe show that there are significant differences in economic culture between West European and European transition countries, as well as within European transition countries. It is in Western European countries that the paternalistic syndrome is lowest and also that the strongest connection between democracy and economic efficiency is identified. Also, different perceptions exist within Europe towards the privilege syndrome that legitimates taking advantage of political power, and the black economy syndrome where tax evasion is justified. Perceptions are even different between religious subgroups – Catholic, Protestant or Orthodox – in Europe.

On the other hand, a different study[45] has analysed cultural developments during the present globalization period based on 'cultural Balkanization', a term that describes the tendency to assert local identities over national ones, in reference to the cultural and ethnic fragmentation that is part of the outcomes and contingencies of globalization. Globalization and cultural Balkanization both undermine national identity. At the same time there is a tension between the two insofar as globalization attacks national identities because it emphasizes universal cultural elements, while cultural Balkanization reasserts local identities at the expense of national ones to avoid a reduction of cultural norms.

Cultural Balkanization has several implications for international business. In international management there has been great interest in creating a global organizational culture within a global organization. If cross-vergence by merging from local and global cultural sources to form a third new mix of culture is not just a temporary phase but also a permanent condition, it may be that such a global organizational culture will never occur, or will only do so under very special conditions.

Under cultural Balkanization, viable configurations of leadership will continue to develop but it makes a universal leadership philosophy, beyond certain core attributes, unlikely even in global companies. In international business the effects of Balkanization have an impact on the increased appreciation of local and ethnic identities. The complex relation between the global and the local is just beginning to be examined in cross-cultural research, and it appears that one of the elements of global culture is local identity.

Hence, culture cannot be ignored when firms internationalize and try to focus on global strategies. Culture itself is one of the basic factors motivating anti-globalization attempts, and a complete understanding of this phenomenon is necessary in order to develop the new dimensions of global business.

Anti-globalization

In this new millennium, various groups – environmental, labour, political, social – have begun to question the value of globalization, arguing that it has done little to reduce poverty and raise living standards in developing countries while multinationals, mostly from economically developed countries, have profited handsomely from it. While some have argued that globalization has resulted in gains for large numbers of people worldwide,[46] others counter that due to the power of corporate interests, organizations such as the WTO are putting corporate profits ahead of issues relating to human development.[47] Critics of globalization contend that emerging markets and their consumers are generally the losers from globalization, although Klein[48] suggests that there is damage from globalization in the developed world as well since global brands give consumers fewer choices and displace local culture. The massive protests at IMF and WTO meetings around the world indicate that the anti-globalization movement enjoys some support. Economists have argued that while free trade and free market capitalism have brought prosperity, these protests may also reflect growing disquiet about human rights, income distribution and other social issues as political power shifts from states to corporations.[49] Others have suggested that the cocktail of free markets and democracy resulting from globalization has had a devastating impact on the developing world.[50]

Not all expressions of the anti-globalization sentiment involve street protests, riot police and massive demonstrations. Indeed, some are rather quirky, whimsical and distinctly peaceful. Take, for example, the Slow Food and Slow Cities movements that originated in Italy and are now resonating with people in other parts of the world. Initially conceived in the 1980s as a response to the opening of a McDonald's restaurant next to the Spanish Steps in Rome,[51] the Slow Food movement emphasizes traditional and local foods and simpler, tastier and slower meals, the very antithesis of fast food. The international movement was founded in Paris in 1989 and boasts

77,000 members in 48 countries.[52] Part of its appeal certainly is its attempt to undo the homogenizing influence of globalization.

In a similar vein, the Slow Cities movement, an offshoot of Slow Food, argues that while globalization has benefits, it 'does tend to level out differences and conceal the peculiar characteristics of single realities'.[53] Cities that sign on to the movement pledge to promote policies that fight what they see as the worst excesses of globalization. They therefore undertake to protect the environment and local culture and tradition. Several cities in Italy have signed the movement's charter, and cities from Brazil, Britain, Germany, Greece and Switzerland have applied for membership.[54] Both these efforts appear to be the stirrings of resentment against globalization and a reassertion of local and national identities.[55]

According to many economists and others, however, multinational entry into emerging markets usually creates overall improvement in working and living conditions,[56] although the benefits may accrue differentially creating greater relative differences.[57] Multinational investment increases the number of jobs available and, despite accusations of worker exploitation, pays higher wages than the going local rate. While some local businesses fail, the competition motivates others to improve their efficiency. However, others suggest that globalization's supposed benefits may be mythical and companies may be best served by operating locally and regionally.[58]

Notwithstanding the resistance to globalization, however, for many emerging markets their domestic markets are too small and they have to become successful exporters in order to survive and eventually develop. In addition, their companies will have to contend with multinational competition at home. While there are lessons to be learned from an overreliance on preferential trading agreements and the dependence they may engender,[59] the rules of world trade, whether fair or not, are very hard for emerging market governments and companies to change. Regional initiatives such as the FTAA do not plan North-to-South budget transfers nor are living-standard gaps between Latin American countries and the USA expected to narrow.[60] Yet FTAA membership will help some countries enhance their export capabilities and facilitate access to the US market. Their companies, and other emerging market companies in similar situations, will have to learn to play by the world trade rules and be globally competitive in order to take advantage of these opportunities or they will surely perish.

True globalization for success is defined by Caslione and Thomas[61] as 'global manifest destiny,' whereby companies develop a system of shared goals, values and behaviours and internalize a global mindset; that is, adapt their corporate culture and processes for the long term with huge insight, understanding and courage to take risk. Hence, just learning about the macro-environmental differences such as in economic, political and technological conditions or learning about the difference in culture and adapting the existing product according to these needs and expectations is not enough to be successful in overseas markets, particularly in EMs. Only internalizing the differences and creating new ways of management in the international arena can help companies to success in the future. This then creates a unique corporate culture, beyond understanding the country-specific values and requirements of these individual cultures.

For a firm to be successful in a global culture, certain criteria should be met:[62] first of all, the top management should be ready for a change in mind-set like Ranbaxy Pharmaceuticals from India from 1993 on. Also, the firm must be ready to integrate new ideas like Desc, S.A. from Mexico and, beyond that, a global customer-service strategy should incorporate customer focus, detecting needs beyond the revealed expectations, being flexible in operations and spotting trends. Hence any company operating in an EM or AM should first work on a cultural synthesis for the company and then for its operations abroad.

The global shift

A brief look at the developments in world trade reveals that an evolving global economy is creating worldwide competition. Kenichi Ohmae first introduced the Triad concept in 1990 to describe the flow of international trade. In this arena, the leaders of world trade today are Japan, North America and Western Europe as the 'Triad Power';[63] therefore, the 'first curve in world trade' occurred between economically advanced nations.[64] However, there are two important points to keep in mind: (1) the Triad not only used to interact within its triangle boundaries, but also grew its trade relations with the countries in geographic proximity: for Western Europe this was Eastern Europe, for North America the Latin American markets, and for Japan the Pacific Rim. (2) Some markets, principally in Western Europe and Japan, will be growing much more slowly over the next two decades than the markets in the rest of the world.[65] Developed markets are becoming saturated and stagnant,[66] and changing demographic patterns such as aging populations are leading to flat or declining sales for many products.[67]

Economic as well as political changes in the world over recent decades have created a new world order; new markets are emerging as a major growth opportunity. They are emerging because of their positive momentum, because they are committed to growth on a world scale, have the potential for growth and show great promise for providing a growing demand in a variety of target markets. They are large in size because they have become magnets for most of the world's most competitive firms, increasing their volume of international trade.[68] They are not only emerging, but also affecting the business expansion and investment strategies of many MNCs from developed economies.[69] Consequently, 'new and evolving markets' become proactive environmental forces influencing an organization and its industry's degree of globalization.[70]

The second curve will belong to emerging markets. But there is a long way to go, because in order to become a real second-curve country, income inequalities have to be eliminated and the middle-class consumer segment needs to increase with a rise in standards of living for all. Besides, the transition will be slow since the first-curve countries with advanced economies hold much of the revenues, most of the capital, and a disproportionate share of consumption.[71]

All these changes have brought new visions to the political and economic scene, with the potential to affect business and other strategies. There are now a significant number of countries in the world with very unique, different structures relevant for them. Based on this variety, the strategies applied and used in world markets so far are questionable in terms of their potential for success in the new markets in the long run. The beginning of the twenty-first century can be seen as a starting point for innovative developments to take place in business in order to create new knowledge tailor-made to fit the newly emerging regions of the world.

Notes

1. S.T. Cavusgil, P.N. Ghauri and M.R. Agarwal, *Doing Business in Emerging Markets. Entry and Negotiation Strategies* (Thousand Oaks, London and New Delhi: Sage Publications, 2002).
2. W. Greider, *One World Ready or Not: The Manic Logic of Global Capitalism* (New York: Simon & Schuster, 1997): 37.
3. Here studies on marketing conducted in the last decade by the Akadémiai Kiadó, Budapest are worth mentioning.
4. D. Yergin and J. Stanislaw, 'Sale of the Century', *Financial Times Weekend*, 24–25 January (1998): 1.
5. W. Greider, *One World Ready or Not: The Manic Logic of Global Capitalism*: 36–7.
6. T. Frasca, 'The Sacking of Argentina', *The Nation* (6 May 2002): 26.
7. H. Tobar, 'The Good Life is No More for Argentina', *Los Angeles Times* (18 February 2003) (www.latimes.com).
8. Thomas L. Friedman, *The Lexus and the Olive Tree* (New York: Anchor Books, 2000): 151–2.
9. www.heritage.org
10. L.A. Manrai and A.K. Manrai, 'Marketing Opportunities and Challenges in Emerging Markets in the New Millennium: A Conceptual Framework and Analysis', *International Business Review*, 10 (2001): 493–504.
11. S. Bakhtiari and N. Daneshvar, 'The Challenges of Globalization and Regionalism for Developing Countries', *Journal of International Marketing and Marketing Research*, 26, 2 (2001): 91–8.
12. M.S. Akman and M. Dartan, 'The Regionalism in the World Economy: Novel Expectations from an Old Habit', *Marmara Journal of European Studies*, 6, 1 (1998): 1–30.
13. V. Sriram and Z. Bilgin, 'Regionalism and Emerging Markets: An Analysis of Turkey's Trade with the BSEC and the EU', *Marmara Journal of European Studies* 10, 1 (2002): 137–61.
14. P. Marber, *From Third World to World Class – The Future of Emerging Markets in the Global Economy* (New York: Perseus Books, 1998): 32–3.

15. C.D. Wadhva, 'Assessing the SAARC Preferential Trading Agreement: An Indian Perspective', in *The Dynamics of South Asia: Regional Cooperation and SAARC* (New Delhi: Sage, 1999): 192–216.
16. A.A. Waqif, 'GATT-1994 and South Asian Regional Cooperation: A Survey of Issues and Approaches', in *The Dynamics of South Asia: Regional Cooperation and SAARC* (New Delhi: Sage, 1999): 217–37.
17. H. Cooper and B. Bahree, 'No "Gattzilla": World's Best Hope for Global Trade Topples Few Barriers', *The Wall Street Journal* (3 December 1996): A8.
18. S. Page, *Regionalism Among Developing Countries* (London: Macmillan, 2000).
19. C. Katz, 'Free Trade Area of the Americas: NAFTA Marches South', *NACLA Report on the Americas* (February 2002): 27–33, 44–5.
20. R. Grynberg, 'The WTO Incompatibility of the Lomé Convention Trade Provisions', Asia Pacific School of Economics and Management, The Australian National University (working paper) (1998) (http://ncdsnet.anu.edu.au/pdf/wp98/sp98–3.pdf): 22.
21. 'Finance Notebook', *The Guardian* (21 February 2003): 25.
22. A. Bernstein, 'Backlash: The Anxiety Over Globalization', *Business Week* (24 April 2000): 38–44.
23. N. Dawar and A. Chattopadhyay, 'Rethinking Marketing Programs for Emerging Markets', The University of Michigan Business School, *William Davidson Institute Working Paper*, no. 320 (June 2000): 1–22.
24. J.A. Caslione and A.R. Thomas, *Global Manifest Destiny – Growing Your Business in a Borderless Economy* (Chicago, IL: Dearborn Trade Publishing, 2002): 10–11.
25. S. Roberts, *Harness the Future – The 9 Keys to Emerging Consumer Behavior* (Ontario: John Wiley & Sons, 1998).
26. N. Dawar and A. Chattopadhyay, 'Rethinking Marketing Programs for Emerging Markets': 1–22.
27. J. Gray, *False Dawn – The Delusions of Global Capitalism* (London: Granta Books, 2002).
28. J.A. Caslione and A.R. Thomas, *Global Manifest Destiny – Growing Your Business in a Borderless Economy*: 23.
29. *Alternatives to Economic Globalization: A Better World Is Possible* (San Francisco, CA: Berrett-Koehler, 2002).
30. G. Soros, *On Globalization* (Oxford: Public Affairs Ltd, 2002).
31. J.E. Stiglitz, *Globalization and Its Discontents* (New York: W.W. Norton, 2002): 35.
32. Ibid.
33. G. Soros, *On Globalization*: 123.
34. See W.L. Keegan, *Global Marketing Management*, 7th edn (Englewood Cliffs, NJ: Prentice Hall – Pearson Education Inc., 2002). In fact, as stated by Keegan on p. 7, the concept of high and low-context as a way to understand different cultural orientations had been introduced by Edward T. Hall, 'How Cultures Collide', *Psychology Today* (July 1976): 67–97; J. Child, 'Theorizing about Organization Cross-Nationally: Part 1 – An Introduction', in M. Warner and P. Joynt (eds), *Managing Across Cultures, Issues and Perspectives* (London: Thomson Learning, 2002): 26–39.
35. G. Hofstede, *Cultures and Organizations – Intercultural Cooperation and its Importance for Survival* (London: HarperCollins, 1994).
36. See F. Trompenaars and C. Hampden-Turner, *Riding the Waves of Culture – Understanding Cultural Diversity in Global Business*, 2nd edn (New York: McGraw-Hill, 1998). In fact the authors focused on Parson's five relational orientations as a starting point. For this see T. Parsons, *The Social System* (New York: The Free Press, 1951).

37 J. Child, 'Theorizing about Organization Cross-Nationally: Part 2 – Towards a Synthesis', in M. Warner and P. Joynt (eds), *Managing Across Cultures, Issues and Perspectives* (2002): 40–56.
38 *Ibid.*: 49.
39 F. Trompenaars and C. Hampden-Turner, *Riding the Waves of Culture – Understanding Cultural Diversity in Global Business*, op. cit.
40 J. Child, 'Theorizing about Organization Cross-Nationally: Part 1 – An Introduction': 26–39.
41 See G.P. Ferrero, *The Cultural Dimensions of International Business*, 3rd edn (Englewood Cliffs, NJ: Prentice Hall, 1998).
42 See for details G. Hofstede, 'Images of Europe: Past, Present and Future', in M. Warner and P. Joynt (eds), (2002): 89–102.
43 F. Trompenaars and C. Hampden-Turner, *Riding the Waves of Culture – Understanding Cultural Diversity in Global Business*, op. cit.
44 See for details Tjasa Zivko, Milan Zver and Vito Bobek, 'Economic Culture in European Countries', paper presented in the 28th EIBA annual conference in Athens entitled 'Regional Integration, Agglomeration and International Business' (8–10 December, 2003).
45 For details, see B.W. Husted, 'Cultural Balkanization and Hybridization in an Era of Globalization: Implications for International Business Research', in M. Kotabe and P. S. Aulakh (eds), *Emerging Issues in International Business Research* (Cheltenham: Edward Elgar): 81–95.
46 J.M. Templeton, 'A Worldwide Rise in Living Standards', *The Futurist* (January 1999): 17–22.
47 M. Albert, 'A Q&A on the WTO, IFM, World Bank and Activism', *Z Magazine*, (January 2000): 24–9.
48 N. Klein, *No Logo* (London: Flamingo, 2000).
49 N. Hertz, *The Silent Takeover: Global Capitalism and the Death of Democracy* (New York: The Free Press, 2001).
50 A. Chua, *World on Fire: How Exporting Free Market Democracy Breeds Ethnic hatred and Global Instability* (New York: Doubleday, 2003).
51 J. Flynn, 'La Dolce Vita', *The Baltimore Sun*, 24 August 2003, 1R, 4R–5R.
52 www.slowfood.com (retrieved on 8 November 2003).
53 *Ibid.*
54 J. Flynn, 'La Dolce Vita', op. cit.
55 D. MacKenzie, 'Brands Have to Meet Customers' "Local" Demands', *Marketing* (30 August 2001): 18 .
56 T.L. Friedman, *The Lexus and the Olive Tree*, op. cit.
57 E.M. Graham, *Fighting the Wrong Enemy: Antiglobal Activists and Multinational Enterprises* (Washington, DC: Institute for International Economics, 2000).
58 A. Rugman, *The End of Globalization* (New York: Amacom, 2001).
59 R. Grynberg, 'The WTO Incompatibility of the Lomé Convention Trade Provisions': 22.
60 C. Katz, 'Free Trade Area of the Americas: NAFTA Marches South', op. cit.
61 J.A. Caslione and A.R. Thomas, *Global Manifest Destiny – Growing Your Business in a Borderless Economy*: 5.
62 For the details about the examples from India and Mexico, see J.A. Caslione and A.R. Thomas, *Global Manifest Destiny – Growing Your Business in a Borderless Economy*: 26 and 29. In fact, the example about the Indian company is based on

A. Gupta and V. Govindarajan, 'Managing Global Expansion', *Business Horizons* (March–April 2000): 50.
63 K. Ohmae, 'Becoming a Triad Power – The New Global Corporation', in H.B. Thorelli and S.T. Cavusgil (eds), *International Marketing Strategy*, 3rd edn (Oxford: Pergamon Press, 1990): 57.
64 I. Morrison, *The Second Curve: Managing the Velocity of Change* (New York: Ballantine Books, 1996): 20 and 99.
65 J.E. Garten, 'The Big Emerging Markets', *op. cit.*: 7.
66 I. Morrison, *The Second Curve: Managing the Velocity of Change*: 18; C. Egan and D. Shipley, 'Strategic Orientation Toward Countertrade Opportunities in Emerging Markets', *International Marketing Review*, 13, 4 (1996): 102.
67 C. Nakata and K. Sivakumar, 'Emerging Market Conditions and their Impact on First Mover Advantages', *International Marketing Review*, 14, 6 (1997): 461, http://www.europe.emerald-library.com/cgi-bin/EMRshowrc.cgi?rn=4720&nfmt=16&jt=36; K. Ohmae (1990) *op. cit.*: 57.
68 C. Nakata and K. Sivakumar, 'Emerging Market Conditions and their Impact on First Mover Advantages': 463; D.J. Arnold and J.A. Quelch, 'New Strategies in Emerging Markets', *Sloan Management Review* 40, 1 (Fall 1998): 8; J.E. Garten, 'The Big Emerging Markets', *op. cit.*: 7; I. Morrison, *The Second Curve: Managing the Velocity of Change*, op. cit.
69 D.J. Arnold and J.A. Quelch, 'New Strategies in Emerging Markets', *op. cit.*: 7; A. O'Reilly, 'Establishing Successful Joint Ventures in Developing Nations – a CEO's Perspective', *Columbia Journal of World Business* 23, 1 (1988): 66.
70 R.T. Moran and J.R. Riesenberger, *The Global Challenge. Presentation in Eighteenth Faculty Consortium on International Marketing* (Ann Arbor MI: American Marketing Association, Michigan State University, 1998).
71 I. Morrison, *The Second Curve: Managing the Velocity of Change, op. cit.*

3
A General Look at Emerging Markets

F. Zeynep Bilgin, Ven Sriram and Gerhard A. Wührer

Until the last decade of the twentieth century, the understanding of the concept of 'emerging markets' (EMs) was not widespread. World trade was assumed to take place between the 'highly industrialized countries', and the rest was considered to be composed of 'developing', 'newly industrializing' or even 'underdeveloped' countries. An interesting point nowadays is that different terms are still used when talking about EMs. Some scholars[1] use the terms 'developing country', 'emerging market' and 'third world' interchangeably when referring to emerging markets, whilst in other sources[2] the phrase 'less-developed countries' is used to describe EMs. The shift in the Triad power necessitates a look at how the 'emerging market' concept evolved, what are the different types of emerging markets, and what are the basic characteristics which differentiate them from each other and from the markets of industrially advanced economies.

Evolution of the emerging markets concept

It is not surprising that different authors have used a variety of indicators[3] to identify countries as emerging markets: rapid economic growth, privatization of state-owned enterprises, an expanding middle class, trade and economic liberalization, developing infrastructure, growth in exports and imports and a general sense of 'globalization' are some of the economic attributes that many emerging markets share. Cavusgil, Ghauri and Agarwal[4] point out that not all developing countries may be considered emerging markets, but only those that have begun a process of economic reform and have a steady rate of GNP growth can be considered truly emerging. In fact, while much of the future growth in world trade is forecasted to come from less-developed countries, a small core of them is expected to account for a substantial portion of that growth.[5]

Hence, as reflected in Table 3.1, a paradigm shift is in general observed. In most of the developing countries, political upheavals and undemocratic systems have inhibited the acceleration of economic development, resulting

Table 3.1 Paradigm shift in international business

Developing countries (prior to 2000)	Emerging markets (2000 and beyond)
• High risk for foreign business • Economically and technologically backward • Consumers had poor purchasing power • Few opportunities for business	• Risk increasingly manageable • Higher income growth than developed nations • Technologically competitive • Increasing purchasing power among customers • Offer many opportunities as large untapped markets and low-cost, high-quality sources

Source: Cavusgil, Ghauri and Agarwal (2002): 3.

in economic instabilities, low purchasing power and insufficient technological infrastructure, and these countries were therefore perceived to be high-risk countries possessing few opportunities for foreign business. But out of the group of developing countries, a new and rapidly evolving group has emerged in recent years. In these countries called emerging markets, risks are seen as increasingly manageable, there is a higher rate of income growth than that in many developed nations, technological competitiveness is increasing, purchasing power among consumers is rising, and they offer many opportunities as large untapped markets and low-cost, high-quality supply sources.[6]

Actually, the biggest consumer boom is observed in EMs[7] and the business world should begin to focus on the group E7 (Brazil, China, India, Indonesia, Mexico, Russia and South Korea).[8] What is striking about the demographic data is the segment of consumers between the ages of 15–40. Here the EMs have higher growth rates of consumption in durable and non-durable consumer goods sectors than the AMs.[9] Besides, consumption is highly related to the increasing affordability of a variety of products in these markets. Although the GDP per capita may not be very promising, it is the purchasing power parity (PPP)[10] that determines the real purchasing potential in a society. Accordingly, using PPP adjustments, the GDP per capita in an EM can appear to be much higher than calculated on the traditional exchange rate basis.[11] So, for any firm from any country in the world, being involved in international business relations with EMs is a promising strategy for long-term operations given all these optimistic projections of growth opportunities.

Khanna and Palepu[12] argue that the most important criterion in defining an emerging market is 'how well an economy helps buyers and sellers come together'. While emerging markets, they believe, have developed some of the institutions necessary to stimulate commerce, market failures still occur and companies therefore have to perform these functions themselves.

Types of emerging markets

Just as the different terms used to describe emerging markets can cause confusion, as discussed earlier, there is an equally bewildering array of categorizations of emerging markets themselves. These groupings do not always relate to the differences in EMs in terms of their level of economic development, political systems, or their market structure based on the level of advancement in infrastructure and the like. The basic distinction revolves around two extremes: big emerging markets (BEMs) and starting emerging markets (SEMs). SEMs can be called starters, or transition economies (TEs), because they are still in the process of transition from the closed, centrally planned (Soviet) system to that of a free market.

A detailed look at the two basic groups, SEMs and BEMs, and the countries falling into these categories or in general into the EM definition reveals the following: the SEMs of transition economies are Poland, the Czech Republic, Slovakia, Albania, Hungary, Romania, Bulgaria, former Yugoslavia, and the former USSR (principally today's Russia, Ukraine, Belarus and the Baltic States).[13] The US Department of Commerce[14] puts great emphasis on the market developments and opportunities open in EMs for international trade, whether it is just for import/export aims or for investment purposes. Accordingly, the countries categorized as being most promising for business operations are the 10 BEMs: Argentina, Brazil, China, India, Mexico, Poland, South Africa, South Korea, Taiwan and Turkey. Garten's[15] definition of BEMs talks about China as the 'Chinese Economic Area', which includes Hong Kong and Taiwan in addition to China. In a broader list, the US Department of Commerce adds Negara Brunei Darussalam, Malaysia, Philippines, Singapore and Vietnam to the group of EMs. In some categorizations,[16] Thailand, Hungary and the Czech Republic are listed as promising EM countries.

A source of some confusion in these EM groupings is that, sometimes, different literature sources reflect different categorizations for the same countries: China, India, Indonesia, Brazil, Russia and South Africa are listed as 'key emerging second-curve countries'[17] instead of BEMs; besides, Indonesia and Russia have not been categorized under the BEMs by most of the authors dealing with EM studies. Table 3.2 lists the countries that fall into each of the common definitions of emerging markets.

Clearly, there are huge variations among the countries in these lists economically and politically, but they represent many regions of the world. Also, the economic crises some have experienced recently – notably Argentina, Indonesia and Turkey – points to their volatility but many people agree that these countries 'are the key swing factor in the future growth of world trade, global financial stability, and the transition to free market economies'.[18]

Table 3.2 Types of emerging markets categorization

EMs	BEMs/second curve	SEMs

• BEMs
    +
• SEMs
    +
• Brunei
• Malaysia
• Phillipines
• Singapore
• Vietnam
• Thailand
	• Argentina
	• Brazil
	• Chinese Economic Area:
	    China + Taiwan + Hong Kong
	• India
	• Mexico
	• Poland
	• South Africa
	• South Korea
	• Turkey
	• Indonesia
	• Russia
		• Poland
		• Czech Republic
		• Slovakia
		• Albania
		• Hungary
		• Romania
		• Bulgaria
		• former Yugoslavia
		• Russia
		• Ukraine
		• Belarus
		• Baltic States

Sources: Compiled based on US Department of Commerce; Morrison (1996); Money and Colton (2000); Czinkota and Ronkainen (1996); Nakata and Sivakumar (1997).

The wide economic disparity of the BEMs, where the most recent development can be looked at under the statistics of the World Bank,[19] suggests that some are more 'emerged' than others. What these data also indicate is the economic volatility in many countries where economies have actually shrunk in the last few years. On the other hand, an examination of the data also reveals that countries like China and India have been enjoying strong GDP growth over several years.

Characteristics of emerging markets

In an emerging market the national economy reflects rapid growth, the structure of the industry is changing, the market is still volatile but promising, its regulatory system favours the free market system and liberalization of the economy, and attempts are being made to reduce bureaucratic and administrative controls over business operations.[20] The spectacular economic growth in emerging markets, 5 per cent annually according to the Organisation for Economic Co-operation and Development (OECD), and population growth, both increasing at a much higher rate than in industrialized nations, has resulted in increasing income levels and the biggest consumer boom in history since these people are expected to create a high demand for different products, assuring higher returns for manufacturers and distributors.[21] Nevertheless, it is important to also note that the GDP per capita in EMs is much lower than that in AMs. As defined by Marber,[22] countries with GDP per capita below $9,385 fall into the category of EMs; the categorization and description of BEMs only started with the attempts of the Clinton administration[23] in the USA in the first half of the 1990s. In writing about

Table 3.3 Classification of the new economic powers, the EMs

BEMs	SEMs
More promising; very fast, more established	Slowly learning to emerge
Larger	Smaller
More advanced in international trade	At infancy stage of trade (esp. for cons. goods)
Marketing orientation already established	Marketing orientation still lacking
Infrastructure developing fast	Infrastructure needs improvement
Stability: higher	Stability: lower
Very many reforms, growth spillover effects to other regions	Reforms slowly come

emerging markets in general[24] from a US perspective,[25] the criteria that have been identified for BEMs may be summarized as in Table 3.3.

When TEs[26] or SEMs[27] are compared to BEMs, one can see that BEMs are more advanced in their marketing orientation and structures while SEMs are in the process of adapting their strategies to the new economic system (Table 3.3). In fact, firms interested in these markets should know that most of the transitional economies[28] are small in size, with a population not more than five million people in many cases. Yet also among them are large markets like Russia and Ukraine. And all these markets, big or small, are slowly evolving into the role of 'future leaders' in international trade operations.[29]

Based on these characteristics, three additional key factors are relevant for all emerging markets:[30] low level of incomes; variability in consumers and infrastructures; and the relative cheapness of labour, which is often substituted for capital. Thus, while emerging markets represent a variety of countries at different stages and with different speeds of economic and political reform, they are all generally committed to freer markets and recognize the potential benefits of globalization.

The dual-economy syndrome

'Being dynamic and uncertain at the same time, driven by technology in the hands of users with rapidly changing consumer preferences.'[31] This sentence captures extremely well a characteristic that is very unique to all developing economies, including EMs. Dual economies are ones with two faces: the modern and the traditional. On the one side are firms purely modern and advanced in the technology they use and highly professional and sophisticated in their management styles, on the other side there are firms run as small family businesses based on traditional values and with limited investments in technology. The desires of the populations in the related societies also reflect a similar pattern. In urban areas, where consumption trends or desires are similar to any of the developed economies, the modern face is represented; while in rural areas the traditional lifestyles prevail. The speed of urbanization along with job opportunities improves the consumption patterns of people. Hence, in a way two different markets need to be served with different strategies.

Also, the rapid economic growth that many emerging markets have enjoyed has not been uniform throughout the country with certain areas, usually the large cities, attracting jobs and investment. As a result, the burgeoning middle-class with disposable incomes that make them attractive target markets are concentrated in those urban areas with the rural provinces still mired in poverty with only limited banking, communication, transportation and other infrastructure. Friedman[32] highlights this 'dual-economy' syndrome of many emerging markets by classifying China as 'DOScapital 1.0' in the rural areas and 4.0 in Shanghai (in his conceptualization, DOScapital 0.0 represents the centrally planned economic system of communist countries, and 6.0 as that of liberalized economies).

The impact of MNCs in emerging markets[33] tends to be more apparent in urban areas where there is relative affluence and demand for their products. In these markets, a lifestyle change based on the changing consumption habits can be observed over time. Besides, with the widespread internationalization of retailing also taking place in EMs, shopping habits of people tend to change. Markets therefore become more and more similar to each other, often with the same products on the shelves and advertised on billboards. Consequently, local consumption habits begin to slowly disappear, especially in urban areas. On the other hand, in small towns and in rural regions, younger generations are the innovators while older people like to stick to their traditional lifestyles, so needs reflect variety. The diffusion of the products to the targeted markets is not very fast, particularly in regions with traditional lifestyles.

Obstacles in EMs: corruption and the shadow economy

It is also important to note that despite the prospects for economic growth in EMs, there are also significant problems: political risk, economic instability, corruption and weak infrastructure make it a challenge to operate businesses successfully. For instance, although an identifiable target market has already emerged in the EMs based on the increase in disposable income levels and the increasing reach of international media contributing to product awareness and perception, in many EMs a marketing infrastructure is still lacking. Market data is frequently missing and the distribution systems and communication channels are still poorly developed; and most of them are characterized by high levels of product diversion within or between countries, product counterfeiting, power and loyalty structures within complex networks of local business and political players; all this reflecting a distinctive marketing environment.[34]

Another persistent difficulty faced by marketers in many emerging markets is the pervasive level of corruption. This is largely the legacy of extensive government controls that existed, and still continue to exist, in some countries, over many areas of economic activity, and the regime of various licences and permits required to start and operate a business. BEMs range in ranking from 36 to 96 out of 102 countries surveyed in Transparency International's Corruption Perceptions Index (CPI),[35] Based on this classification the most highly corrupt BEMs are Indonesia, India and Argentina, followed by Turkey, China, Mexico, Poland, Brazil, South Korea and South Africa.

Nevertheless, some of the basic characteristics to be taken into consideration while operating in the markets of transitional economies are as follows:[36] because the income distribution and wealth are unequal in these societies, for many segments renewal demand cannot even take place and hence consumption is negatively affected necessitating a high level of marketing mix adaptation for many sub-markets; sellers'-market, black-market and 'gray-market' conditions as well as corruption in the local political and regulatory environments or rigid labour regulations still prevail; and some industries are still subsidized by the state so that certain parties take advantage of market shortages and market growth. Infrastructure problems relate to inadequate physical distribution and logistics, the causes[37] of which may be related to political, social, historical and cultural factors which influence market partners.

Another aspect to consider for EMs is that the traditional frameworks for foreign market evaluation do not always apply very well because:[38]

1. most of the macro economic and population data are either inaccurate or outdated;
2. the size of the 'gray economy' is not reflected in the official statistical data. It has been suggested that the shadow economy or informal economy may account for up to one-seventh of the output of the world's wealthiest nations and a much higher proportion in emerging markets, and that this part of the economy is growing faster than the formal part. As a consequence, the informal economy often competes directly with the formal economy, but without the constraints of regulation or taxation;
3. in many cases, data about the level of sales or number of distributors is also lacking; and
4. the data available is just a snapshot assessment in an ever-changing, dynamically growing market environment. Additionally, there is the 'problem of fit'[39] when data from different EMs is to be compared.

Above and beyond the still relevant economic and political instabilities, and lack of market orientation, these EMs are going through drastic economic and political reforms, have significant growth rates, and are slowly building a developing free market system.[40] Hence, a great shift of productive wealth is thought to be underway, based on the extraordinary growth rates of some of the EMs such as Korea, Taiwan, Indonesia, Chile, Malaysia, Thailand and Turkey. In addition, China, India and Brazil are racing to become the world's next major manufacturing economies.[41] In all these EMs, big or small, a new global middle class of consumers is slowly emerging. The important point now is that many large emerging markets are beginning to have an increasing influence on the global stage, and what is happening in these countries is of vital consequence to the world of the future.

The importance of emerging markets

We now take a look at why emerging markets are important – both from a macro viewpoint in terms of world trade and from a micro point of view by highlighting the success that many emerging market firms are beginning to enjoy around the world.

Emerging markets and global trade and investment

BEMs are important in terms of their populations and also because of the rapid growth in their economies. Other indicators of the significance of emerging markets can be seen from Tables 3.4 and 3.5, which show the share of each BEM in the world's total exports and imports in 1995 and 2001.

As Table 3.4 shows, BEMs now account for almost 14 per cent of world exports, up from a little over 11 per cent in 1995. The data in Table 3.5 again provide an important reminder of the significance of BEMs. The UNCTAD data also reveal that in 2001, 31.46 per cent of the world's exports

Table 3.4 Percentage share of world exports

Country	1995	2001
Argentina	0.41	0.44
Brazil	0.91	0.95
China	2.90	4.35
India	0.60	0.71
Indonesia	0.89	0.92
Mexico	1.55	2.59
Poland	0.45	0.59
South Africa	0.54	0.48
South Korea	2.44	2.46
Turkey	0.42	0.45
Total BEM	11.11	13.94

Source: Value and shares of exports and imports, UNCTAD.[42]

Table 3.5 Percentage share of world imports

Country	1995	2001
Argentina	0.39	0.32
Brazil	1.03	0.93
China	2.48	3.87
India	0.67	0.79
Indonesia	0.78	0.59
Mexico	1.46	2.75
Poland	0.56	0.80
South Africa	0.59	0.45
South Korea	2.60	2.24
Turkey	0.69	0.67
Total BEM	11.25	13.41

Source: Value and shares of exports and imports, UNCTAD.[42]

came from developing countries, up from 23.85 per cent in 1990. At the same time, the developed world's share has reduced from 71.51 per cent to 64.12 per cent over the same period. The figures point to the increasing importance of emerging markets in general, and BEMs in particular, to future world trade.

The spurt in cross-border investments over the past decade or more has meant that trade statistics do not often tell the whole story since products that were once manufactured in a country may subsequently be imported into that same country if production shifted overseas. As a result, foreign direct investment (FDI) statistics are also a useful indicator of the importance of countries since an inflow in FDI may be a signal of investor confidence in the country, the potential in the domestic market and the desire of foreign investors to take advantage of labour, raw material and other cost savings. Here again, the numbers[43] indicate that emerging markets, particularly Brazil, China and Mexico are seen as very important and dynamic players in the future of world economic activity. Of course it should be kept in mind that investor size and the geographic proximity of the head-office to the country targeted for investment can also play an important role in the flow of FDI in addition to the market attractiveness and the relevant legal regulations for FDI in these EMs.[44]

Global impact of emerging market companies

While the trade data presented earlier provide some evidence of the importance of emerging markets, behind these data lie companies who are responsible for all this economic activity. Some of them are successful domestic firms who have built a thriving export business, others are more directly involved in the global activity of their countries in many ways, though their role as contract manufacturers, as partners in licensing and joint venture agreements or as multinational corporations that engage in all these activities. In the past decade or so, South Korean companies such as Hyundai and Kia in automobiles, Samsung and LG in consumer electronics and other products, and the Taiwanese company Acer in computers are slowly becoming household names in many parts of the world. There are several other emerging market companies that are major players in sectors such as banking, petroleum and communications that are not quite as well-known. However, they are competing successfully against multinationals from the Triad and have become serious global challengers for market share in many key areas. Table 3.6 highlights some of the major emerging market companies. All of the companies on this list are large enough to feature in *Fortune* magazine's 2002 list of 500 largest global companies.[45] While many of these top emerging market companies are state-owned corporations operating in industries that are traditionally public-sector monopolies, some have been privatized and others are in industries where the competition comes from global multinationals.

As discussed earlier, as emerging markets continue to privatize their economies, local companies will have to adapt in order to succeed against these rivals that typically have substantial financial resources, strong marketing and management skills, superior technology, and globally recognized brands.

Many have felt that the only options for such emerging market companies was to look for government support, become junior alliance partners to the multinationals, or exit the industry.[46] However, many companies, such as some of those in Table 3.6, have found other viable options and formulated

Table 3.6 Top emerging market companies

Company	Country	Sales (US$ mil.)	Profits (US$ mil.)	Assets (US$ mil.)	Return on equity (%)
SINOPEC	China	36,772	1,936	41,975	10.9
Petrochina	China	28,864	5,656	51,722	16.0
Samsung Electronics	South Korea	26,407	2,403	22,769	15.1
Indian Oil	India	23,154	555	n.a.	14.0
Petrobras	Brazil	22,736	3,901	29,713	34.1
Anglo American	South Africa	19,282	1,770	25,501	13.2
Hyundai Motor	South Korea	18,354	950	16,011	13.3
Gazprom	Russia	17,230	9,132	60,000	22.9
Korea Electric Power	South Korea	14,886	1,462	52,619	4.7
LG Electronics	South Korea	13,539	414	9,454	n.a.

Sources: *Business Week*, 15 July 2002.

and implemented effective strategies that have made them formidable competitors. These responses, coupled with the 'imperialist mind-set'[47] with which many multinationals initially approached emerging markets (for example trying to sell old products or squeeze profits from sunset technologies) have proven that emerging market companies can not only survive the competition from multinationals but can in fact become powerful global players themselves.

Some of the competitive response strategies that are viable for emerging market companies depend on the globalization pressures in the industry and whether the company's competitive assets are customized to the home market or transferable abroad. Dawar and Frost[48] describe how the Indian motor scooter company, Bajaj, used its low-cost structure and extensive distribution network to successfully defend its market share against Honda. On the other hand, when emerging market companies have assets that are transferable abroad, such as in the case of Mexico's media company Televisa (a producer of soap operas) or Indonesia's Indah Kiat Pulp and Paper (low production costs in paper); they can become serious regional and even global contenders. Many Turkish companies are becoming important global players: as an example Eczacıbaşı Vitra meets 6.5 per cent of the total demand of sanitary ceramics products in Europe; Vestel is starting production of TVs for the Russian market in its own plant located in Russia;[49] in the steel industry, Borusan Group bought 35 per cent of Bamesa Aceros from Spain, one of the world's largest steel manufacturers, and is starting to manufacture for global automobile giants;[50] and Sabancı Çimsa, the cement manufacturer, has captured 20 per cent of the market share in the world's largest white-cement market, Spain.[51]

Clearly, emerging markets are an important battleground in the future sales and profit efforts of companies around the world. However, companies from these markets are not just local defenders of their turf, but many now have the resources, technology and knowledge to engage multinationals in a challenge for global market share. Given the success these companies are having, it is important to understand the strategies that are bringing them that success.

Notes

1 P. Marber, *From Third World to World Class – The Future of Emerging Markets in the Global Economy* (New York: Perseus Books, 1998).
2 'Big Emerging Markets', *Business America* (March 1994): 4–6.
3 For details see http://globaledge.msu.edu/ibrd/marketpot.asp
4 S.T. Cavusgil, P.N. Ghauri and M.R. Agarwal, *Doing Business in Emerging Markets: Entry and Negotiation Strategies* (Thousand Oaks: Sage, 2002); see also http://globaledge.msu.edu/ibrd/marketpot.asp, and 'Emerging Market Indicators', *The Economist* (13 January 2001): 110.
5 'Big Emerging Markets' (March 1994): 4–6, and alternatively 'Emerging Market Indicators', *The Economist* (13 January 2001): 110.

6. S.T. Cavusgil, P.N. Ghauri and M.R. Agarwal, *Doing Business in Emerging Markets: Entry and Negotiation Strategies, op. cit.*: 3.
7. J.A. Caslione and A.R. Thomas, *Global Manifest Destiny – Growing Your Business in a Borderless Economy* (Chicago, IL: Deenborn Trade Publishing, 2002).
8. For details about the E7, see P. Marber, *From Third World to World Class – The Future of Emerging Markets in the Global Economy, op. cit.*: x and 213–14.
9. P. Marber, *From Third World to World Class – The Future of Emerging Markets in the Global Economy, op. cit.*: 112.
10. PPP = what people located in different countries can afford with the same amount of money; or number of currency units required to purchase the same amount of goods in different markets.
11. P. Marber, *From Third World to World Class – The Future of Emerging Markets in the Global Economy, op. cit.*: 112.
12. T. Khanna and K. Palepu, 'Why Focused Strategies may be Wrong for Emerging Markets', in J.E. Garten (ed.), *World View: Global Strategies for the New Economy*, (Boston, MA: Harvard Business Review Books, 2000): 23.
13. R.B. Money and D. Colton, 'The Response of the New Consumer to Promotion in the Transition Economies of the Former Soviet Block', *Journal of World Business*, 2, 35 (2000): 189–206; M.A. Czinkota and I.A. Ronkainen, *Global Marketing* (Orlando, FL: The Dryden Press – Harcourt Brace & Co., 1996): 156.
14. http://www.ita.doc.gov/bems
15. J.E. Garten, 'The Big Emerging Markets', *The Columbia Journal of World Business* (Summer 1996): 7–31; J.E. Garten, *The Big Ten: The Big Emerging Markets and How They Will Change our Lives* (New York: Basic Books, 1997).
16. C. Nakata and K. Sivakumar, 'Emerging Market Conditions and their Impact on First Mover Advantages', *International Marketing Review*, 14, 6 (1997): 461–85.
17. I. Morrison, *The Second Curve – Managing the Velocity of Change* (New York: Ballantine Books, 1996): 96, 97, 99.
18. J.E. Garten, *The Big Ten: The Big Emerging Markets and How They Will Change our Lives op. cit.*: 3.
19. http://www.worldbank.org/data/countrydata/countrydata.html (retrieved 1 March 2003).
20. Y. Luo, *Multinational Enterprises in Emerging Markets* (Copenhagen: Copenhagen Business School Press, 2002): 5.
21. J.A. Caslione and A.R. Thomas, *Global Manifest Destiny – Growing your Business in a Borderless Economy, op. cit.*
22. P. Marber, *From Third World to World Class – The Future of Emerging Markets in the Global Economy, op. cit.*
23. 'Big Emerging Markets,' *Business America*, March 1994: 4–6.
24. P. Marber, *From Third World to World Class – The Future of Emerging Markets in the Global Economy, op. cit.*, and J.E. Garten, 'The Big Emerging Markets', *The Columbia Journal of World Business* (Summer 1996): 7–31.
25. J.E. Garten, *The Big Ten: The Big Emerging Markets and How They Will Change Our Lives, op. cit.*; I. Morrison, *The Second Curve – Managing the Velocity of Change, op. cit.*: 10; J.E. Garten, 'The Big Emerging Markets', *op. cit.*: 11; P.R. Cateora and J.L. Graham, *International Marketing*, 10th edn (New York: Irwin/McGraw-Hill, *op. cit.*: 1999).
26. R. Batra, 'Marketing Issues and Challenges in Transition Economies', in R. Batra (ed.), *Marketing Issues in Transitional Economies* (Boston, MA: Kluwer Academic Publishers, 1999): 3.

27 Z. Bilgin, 'The Changing Market Structure in Starting Emerging Markets (SEMs) of Transition Economies', in S.G. Kräuter and G.A. Wührer (eds), *Trends im internationalen Management – Strategien, Instrumente und Methoden* (Linz: Universitätsverlag Rudolf Trauner, 2001).
28 Y. Luo, *Multinational Enterprises in Emerging Markets*, op. cit.: 5–6.
29 Z. Bilgin, 'The Changing Market Structure in Starting Emerging Markets (SEMs) of Transition Economies', op. cit.: 100.
30 N. Dawar and Amitava Chattopadhyay, 'Rethinking Marketing Programs for Emerging Markets', The University of Michigan Business School, William Davidson Institute, Working Paper, 320 (June 2000): 1–22.
31 I. Morrison, *The Second Curve – Managing the Velocity of Change*, op. cit.: 15.
32 T. Friedman, *The Lexus and the Olive Tree* (New York: Anchor Books, 2000) 151–2.
33 S.T. Cavusgil, P.N. Ghauri and M.R. Agarwal, *Doing Business in Emerging Markets: Entry and Negotiation Strategies*, op. cit.: 2–4.
34 D.J. Arnold and J.A. Quelch, 'New Strategies in Emerging Markets', *Sloan Management Review*, 40, 1 (Fall 1998): 9; A. Shama, 'Transforming the Consumer in Russia and Eastern Europe', *International Marketing Review*, 9, 2 (1992): 43–59.
35 'Corruption Perceptions Index 2002', *Transparency International*, www.tranparency.org (retrieved 28 February 2003).
36 R. Batra, 'Marketing Issues and Challenges in Transition Economies', op. cit.: 5–10.
37 See in detail Y. Luo, *Multinational Enterprises in Emerging Markets*, op. cit.: 5–6.
38 D.J. Arnold and J.A. Quelch, 'New Strategies in Emerging Markets', *Sloan Management Review* 40, 1 (Fall 1998): 11,12.
39 G.A. Churchill, *Marketing Research – Methodological Foundations*, 6th edn (New York: The Dryden Press, 1994): 273.
40 G.J. Hooley, J. Berács and K. Kolos, 'Marketing Strategy Typologies in Hungary', *European Journal of Marketing* 27, 11–12 (1993): 80–101.
41 W. Greider, *One World, Ready or Not – The Manic Logic of Global Capitalism* (New York: Touchstone/Simon & Schuster, 1998): 32.
42 UNCTAD Handbook of Statistics, www.stats.unctad.org (retrieved 13 June 2003).
43 United Nations Conference on Trade and Development, http://stats.unctad.org/fdi (retrieved 1 March 2003).
44 For details see the website of UNCTAD where a list states the top 100 transnational companies based on their country of origin, http://r0.unctad.org/en/Subsites/dite/fdistats_files/Top100pdfs/Top100WIR2002.pdf (retrieved 16 June 2003).
45 'The 2002 Global 500', Fortune, www.fortune.com (retrieved 1 March 2003).
46 N. Dawar and T. Frost, 'Competing with Giants: Survival Strategies for Local Companies in Emerging Markets', in J.E. Garten (ed.) (2000): *World View: Global Strategies for the New Economy*, op. cit. 37.
47 C.K. Prahalad and K. Lieberthal, 'The End of Corporate Imperialism', in J.E. Garten (ed.) *World View: Global Strategies for the New Economy*, op. cit.: 3.
48 N. Dawar and T. Frost, 'Competing with Giants: Survival Strategies for Local Companies in Emerging Markets', op. cit.
49 'Vitra Büyük Oynuyor' (26 December 2002), *Türkiye'ye Döviz Kazandıranlar*, Radikal Newspaper Supplement: 5, 8.
50 'Borusan Devlere Üretecek', *Ekonomi*, Radikal Newspaper (13 November 2002): 12.
51 'Sabancı'nın Ispanya'da Beyaz Çimento Zaferi', *Pazar Ekonomi* (20 October 2002), Hürriyet Newspaper: 11.

Part II

Views on Emerging Markets: Management Thinking in Transition

4
Market Orientation from a Hungarian Perspective

József Berács

Introduction

Marie Lavigne, in her excellent book on the economic transformation of the former socialist countries, analyses systematically the economic categories that characterize former socialist countries in the past and in the present transition period. At the end of the book the writer puts the question to herself: when does the transition reach its end? Logically, one would expect to see some formulation of the instruments discussed before. Instead, we receive three highly illuminating answers. For a better understanding of what is to follow we quote:

> A *straightforward* answer to the question would be when a young German, or British tourist walking in the streets of Budapest or Vilnius would never be reminded that once that was a different world. A more *sophisticated* way to put it is to say that transition will be over when developments in these countries erase the economic connotations of the adjective *Western* European. My *personal* answer would be that as the European Union requires that its members be 'functioning market economies', all the countries admitted into the EU would have by definition completed their transition.[1] [My emphasis]

Let us make two statements, which are at the same time the starting point of this study and to help its understanding. First, it is surprising that the 'most obvious' answer is not what traditional economics would deal with. Standard books on economics[2] do not deal with when and why tourists enjoy themselves in a foreign town. Marketing books such as Kotler[3] on the other hand deal exactly with this question. How can we 'dazzle' the buyer, the customer? Marketing enlists a whole arsenal to make Mr Smith feel 'at home' when abroad. This, however, needs a group of entrepreneurs and managers who understand these questions and try to answer them; to put it simply, who behave in a market-oriented way.

The second thing we would like to emphasize is that the view qualified as personal opinion gives the most acceptable answer from the point of view of economics as the European Union defines a set of measurable and verifiable criteria candidate countries will have to respond to. Hungary was able to fulfil these requirements by the end of 2002 and the contract of membership was signed by EU and Hungarian officials in Athens, 2003.

Will Mr Smith feel at home on 2 May 2004 after the official acceptance of Hungary's EU-membership? Undoubtedly he will be more comfortable when walking in the streets; he will know this is an allied country. But perceptions will change. He will not look wide-eyed 'oh, is this a McDonald's here?' but take for granted that he can go to McDonald's in this country, too, when he becomes hungry. When paying, he can use his usual credit card or soon pay with euros.

The interest of the West in researching market-oriented enterprise behaviour as a theoretical construction has not decreased at the beginning of the new decade either.[4] The *Journal of Marketing*, undoubtedly the most influential scientific review for marketing, devoted a whole issue in 1999 to the scientific situation of marketing, and several articles dealt with market orientation.[5] There is substantial research on the *sine qua non* of a market economy outside the USA as well,[6] referring to examples from Germany, France, Belgium, the UK, Finland, New Zealand or the Netherlands.

When I was looking for an explanation for the above-outlined situation, the interest of researchers in market orientation, I did not find it within marketing, but outside it in books and articles on economic transformation.[7] Maturity of market economies and meeting requirements of Western standards are basic elements of conceptualizations of Hungarian economists.[8] My own interest in this direction was reconfirmed by the fact that I have, within the frame of an international research team,[9] systematically dealt with the transformation of the Hungarian economy, with the emergence of marketing as an enterprise function, for ten years.

Market orientation, theoretic hypotheses and practical measurements

The core category of economic sciences is the market. An economy where the market has an outstanding and defining role among the various coordination mechanisms is called a market economy.[10] Among the institutions of a market economy, the enterprise has a major role and company theories concentrate on three core issues: what are the basic reasons for the existence of a company, where are its limits and what is its internal structure? The evolutionary theory of enterprises, which developed from the evolutionary economic sciences,[11] is a principle based on skills. Kapás[12] analyses the evolutionary theory of enterprises in detail and comes to the conclusion that we need a multidimensional enterprise theory, where short-term and long-term issues are in harmony – which is one of the least manageable things.

Desphande,[13] with an eye to the future, prepared a summary of the priorities of the Marketing Science Institute in its research over three-year periods during the past ten years. There is some kind of circulation of topics like product development, labelling, customer relations, and the like. In 1994–96, market orientation was in second place. But what is this marketing concept? There is an overall agreement in the discipline that it basically includes three factors: customer orientation, integration within the enterprise, and long-term profit-making.

What we shall discuss is the role and weight of the different elements. How can people responsible for the marketing function guarantee success in the different areas? There is agreement on customer focus as a distinguishing characteristic of marketing, but quantification of the usual 'customer is king' approach is no easy task. Those who refer to the recent decline of the role of marketing[14] often mention the fact that marketing responsibilities – especially those related to strategy – are covered by actors of other corporate functions. To counterbalance this, Moorman and Rust[15] state and recommend, 'The effectiveness of a market orientation depends on the presence of strong functions that include marketing'. The basis for this is a strong marketing organization – they add, concluding from company surveys. In other words, the company must have a market orientation penetrating throughout its structures, where 'the market is the set of all actual and potential buyers of a product or service,'[16] and at the same time the company possess a marketing organization.

Measuring market orientation

The term market orientation was in use by the end of the 1980s. Due to the loose terminology of the Anglo-Saxon literature, Shapiro[17] wrote a provocative article on 'What the hell is market oriented?' Reading the article, marketing experts from Central and Eastern Europe facing political and economic changes indeed have the right to ask this. How the hell is it possible that a professor of Harvard living and teaching marketing in the most developed market economy does not know what market orientation means. How can he not know the term Hungary has talked about since 1968, for example the introduction of the 'new economic mechanism'?

The question is not left without any consequences, and in 1990 two articles were published in the *Journal of Marketing* which tried to make a theoretic construction of the term market orientation, and so measurable by companies. For Kohli-Jaworski,[18] market orientation is made up of three elements:

1 A comprehensive generation of market information throughout the whole organization on current and future customers' needs;

2 Dissemination of this information among the units of the organization; and
3 Responsiveness of the organization as a whole.

Narver and Slater[19] also define three parts of market orientation: customer and competition orientations, and interfunctional coordination. Around the end of the 1990s, new approaches emerged, but none could ignore these two approaches when measuring market orientation. On the basis of the scales recommended in the above-mentioned studies, different countries and sectors measured[20] their market orientations, where the scale reliabilities proved to be sufficient by standards of social research. Hungary is also included in the four-country survey (Bulgaria, Poland, Slovenia) where the three-dimensional model by Narver–Slater was tested in 1996. According to the analysis based on the Hungarian, Slovenian and Polish data, the Narver and Slater instrument for measuring market orientation proved to be valid and reliable in the transition economies of Central Europe.[21]

Measuring market orientation on the basis of the Narver and Slater scales

Against the background discussed, in 1992 immediately after the change of the political system, the three countries Hungary, Poland and Bulgaria were included in an analysis of the marketing situation, the measurement of market orientation as defined above. The survey led to surprising results in Hungary. In a national group of 3,000 representative companies, each with more than 20 employees, 893 answers could be evaluated with a spread as follows:[22]

Production orientation	19 per cent
Sales and promotion orientation	18 per cent
Customer (marketing orientation)	63 per cent

Concerning customer orientation, the values were much lower in Poland and especially in Bulgaria. However, the Hungarian result did not differ substantially from those of a former British survey, where 67 per cent of company managers of a similar group in the UK claimed that they and their companies were customer-oriented. We cannot give an adequate explanation for the surprising resemblance between Hungary at the early stage of transition and the UK with her developed market economy. We did not think that the Hungarian respondees were conscious of painting a more beautiful picture about themselves (the questions were sent out by mail in written form), in our view the results were to be explained by the weakness of the measuring instrument.

When the second comprehensive analysis of the marketing situation started in 1996, we mainly wanted to assess the impact of privatization and foreign capital investment in Hungary and the Central European regions.[23]

Another objective of the research was to use the Narver–Slater scale developed specifically for the measurement of market orientation, which had not been tested in the Central European environment. Hooley[24] describes these results in detail. The scale met the reliability and validity criteria of theoretic constructions,[25] and one of the most exciting issues here was the proof of nomological validity. We therefore formulated different hypotheses and tested them on the basis of the data from the three countries (Poland, Hungary, Slovenia). For the sake of illustration, let us quote one hypothesis and its testing:

> *Proposal*: Firms exhibiting a higher degree of market orientation will exhibit more aggressive, externally focused, long-term strategic priorities than less market-oriented firms.[26]

The items of the Narver–Slater scales will be described later on the basis of the Hungarian survey, 2000. The average of the scale was made up of 14 items and the answers were grouped into three categories with approximately equal numbers of elements. On that basis, we arrived at groups of companies with low, medium and high market orientation. There was a statistically significant difference[27] among companies with low and high market orientation in the three strategic areas examined. Companies with high market orientation justified the connections measured in theory:

(a) Strategic priorities focus much more on long-term market expansion than survival.
(b) The main focus of strategy is to decrease costs and to increase efficiency (58.4 per cent). Market-oriented companies, however, are *not* distinguished by this, but by much greater efforts to penetrate the market through the disadvantage in market share of competitors.
(c) Concerning the objectives of marketing strategy, 63 per cent of the companies follow the objective of an even increase of sales, yet aggressive efforts for market dominance are much more typical (9.7 per cent versus 4.8 per cent).

On the basis of a comprehensive analysis of the marketing activity of Hungarian companies and their assessment through their performance, we drew the general conclusions[28] that already in 1996, 10 per cent of the best-performing companies were following Western standards and were prepared to respond to the challenges of the twenty-first century. Not having any data on Western countries, we can only rely on assessments of proportions there of 20–30 per cent. The question we will revisit at the end of the study is: when will Hungarian companies reach this presumed Western European level?

Continuing the description of the Narver–Slater market orientation construction, company managers were approached in the autumn of the year 2000 with a response rate of 19 per cent. The sampling rules ($n=3000$) were the almost the same as in 1992 and 1996, and 15 questions were used to measure market orientation from which seven related to customer orientation, four to competition orientation and four to coordination among company functions. The high value of the whole scale (Cronbach's alpha = 0.89) reflects that the scale can be used reliably in Hungarian conditions.

In the 1996 survey we studied the validity of the three orientations – customer, competitor, coordination among functions[29] – but in contrast to Moorman–Rust[30] we found that such orientations did not prevail. We were curious to see if there had been any change by 2000. (This survey has not been published, but the Hungarian results from 1996 did not differ on this point from the results of Central Europe.) The factor analysis of the variables (Table 4.1) shows that this method cannot appropriately reflect the internal structure of the model. Naming the factors, we seemed to have much more the Kohli–Jaworski construction than what Narver–Slater had envisioned. This reconfirmed our previous recognition[31] that the segments of the two scales measure phenomena very similar to one another–they measure market orientation.

Of the 15 original variables, 12 were included in the three factors, which explain 56 per cent of the total variance. The four variables in the first factor are related to the transfer and use of market knowledge within the company, and were thus called *market knowledge* (cf Kohli–Jaworski's term on the dissemination of information). The second factor includes three variables and measures the more formal capacity of companies in collecting information, therefore this factor is called *generation of information* (cf Kohli–Jaworski's intelligence generation). Finally, the third factor includes variables related to how customer needs influence the definition of long-term, formal strategic and economic plans. This factor is called *strategic responsiveness* (cf Kohli–Jaworski's responsiveness). Three variables were not included in the factors (one from each of the groups planned to measure consumer, competitor and coordination orientations). It is interesting to see that the average mean of the 15 variables, 4.66, is higher than what was measured for the three countries in 1996 (4.03). The weight of the different factors gives the bottom-up ranking of what we would get on the basis of the averages of the factor variables. Variables (with the original number) with the highest average values were:

3. Our objectives and strategies are driven by the creation of customer satisfaction (5.41).
9. Business strategies are driven by increasing value for customers (5.44).

Table 4.1 Factor analyses results of the market orientation items of Narver–Slater, Hungary 2000 (*n* = 572)

Market orientation items	Market knowledge	Information gathering	Strategic responsiveness	Mean
2. Sales people share information on competitors	0.732			4.04
12. Top management regularly discuss competitors' strength and weaknesses	0.680			4.52
13. Our managers understand how employees can contribute to the value for customers	0.598			4.44
14. Customers are targeted when we have an opportunity for competitive advantage	0.582			4.82
10. Customer satisfaction is frequently assessed		0.758		4.55
11. Close attention is given to after sales service		0.725		5.20
15. The results of customer satisfaction measurements appear in internal reports		0.682		3.74
3. Our objectives and strategies are driven by the creation of customer satisfaction			0.732	5.41
1. Our commitment to serving customer needs is closely monitored			0.681	4.91
9. Business strategies are driven by increasing value for customers			0.640	5.44
7. Competitive strategies are based on understanding customers' needs			0.633	4.78
8. Business functions are integrated to serve market needs			0.560	4.44
4. We achieve rapid response to competitive actions				4.40
5. Top management regularly visits important customers				4.81
6. Information about customers is freely communicated throughout the company				4.37

KMO = 0.906, *Sig.* = 0.0000, total variance 0.56, varimax rotation; Average mean of 15 items is 4.66.
Source: J. Berács, T. Keszey and L. Sajtos, 'The Marketing Approach, Strategy and Performance of Hungarian Companies in 2000' (in Hungarian), *OTKA Kutatási jelentés*, T 030028, BKÁE Marketing tanszék (Budapest, 2001): 178.

These reflect how strongly strategic and customer orientation are interlinked. There are also many other connections between market orientation and company characteristics. Companies with high market orientation are – according to *sectors* – in the wholesale sector, according to *size*: with less than 20 and more than 500 employees, and according to *ownership*: foreign companies. Low market orientation is typical in the agriculture and financial services sectors, with 300–500 employees and in companies owned by the state or municipalities.

Changes in strategic priorities in the 1990s

According to the evolutionary company theory,[32] one of the eternal dilemmas is how short-term and long-term objectives can be harmonized and how to guarantee the dominance of long-term objectives. A general problem of marketing research is that interviews with repeated methodology are rare, and so the possibilities of longitudinal analyses are limited. From this point of view, our survey series revealing the position of marketing in Hungary is unique as it also covers ongoing issues – for example the problem of strategic priorities, which is extremely important for an economy in transition or simply in turbulence. Table 4.2 reflects this transformation in Hungary between 1992–2000.

In the period of the change of the economic system, 1990–96, the primary objective was survival. Looking at the time series evaluating the past two years, we see a gradual change in the roles and, by 2000, half of the companies intended to concentrate on long-term market presence. This is even truer for the expectations of company managers. Company managers are optimistic about the future, but this optimism tends to turn increasingly into a 'normal' optimism.

This can be seen in the numbers derived from the variance of assessments on the past and future figures. Concerning survival, in the series we may call the 'optimism factor', the percentages change: 67–42=25, 57–27=30, and

Table 4.2 The strategic priorities of Hungarian companies, 1992, 1996 and 2000 (per cent)

Strategic priorities	Past two years			Next two years		
	1992 $N=893$	1996 $N=589$	2000 $N=572$	1992 $N=893$	1996 $N=589$	2000 $N=572$
Survival	67	57	39	42	27	25
Short-term financial returns or profit	8	7	11	4	5	4
Long-term building of market position	25	36	50	54	68	71
Total	100	100	100	100	100	100

39–25 = 12 (Table 4.2). Thus the beginning of the change in the political system, the number of companies focusing on survival was high (67 per cent) and relatively many (25 per cent) thought that this would change. The most difficult part of the system change, however, was still ahead – which could not be anticipated in 1992. The period between 1994–96 was difficult as the macroeconomic data and economic policy measures also reflect. For that reason, the greatest challenge for the majority of the companies (57 per cent) was their survival. But this was the year when transition to a market economy, the transformation of the legal system, the 'marketization' of company structures, privatization and the influx of foreign companies resulted in a dominance of private ownership. On the basis of the attitudes and views of company managers, we asserted that the market transformation of the economic sector had been completed, and the employment research programme on competitiveness arrived at the same conclusions.[33] This is reflected by the 30 per cent value of the 'optimism factor', which macroeconomists would probably have considered at the time exaggerated. It turned out that it was not. By the year 2000, the number of those concerned about survival decreased drastically. Parallel with this there was hardly any change among those who projected the same for the future; the change was from 27 per cent to 25 per cent. This also means that we can state with relative safety on the basis of the 12 per cent 'optimism factor', that about one-third of the companies will strive for survival in the period 2000–04. This is already a normal value in a market economy and its spread is determined mainly by the situation and conditions of sectors, changes in the world market, and so on.

Marketing to serve economic growth

The starting presumption in the definition of the theoretical construction of market orientation was that it should contribute to the increase of company performance, and the research results have reliably justified this theoretical presumption. Researchers had previously presumed that a more intensive use of marketing instruments would positively influence the development of the economy. The most sophisticated marketing in the world is used in the USA and indeed the USA is the leading power of the world.

From an economic point of view, an appropriate combination of resources produces new values and economic growth. The basic issue of economics is the management of scarce resources, while the basic issue of marketing is the management of the exchange of goods.[34] The relationship between the two can most easily be set up when we put the question: how can marketing contribute to resolving the problem of scarce resources; in other words, does marketing possess anything that responds to the economic term 'resource', and, more exactly, has it got an element which can function as a resource? The answer is a definite yes. And on that basis, Hunt and

Morgan[35] defined their model of market competition based on the principle of resources as opposed to the neoclassical competition theory of the microeconomy. Market orientation is not at our unlimited disposal, and it is at the same time the instrument of efficient company operations – it functions by definition as a resource. Returning to the original problem, we try to find the answer to two questions. What are the benefits for the Hungarian economy from point of view of its development if a greater proportion of companies is market-oriented? What limitations are there in the Hungarian economy in the way of increasing market orientation?

Conclusions regarding the research of market orientation

Market orientation was already a frequently used term in Hungary before the change in the political system, and both economists and marketing experts were keen on using it. Their approach was typically macro-economic. Toying with the idea of market economy (implementing reform), there was a recurring question of what would better guarantee the supply of the population with products, market orientation (that is, market economy) or the responsibility of supply (for example redistribution)?[36]

According to the model of Western economies, the market is more efficient than redistribution. It would be interesting to study in historic perspectives to what extent relations of market orientation learned in the corporate sector can be transferred to other organizations. It is worth investigating what characteristics might be observed in the mature market economies of the European Union, the Far East and the USA.[37]

In our study we analysed, besides other topics, the time series of strategic priorities, and we found connections between the macro-economic processes and the views of company managers, and some concluding remarks may be appropriate:

1 In corporate theory based on resources and in the related strategy and competition theories, it would be expedient to mention the contribution marketing makes to the profitability of an enterprise. The measuring tool of market orientation is only one of the possibilities by which marketing capabilities can be measured. From the economic science point of view, it has to be acknowledged that a picture based on subjective views is also appropriate to assess a company's market situation objectively.
2 A greater emphasis should be put on the analysis of the marketing function based on cost–benefit principles. An indicator system should be developed which helps to interpret the problem of what is done and why, and at what costs, how much. The instruments of economic science should be more intensively used here. Branding is also one of the major activities of marketing. Branding and brand values are among the most interesting topics to be considered. Here it is important how the structure of the

media industry develops, which sectors and companies lead the rank lists, and how do these indices relate to other countries? Similarly, the macro-economic analysis of other marketing areas is also needed. What is new product development and innovation like in the different sectors: how does the transformation of sales and the trading system progress? All this has to be related to human capital, to the pool, the distribution and intellectual capacities of marketing experts, and market orientation.

3 Market information is valuable in the business sector, and therefore whoever possesses it does not want to share it with others free of charge. According to the definition, market orientation is the knowledge of and interpretation of market information, and turning that into action. There is a need to develop a methodology for how this activity within an organization can be translated into money. At the same time, it has to be acknowledged that the amount of information available for purposes of academic research is partial and poor. Therefore, it permits very little pioneering research.

Notes

1 M. Lavigne, *The Economics of Transition; From Socialist Economy to Market Economy*, 2nd edn (New York: St. Martin's Press, 1999): 276.
2 A. Samuelson and W.D. Nordhaus, *Közgazdaságtan I–II* (Economics), Közgazdasági és Jogi Könyvkiadó (Budapest, 1998).
3 P. Kotler, *Marketing Management*, 9th edn (Englewood Cliffs, NJ: Prentice Hall, 1997).
4 A.K. Kohli and B.J. Jaworski, 'Market Orientation: The Construct, Research Propositions, and Managerial Implications', *Journal of Marketing*, 54 (April 1990): 1–18; J.C. Narver and S.F. Slater, 'The Effect of Marketing Orientation on Business Profitability', *Journal of Marketing*, 54 (1990): 20–35; G.S. Day, 'The capabilities of market-driven organizations', *Journal of Marketing*, 58 (October 1994): 37–52; B.J. Jaworski and A.K. Kohli, 'Market Orientation: Review Refinement and Roadmap', *Journal of Market Focused Management*, 1, 2 (1996): 119–35; G.S. Day, 'Misconceptions About Market Orientation', *Journal of Market Focused Management*, 4, 2 (1999): 5–16.
5 C. Moorman and R.T. Rust, 'The Role of Marketing', *Journal of Marketing*, 63, special issue (1999): 180–97; R.S. Achrol and P. Kotler, 'Marketing in the Network Economy', *Journal of Marketing*, 63, special issue (1999): 146–63; R. Deshpande, ' "Foreseeing" Marketing', *Journal of Marketing*, 63, special issue (1999): 164–7.
6 R. Köhler, 'Die Marketingimplementierung – Was hat die deutschsprachige Marketingforschung an Erkenntniszugewinn erbracht?', in K. Backhaus (ed.), *Deutschsprachige Marketingforschung* (Stuttgart: Schaffer-Poeschel Verlag, 2000); J.F. Trinquecoste, 'Pour une clarification du lien marketing-stratégie', *Cahiers de Recherche*, Laboratoire de Recherche en Management, Bordeaux Business School (1999); J.W. Cadogan, N.J. Paul, R.T. Salminen, K. Puumualainen and S. Sundquist, 'Key Antecedents to Export, Market-Oriented Behaviors: A Cross-National Empirical Examination', *International Journal of Research in Marketing*, 18, 3 (2001): 261–82; F. Langerak, 'Effects of Market Orientation on the Behaviors of Salespersons and Purchasers, Channel Relationships, and Performance of Manufacturers', *International Journal of Research in Marketing*, 18, 3 (2001): 221–34; J.J. Lambin and R. Chumpitaz,

'Being Customer-Driven is Not Enough', *European Business Forum*, issue 2 (Summer 2000): 28-34.
7   P. Drucker, *Management Challenges for the 21st Century* (New York: HarperCollins, 1999); K. János, 'The System Paradigm' (in Hungarian), *Közgazdasági Szemle*, 46, 7-8 (1999): 585-99; T. Tamás, 'The Theory of Jánossy; Comparing to the New Economic Growth Theories' (in Hungarian), *Közgazdasági Szemle*,47, 5 (2000): 457-72; M.E. Porter, *The Competitive Advantage of Nations*, (New York: The Free Press,1990, 1998); F.A. Hayek, '*Economics and Knowledge*', in, *Individualism and Economic Order* (London: Routledge & Kegan Paul, 1936).
8   P. Gedeon, 'The Economics of Transition and the Transition of Economics; From the Comparative Theory of Economic Systems to the Comparative Political Economy' (in Hungarian), *Közgazdasági Szemle*, 46, 1 (1997): 56-68; T. Szentes, 'Imprisoned by Ideologies or at the Eve of the New Enlightenment? Thoughts About Present Situation of Economics and Development Theories and About Their Education' (in Hungarian), in *Új utak a közgazdasági, üzleti és társadalomtudományi képzésben*, BKE Jubileumi Konferencia I. kötet (1995): 31-45; Á. Török, 'Several Ways to Market Economy Maturity? Interpreting and Applying some Basic Concepts in the Three Great Regions of the World Economy' (in Hungarian), *Közgazdasági Szemle*, 48, 9 (2001): 707-25.
9   J. Berács and K. Kolos, 'Marketing in Hungary in 1992, 2nd part' (in Hungarian), *Marketing*, 28, 1 (1994): 7-12; J. Berács, I. Agárdi and K. Kolos, 'The Effect of Privatization and Foreign Direct Investments on Marketing Activities of Hungarian Companies' (in Hungarian), *Marketing és Menedzsment*, 31, 3 (1997): 11-19; J. Fahy, G. Hooley, T. Cox, J. Berács, K. Fonfara and B. Snoj, 'The Development and Impact of Marketing Capabilities in Central Europe', *Journal of International Business Studies*, 31, 1 (2000): 63-81; G. Hooley and J. Berács, 'Marketing Strategies for the 21st Century: Lessons from the Top Hungarian Companies', *Journal of Strategic Marketing*, 5 (1997): 143-65; G. Hooley, J. Fahy, T. Cox, J. Berács, K. Fonfara and B. Snoj, 'Marketing Capabilities and Firm Performance: A Hierarchical Model', *Journal of Market Focused Management*, 4 (1999): 259-78; G. Hooley, T. Cox, J. Fahy, D. Shipley, J. Berács, K. Fonfara and B. Snoj, 'Market Orientation in the Transition Economies of Central Europe: Tests of the Narver and Slater Market Orientation Scales', *Journal of Business Research*, 50, 3 (2000): 273-86.
10 M. Lavigne, *The Economics of Transition; From Socialist Economy to Market Economy*, op. cit.
11 R.R. Nelson and S.G. Winter, *An Evolutionary Theory of Economic Change* (Cambridge, MA, and London: Harvard University Press , 1982).
12 J. Kapás, 'Szükséges-e többdimenziós vállalatelmélet? Az evolúciós vállalatelmélet kritikai összefoglalása', *Közgazdasági Szemle*, 46, 9 (1999): 823-41.
13 R. Deshpande, ' "Foreseeing" Marketing', *Journal of Marketing*, op. cit.
14 G.S. Day, 'Misconceptions about Market Orientation', op. cit.
15 C. Moorman and R.T. Rust, 'The Role of Marketing', op. cit.: 180.
16 P. Kotler, *Marketing Management*, op. cit.
17 B. Shapiro, 'What the Hell is Market-Oriented?', *Harvard Business Review*, 66 (November-December, 1988): 119-25.
18 A.K. Kohli and B.J. Jaworski, 'Market Orientation: The Construct, Research Propositions, and Managerial Implications', op. cit.
19 J.C. Narver and S.F. Slater, 'The Effect of Marketing Orientation on Business Profitability', *Journal of Marketing*, op. cit.

20 J.A. Siguaw, P.M. Simpson and T.L. Baker, 'Effects of Supplier Market Orientation on Distributor Market Orientation and the Channel Relationship: The Distributor Perspective', *Journal of Marketing*, 62 (July 1998): 99–111; G.B.Voss, Z.G. Voss, 'Strategic Orientation and Firm Performance in an Artistic Environment', *Journal of Marketing*, 64 (January, 2000): 67–83; F. Langerak, 'Effects of Market Orientation on the Behaviors of Salespersons and Purchasers, Channel Relationships, and Performance of Manufacturers'; J.W. Cadogan *et al.*, 'Key Antecedents to Export, Market-Oriented Behaviors: A Cross-National Empirical Examination', *op. cit.* C. Moorman and R.T. Rust, 'The Role of Marketing', *op. cit.*; B.J. Jaworski and A.K. Kohli, 'Market Orientation: Review Refinement and Roadmap', *op. cit.*; G. Rekettye and A.K. Gupta, 'Half-Way Towards Market Economy: Market Orientation of the Hungarian Manufacturing Companies', *Marketing and Management*, 29, 1 (1995): 27–32.
21 G. Hooley *et al.*, 'Market Orientation in the Transition Economies of Central Europe: Tests of the Narver and Slater Market Orientation Scales', *op. cit.*
22 J. Berács and K. Kolos (1994), *op. cit.*
23 J. Berács, I. Agárdi and K. Kolos (1997), *op. cit.*
24 G. Hooley *et al.*, 'Market Orientation in the Transition Economies of Central Europe: Tests of the Narver and Slater Market Orientation Scales', *op. cit.*
25 N.K. Malhotra, *Marketing Research – An Applied Orientation*, 3rd edn (Englewood Cliffs, NJ: Prentice Hall, 1999).
26 G. Hooley *et al.*, 'Market Orientation in the Transition Economies of Central Europe: Tests of the Narver and Slater Market Orientation Scales', *op. cit.*: 275.
27 *Ibid.*: 281.
28 G. Hooley and J. Berács, 'Marketing Strategies for the 21st Century: Lessons from the Top Hungarian Companies', *op. cit.*
29 G. Hooley *et al.*, 'Market Orientation in the Transition Economies of Central Europe: Tests of the Narver and Slater Market Orientation Scales', *op. cit.*
30 C. Moorman and R.T. Rust, 'The Role of Marketing', *op. cit.*
31 G. Hooley *et al.*, 'Market Orientation in the Transition Economies of Central Europe: Tests of the Narver and Slater Market Orientation Scales', *op. cit.*
32 J. Kapás, 'Szükséges-e többdimenziós vállalatelmélet? Az evolúciós vállalatelmélet kritikai összefoglalása', *op. cit.*
33 A. Chikán, 'Company Networks in the Hungarian Economy' (in Hungarian), *Gazdaság, Vállalkozás, Vezetés*, 6–7 (1997): 25–33.
34 P. Kotler, *Marketing Management*, *op. cit.*
35 S.D. Hunt, and R.M. Morgan, 'The Resource-Advantage Theory of Competition: Dynamics, Path Dependencies, and Evolutionary Dimensions', *Journal of Marketing*, 60 (October, 1996): 107–14.
36 G. Karsai, 'Supply Responsibility or Market Orientation?' (in Hungarian) (Budapest: KJK, 1988).
37 Á. Török, 'Several Ways to Market Economy Maturity? Interpreting and Applying some Basic Concepts in the Three Great Regions of the World Economy' (in Hungarian), *op. cit.*

5
Leadership in Central and Eastern European Countries

Manfred Reichl, Gerhard A. Wührer and Ven Sriram

Introduction

Since the fall of the Iron Curtain in the 1980s, issues related to the leadership style and managerial competence of Eastern European managers has been a focus of interest,[1] both for Western and Eastern European academics and companies. Given the emphasis on state-planned microeconomic behaviour and production, where managerial decisions in companies had to contribute to a central economic plan to fulfil the obligations of a five-year development perspective, managerial thinking consisted of values, norms, skills and techniques[2] that were more or less appropriate for a different decision situation, unlike that of 'Western'-style economic situations.

The conditions in which changes take place have to be accomplished from social, industrial and agricultural bases[3] that have been weakened by some years of turmoil and uncertainty, particularly in the countries in the former Soviet Union. Although the former socialist countries in Central and Eastern Europe (CEE) are not a uniform group, similar leadership models and HRM (human resource management) systems evolved in all of them during the Communist era in response to the requirements of the system. While many of the leadership skills required of CEE managers, such as strategic thinking, the willingness to take initiative and cost containment, are not different from those expected of managers elsewhere. The central-planning model followed under Communism meant that few CEE managers possessed these skills at the time of the transition to a free market system.[4]

Sample and methodology

In an attempt to understand current perspectives on leadership in CEE, an exploratory study was conducted in 2002–03 by Roland Berger, a leading German strategic management-consulting firm based on personal interviews with a convenience sample of CEE and EU managers. Seventy interviews with top managers of CEE companies (from Poland, the Czech Republic, Slovakia,

Hungary and Romania) and 25 from six Western European countries (Spain, France, the United Kingdom, the Netherlands, Germany and Switzerland) were conducted.

The semi-structured questionnaire[5] for self assessment covered variables such as: characteristics of management style, perceived handling of stakeholders, perceived competitiveness, perceived importance of improving competitiveness, reorganization of the company, handling of non-core activities, usage of cross-charging systems in companies, performance measurement and shareholder value, management recruitment, and management development.

Main findings of the study

When asked to assess their management style, CEE managers rated themselves higher on each dimension than did EU managers (see Figure 5.1). They saw themselves as more professional, more dynamic, tougher and more client-oriented. There are several reasons that might account for this self-assessment, which is markedly above their Western European counterparts.

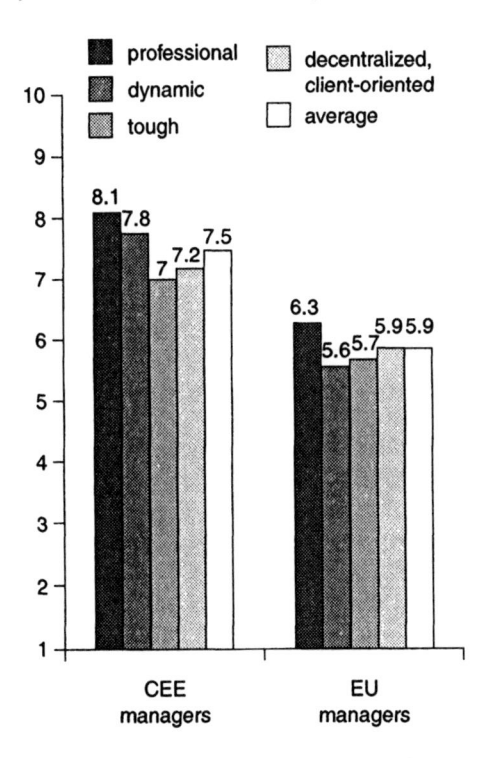

1 denotes no style at all; 10 very good.

Figure 5.1 Assessment of management style

Table 5.1 Perceived management style in CEE countries (CEE managers' views)

+	Managers in CEE countries...	−
...are more entrepreneurial ...are faster decision-makers ...have a more improvization-based style ...are more flexible/adaptable		...have less market knowledge ...have a less market-oriented managerial approach ...have a political rather than economic base of decision-making ...are less driven by shareholders' interests ...are less client-oriented ...are less dynamic ...pay more attention to political networking ...are more hierarchical

Some of the differences might be explained by different cultural backgrounds, management experiences of the past, a dissimilar economic environment, changing legal and political situations, different organizational structures and cultures, and overcompensation for a lack in managerial expertise during the transition process. It is worth pointing out that our knowledge of the management behaviour of managers during the transformation is scant and anecdotal, a view also supported by a survey of literature which revealed only very few leadership[6] studies that have included CEE countries. Some of these differences may also reflect a high power distance and the value placed on charismatic leadership in some Eastern European countries.[7]

Given the fact that there are some differences in the characterization of leadership styles, one of the superficial consequences could be that CEE managers should change their characterization of their leadership styles. The more intriguing questions are which dimensions of leadership styles are shared by both groups of managers and where are the differences in detail?

A summarized view (Table 5.1) presents the typical self-assessments of CEE management style. The strengths are based on a more entrepreneurial impetus, faster decision-making, an inclination to deal in unstructured situations with improvisation, and, as an add-on, a more flexible and adaptable approach to managerial situations. That strength is diluted by a lack of market knowledge, a less market-oriented approach, a strong tendency to decision-making based on political matters, little attention to shareholders' interests, less client-orientation, a less dynamic managerial behaviour, political networking,[8] and an influence of enterprise hierarchies or hierarchical thinking[9] in general business matters. It is necessary to stress the point that these weaknesses seem consistent in that they appear to reflect a lack of attention paid to vital external constituencies such as customers and shareholders. This again may be due to the relative unimportance of market forces under communism, where production was emphasized more than the market.

The self-characterization of management style is mirrored by the views of EU managers, who share some of the judgments of their CEE counterparts but also mention differences. The 'good news' is on the positive side. Here EU managers attribute 'a more pragmatic' approach to leadership, which is also fairly consistent with a more improvization-based style. The larger differences are found on the negative side.

To an extent there is a small overlap between CEE and EU managers' perceptions that cover the political base of decision-making, which really is a shared common view and a reflection of the influence of the economic and political establishment in CEE countries. But in addition there are some aspects of leadership that are far more important and are lacking in CEE managers, at least in the self-assessment of EU managers. The EU managers estimate the work of their colleagues in CEE to be less formal and organized, which may concern the planning process, control procedures, and their support by information technology. But it may also apply to management systems in general, for example formalized incentive systems, performance measurements and other measures to control the primary and secondary processes in the value chain. Typically, companies in CEE countries seem to be less focused on strategic issues, which means that they are assumed to have less explicitly defined core competencies. Competencies are always built on some specific resources,[10] developed by the firm or acquired and shared by partners.

Company strengths and weaknesses, personal values[11] of key implementers, have to be seen in the context[12] of industry, economic and technical opportunities and threats, and also broader societal expectations. Regarding this framework, it is not surprising that companies have a lack of clear priorities in improving competitiveness. Interestingly, both CEE and EU managers' perceptions of the management style of CEE managers is consistent with findings that Eastern Europeans preferred hierarchy rather than equality[13] and tended to be non-achievement-oriented.[14] More recent evidence[15] appears to suggest, however, that Eastern European managers are putting high value on their societies becoming more performance-oriented and less hierarchical in the future.

A comparison of the top priorities for improving competitiveness shows remarkable differences. Where EU managers tend to focus on one or some approaches to meet the demands of the future, their CEE counterparts tend to focus on multiple leverage points. CEE managers seem to place relatively more emphasis than EU managers (with the exception of management development and employee development) on internal issues. They appear to place less priority on market development and global markets than do their EU counterparts. Perhaps this may suggest that they feel the need to improve internal procedures and increase their efficiency in the domestic market before attempting to take on the far more risky strategy of going global. EU managers count on continuous management improvement, where most of the other exercises have been done, or are of minor importance in comparison.

These research findings contrast somewhat with the excellent self-assessments in management style that have been done (cf Table 5.1) by CEE managers, which once again gives the impression of an overestimation of their capabilities, especially in comparison with EU managers. It is remarkable that the competitiveness agenda 'management development' seems to be of minor importance for CEE managers.

Suggestions for the contents of management training include three categories[16] of personal attributes: *operational skills* to cover the basic technical areas of management such as accounting, finance, marketing and so on; *organizational skills* to manage perhaps large numbers of people who possess the operational skills, and *strategic skills* that enable the understanding of the basic nature of market-oriented business, the importance of strategic goals, and the social responsibilities and community obligations of business in a modern market-based society. Some of the skills are of course already developed as the research findings show, for instance social responsibilities and the need to deal with political obligations. The aspirations of management development programmes are therefore at least threefold: (1) a realistic and balanced assessment of skills deficits on all three levels; (2) development and/or acquisition of in- or out-house training programmes to deliver training success; and (3) an ongoing update of the programmes as the environment[17] changes. This view might be too concentrated on cognitive contents of management development programmes. As Chatterji points out, there is a demand for a balance[18] between cognitive knowledge based on empirical evidence and non-cognitive matters like leadership and communications skills, where the currently the ratio is 40 to 60 per cent.

It turns out that management qualifications and in addition management recruiting are the critical processes in the years ahead. As there is a tight labour market for skilled and experienced managers of all levels, external recruiting is done less on an 'often/regularly' basis in CEE companies. Even recruiting from internal labour markets is relatively more difficult in CEE countries. So the important need for management development is once again stressed.

Conclusions

The research findings of this recent exploratory study, which was done from a managerial and consultant perspective, reveal the crucial factors that might hamper the success of companies from the emerging markets of CEE countries. Leadership in CEE countries depends on a realistic assessment of skills and motivations available. It appears that while CEE managers understand the need to recruit good managers, they don't appear to rely on external recruiting as much as EU managers, partly because they feel that there is greater difficulty in finding managers externally than internally. This points very clearly to the need for management development in CEE countries. Additionally, many of the managers in CEE may be underestimating the challenges of EU accession while not concentrating enough on improvement measures.

On the other hand the quest for further modernization is important. There are still inefficiencies in existing organizations, despite the reorganizations undergone so far. In fact, CEE companies report having undergone more reorganization on average than EU companies in the past 10 years (four versus three), and 74 per cent of CEE companies report having gone through reorganization in the last two years, versus 59 per cent of the EU companies interviewed. But unless this restructuring is done strategically,[19] CEE managers are going to find it difficult to transform their companies to compete successfully in a market-based economy.

The data from this study also point to the powerful impact that culture has on management and leadership styles. Although the data presented were collected more than 10 years after CEE countries began their transition from a communist system, the findings show that many significant differences remain in the way Eastern and Western European executives manage their companies and what they see as their important priorities for the future. While some of these differences are undoubtedly due to the differences that still exist in infrastructure, human and financial resources, technology and in other areas between these two parts of Europe, some differences in management style will probably still remain long after the economic gap has been bridged. As the business world globalizes it does not necessarily follow that cultural differences will disappear or diminish.[20] The findings reported here provide us with a strong reminder of that.

Notes

1 V. Suutari and K. Riusala, 'Leadership Styles in Central Eastern Europe: Experiences of Finnish expatriates in the Czech Republic, Hungary and Poland', *Scandinavian Journal of Management*, 17 (2001): 249–80.
2 W.M. Danis, 'Differences in Values, Practices, and Systems among Hungarian Managers and Western Expatriates: An Organizing Framework and Typology', *Journal of World Business*, 38 (2003): 224–44.
3 M.C. Frazer, 'Management Education for Societies in Transition', in M.C. Frazer and M. Chatterji (eds), *Management Education in Countries in Transition* (Basingstoke: Macmillan – now Palgrave, 1999): 1–12.
4 K.L. Newman, 'Leading Radical Change in Transition Economies', *Leadership and Organization Development Journal*, 19 (1998): 309–24.
5 The questionnaire is available on request from Roland Berger Strategy Consultants, Vienna.
6 V. Suutari and K. Riusala, 'Leadership Styles in Central Eastern Europe: Experiences of Finnish Expatriates in the Czech Republic, Hungary and Poland', *op. cit.*: 252.

7   G. Bakacsi, T. Sandor, K. Andras and I. Viktor, 'Eastern European Cluster: Tradition and Transition', *Journal of World Business*, 37 (2002): 69–80.
8   See also W.M. Danis, 'Differences in Values, Practices, and Systems among Hungarian Managers and Western Expatriates: An Organizing Framework and Typology', *op. cit.*: 233.
9   *Ibid.*: 237.
10 M. Humbert, D. Jolly and F. Thérin, 'Building Strategy on Technological Resources and Commercial Proactiveness: The Gemplus Case', *European Management Journal*, 15 (1997): 658–66; J.A. Mathews, 'A Resource-based View on Schumpeterian Economic Dynamics', *Journal of Evolutionary Economics* (2002): 29–54.
11 W.M. Danis, 'Differences in Values, Practices, and Systems among Hungarian Managers and Western Expatriates: An Organizing Framework and Typology', *op. cit.*: 234.
12 J. Fahy and A. Smithee, 'Strategic Marketing and the Resource Based View of the Firm', Academy *of Marketing Science Review*, 10 (1999), available at http/www.amsreview.org/articles/fahy 10-1999.pdf
13 B.P. Smith, 'Leadership in Europe – Euro-Management or the Footprint of History? *European Journal of Work and Organizational Psychology*, 6 (1997): 375–86.
14 C. Hampden-Turner and F. Trompenaars, *Building Cross-Cultural Competence: How to Create Wealth From Conflicting Values* (London: Yale University Press, 2000).
15 G. Bakacsi *et al.*, 'Eastern European Cluster: Tradition and Transition', *op. cit.*
16 M.C. Frazer, 'Management Education for Societies in Transition', *op. cit.*: 3.
17 M. Chatterji, 'Management Education: Past, Present and Future', in M.C. Frazer and M. Chatterji (eds), *Management Education in Countries in Transition* (Basingstoke: Macmillan – now Palgrave, 1999): 225–41.
18 *Ibid.*: 227.
19 K. Uhlenbruck, K.E. Meyer and M.A. Hitt, 'Organizational Transformation in Transition Economies: Resource-based and Organizational Learning Perspectives', *Journal of Management Studies*, 40 (2003): 257–82.
20 M. Javidan and R.J. House, 'Leadership and Culture Around the World: Findings From GLOBE', *Journal of World Business*, 37 (2002): 1–2.

6
Market Entry Strategy of a Slovenian Jewellery Producer

Vito Bobek

Introduction

Zlatarna Celje, a Slovene producer of jewellery, is presently only in Slovenia and in some markets of former Yugoslavia. The company would like to expand to new markets, starting with Central and Eastern Europe, and the first of those markets should be the Czech Republic. Until now, there have been two subsidiary companies established: one in Zagreb, the capital of Croatia, and the other in Sarajevo, the capital of Bosnia and Herzegovina, with two branch offices, respectively.

The main objective of this chapter is to develop a market entry strategy for Zlatarna Celje in order to achieve a competitive position of the company in the Czech Republic. For this objective to be achieved, there are first some minor objectives to be completed:

- The market itself should be precisely analysed, along with the political and economic environment.
- On the basis of collected information, the best possible market entry strategies should be developed.
- It is necessary to define target segments of customers as well as the market positioning of the company and the products' brand name.
- In the end, a marketing mix should be developed.

The *first proposition* is that the market of the Czech Republic has many similarities to the Slovene market, and that it is therefore appropriate for Zlatarna Celje to start its foreign operations there.

The *second proposition* is that the target segment should be the newly established high class of Czechs, which includes successful entrepreneurs, managers and foreigners working in the Czech Republic.

The *third proposition* is that the company should concentrate its sales in Prague at the beginning, for two reasons: the highest living standard in the country and the large number of tourists visiting Prague.

It is assumed that competition in this market is severe since it is also an attractive market for other companies which would like to take advantage of this situation. The next assumption is that no major adaptations in the design of exported products would be needed, since there is now a global trend in jewellery design.

The company: Zlatarna Celje

Founded in 1844, the company was the biggest jewellery company during the Austro-Hungarian monarchy. The company's largest expansion was achieved in the period 1976–91, when practically the whole market of former Yugoslavia was covered and more than 1,000 people were employed. After the collapse of the former Yugoslav market in 1991, the company has successfully transformed into a competitive and profitable enterprise. In 2000, the company received the international certificate of quality ISO 9001, and the company is now privately owned with a dispersed ownership structure. Three business units form the company: jewellery production, a dental programme, and industrial programmes. The company has several sources of success factors: recognition of the brand name, design, skilled labour, high productivity, low wages, and a quality orientation.

As Slovenia is one of the best-developed Central European transition economies according to many criteria, and one that has had relatively well-developed relations with Western firms for some time, it is to be expected that Slovene firms will exhibit a market orientation that could lead to success.

The company has two strategic goals: specialization in high-quality and high-class jewellery, and to enter foreign markets (Central and Eastern Europe, the USA and Japan) and export the majority of its production.

Country risk and opportunity analysis for the Czech Republic

Trade environment

The Czech Republic is traditionally an important trading partner of Slovenia. In 2001, Slovene exports to this market amounted for 1.8 per cent of total exports, while imports from the Czech Republic amounted for 2.4 per cent of total Slovene imports.

For the Czech Republic, duties and taxes are levied on *ad valorem* basis, that is on the basis of the declared value of the goods sold.[1] In addition to customs tariffs, imported goods are liable to taxes (value added tax and excise tax on some kinds of goods). In harmony with the Czech Republic's international obligations, identical rates of these taxes apply to both domestic and imported goods.[2] The labelling requirements of the Czech Republic were fully harmonized with those of the EU by the end of 1999. Czech importers and distributors are responsible for the correct labelling of products that are put on the Czech market, and can typically advise foreign exporters on specific requirements regarding labelling and marking.[3]

Cultural environment

Cultural differences require special attention when entering new markets, and their segmentation.[4] Czech culture is free and democratic, incredibly broad, diverse and multilayered. Among the most significant features of Czech culture are mobility, concept of time and status. Czechs are by nature egalitarian and frown on status and its outside representation. A high importance is attached to academic titles, which are used very often in addressing people. Also, a sense of humour is a very important characteristic of a person, while modesty is an important virtue that Czech people appreciate. Czechs' attitudes towards foreigners are sometimes inferior and sometimes superior. They may ridicule them for strange habits and behaviours typical of tourists, while on the other hand they may feel respect for other countries for their economical, political or cultural achievements.[5]

Social environment

After 1989, Czech society experienced a significant increase in income and wealth inequality. Consequently, it has been divided into a minor part of the very rich, and a major part of the relatively poor. Also a new middle class has appeared, structured mostly of white-collar workers and entrepreneurs. One of the factors that has prevented faster development of the middle class has been the relatively slow transformation[6] of the occupation structure. The consequences of social and economic changes have dramatically altered some factors acting on lifestyles as a complex phenomenon concerning attitudes towards personal and social life. The factors might be labelled 'polarization' in income, demonstrative consumption, fragmentation of society into those who follow, and those who resist globalization and post-modernism.

Target positioning in the Czech market

The general conditions of the Czech market might be described as follows: the market has had to face the presence of multinational companies coping with brand-supporting activities, while consumers have had to develop brand awareness; domestic companies have lost ground being unable to adapt to the emerging market environment that requires professional marketing activities; and market and consumer behaviour research has become more and more vital for companies.

Czech jewellery market research

To gain more insight, research into the Czech jewellery market was conducted in five steps:[7]

1. *Definition of the problem.* Obtaining an overview of the present situation in the Czech jewellery market: who is present on the market, how strong are competitors, where jewellery is being sold. On this basis, the right marketing mix strategy may be created for target segments.
2. *Analysing the situation.* Secondary up-to-date data analyses on the situation in the Czech jewellery market are not available. Therefore, most of the information included in this research was collected onsite via observation.
3. *Collecting specific data.* Two basic methods were used for obtaining primary data: questioning and observing.
4. *Interpreting the data.* After the data were collected, they were interpreted through statistical processing and analysis.
5. *Solving the problem.* The research results were used to conduct marketing decisions – the Four Ps strategy.

Specific data

Larger jewellery selling companies (the criterion for larger companies was their sales networks) are present throughout the whole territory of the Czech Republic, and most commonly also in the Slovak Republic. These companies are Primossa, Klenoty Aurum, Lucie Hubacova and others. They usually have their own stores where they sell their own products, and also work as wholesalers selling their products to smaller jewellery shops, usually called 'zlatnıtn'.

Large chains with outlets represent the second kind of jewellery sellers, and there are two kinds of such stores: Czech chains like Klenoty Aurum and Primossa have their outlets all over the Czech Republic, while foreign-owned chains like Allure and Folli Follie have their outlets most commonly only in Prague and sometimes in other tourist cities. They sell their jewellery under their own brand name.

A third kind of jewellery store sells only garnet jewellery and is focused on tourists. These stores are owned by small entrepreneurs and have their outlets in tourist parts of Prague and other tourist cities like Karlovy Vary.

Media used for advertising are fliers (mainly small stores), web pages on the Internet, Czech versions of magazines such as *Elle* or *Cosmopolitan* (for women) and *Status Quo* (for men).

As far as the jewellery market is concerned, according to the Czech Assay Office,[8] sales of jewellery have grown since 1989, with an annual growth rate of 20 per cent during 1995 and 1996.

Segmentation of the Czech market: a seven-step approach

To identify market segments the criteria[9] 'effective', 'identifiable', 'profitable', 'accessible' and 'actionable' were used. The seven-step approach for segmenting products markets developed by McCarthy and Perreault[10] was then used:

1. *Name the broad product market.* In our case, the broad product market is represented by jewellery, made of gold and silver in various price classes.
2. *List potential customer needs.* This is a brainstorming step. In our case, needs that could be satisfied by jewellery products are: (i) some people buy jewellery because of status, (ii) people buy jewellery for others as presents, (iii) jewellery is bought on special occasions such as weddings, engagements, (iv) jewellery is also a fashion accessory, so it is bought by some people in order to be fashionable, and (v) as a long-lasting product, jewellery can fulfill the need for permanency.
3. *Form homogeneous sub-markets.* In our case, homogeneous sub-markets could be: (a) people looking for a present for a special occasion such as Christmas or a birthday. This is a mass market where one of the most important determinants is price; (b) Czechs and foreign young women with good social status, who also pay great attention to fashion, can afford and are willing to spend a lot of money in order to achieve this, including on jewellery even on no special occasions; (c) Czechs and foreign young professionals working in high positions in companies; they may have problems with what to buy for partners or relatives; (d) people who have spent the majority of their lives under communism, but now belong to the highest social class. In this class are mostly people in their 50s and 60s who are not willing to spend their money for no reason; they need to see it as an investment since they feel their money was hard-earned; (e) tourists who are not oriented towards lower-priced garnet jewellery that is being sold all over the Czech Republic as a typical present from this country; (f) people anticipating getting married and looking for wedding rings. In this case price is commonly less important than design.
4. *Identify the determining dimensions.* From the previous step, dimensions for identified sub-markets could be for segment (a) – price against value; a good deal, special offers, good design. For segment (b) – price is less important than modern design, brand name and accessibility. For segment (c) – service is the most important element since young professionals constantly lack time, and also need a lot of help when choosing what to buy. Price is not very important for them, but accessibility is. For segment (d) – these people are also looking for a good value, although they do not miss the money. But having lived most of their lives made communism, they are used to saving. They are willing to spend a lot of money, but only if they see it as a good investment. Segment (e) – seeks something special, they do not care a lot about price, and they do not have much time for shopping. It is important that products are accessible to them. For segment (f) – this group seeks a long-lasting good design. Price is mostly not of primary importance, although most cannot afford very expensive items since they are starting a new life.

5 *Name the possible product markets.* In our case, the following names could be attached to each product market: (a) *good dealers*, (b) *design seekers*, (c) *service seekers*, (d) *investors*, (e) *specialty seekers*, (f) *durable design seekers*; and
6 *Evaluate why product market segments behave as they do.* For design seekers it is very important to understand that they mostly look for products for themselves, while service seekers mostly look for products as presents and usually don't know exactly what they want. However, design seekers sometimes also look for products for others. For specialty seekers, it is important that they are fully informed quickly and effectively. They do not have much time to think about their purchase and they do not spend much time in the country, so the speed of acquiring them as customers is very important.
7 *Make a rough estimate of the size of each product-market segment.* The segments of design and service seekers mainly belong to the middle and upper-middle social classes, and the middle class, according to social studies, makes up about 30 per cent of the economically active population of the Czech Republic. However, it is important to realize that other people not targeted by this strategy also belong to the middle and upper-middle class, not only the two targeted segments. Good dealers, who comprise the mass market, belong mainly to the lower-middle class and blue-collar workers. About 57 per cent of the active population belongs to these latter two classes.[11]

Positioning in the Czech market

Our goal is to position the company within the Czech market according to targeted segments in two different ways. For the segment of 'good dealers' we would position the company as 'unnamed', and offer products through the big chain stores such as Tesco, Hypernova, Carrefour and Globus. For the segments of 'design seekers', 'service seekers' and 'specialty seekers', the company would be positioned as a premium-class jewellery house with own outlet somewhere in the centre of Prague. Products would be sold under special brand names. Of particular interest for SWOT analysis (Figure 6.1) are the segments 'investors', 'specialty seekers' and 'durable design seekers'.

Market strategy

Market-entry strategy

On the basis of the company's internal goals and research into the political, legal, cultural and economic environment of the Czech Republic, the recommended entry strategy to the Czech Republic market would be as a company-owned sales subsidiary. The strategy would first concentrate on Prague by opening a first sales subsidiary there, but in addition would also market products to hypermarket chains with outlets all over the Czech Republic.

Strength	Weakness
Experience in foreign markets, modern and traditional design, products in price class, country of origin Slovenia, young and enthusiastic board of directors, own distribution network to foreign markets	Large geographic distance to Czech market as cost factor, no previous experience in Czech market
Opportunities	**Threats**
Size of Czech market, building up a new brand name, new potential customers every day – tourists, CEFTA-membership, foreigners living in Czech Republic, formation of new wealthy social class after 1989	Small purchasing power of average Czech citizen, very severe competition, level of rents in Prague, corruption, bureaucracy, weak demand from foreigners/tourists

Figure 6.1 SWOT analysis of Zlatarna Celje in the Czech market

Zlatarna Celje will appoint a specialist from its home company to be based in the Czech Republic for a starting period and to be responsible for setting up an own sales subsidiary.[12]

Marketing-mix strategies

The marketing mix is a set of marketing tools that a firm uses to achieve its goals in target markets.[13] There are basically three possible approaches in developing a market-oriented strategy in a broad product market:[14] undifferentiated, differentiated and focused. In our case, a differentiated approach will be used to serve customers better, even if this strategy requires higher costs.

A single strategy A will be adopted for the mass-market segment of good dealers. A second strategy B will be adopted for the rest of the targeted segments, but will differ according to each of the segments, design seekers, service seekers and specialty seekers. Here the primary concern is promotion and distribution, since products are not going to be adapted substantially. In this kind of production, it is possible to talk about European or even Western styles with the preferences and refined taste of the Czech people and foreigners living there.

Product, price and place

The company will not adapt its products substantially. For strategy A, the product will be will designed but will not contain any expensive stones that will result in too high a price. A private branding strategy will be followed and the company will produce and deliver the product to the stores, thus enabling prices to be kept low. The distribution will be through large hypermarket chains such as Tesco, Globus, Hypernova and Carrefour where the mass-market segment tends to shop.

For the more discerning customers, strategy B will be followed. Here products will be developed especially for the Czech market, sold through company-owned stores and carry the company's brand name. Prices will be higher due to lower price sensitivity of these consumers, uniqueness of the product and to support the higher marketing costs such as advertising and sales force as well as additional expenses such as rents and salaries. The stores will be located in areas where the design, service and specialty seekers tend to shop.

Promotion

For strategy A customers, there will be no promotion provided by the producer; promotion will only be carried out by the chain stores themselves in their weekly, monthly and seasonal offers, distributed to Czech homes.

Strategy B design seekers constitute a segment of young, educated Czech and foreign women living in Prague who enjoy well-paid professional positions. For them, promotion will be carried out through the Czech editions of international women's magazines, as well as professional magazines, such as the *Prague Business Journal, Dnes* or *Euro*. Advertising will emphasize design, since this is the most important attribute for this segment of customers where price is not of primary importance. Since foreign women do not commonly read these magazines, the foreign part of this segment will be covered by placing leaflets, written in English, into some of Prague's best restaurants, as well as in the *Prague Post* newspaper which provides basic information for foreigners in Prague.

For strategy B service seekers, mainly young men, entrepreneurs or managers of international companies, advertising will be carried out through professional magazines like *Euro* and *Prague Business Journal*, as well as some male magazines like *Status Quo*. Advertisement emphasis will be on store location, since these customers are always very busy. The other emphasis should be on services that the company provides for choosing jewellery. Foreigners within this segment will again be covered by English-language leaflets placed in some of Prague's best restaurants, as well as in the *Prague Post*.

Strategy B specialty seekers mostly include tourists willing to spend a relatively high sum of money on their presents from Prague, and for them attractive leaflets will be placed in the lounges of Prague's best hotels, as well as in clubs, restaurants and theatres.

Conclusions

The main purpose of this chapter has been to highlight the Czech market in general and identify the best market entry and marketing-mix strategies for the jewellery producer Zlatarna Celje.

A combination of business research (market entry strategy for the Czech Republic) and microeconomic research (demand and supply of jewellery products in the Czech Republic) was adopted, but macroeconomic research (economic situation of the market at the national level) also has been used. The assumption stated at the beginning of the chapter, that the Czech market is appropriate for the company to start such operations due to the high level of achieved transformation and its position in Central Europe, turned out to be correct. The market has been segmented and targeted into several buyer groups for jewellery.

We identified several possible market-entry strategies for the company, such as a chain of outlets spread across the country under a common name, targeting all segments at once, or the option of giving exclusive rights to a company in the Czech Republic to sell the products.

The strategy we thought best is that of opening an own-outlet on one of the most saturated streets in Prague. In-store products would be sold under a specially developed brand name for the Czech market. At the same time, the store would also serve as a sales subsidiary from where products of lower prices, and unbranded, would be distributed to hypermarket chains to serve that largest segment, mainly 'good dealers'.

On the whole, it is possible to conclude that conditions in the Czech jewellery market are very good at the moment. There are large potential profits provided the company's approach is differentiated according to the society structure. Also, politically, the Czech Republic is a very stable country, but attention has to be given to currency exchange rates and their development.

Since Zlatarna Celje is present only in the markets of the former Yugoslavia at the moment, it is expected that it will be a good experience for the company to start its foreign operations in the Czech Republic, where conditions are so similar to those in Slovenia and where there are thousands of potential new customers arriving in the country every day. We conclude that the company has very good chances of long-term successful operations in the Czech Republic, as a spring board to entering other international markets.

Notes

1 (USDC), US Department of Commerce National Trade Data Bank, Czech Republic: Country Reports on Economic Policies and Trade Practices (1999), http://www.tradeport.org/ts/countries/czechrep/regs.html (retrieved 15 January 2003).
2 J. Maceska, Commercial Policy of the Czech Republic (2001), http://www.doingbusiness.cz/article.asp?ArticleID = 50 (retrieved 20 December 2002).
3 (USDC), US Department of Commerce National Trade Data Bank, Czech Republic: Country Reports on Economic Policies and Trade Practices (1999), *op. cit.*
4 J.E. McCarthy and W.D. Perreault, *Basic Marketing* (Boston, MA: Irwin, 1993): 131.
5 D. Lukes, Czech Culture Guide (2002), http://www.bohemica.com/czechculture/index.htm (retrieved 15 February 2002).
6 P. Mateju, The Middle Class Formation in the Czech Republic (1998), http://archiv.soc.cas.cz/stwp/98-6.doc (retrieved 10 January 2003).
7 J.E. McCarthy and W.D. Perreault, *Basic Marketing, op. cit.*: 149.
8 Czech Assay Office, Mission and Legal Status (1998), http://www.puncovniurad.cz/eng/poslani/poslani.html (retrieved 1 February 2003).
9 P. Doyle, *Marketing Management and Strategy*, 2nd edn (London: Prentice Hall Europe, 1998): 74.

10 J.E. McCarthy and W.D. Perreault, *Basic Marketing, op. cit.*: 97–101.
11 P. Mateju, The Middle Class Formation in the Czech Republic, *op. cit.*
12 M. Bohacek, *International Business Law* (Prague: University of Economics, 2001).
13 S. Mercado, R. Welford and K. Prescott, *European Business* (Harlow: Pearson Education, 2001).
14 P. Doyle, *Marketing Management and Strategy, op. cit.*: 75–7.

Part III
Views on Emerging Markets: Management in Practice

7
Give a 'FILIP' to Your Marketing Programme

Rajan Chhibba

The march of globalization has brought about a new meaning to the term 'global marketing'. If one thinks of global marketing as the ability to effectively compete in one's chosen market against all forms of global competition, there are hundreds of global firms which are global from the competitiveness perspective, even though they do not necessarily service global markets. In this regard India and China potentially have a large number of globally competitive firms. This chapter focuses on firms in India, and tries to draw globally relevant lessons from their experiences.

Why India?

Many multinationals such as Unilever, Whirlpool, American Express and Timex have senior executives who have cut their teeth in the same market – the Indian subcontinent. Their organizations have recognized that although the value of business handled by them was small by global standards, successfully handling the emerging-economy marketplace of India had developed them as effective global managers.

If the Indian experience is an MNC HR manager's happy-hunting-ground for global managers, both in the above organizations as well as others such as GE, Stanchart, HSBC, Nestlé, Alstom, and Colgate Palmolive, it stands to reason that there will be lessons learned from the Indian experience that will have global relevance.

India is a microcosm of the global marketplace for the following important reasons:

- *India's size.* As home to over a billion people representing over a fifth of the world's population, India certainly qualifies to represent the world on a traditional sample size basis. Added to that is its geography which, besides making it the fourth largest country by area, is also home to all the climatic conditions of the world.

- *India's growth potential.* India has in place drivers for its economic growth which go beyond merely rising incomes. It is one of the handful of countries in the world whose 'spending' age group of 20–49 is set to grow in the next seven years representing an unmatched growth engine.
- *India's diversity.* India is a unique cultural melting pot where the number of distinct religions, languages and cuisines are perhaps the highest for any country in the world. From the Indian Census 2001, on the basis of religion, while the majority of the population is Hindu (750 million), the absolute numbers of Muslims (150 million), Christians (25 million), Sikhs (22 million), Buddhists (10 million) and Jains (7 million) would each be larger than the population of many nations of the world.[1] Even the Hindus are segmented into various sects and do not represent a unified religious entity. This multiethnicity transforms itself actually into a political entity which is perhaps as diverse as Europe – 28 states, 17 official languages (with over 5,000 dialects), over 3,000 cuisines, over 500 different recognized dance forms, and so on. The sheer diversity under one roof again makes a strong case for India being seen as a global microcosm.
- *India's wealth profile.* In terms of income and wealth (see Table 7.1), the profile of the Indian population represents everything from the richest to the poorest in the world. On the one hand India has the largest number of 'dollar' millionaires in the world outside the USA (unfortunately most of it invested in real estate and gold),[2] while on the other 29 per cent of the population are below the poverty line, representing the poorest segment of the world's population. Between the rich and the poor is a consuming class, which by itself is a population equivalent to that of the USA and which represents a significant spending power.
- *Indians' global exposure.* In the last 20 years, the Indian consumer has been exposed to global products, services and cultures thanks to comprehensive media coverage, strong family linkages with the over one million-

Table 7.1 A profile of the Indian consumer[3]

Annual Income (US$)	Number of Households (millions)	
	1997–98	2006–07
>4674	1	5
979–4674	33	75
478–979	54	82
347–478	44	20
<347	33	17

Source: National Council of Applied Economic Research.

strong Indian diaspora – non-resident Indians – and extensive international travel by resident Indians. In fact, in 2002 Indians were the highest-spending tourists in tourist destination economies like Singapore, Switzerland and Thailand.[4]

- *India's thriving private enterprise.* Despite its brush with socialism, private enterprise has always thrived in India and has been an engine of economic growth. India has the largest number of companies (7,500) listed on the Stock Exchange[5] representing largely the manufacturing sector and over 12 million retail outlets constituting a very strong service sector.[6] Add to that the largest number of bank branches, post-offices, railway stations and transportation fleets – and you have a business structure that again provides a robust global sample.

Indian private enterprise is vibrant because Indians prefer being self-employed to working in the organized sector. According to an International Labour Organization study in 1991, India is the only country in the world where the labour flow from organized-sector employment is higher than the inflow from unorganized to organized. This helps private enterprise nurture itself, and grow.

- *India's vibrant and functioning democratic institutions.* With a strong tradition of democratic institutions like the national parliament, elected state and local governments and a strong legal system, India offers an open environment for marketing. At the same time, globally current legislation on women's empowerment, child labour, equal opportunities, labour laws and the environment make the legal operating environment as complex as in the developed world, if not more so. At the same time, India has its fair share of scandals like Enron, which provide an impetus for strengthening the regulatory mechanisms as is happening in the rest of the world. The scandals include the stockmarket scam of 1992, where bank funds were illegally channelled into the stockmarket creating an artificial bull run, the unit-trust scandal of mismanagement of the country's largest mutual funds, and the disappearance of over 800 listed companies.

The study

Having established the global relevance of studying the Indian business experience, a study of the success factors of companies operating in India was undertaken. The sample consisted of 80 companies/brands that have achieved strong brand strength. The sample was evenly divided among those that have been in the country over 20 years, and those for fewer than 20 years. Within that, the sample had both Indian and foreign companies. The companies were picked from six broad sectors of the economy to ensure that different product categories were adequately represented. At this juncture, it may be useful to point out that in 2002, as can be seen in Table 7.2 eight of the ten fastest growing brands in the fast-moving consumer goods

Table 7.2 Fastest growing Indian FMCG companies

Top 10 companies by growth

(Sales of above INR 1,000 million = US$ 20million)

	Brand name	Growth rate (%)
1	Parakh Foods	32.4
2	Haldirams	26.9
3	Anchor Health	21.4
4	Dhara Veg Oil & Foods	14.5
5	Perfetti India	14.1
6	Kanpur Detergents	14.5
7	CavinKare	13.3
8	Marico Industries	11.6
9	Godrej Hi-Care	7.9
10	Cadbury	6.5

Source: AC Nielsen Connect 2003 (released in May 2003).

(FMCG) category where the MNCs are supposedly dominant, were domestic Indian companies.

This story is repeated in other sectors like automobiles (Tata, Mahindra & Mahindra), telecom services (Bharti, Reliance, Tata and BSNL) and banking (SBI, HDFC, ICICI). Even brands of MNCs that have been successful such as Dettol, Colgate, Lux and Pepsi have had to change their marketing strategies to suit the environment and to ensure their success. For instance, the snack food business of Pepsi had to relaunch itself around Indian snacks, and Colgate had to develop a business around toothpowder.

The study was a two-step process. In the first step, executives/academics/consultants known to the author were asked to define marketing success by assessing common underlying patterns that separated successful companies from others. This was necessary because strong parameters for measuring success in terms of shareholder wealth and other such factors were not available. Next, interviews were conducted with executives/customers/vendors from the sample companies to identify the key lessons for success, which may have global relevance.

Defining marketing success

Most organizations measure their successes or failures against their own goals and objectives. While this makes sense from their own viewpoint, some common benchmarks need to be established to see if there is pattern which cuts across product categories. Typically, success is measured by sales turnover or market share, and very often these are related to each other. Each of these measures works well in mature product categories, but fail to reflect the true picture in evolving markets. This is particularly true in cases where products are successful in sales but fail to make money because sales are bought at a price through deep discounting and consumer/trade push. In many cases, market shares are difficult to define since market segments are highly fragmented by geography, mode of purchase, price levels and so on.

Therefore for the purpose of this analysis, it was decided to assess both the external consumer-facing strategies and the internal systemic processes of all successful brands/services in which there was unanimity among the sample set of 30 executives, as being factors that reflected success. These products, which were checked for common traits, were chosen from across various categories such as FMCG (ChiK Shampoo), Food Service (Nirulas), service providers (HDFC Bank), fashion products (Newport Jeans), snack foods (Haldiram), and automobiles (Tata Indica).

From the interviews, three traits emerged that were common to all the successes: (1) a repeat business rate of 30 per cent or more; (2) profitability by the end of year 3 from start; and (3) world class.

While most of the companies/brands selected were considered successful, the main examples of unsuccessful ones were Tang, Ariel's initial launch, KFC, Baskin Robbins, and HMT. In addition, the author examined other well-known unsuccessful ones such as American Tourister, Fiat, Piaggio and others based on his own consulting experience.

Findings: successful companies give a 'FILIP' to their marketing programmes

The starting block of our thinking was that the fundamental 4Ps of marketing – product, pricing, place and promotion – were addressed by every marketer, yet some succeeded while others failed. Strategizing the Ps emerged as basic factors, which everyone addressed, in all the cases discussed. The successful companies in fact frequently went beyond the Ps to execute total business plans that continually bootstrapped the marketing effort.

What emerged was a consistent pattern to what the successful firms did beyond the Ps to develop a sustained marketing advantage. The success formula emerged as a five-pronged framework, which we have called the 'FILIP' model of ensuring marketing success. In short, successful companies give an extra FILIP to their marketing programmes by design. FILIP stands for:

F: Fraternity building as the most important brand-building investment.
I: Institution building outside the firm's environment as a key strategic marketing weapon.
L: Logically modular and phased capital investments.
I: Indigenous innovation as a tool for delivering customer value.
P: Portfolio management of market segments from day one.

These five initiatives represent a balance of proactive initiatives and de-risking strategies. Three of these initiatives are proactive – fraternity building, institution building and indigenous innovation. These all lead to long-term sustainable competitive advantages for the firms. The other two, logically modular and phased capital investments and portfolio segmentation, are de-risking strategies which help the firm cope with the vagaries of the dynamic and turbulent environment in which a firm functions. Successful marketers impose these FILIP factors over and above the strategy that emerges from the classic Ps of marketing.

F: Fraternity building as the critical brand investment

Any brand launch, by definition, involves making investments in media, below-the-line promotions, channel promotions, and other areas. Since all the cases studied were of brands that figure in the top hundred media spenders in the country, we had expected that the key aspect of brand building would be some insights into successful communication and media strategies. In fact in case after case the most important brand-building initiative was actually the investments made early on in 'fraternity building' to support the brand. These fraternities were consumers, trade partners, governments, social groups, or vendors. These fraternities assumed a life of their own and gave soft support to the brand by way of localization, cost-sharing, financial de-risking or spreading product usage.

Interesting models of fraternity development were found. Hindustan Lever, the Unilever subsidiary, is currently building a consumer 'fraternity' of self-help groups in villages which will one day give them unique distribution muscle. Mother Dairy, the leading milk brand, created a fraternity of retired ex-soldiers as the team of operating franchises giving itself teeth to get low-cost and disciplined manpower for its retail outlets virtually on tap. Asian Paints built a trade fraternity of non-paint paint retailer dealers and supported them with business models that were customized to their needs. This fraternity displays a loyalty that ensures that Asian Paints sales stay always twice that of the next competitor.

Amul, the milk-food cooperative, focused its fraternity building on a cooperative model of sourcing which converted thousands of dairy farmers with even one cow as vendors and in turn provided the initial captive market base to sustain the brand launch. Lijjat Papad, the women's self-help group, formed a manufacturing fraternity of housewives to produce low cost *papad* (an Indian snack). Maruti Suzuki cars and Bajaj Scooters created fraternities of independent service mechanics who could earn their livelihoods with minimum investments in working capital. Hero Motors, the motorcycle brand, chose the route of creating a fraternity of bicycle traders who became motorcycle dealers. They became the motorcycle protagonists upgrading the cycle-using population to motorcycles and not motor scooters as was the norm till then. Delhi's Hyatt Regency hotel made its most important investment in the taxi-driver fraternity – free meals for over a month for each of them. In every case, whether one looks at Tata Salt, Lux, Colgate, Nirlep (the non-stick cookware brand) or any other, investments made in fraternity building were perceived as the key success factor.

The point to note is that more mileage has been gained by the successful brands by a focused attempt at fraternity building than by all the advertising and promotions put together. Although not part of the sample, the marketplace is replete with examples of very successful media launches but the products failing because there was no fraternity with a stake in its success. A case in point is Catch – the table-salt and spice brand. It has almost 100 per cent recall and trial and product satisfaction but very low sales. While its competitor MDH, a spice brand, has a fraternity of 'chefs of private caterers' who carry the brand on their shoulders. In India, social functions like marriages and parties are catered by a huge base of *halwais* or sweet-shop owners who act as caterers. The chefs of these caterers are a unique community, which the brand has helped knit together.

I: Institution building outside the firm's environment as a strategic competitive weapon

Emerging markets have relatively weak institutional frameworks such as market information, financial systems, labour markets, social infrastructure and logistics infrastructure to support business in general. While many players lament the absence of these frameworks, successful marketers see these as strategic opportunities. They have seized these gaps as opportunities to develop and create their own 'managed institutions,' then leveraging them for competitive advantage. This flies in the face of the core competence mantra, but actually has served successful marketers well as a source of sustainable competitive advantage.

Hindustan Lever, the Indian arm of Unilever, found that market information was a weak area in the Indian market. It created its own market research department, as well as virtually spawned two outside research agencies, to help develop a market research framework for the country for consumer products. Even today, 60 years later, its core advantage stems from its own research department, which is the largest agency in India.

Reliance Industries found that the country's financial system was not robust enough to support its growth ambitions. So it created the equity cult by selling the idea of equity investing for the retail investor by leveraging its 'consumer' and 'dealer' fraternities to create the necessary financial markets to feed its appetite to become the most integrated manmade textile manufacturer in the world. In the process Reliance created a fraternity of over two million retail investors.

The house of Tata, through its focus on social development, virtually creates its own labour markets by developing townships, investing in healthcare, education and so on. These labour markets have in turn benefited them by allowing Tata to become the lowest-cost steel producer in the world (Tata Steel) and the lowest cost car manufacturer in the world (Tata Indica).[7]

Virtually every successful brand has developed some institutions, big or small, in education, healthcare and poverty reduction. It is interesting to note that even with the maturing of the markets, successful marketers do not feel the need to exit these institutions, but actually feel that they need to reinvest in them to meet future challenges. Investments in these institutions provide a strong back-end cost advantage which helps these companies compete with others. For example, by creating a village-craftsman NGO for watch-part manufacture, Titan Watches is able to design, develop and market watches at the lowest cost.

This investment in institution building seems inconsistent with the core-competence mantra, but it is actually a source of sustainable competitive advantage if leveraged successfully. The trick is to carefully identify the external institutions that will give the brand a key strategic advantage.

L: Logically modular and phased capital investment

Any successful launch requires long-term investments not only in manufacturing but in marketing as well. The intuitive method is to estimate the need and then hurl everything behind the brand – a kind of 'shock and awe' strategy.

The study found that virtually all cases of such 'shock and awe' tactics did not succeed. Examples include the initial Timex launch, the Sony TV and Walkman launch, the Indo Nissin Foods' Top Ramen noodles launch, and Baskin Robbins. In reality, successful marketers broke their marketing investments into logical modules and then phased them out in a balanced manner. This not only de-risked the launch as costs of mistakes were lower, but also often allowed companies to plough back the benefits of the early phases into the next phase. The best example would be that of McDonald's, which for the first year had just three outlets and now, seven years after entry, has 40 outlets. In the initial years they focused on developing supplier fraternities, followed by a logistics institution called the cold chain, the refrigerated logistics chain and only then started investing in brand building.

To illustrate comparatively – two of the leading new retail clothing chains Shopper's Stop and Westside followed two different strategies. Shopper's Stop went full-speed ahead with brand advertising, national roll out, IT investments and loyalty programmes. It spent the first five years rolling out full steam and the last five recouping its losses. Westside, on the other hand, invested the same amount but phased it as follows: merchandising investments, minimal loyalty programmes, roll-outs and, after turning profitable, is finally investing in media and top-end IT (with a more sophisticated loyalty programme, which besides other things has taken segmentation of the consumer to a higher level of a 'consumer of promotions' differentiated from a 'consumer of Westside'). Meanwhile it has built successful modular fraternities of vendors, sources of staff, and a real-estate fraternity of mall developers that sees it as an ideal anchor partner. Overall, in the same ten years, Westside is profitable for the same investment while Shopper's Stop is not.

Banks like HDFC and ICICI have also followed a sequence balancing technology and face-to-face banking by maintaining a healthy mix of bricks and mortar branches (front-end oriented) and ATMs (back-end oriented), unlike others who relied either on branches or totally on ATMs to expand their reach. This way each stream of investment builds on the other. The trick here is not just to figure out whether to invest, but when to invest. Typically this calls for a fine balance between front-end consumer acquisition investments and back-end investments that give sustainable mileage that can then be leveraged for the back end.

I: Indigenous innovation to deliver consumer value

Innovations in product, packaging, pricing and other areas are a necessary tool for differentiation that leads to marketing success. Most such innovations are, however, easily copied and very often fail to give sustainable value to consumers over competing products. Successful marketers have added new teeth to the innovation game. They have successfully identified their own indigenous innovations – more often in processes than products – and leveraged them to deliver lasting consumer value.

Godrej, the white-goods manufacturer, recognized its unique reverse logistics capabilities of receiving faulty equipment and turning it around faster, developed originally as a service need, and leveraged it to a consumer value of the best trade-ins in the business.

Nirma, which is today one of the largest-selling washing-powder brands in the world with a turnover of nearly half a million tons, was successful because it leveraged its innovation in a low-cost distribution system to develop a consumer value of economy products. Mr Patel built the entire national network as a modular multiple of his home-selling experience, which eliminated lot of sales and distribution costs by using a cluster approach to selling and achieved very low distribution costs. The key to the success was in not just developing the network, but in successfully passing on the benefits to both consumers and trade partners.

Tata's Indica and Scorpio from Mahindra have leveraged their low-cost R&D to develop cars at one-sixth global norms, since they developed the vehicles from start to finish for costs between US$50–70 million, converting this to consumer advantage. Rajanigandha (a chewing tobacco brand) has innovated in a locationally-flexible production system which has the ability to shift production centres within 30 days to lowest cost locations, using local labour in each location to help keep costs the lowest in the industry. Cost benefits are largely passed on to the trade, which finds a reason to be its partner even in a declining market.

Mother Dairy's innovation in bulk transportation of unpackaged milk right up to the retail point was used to deliver quality right next door, and at a price with matched the unorganized dairy sector, making it a dominant milk brand in Delhi. Raymonds, the largest brand of men's formal wear, gained access to unique databases of tailors' measurements of trousers to design the best-fitting ready-made clothing for Indian males. Unfortunately, they stopped leveraging this innovation in the last 10 years and have hence lost market share. KSA Technopak, a consulting firm, could not compete with the global majors in attracting talent based on salaries. It therefore created a website designed to help MBA students in their studies by providing data for their project work. From then on, unsolicited applications reduced its recruitment costs to zero – a benefit it leveraged to translate into effective assignment costs to clients. The cement brand Gujarat Amboja used innovation in multi-modal logistics to bring cement prices down in distant markets thereby expanding consumption in many new consuming markets.

These forms of process innovation are very strong since they are unique and not easy to replicate. The point to be noted is that process innovation has to be understood as an activity which an organization is doing in a unique way – often by historical accident – and then leveraging to consumer advantage. All organizations intrinsically innovate on processes, but the successful ones actually leverage these innovations to deliver consumer value.

P: *Portfolio of market segments serviced from day one*

Since emerging markets present many heterogenous markets, successful marketers realize that focusing products on one market segment alone is fraught with risk. Successful marketing strategies have always centred on ways to address multiple segments simultaneously. These market segments can be created on consumption patterns, buying processes and price points or any other basis. All the successful companies traded in the concept of focus in favour of servicing a portfolio of market segments through a multiple channel strategy. Brands developed exclusive outlets, multi-brand preferred outlets as channels, mass channels and institutional channels as part of the initial mix rather than focusing on any one and then expanding into other channels later.

All fast-moving consumer goods like Parachute Oil or Dabur Vatika Hair Oil, addressed all the channels, including general merchants, *kirana* (small, neighbourhood grocery store) shops, chains, kiosks and others with the same brand. Even in the case of durables, Whirlpool, LG and Samsung each developed at least six different types of channels, that is, exclusive company-owned showrooms, franchise showrooms, multi-brand shop-in-shops, traffic discount outlets, sales booking outlets and department store outlets, each serving a different niche. Most new product categories took volume support from institutional channels while consumer markets were being evolved. Even the car brand Tata Indica addressed the household and taxi markets simultaneously.

Another consequence of the need to address multiple segments is the need to launch a minimum range of product variants either by size, use or features. Ayur, the natural products-based cosmetics company, launched 12 categories of products simultaneously. So did Biotique. Samsung launched 30 products in the first year, and even Coke has had to run two cola brands – Thums Up and Coke – to service multiple segments.

The key success factor is therefore to ensure that the customer acquisition strategy is de-risked by addressing multiple segments simultaneously through a multiple-channel strategy as well as a product variant strategy.

Failure to give a FILIP to a marketing programme

Although the study did not focus on assessing the impact of failure to add the FILIP strategy, some anecdotal evidence seems to suggest that those who had ignored fraternity building and institution building may have enjoyed high initial sales. However, they were not able to sustain themselves at the high level of business. Those weak on indigenous innovation could achieve sales goals but tended not to achieve profit goals and were not considered world-class according to the norms given earlier. Those that failed to logically phase their investments and had a single market segment focus could never generate enough cash to support their businesses.

Conclusion

The key lessons that emerged from the study were that successful marketers go beyond the management of the Ps of marketing to tactically give a FILIP to their programmes. They invest in Fraternity building as the core brand investment, build external Institutions to support the cause of the brands, Logically phase the marketing investments, Leverage Indigenous innovation to deliver consumer value, and address a Portfolio of market segments as part of the launch.

As a consequence, not only do they succeed by way of sales, market shares and profits, they become world class in their own right, and this gives them a sustainability that helps create enduring brands. For global marketers the value of this framework becomes clear in both developed markets as well as in cross-border marketing. Firstly, as developed markets tend to become more heterogenous, ethnically and otherwise, the same lessons would be applicable as in the Indian context. Secondly, as managers become more global, the same rules apply to addressing global brands across countries. It is therefore no surprise that many MNCs are placing managers who have been the architects of their respective FILIP-based marketing programmes in key global positions.

Notes

1. CD on Indian Census (2001) (released March 2003).
2. India Market Demographics Report 2002, National Council of Applied Economic Research, New Delhi.
3. *Ibid.*
4. Pacific Asia Travel Agencies Conference (2003).
5. Stock Exchange Directory of India (2003).
6. Confederation of Indian Industries White Paper on Retailing prepared by KSA Technopak (December 2002).
7. 'Study on Steel Industry', India Infoline and *Business World* (July 2003).

8
Export Success: Lessons from Award-Winning Pakistani Firms

Farrah Arif and Irfan Amir

Introduction

There is a growing body of literature focusing on factors for achieving export success. Some of the key studies include Katsikeas,[1] Lages,[2] Zou and Stan,[3] Katsikeas et al.,[4] Katsikeas and Piercy,[5] Cavusgil and Zou,[6] Aaby and Slater,[7] Madsen,[8] Burton and Schlegelmilch,[9] Cavusgil,[10] Bilkey,[11] and Michell.[12] The key determinants of export success fall under three categories: *marketing policy elements, firm-specific factors*, and *external factors*. The marketing policy factors include export market selection, competitive pricing, payment terms, packaging, new product development, promotional efforts, after-sales support, distribution network, and physical distribution. Firm-specific factors include technology superiority in product and/or process, export market planning, close monitoring of export operations by management, quality of staff, product quality control and financial strength. The external factors include diplomatic relations between countries, multilateral, bilateral and counter-trade arrangements, export subsidies, lack of import/export restrictions, national credibility in overseas markets, tax incentives, absence of import tariffs, stability of foreign economy, low risk in export market operations, sales potential, state of economy in overseas market, and export market accessibility.[13]

While most of the export success studies have focused on the more industrialized (advanced) countries, a relatively small number of studies have also been conducted on the developing (emerging) countries.[14] Several studies have emphasized the need to replicate the work in different country, culture and industry settings to check results for validity and generalizability.[15]

This study seeks to contribute to the export success literature by examining the export success factors of Pakistani companies. The study will not only provide much-needed validation of previous empirical work, but will also contribute significantly to the scant inventory of knowledge on the determinants of export success in the context of emerging countries, such as Pakistan. To generate more empirical richness, the export success factors will be examined on several market and company dimensions, such us *export direction* (emerging market versus advanced market orientation), *market coverage* (number of foreign markets), *company size* (number of full-time employees), *export experience* (number of years exporting), and *consistent performance* (frequency of awards).[16]

The material in this study is organized in five sections: (i) methodology, (ii) findings, (iii) discussion, (iv) implications and guidelines, and (v) limitations and directions for future research.

Methodology

The sampling frame was drawn from the export directories published annually by the Federation of Pakistan Chambers of Commerce and Industry (FPCCI).[17] A sampling frame of 149 companies was developed from the listings using the directories for the three years 1999–2001. These directories give a detailed profile of top exporters of the year. The information on each company includes company name, address, products, export markets and sales performance. Each year FPCCI gives away a number of export performance awards. These include Businessmen of the Year Gold Medal, President of Pakistan Trophy, Best Export Performance Trophies, Merit Trophies in the Exports of Non-traditional Items/Markets, and Special Merit Trophy. The awards are targeted at both large and small exporters.

Data were collected through a mail survey. The questionnaire included 29 of the 32 items used in a study[18] on the export success factors of small and medium-sized Canadian firms, a study that had been well-grounded in the pertinent literature.

The questionnaire was pre-tested through interviewing five exporting companies representing different industry sectors. Based on feedback from these interviews a couple of items were dropped. Additionally, some items were expanded for a better understanding of the respondents. The item list followed the questionnaire used by Katsikeas *et al.*[19] The three items not included in the list of the factors in the current study were *foreign market connections, industry-specific regulations* and *disposable income in host country*. These items were deleted because in the pre-test interviews respondents considered them either confusing or not relevant in their context.[20] A five-point scale was used to assess respondents' perceived importance on each of the listed export success factors, the scale ranging from 1=no importance/not relevant, 2=little importance, 3=some importance, 4=important to 5=crucial.[21]

Of the 149 questionnaires, 61 (41%) were finally received after one follow-up. Senior management, such as chief executives and directors, completed 90 per cent of the questionnaires. Fifty-four per cent of the firms focused their export efforts on emerging markets, while 46 per cent were oriented towards advanced markets. The participating firms were largely of small and medium size. The median values of sales, number of full-time employees, and number of years of export experience were $15.34 million, 365 employees and 15 years respectively. The smallest sales value was of $100,000 and the largest was $1.8 billion.

Findings

The findings are based on the calculation of mean scores and *t*-test analysis.[22] Table 8.1 ranks the mean scores for each of the 29 items, and the top three items are seen to be *product quality control, close monitoring of export operations by management*, and *quality of staff*.

Table 8.1 Ranking of success factors

Success factors	Means
Product quality control	4.82
Close monitoring of export operations by management	4.40
Quality of staff	4.38
Product adaptation according to the foreign market (R&D and new product development)	4.36
Export market selection at the start of your export venture	4.28
Credibility of Pakistan in foreign markets	4.28
Technological superiority in product and/or process	4.21
Export market planning	4.18
Distribution network (good and effective relations with distributors)	4.13
Sales potential in foreign markets	4.13
After-sales service support to overseas customers	4.10
Financial strength of your company	4.08
Stability of foreign economy (political & economic stability)	4.07
State of economy in foreign market (e.g. growing/stagnant)	4.00
Access to export markets (e.g. good infrastructure, conducive procedures & policies of the importing country)	3.98
Competitive pricing (lower price than competitors)	3.89
Physical distribution (effective distribution of your product in the foreign market)	3.81
Terms of payments	3.80
Packaging characteristics	3.73
Absence of import tariffs (e.g. on raw material & machinery)	3.73
Diplomatic relations between Pakistan and the importing country	3.64
Low risk in export market operations	3.60
Multilateral trade agreements (e.g. WTO agreements)	3.59
Promotional efforts/campaigns	3.53
Lack of import/export restrictions	3.52
Counter trade arrangements (e.g. product buy-back, trade-for-debt or debt-for-goods)	3.39
Tax incentives (e.g. tax holidays)	3.38
Export subsidies	3.36
Bilateral trade agreements (e.g. bilateral investment treaty with USA)	3.33

A series of *t*-tests were run for each of the 29 items by grouping the sample on a number of market and company dimensions (export direction, market coverage, company size, export experience, and consistent performance). With regard to export direction, the two groups were firms exporting to the more advanced markets and those focusing on emerging markets. The countries falling in the 'advanced markets' category include the USA, the UK, Germany and Japan; the countries falling in the 'emerging markets' category include China, Bangladesh, the United Arab Emirates and Hong Kong. For market coverage, the sample was divided into two groups of exporters, those exporting to fewer than 10 foreign markets and those exporting to 10 or more foreign markets; for company size the sample was divided into companies having fewer than 500 employees, and those having 500 or more employees; with regard to export experience, the two groups were firms with less than 10 years versus 10 or more years of export experience; for consistent performance, the groups were firms that had won awards four or more times in the last 10 years, and those firms that had won awards fewer than four times in the same period.

Table 8.2 shows that only in the case of export direction, company size and market coverage were there some success factors that were statistically significant. The data were further explored by comparing consistent and inconsistent performers by export direction. The three categories for comparison were *consistent performers to emerging markets versus consistent performers to advanced markets, consistent versus inconsistent performers to advanced markets,* and *consistent versus inconsistent performers to emerging markets*. In the case of consistent performers to EMs versus consistent performers to AMs, and consistent versus inconsistent performers to AMs, some success factors were found to be statistically significant. The results are shown in Table 8.3.

Further *t*-test analyses were run to examine possible differences between firms with 'emerging market' and those with 'advanced market' focus using different market and company dimensions. The results are shown in Table 8.4. The dimensions of consistent performance and export experience were found to be statistically significant.

Discussion

Validity of export success factors

All the 29 items used in this study to measure export success were found to be both relevant and important, albeit to different degrees. This provides evidence for the validity of the success factors derived from the literature.[23] Furthermore, a number of factors listed in response to an open-ended question with regard to determinants of export success were similar to the 29 factors tested in the current study. The additional factors mentioned by the respondent companies included *support form the government and other relevant agencies*,

Table 8.2 Significant success factors across market and company dimensions

Export success factors	Market and company dimensions*		t-value**
	Export direction		
	Emerging markets	Advanced markets	
Physical distribution (effective distribution of your product in the foreign market)	3.50	4.19	−2.74
	Company size (full-time employees)		
	Greater than and equal to 500	Less than 500	
Quality of staff	4.54	4.24	2.13
Bilateral trade agreements (e.g. bilateral investment treaty with USA)	3.73	2.97	2.33
Absence of import tariffs (e.g. on raw material & machinery)	3.38	3.97	−2.06
	Market coverage (number of foreign markets)		
	Greater than and equal to 10	Less than 10	
Access to export markets (e.g. good infrastructure, conducive procedures & policies of the importing country)	4.23	3.80	2.04

* Average values, ** significant at alpha ≤0.05.

simplicity of import/export policies and procedures, efficient financial and credit support, foreign exchange parity, development of an export-oriented culture, emphasis upon shorter lead times, and *honouring delivery commitments.*

Emphasis on quality

The top performers rated *product quality, close monitoring of export operations,* and *quality of staff* as the top three success factors. This implies that the quality of product and management were considered to be critical success factors. Several studies have invariably found quality of product as a key export success factor.[24] Some studies have found managerial competence (sometimes also termed 'export competence') as a significant export success factor; they have included staffing, market planning, management control, new product development and after-sales service as part of export competence.[25]

Table 8.3 Significant success factors by consistent and inconsistent performers and export direction

Export success factors	Performance consistency and export direction*		t-value**
	Consistent performers to emerging markets (EMs)	Consistent performers to advanced markets (AMs)	
Tax incentives (e.g. tax holidays)	4.00	2.85	2.11
	Consistent performers to AMs	Inconsistent performers to AMs	
Export market selection at the start of your export venture	4.50	3.79	2.73
State of economy in the foreign market (e.g. growing/stagnant)	3.69	4.27	−2.28

* Average values, ** significant at alpha ≤ 0.05.

Table 8.4 Differences in market and company dimensions by export direction

Market and company dimensions	Export direction*		t-value
	Emerging markets	Advanced markets	
Consistent performance (frequency of awards)	2.88	5.04	−2.70**
Company size (number of full-time employees)	870.84	1442.25	−1.09
Market coverage (number of foreign markets)	10.39	12.04	−0.75
Export experience (number of years exporting)	14.09	21.29	−2.51**

* Average values, ** Significant at alpha ≤0.05.

Governmental support

Government support in the form of export subsidies, tax incentives and bilateral and counter-trade arrangements was perceived to be of relatively less importance as drivers of export success. In the developing-country context, contrary to much-claimed demand for government subsidies, and other export promotional support, the respondents in the current survey did not attach much importance to such support in their endeavours to achieve higher export performance.

Export success factors across market and company dimensions

With regard to the *export direction*, only one success factor (*physical distribution*) was found to be statistically significant. Firms focusing on advanced markets deemed this factor more important compared to firms focusing on emerging markets. This finding implies that getting closer to the customer is a more uphill task in the fiercely competitive advanced markets. Perhaps due to the involvement of several players vying for bigger slices of the target market, the channel power is tilted more towards the buying agent and other channel members, thus making distribution arrangements (including effective physical distribution) a critical factor for export success. The finding of almost all success factors to be insignificant indicates that these factors may be equally applicable for emerging and advanced markets. However, one caveat in this context is that the respondent companies may be oblivious to some of the important aspects that need to be factored in while developing export plans for the two export markets. For example, one would expect that factors such as product quality control and high-quality personnel would be relatively more critical in the case of companies targeting advanced markets as opposed to those oriented towards emerging markets. It is also important to note that in the fiercely competitive international markets in general, and advanced markets in particular, there is a need to place higher emphasis on all the stated export success factors. Furthermore, the companies focusing on advanced markets need to look for new vistas to sustain and increase penetration in these sophisticated markets.

With regard to company size, *quality of staff, bilateral trade agreements* and *absence of import tariffs* were found to be statistically significant. The large companies (500 and more employees) considered quality of staff and bilateral trade agreements to be of greater importance in their export success compared to smaller firms. It is possible that larger firms realize not only the importance of high quality of export and other staff, but can also afford to pay for high-quality staff. One would expect the bilateral trade agreements to be equally beneficial for both small and large firms; however, the high importance attached to this factor by the larger firms might be indicative of the ability of these firms to capitalize more from this arrangement because of a stronger resource base. Smaller firms placed more importance on the absence of import tariffs (on raw material and machinery, and the like) compared to larger firms. This finding confirms the notion that smaller firms strive to seek all possible concessions to make them more competitive in the export arena.

Companies with more diversified market coverage placed significantly higher emphasis on *access to export markets* compared to the geographically less-diversified exporting firms. This might be because of the increasing desire of these firms to cover more markets in different exporting zones. Surely, one would expect marked differences with respect to infrastructure, and import policies and procedures across different countries.

Consistent and inconsistent performers by export direction

Analysis of consistent and inconsistent performers across the two categories of export orientation (emerging versus advanced markets) showed that only a few export success factors were statistically significant. More specifically, comparison of consistent performers to emerging markets versus advanced markets found only one factor (tax incentives) to be statistically significant. The consistent performers in EMs considered tax incentives to be extremely important compared to consistent performers in AMs. This indicates that high performers oriented towards EMs are keenly looking towards more and more support from the government, thus showing their higher reliance on support from external sources rather than relying on their own competences to achieve market success. Comparison between consistent and inconsistent performers in AMs found only two factors, namely *export market selection at the start of the export venture* and *state of the economy in the foreign market* to be statistically significant. The consistent performers in AMs considered export-market selection at the start of their export venture as a key factor. This clearly shows the importance of initial market research and correct target-market selection as necessary activities to increase the chances of export success. It is interesting to note that inconsistent performers in AMs placed a higher emphasis on *state of the economy in the foreign market* compared to the more consistent performers. This difference could be attributed to the export competency of and approach adopted by the two groups of companies. A higher emphasis on *the state of the economy* by the inconsistent performers points towards a more passive or reactive approach of such companies to gain better results in the targeted export markets. In other words, the consistent performers were more aggressive and proactive to seek more business without putting undue emphasis on the state of the economy in the target markets. The fact that in the comparative analysis of the importance of *performance consistency* and *export direction* only a small number of factors were found to be significant, indicates that export performance is not strongly impacted by export direction.

Market and company dimensions by export direction

Analysis of export direction by market and company dimensions (consistent performance, company size, market coverage and export experience) revealed that the two groups of companies differed significantly with regard to *consistent performance* and *export experience*. Firms oriented towards advanced markets were found to be more consistent performers (with a 5.04 value of frequency of awards in the last 10 years compared to a frequency value of 2.88 for firms focusing on emerging markets) and had more export experience (21 years versus 14 years). These findings indicate that firms focusing on advanced markets had been in the exporting business for an extended period of time and their efforts and experience had increased their chances of achieving higher export success. No significant difference was found in the two groups of companies with regard to company size and market coverage. This finding is very encouraging from a more macro perspective in that even the smaller companies are endeavouring to cover both emerging and advanced markets as well as attempting to increase market coverage.

Implications and guidelines

In this section, insights and guidelines are offered for exporters as well as government and non-governmental agencies engaged in export promotional activities.

Guidelines for exporters

The top exporters surveyed in this study show a number of characteristics that could be useful for other exporting companies as well as potential exporters. First, the *winners* do not compromise on quality. The quality dimension is based on product and high-level managerial skills of both export and other staff. Second, these firms rely more on their own managerial and financial prowess than worrying either about the macro-level 'external factors' or looking up to the government to provide 'incentives' for export growth. Surely, the macro level factors such as socio-economic and political stability as well as conducive government support mechanisms are important factors for export activities. However, the larger and more established high-performing exporting firms tend to focus more on the controllable 'internal' factors as drivers of their success. The internal factors include total quality emphasis, export-oriented culture, and sophisticated marketing strategies and implementation. In fact, the high level of managerial skills is, perhaps, the lynchpin for spearheading the overall export endeavour to make successful inroads into the sophisticated and fiercely competitive international markets. Third, the findings validate the factors identified in the literature.[26] Most of the factors had a relatively high mean score (with 3.33 being the lowest mean score on a scale of one to five). Furthermore, only a few factors were found to be significantly different across the market and company dimensions of export direction, consistent performance, company size, market coverage and export experience. Although this study did not include other contextual variables such as industry type (manufacturing versus service) and product type (industrial versus consumer), the findings provide support for the universal relevance of the success factors tested in this study. Fourth, a sustained orientation towards advanced markets increases the odds for consistent performance compared to an orientation towards emerging markets. This implies that firms should seek to 'upgrade' themselves by enhancing their export competences to win a higher share of the market in the sophisticated and competitive advanced markets. Fifth, while the broad market coverage by both small and large companies shows that Pakistani exporters want to try out their exporting skills and strengths far afield, with corresponding benefits of market diversification, it is more advisable for exporters to approach international markets in a more gradual and focused fashion. This is, perhaps, especially applicable in the case of small as well as new exporters, helping them deploy their resources more efficiently and effectively for achieving success. It is wiser for these firms to first try out their export capabilities and potential in domestic and emerging (developing countries) markets before approaching the more challenging markets of advanced countries such as the USA and Western Europe. Challenges in the more sophisticated Western markets include stringent quality controls, environmental regulations, stiff competition and sophisticated and demanding buyers.

Guidelines for export promotion agencies

The respondent companies considered the role of government and export promotional agencies to be both supportive as well as restricting. This paradoxical situation needs careful attention. For example, some respondents considered the provision of export subsidies and other incentives as critical in boosting their export performance; while other firms considered these incentives as 'crutches' and relied more on their own capabilities to achieve success. However, almost all respondents were emphatic on the need for the government to provide fiscal (access to finances) and infrastructural support. A large majority of respondents also pointed out the need to decrease the prices of inputs (raw materials and utilities). Another key aspect for governments to take into consideration is the proper 'targeting' of scarce export promotional funds. The study findings suggest that small and less-experienced firms were more inclined to seek government support in various forms. Large firms also need support from the government in the form of bilateral and multilateral trade agreements, greater access to foreign markets, and socio-economic stability in the home country to make long-term plans for investment and expansion in export operations. Furthermore, most firms were critical of the complex and inefficient policies and procedures in the processing of export documentation and other methods. The issue of 'red-tapism' was frequently raised. There is strong support in the literature on two basic issues with regard to government support for export activities. One is that minimum intervention by the government is usually a better approach to support private initiative for export promotion; the second is the critical importance of careful targeting of resources.[27]

Limitations and directions for future research

The foremost limitation of our study is the small sample size. A related issue is that of non-response. For mail surveys, the current study's response rate of 42 per cent is respectable; however, given the well-targeted sampling frame of 149 'export award winners' and the use of a short and precise questionnaire, a much higher response rate was expected. Aside from the response rate, a key issue is that the non-response category might have included a higher proportion of well-established large exporting firms. Another limiting factor in this study is the method of data collection deployed. The use of in-depth interviews and/or case studies could provide a better understanding of the construct of export success compared to the survey method, but resource constraints did not allow the use of such data collection techniques.

A number of suggestions are offered for future research. As stated earlier, there has been relatively less emphasis in the literature on the export success factors of emerging markets (developing countries). An interesting line for future endeavours would be to undertake more cross-cultural studies using matched samples from advanced countries, advanced and developing countries, and developing countries. In the Pakistani context, a significant effort is required to develop an inventory of knowledge on a broad spectrum of matters relating to export development and performance.

Notes

1. C. Katsikeas, 'Firm Level Export Performance Assessment: Review, Evaluation and Development', *Journal of the Academy of Marketing Science*, 28, 4 (2000): 493–512.
2. L.F. Lages, 'A Conceptual Framework of the Determinants of Export Performance: Reorganizing Key Variables and Shifting Contingencies in Export Marketing', *Journal of Global Marketing*, 13, 3 (2000): 29–51.
3. S. Zou and S. Stan, 'The Determinants of Export Performance: A Review of the Empirical Literature between 1987 and 1997', *International Marketing Review*, 15, 5 (1998): 333–57.
4. C. Katsikeas, S. Deng and L. Wortzel, 'Perceived Export Success Factors of Small and Medium-Sized Canadian Firms', *Journal of International Marketing*, 5, 4 (1997): 53–72.
5. C.S. Katsikeas and N.F. Piercy, 'Determinants of Export Performance in a European Context', *European Journal of Marketing*, 30, 6 (1996): 6–36.
6. S.T. Cavusgil and S. Zou, 'Marketing Strategy-Performance Relationship: An Investigation of the Empirical Link in Export Market Ventures', *Journal of Marketing*, 58, 1 (1994): 1–21.
7. N.E. Aaby and S.F. Slater, 'Management Influences on Export Performance: A Review of the Empirical Literature 1978–88', *International Marketing Review*, 6, 4 (1989): 7–26.
8. T.K. Madsen, 'Successful Export Marketing Management: Some Empirical Evidence', *International Marketing Review*, 6, 4 (1987): 41–57.
9. F.N. Burton and B.B. Schlegelmilch, 'Profile Analysis of Non-Exporters versus Exporters Grouped by Export Involvement', *Management International Review*, 27, 1 (1987): 38–49.
10. S.T. Cavusgil, 'Success Factors in Export Marketing: An Empirical Analysis', *Journal of International Marketing and Marketing Research*, 8, 2 (1983): 63–73.
11. W.J. Bilkey, 'Variables Associated with Export Profitability', *Journal of International Business Studies*, 13, 2 (1982): 39–55.
12. P. Michell, 'Infrastructure and International Marketing Effectiveness', *Columbia Journal of World Business*, Spring (1979): 91–101.
13. C. Katsikeas, S. Deng and L. Wortzel, 'Perceived Export Success Factors of Small and Medium-Sized Canadian Firms', *op. cit.*

14 S. Zou, D.M. Andrus and D.W. Norvell, 'Standardization of International Marketing Strategy by Firms from a Developing Country', *International Marketing Review*, 14, 2 (1997): 107–23; M. Das, 'Successful and Unsuccessful Exporters from Developing Countries: Some Preliminary Findings', *European Journal of Marketing*, 28, 12 (1994): 19–23; M. De Luz, 'Relationship between Export Strategy Variables and Export Performance for Brazil-based Manufacturers', *Journal of Global Marketing*, 7, 1 (1993): 87–110; J.S. Hill and R.R. Still, 'Adapting Products to LDC Tastes', *Harvard Business Review*, 62, March–April (1984): 92–101; C. Christensen, A. Rocha and R. Gertner, 'An Empirical Investigation of the Factors Influencing Exporting Success of Brazilian Firms', *Journal of International Business Studies*, 18, 3 (1987): 61–77.

15 S.T. Cavusgil and S. Zou, 'Marketing Strategy-Performance Relationship: An Investigation of the Empirical Link in Export Market Ventures', *op. cit.*

16 L. Leonidou, C. Katsikeas and J. Hadjimarcou, 'Executive Insights: Building Successful Export Business Relationships: A Behavioral Perspective', *Journal of International Marketing*, 10, 3 (2002): 96–115.

17 Federation of Pakistani Chambers of Commerce and Industry (FPCCI), *23rd Export Trophy Souvenir 1998–1999* (Karachi: 2000); FPCCI, *24th Export Trophy Souvenir 1999–2000* (Karachi: 2001); FPCCI, *25th Export Trophy Souvenir 2000–2001* (Karachi: 2002).

18 C. Katsikeas, S. Deng and L. Wortzel, 'Perceived Export Success Factors of Small and Medium-Sized Canadian Firms', *op. cit.*

19 *Ibid.*

20 The final questionnaire used in the survey is available from the authors upon request.

21 C. Styles and T. Ambler, 'Successful Export Practice: The UK Experience', *International Marketing Review*, 11, 6 (1994): 23–47.

22 Statistical Package for the Social Sciences (SPSS) Inc., *SPSS Base 9.0 Applications Guide* (Chicago, 1999); M. Norusis, *SPSS 8.0 Guide to Data Analysis* (New Jersey: Prentice Hall, 1998).

23 C. Katsikeas, S. Deng and L. Wortzel, 'Perceived Export Success Factors of Small and Medium-Sized Canadian Firms', *op. cit.*

24 See note 20 and also Michell, 'Infrastructure and International Marketing Effectiveness', *op. cit.*

25 C. Katsikeas, S. Deng and L. Wortzel, 'Perceived Export Success Factors of Small and Medium-Sized Canadian Firms', *op. cit.*; S.T. Cavusgil and S. Zou, 'Marketing Strategy-Performance Relationship: An Investigation of the Empirical Link in Export Market Ventures', *op. cit.*

26 C. Katsikeas, S. Deng and L. Wortzel, 'Perceived Export Success Factors of Small and Medium-Sized Canadian Firms', *op. cit.*

27 C. Christensen, A. Rocha and R. Gertner, 'An Empirical Investigation of the Factors Influencing Exporting Success of Brazilian Firms', *op. cit.*

9
Gerdau: Multinational Steel Giant from Brazil

Rusty Mae Moore

Introduction

Gerdau is a multinational steel producer based in Brazil, with extensive operations throughout South and North America. It is a family-controlled company, with its origin in the southern part of Brazil at the turn of the twentieth century. Today the company is the largest producer of 'long' steel products (such as angles, round bars, square bars and reinforcing bars) in the Western hemisphere, and one of the most profitable companies in the global steel industry. It currently ranks 14th worldwide in steel production. Gerdau is an example of the global enterprises that are emerging from developing countries and achieving success in extremely difficult conditions.

Global steel trends

Steel producers throughout the world are undergoing a profound restructuring process at the present time caused by overcapacity, overproduction and weak prices. Six of the fundamental trends present in the steel industry which make the outlook for any steel company uncertain are: (1) the relocation of steel production centres from the USA and Europe to the emerging industrial countries such as China, Korea, India and Brazil; (2) consolidation of steel companies within countries and across national borders; (3) the need for global alliances between steel producers; (4) the emergence of China as the location of the largest steel industry in the world; (5) the reemergence of the steel industries of Ukraine, Russia and Kazakhstan as important steel export platforms; and (6) the increasing globalization of the industry, and steel markets.[1] Steel is one of the most fragmented major industries in the world as a result of the perceived national interest that the industry has represented to governments. Many people still take it as an article of faith that a country cannot develop without its own steel industry. Steel companies in many countries have received special protections and subsidies because of this belief, with the result that the total steel production capacity in the world is much greater than the demand for steel at the present time.

The production of steel in the economically developed countries today represents a smaller proportion of the world supply than the past, while steel produced in emerging markets now dominates world supply. In spite of this trend, the steel markets in developed countries remain among the largest in the world.

Brazil is considered to be one of the key centres of the emerging global steel industry. It has location advantages for producing steel which include a large and growing domestic market, low-cost/high-quality labour, huge supplies of high-quality iron ore, state of the art production technology, abundant steel scrap, specialized coal-handling ports, economies of scale, and a supportive government. Table 9.1 shows an estimate of the world market prices in the United States, Brazil and Europe and Japan, compared to the production costs for hot rolled steel of selected steel producers around the world. The figures indicate that the costs of Brazil's Companhia Siderúrgica

Table 9.1 Direct costs of production for hot-rolled steel versus domestic sales prices, 2001

Company	Base country	Price per ton US $
CSN	Brazil	105
Posco	Korea	170
China Steel	China	175
Usinor	France	215
Nippon Steel	Japan	220
Nucor	USA	220
Tokyo Steel	Japan	225
SAIL	India	230
Steel Dynamics	USA	230
Avg Price Europe/Japan		235
Domestic Brazil price		242
Essar	India	245
Domestic US price		260
US Steel	USA	310
Bethlehem	USA	325

Sources: Costs, Goldman Sachs research estimates, first half of 2001; Prices, 'Metal Bulletin', December 2001. National base of companies: CSN, Brazil; Posco, Korea; China Steel, China; Nippon Steel, Japan; Tokyo Steel, Japan; SAIL, India; Essar, India; Nucor (mini mills) USA; Steel Dynamics, (mini mills) USA; US Steel (integrated), USA; Bethlehem, (integrated), USA; Usinor (integrated), Belgium, reproduced in Maria Silvia Bastos Marques, Associação Comercial do Rio de Janeiro, 'A CSN e o novo cenário da Siderurgia Mundial' (CSN and the New Reality of World Steel), 20 February 2002; published on the CSN website, http://csna0004.csn.com.br/portal/page?_pageid = 1004,83485&_dad=ebiz&_schema = PORTAL

Table 9.2 World's largest steel producers, 2002

Rank	Company	Home	2002	Rank	Company	Home	2002
1	Arcelor	France	44.0	24	NISCO	Iran	7.3
2	LNM Group	Neth/UK	34.8	25	INI Steel	Korea	7.3
3	Nippon Steel	Japan	29.8	26	Krivorozstal	Ukraine	6.9
4	Posco	Korea	28.1	27	Kobe Steel	Japan	6.6
5	Baosteel	China	19.5	28	BHP	Australia	6.4
6	Corus	UK/Neth.	16.8	29	Benxi	China	6.2
7	Thyssen Krupp	Germany	16.4	30	Mariupo Illyich	Ukraine	6.1
8	NKK	Japan	15.2	31	Polski Huti St	Poland	5.9
9	Riva	Italy	15.0	37	National Steel	USA	5.2
10	US Steel	USA	14.4	38	Salzgitter	Germany	5.1
11	Kawasaki	Japan	13.7	39	CSN	Brazil	5.1
12	Nucor	USA	12.4	41	Panzihua	China	5.0
13	Sumitomo	Japan	11.8	43	CST	Brazil	4.9
14	Gerdau	Brazil	11.5	46	Stelco	Canada	4.7
15	SAIL	Russia	11.4	47	Usiminas	Brazil	4.6
16	Magnitogorsk	Russia	11.0	48	Erdemir Grp	Turkey	4.6
17	China Steel	China	10.5	50	Techint	Italy/Arg	4.5
18	Anshan	China	10.1	51	Dofasco	Canada	4.4
19	Severstal	Ukraine	9.6	52	Ratarukki	Finland	4.2
20	Novolipetsk	Russia	8.6	55	Zaparozstahl	Ukraine	3.9
21	Shougang Bethlehem	China	8.2	57	COSIPA	Brazil	3.9
22	Steel	USA	8.1	63	SIDOR	Venezuela	3.7
23	Wuhan	China	7.6	65	Hadeed	S. Arabia	3.6
				78	Hylsamex	Mexico	2.8

Source: International Iron and Steel Institute, http://www.worldsteel.org/wsif200302.php

Nacional (CSN) are about half the world market prices, and less than any of the other companies listed. In contrast, the costs of USX (US Steel) and Bethlehem, two of the largest US-based integrated steel companies, are well-above world market prices, an untenable situation which has forced the drastic restructuring of steel-producing enterprises in the United States.

Table 9.2 lists the largest steel companies in the world as of 2002, although these rankings are in a state of flux because of the ongoing worldwide consolidation that has been mentioned. Many of these companies have subsidiaries, affiliates and alliances with Brazilian operations due to the potential importance of Brazil as a steel-producing country. Some of the global strategies of the leading companies include the following:

1 Arcelor, the world's largest steel company at present, is the result of an alliance between Arbed (Luxembourg), Aceralia (Spain), and Usinor (France). Arcelor controls Belgo-Mineira, one of the leading Brazilian steel companies, and several smaller Brazilian companies.[2] Arcelor has allied with Tata

Steel in India and Baosteel in China in specific products. A three-way joint venture in Brazil was announced between Arcelor, Shanghai Baosteel and Brazil's Companhia Vale do Rio Doce in Fall 2003. A Greenfield investment of US$1.5 million will be made in the North of Brazil to create a plant for export to the US market and other overseas destinations.[3]

2 Ispat-LNM is the prototype of a global steel producer based on cross-national takeovers. The company does not have major operations in Brazil, but controls the former Inland Steel Company of the USA, which is a major producer of flat-rolled steel in North America. Ispat-LNM also has operations in Europe, Eastern Europe and the countries of the former Soviet Union. The original base for this global company was a steel mill in India.[4]

3 Nippon Steel is traditionally the largest Japanese steel company. Nippon has alliances and joint ventures in the NAFTA, and is also a major shareholder of Usiminas, one of the largest integrated steel producers in Brazil.[5] Nippon has also had a technical assistance agreement with Gerdau for many years.[6]

4 Posco, the dominant Korean company, enjoys one of the lowest production cost levels in the world. Posco does not have operations in Brazil at this time, but has affiliates in the NAFTA market.[7]

5 Shanghai Bao-Steel is concentrated on the Chinese market for now, but the recently announced Brazilian joint venture with Arcelor and CVRD is a step out of China for the company.[8]

6 Corus is the British–Dutch steel giant which resulted from the Merger of British Steel and Hoogovens of the Netherlands. The company at one time intended to take control of the important Brazilian steel pioneer CSN, but the deal was cancelled as a result of continued problems at Corus and a rethinking of strategy at CSN.[9]

7 Thyssen-Krupp is the resultant company after the merger of the famous German steel companies, Thyssen and Krupp. Thyssen was an early partner of Gerdau in the Consigua Steel operations in Rio de Janeiro, and there continues to be collaboration between the companies.[10]

8 NKK and Kawasaki in Japan have merged since the 2001 listing, and they now comprise the largest steel producer in Japan.[11]

9 Riva is totally dominant as a producer in the Italian national market.[12]

10 US Steel is traditionally the largest integrated steel producer in the USA. The company acquired National Steel in 2002, but is now smaller than both ISG, comprising the liquidated LTV Company and the bankrupt Bethlehem Steel, and Nucor, the number-one mini-mill company in the USA. US Steel acquired USS Košice in Slovakia in the late 1990s. This Eastern European operation is now rumoured to be the only basic steel-producing unit of US Steel that makes a profit.[13]

11 Nucor is the prototype for successful steel production operations in North America at the present time. The mini-mill company now produces

more steel than US Steel, and does it consistently with a substantial profit. Gerdau's Ameristeel Unit is now the second largest US mini-mill operation after Nucor. Nucor recently announced a joint venture with the giant Brazilian iron-ore producer CVRD to create a direct reduction operation in Brazil. The crude steel produced at this operation could be sold in the Brazilian market, used to supply Nucor's North American operations, or exported to other markets.[14]

Access to Brazilian resources and the Brazilian market is of great interest to steel companies from the traditional steel companies in the USA, Europe and Japan. Every steel company in Brazil has links of ownership and/or technology-sharing with steel groups in other countries, but Gerdau is the only Brazil-based company that has made a major move to become a significant international player itself. It had become the 14th-largest steel company in the world by 2003.[15]

The historical development of Gerdau Steel

The story of Gerdau Steel begins at the turn of the twentieth century in Pôrto Alegre, Rio Grande do Sul, in the far south of Brazil next to Uruguay and Argentina. João Gerdau, the company founder, emigrated from Germany to southern Brazil in 1868, and bought the 'Paris Pointed Nail Factory' (*Fábrica de Pregas Pontas de Paris*) in 1901 in Pôrto Alegre.[16] In 1933 the Gerdaus built a new nail factory, which used state-of-the-art technology for that time. The expanded production from the new factory meant that there was no need to import nails in the southern part of Brazil either from overseas, or even from the northern part of the country. Also in 1933 João's granddaughter Helda married Curt Johannpeter, a young German banker who became well-versed in the nail business and took an increasingly important role in the business affairs of the Gerdau family. He assumed the leadership of the family company in 1946 and initiated the development of the corporate culture on which the later success of the Gerdau Group would be based. His focus, which carries through to the present, was on the achievement and capability of people in the organization.

In 1947 the legal organization of the nail company, Fábrica de Pregas Pontas de Paris, was changed from a private limited liability corporation (*Limitada*) to a public joint stock corporation (*Sociedade Anónima*). The capital from the initial public offering was used to help finance the first entry of Gerdau into steel production. The steel company 'Siderúrgica Riograndense' began operations under Gerdau management in Pôrto Alegre in 1948. Part of the motivation for the backward integration into steel production was to obtain a secure steel supply for the nail factory in the context of an economy with constant supply shortages. Reinforcing this factor was the fact that the late 1930s and the 1940s were the period in which the Brazilian government stressed the creation of a steel industry as a necessary building block in the industrialization of the country. The first integrated steel producer, CSN, was founded in 1942 and began producing steel in 1946. Steel production in Brazil seemed to have a great future.

Huge programmes of capital investment for industry and civil construction in the 1950s and 1960s created great opportunities for the steel industry, which experienced a marked expansion during this period. A second large integrated steel producer, Usiminas, was established during this period, located in the rich iron-ore region in the centre-south state of Minas Gerais. In 1957 Gerdau put the second mill of Siderúrgica Riograndense into operation to keep up with the demand from the economic growth spurt being experienced by the entire country. A key development for Gerdau during this period was the introduction of the first continuous casting operations at Siderúrgica Riograndense in 1961. Continuous casting is a technique in which the molten steel produced from scrap and pig iron in the electric or basic oxygen furnaces is continuously cast into shapes which are close to the form which will be used as the final product. The castings can later be rolled or drawn into the final products. Continuous casting is one of the most important technological advances in steel-making in the last half century.

Gerdau initiated steel-plate production at a new plant, São Judas Tadeu, in São Paulo in 1967. This investment was the first move of the company out of southern Brazil into the industrial core focusing on São Paulo, which was becoming the largest manufacturing/financial complex in the Western hemisphere. In 1969 the company acquired Siderúrgica Aço-Norte, in the northern state of Pernambuco. By the end of the decade Gerdau was well launched in the implementation of its strategy of locating production units in the country's geographical regions closest to buyers needing steel. A critical step for the company came in 1968 with the installation of computerized information systems; at the time Gerdau was one of the first companies in Brazil to invest heavily in computerization. An additional development to be highlighted in the 1960s was the creation of Fundação Gerdau in 1963. This autonomous foundation was for the purpose of assisting employees (called collaborators) and their families. The Gerdau Group was ahead of the curve of Brazilian firms in terms of providing private pension and health benefits for employees.

Gerdau made one of its most critical strategic moves in 1971 by investing in a joint venture company named Companhia Siderúrgica de Guanabara (Cosigua) near Rio de Janeiro, the second largest industrial city in the country. Gerdau's foreign partner was Thyssen, the famous German industrial group. This venture gave Gerdau even greater access to the latest in steel-making technology from one of the oldest world-class steel companies. Apart from strategic moves in steel production and technology, Gerdau also made a significant step in the marketing area in 1971 by forming 'Gerdau Comercial' to handle the distribution of the long steel products and rolled products that were its main concentration. Gerdau created a new company named

SEIVA in 1971 that focused on reforestation in southern Brazil; this important environmental initiative was an expression of the social responsibility, traditionally at the core of the company's values.

By the end of the 1970s, Brazil had run up a huge foreign debt, economic growth slowed, inflation rose, the currency steadily devalued, and a debt crisis loomed. The Brazilian government pushed for exports to earn the foreign exchange to service the debt. Brazil's emerging global advantage in steel production made it possible for Brazilian steel companies such as Gerdau to enter the world market. Steel exports rose, but Brazilian companies soon found protectionist opposition in countries with high-cost steel producers, such as the United States.

The Gerdau Group under the leadership of Jorge Gerdau Johannpeter and his brothers continued the aggressive development strategy during the 1980s. A critical strategic step in 1980 was the establishment of technical assistance agreements with two Japanese firms, Funabashi Steel and Nippon Steel, which focused on the installation of quality-control systems. A strong focus on quality as a part of the corporate culture was implanted, and the company began its focus on achieving awards for quality, which demonstrate the high quality of the company's products based on third-party evaluation. As Table 9.3 illustrates, the Gerdau Group was able to continue its expansion during the 'lost decade' of the 1980s even in the face of the national macroeconomic instability. The company embarked on its first international investment in 1981 by taking control of Laisa, a mini-mill steel producer of long products in Uruguay. The base of Gerdau in the southern state of Rio Grande do Sul made expansion into Uruguay a natural step because of traditionally close cultural and economic ties. The Laisa operations were closer to the Gerdau headquarters in Pôrto Alegre than the major steel markets in the centre-south of Brazil (São Paulo, Minas Gerais and Rio de Janeiro). The Laisa investment showed that the Gerdau management intended to reach out into the Mercosur regional market (Brazil, Argentina, Uruguay and Paraguay) that was being established.

Gerdau also expanded geographically within the Brazilian market by setting up operations in the northern state Pernambuco, at Aracaria in 1981, and in another northern state, Ceara, in 1982. The company also expanded operations in Guáira in the southern state of Paraná in 1982, midway between the Rio Grande do Sul base of the company and the giant São Paulo industrial megalopolis. Other expansions during the 1980s included the plant in Hime in 1985, in Barão de Cocais in the 'iron triangle' of Minas Gerais in 1988, and in Usiba in the growing northeastern state of Bahia in 1989. The new operations integrated into the company were achieved in some cases by mergers with existing companies, in other cases by winning privatization auctions, and in still other cases by creating greenfield plants.

At the end of the decade the Gerdau Group took the major step of acquiring a steel operation in North America by buying the Courtice Steel Company

Table 9.3 Gerdau expansion, 1980–2003

Name of operation	Country	Year	Type of Operation
Laisa	Uruguay	1981	Market Minimill
Cearense	Northern Brazil	1982	Market Minimill
Guaira	Southern Brazil	1982	Market Minimill
Hime	Centre-South Brazil	1985	Market Minimill
Barão de Cocais	North Eastern Brazil	1988	Market Minimill
Usiba	North Eastern Brazil	1989	Market Minimill
Courtice	Mid-East Canada	1989	Market Minimill
Piratini	Southern Brazil	1992	Market Minimill Specialty Steels
Aza	Central Chile	1992	Market Minimill
Pains	Centre South Brazil	1994	Market Minimill
MRM	Mid-West Canada	1995	Market Minimill
Açominas	Centre-South Brazil	1997	Integrated Steelmill (minority share)
Sipsa	North Central Argentina	1997	Market Minimill
Sipar**	North Central Argentina	1998	Rolling Mill (minority share)
Ameristeel	South Eastern USA	1999	Chain of Minimills
Co-Steel	Mid-East Canada	2002	Chain of Minimills
Açominas	Centre-South Brazil	2002	Integrated Steelmill (took control)

* Average rate of growth 1980–2002 for crude steel output was 10.4 per cent per year, while average rate of growth for rolled products in the same period was 9.6 per cent annually.
** Rolling mill, 38 per cent ownership.
Source: Gerdau presentation at Morgan Guaranty Natural Resource Conference, São Paulo (February 2003); at http://www.Gerdau.com, Investor Information.

in Canada. This investment followed years of growing exports to the extremely competitive North American market. Gerdau had already faced the protectionism of the United States with respect to steel products, and the Canadian venture gave Gerdau a means of gaining experience in managing a distant overseas subsidiary. Moreover, the Canadian operation could be seen as a stepping-stone into the US market through the US–Canada Free Trade Area, as well as the proposed North American Free Trade Agreement, which was under negotiation at that time.

Despite severe economic problems in the 1990s, Brazil did not implement the policy of privatization with alacrity. There was great scepticism about giving up control of firms such as CSN and Usiminas which were national flagships, especially if it would mean control of these assets by foreigners. At the same time, privatization presented tremendous opportunities for making fortunes and expansion of economic empires to astute Brazilian business groups. The privatization of the state-owned steel firms was a major change in the structure of the Brazilian steel industry. The state firms were large integrated steel-makers literally located on top of mountains containing high-quality iron ore, but were not always efficient producers. The Gerdau Group was something of an outsider in the steel industry from the standpoint that they were based in the south, outside the orbit of the São Paulo–Rio de Janeiro economic centre, their history was one of backward integration from the marketing of specific products for well-defined markets, and their steel mills were based on the mini-mill (electric-arc furnace) technology using recycled steel scrap rather than raw iron ore.

Gerdau participated in joint-venture bidding consortia in the privatization auctions for state and federally owned steel companies. The major victory was winning the privatization auction for Açominas, an integrated producer that had been operating since 1986 and was considered to have the potential to be one of the lowest-cost steel producers in the world.

Brazilian steel producers are often linked by cross-holdings in each other, so that the steel-making capacity of each group depends on how the cross-holdings are presented. Table 9.4 based on a Gerdau Group presentation to investment bankers, shows that Gerdau had achieved third place in Brazilian steel production by 2002.

The Gerdau Group also maintained an aggressive international expansion during the 1990s. Referring again to Table 9.3 the Chilean steel producer, Aza, was acquired in 1992, and Gerdau followed the acquisition by investing in a new state of the art mini-mill to be a part of Aza.[17] Chile is a small market, but is endowed with iron-ore resources, and the national economy has shown steady growth throughout the 1980s and 1990s.

In 1995 MRM was acquired in the prairie province of Manitoba, Canada, covering another geographic region where Gerdau had previously not had a mill. In 1997 Gerdau acquired a minority participation in the Argentine

Table 9.4 Steel production in Brazil by company, 2002

Company	Millions of tons	% of Brazil total
1 Usiminas/COSIPA (Nippon Steel affiliates)	8,447	29.6
2 Belgo/CST/Acesita (Arcelor affiliates)	8,439	28.5
3 Gerdau/Açominas	5,999	20.3
4 Companhia Siderúrgica Nacional	5,107	17.3
5 Aços Villares	700	.2
6 V & M do Brasil	500	.2
7 Barra Mansa	387	.1
8 Other	1,168	3.8
Total	30,747	100.0

Source: Gerdau, Merrill Lynch presentation, São Paulo (25 June 2003), http://www.gerdau.com.br/port/ri/download.asp?cd_idioma = 1&categoria = 4&menu = apresentaçoes

firm Sipsa, which was followed in 1998 by a second minority participation in Sipar, also in Argentina.

Another major strategic step was taken in 1999 when Gerdau bought a controlling interest in Ameristeel, a US-based mini-mill company. This company had half a dozen mini-mills spread through the growing industrial market in southeastern United States. Table 9.5 shows the geographical distribution of Gerdau Group's steel production units by the end of the 1990s.

A final Gerdau project of significance in the 1990s was the establishment of specialty steel production in Piratini, near the company's Rio Grande do Sul home base in 1992. This production unit put the company into the growing market in Brazil for specialty steels of particular metallurgical characteristics required by the market.

There were two major developments in the implementation of Gerdau's broad strategy by 2002. First, the company achieved complete control of Açominas, and was able to legitimately include the Açominas volume as

Table 9.5 Geographic locations of Gerdau production units

South America	North America
Brazil	**United States**
Riograndense	Gerdau Ameristeel
Piratini	Cartersville
Guáira	Charlotte
Cosigua	Jackson
Divinopolis	Jacksonville
Barão de Cocais	Knoxvillle
Usiba	Perth Amboy
Açonorte	Sayreville
Cearense	Gallatin***
Açominas*	
Uruguay	**Canada**
Laisa	Cambridge
	Whitby
Argentina	MRM
Sipar**	
Chile	
Aza	

* Integrated mill, 79 per cent controlled
** Rolling mill, 38 per cent ownership
*** 50 per cent joint venture
Sources: 'Merger Documents', on the old Co-Steel website, explanation of the reverse merger transaction, http://www.gerdauameristeel.com/invrel/fd.cfm (2002). See also http://www.gerdau.com.br/port/ri/download. asp?cd_ idioma=1&categoria =4&menu=apresentaçoes

a part of its own. Second, the company merged its North American operations with Co-Steel of Canada, with the resultant company controlled by Gerdau named Gerdau Ameristeel. This merger reinforced Gerdau's position as a player in the process of restructuring the North American steel industry. Gerdau now has the fourth-largest steel-making capacity in the USA, and is second only to the legendary Nucor as a mini-mill producer. Gerdau's traditional policy of focusing production on targeted end-use markets has been followed in North America. The challenge for the company now will be to raise the profitability of North American operations, which are the weakest performing sector of the company.

Gerdau executives have always been active in industry and community affairs in Brazil. This approach of public involvement has been followed in North America, where the President of Gerdau Ameristeel is the Chairman of the Steel Manufacturing Association, which represents mini-mill producers in industry and government councils. Gerdau has become a North American insider at this point, and is assured access to the giant NAFTA market.

The Gerdau family controls 56 per cent of the company named Metalúrgica Gerdau. Gerdau Internacional controls Aza in Chile, Laisa in Uruguay and Sipar in Argentina from their headquarters in Pôrto Alegre. Gerdau Internacional controls its North American operations through Gerdau Ameristeel Corporation that is 67 per cent Gerdau-controlled. Gerdau Ameristeel, in turn, controls the Canadian operations of Courtice, MRM and the former Co-Steel, as well as the former Ameristeel operations in the USA.

Jorge Gerdau Johannpeter also heads the Executive Committee of the company (Comite Executivo) which focuses on strategy and stakeholder relations. Frederico Gerdau Johannpeter has an 'inside' role as Senior Vice-President, supervising accounting and auditing, juridical issues, management of the holding company and the reforestation programme. Carlos Petry as the other Senior Vice-President is in charge of Human Resources, Logistics and Transportation and Supply. Andre Gerdau Johannpeter (from the fourth generation of the family) is the Vice-President in charge of North American operations as well as information technology in the company. Claudio Gerdau Johannpeter (also fourth generation) is the Vice-President in charge of Brazilian long steel, specialty steel and industry. Vice-President Osvaldo Schirmer is in charge of Finance, Investor Relations and Operations in Argentina, Chile and Uruguay, and the operations of Banco Gerdau. Vice-President Paulo Vasconcellos supervises Açominas, Marketing, Technology and Quality, and steel scrap-collection operations.[18] The achievement of a smooth management transition from the present top leadership to the new people who are being developed is an important management objective.[19]

Investor relations are critical to the company in its expansion programme. The indebtedness of the company has increased substantially due to the takeover of Açominas in Brazil and the North American acquisitions, and one of the current financial objectives is to lengthen the debt maturities of the company.[20] The profitability of the company has been high enough to service the debt, held largely by Brazilian and foreign institutional investors. Key foreign banks that have supported the creation of Gerdau-Ameristeel in North America include Bank of America, GE Capital, Toronto Dominium, ABN LaSalle Bank, JP Morgan Chase Bank, Comerica Bank, CIBC and CIT.[21] These financiers will have to continue to be satisfied as Gerdau digests its overseas acquisitions and continues to expand.

Market strategy

Gerdau's fundamental market strategy is to achieve dominant market share in standard 'long' products such as reinforcing bars, merchantable bars and wire rods by locating production units (so-called 'market mills') close to buyers, and achieving low costs. Table 9.6 shows that the company had achieved a 48 per cent share of the long-products market in Brazil by 2001. Belgo-Mineira of the Arcelor Group was in second place with 36 per cent. The table also shows the large increase in Gerdau's share of Brazilian crude steel production, reflecting the takeover of Açominas.

Industrial demand provides slightly more than half the total market for Gerdau steel products in Brazil, while civil construction accounts for 46 per cent of the demand, and the agricultural sector accounts for the remaining 3 per cent. In terms of product lines, common long-rolled products comprise 67 per cent of company sales, followed by semi-finished products, drawn products, flat products, and specialty products.

Specific products sold by the company include reinforcing bar ('rebar' for the construction industry), 'merchantable bars' for industrial markets, wire rod for both construction and industry, hot and cold-rolled flat products for construction and industry, and crude steel for further processing by third parties.

The Gerdau 'brand'

Steel is a commodity product, and the strength of a steel brand depends on factors other than the basic metallurgical design of the product in most cases. Gerdau has established its brand through a strong commitment to quality, and the company has been recognized through receiving many awards for product quality in the markets in which it operates. Apart from quality awards, Gerdau has been successful in receiving the ISO certifications for

Table 9.6 Gerdau market share in Brazilian market (%)

	1980	1990	2001
Long-rolled steel	21	32	48
Crude steel	9	12	17

Source: http://www.Gerdau.com.br

company commitment to quality in the steel industry. These certifications are recognized as standards around the world.

Gerdau has also maintained a well-communicated public involvement in supporting education and preserving the environment. SEIVA, one of the subsidiaries of the company, is well-known in the area of reforestation in southern Brazil. The company's support for education is exemplified by the fact that almost 1,000 trainees were working with the company's operations in Brazil during 2003, representing one trainee or intern for every 16 employees.

The Gerdau 'brand' has also been supported by the financial success and expansion of Gerdau, and its listing on several major stock exchanges, including the Bôlsa de Valores de São Paulo (BOVESPA) which is the most important stock exchange in Brazil. Gerdau American Depository Receipts are listed on the New York stock exchange, and company shares are trades in the Latibex Section of the Madrid stock exchange. The shares of Gerdau Ameristeel, the company's North American subsidiary, are traded on the Toronto stock exchange. Gerdau maintains close relationships with the investment community, and presents data on how the shares of the company have out-performed the shares of most companies in the past five years.

Price

Given that steel is a commodity, it is difficult for individual companies to maintain control over price. Price leadership by the largest companies in individual national markets was a characteristic of the steel industry in the era prior to the globalization that prevails today. Companies are confronted today with world market prices unless there are protectionist barriers in particular national or regional markets for particular products. Successful steel producers in the long run must have production costs that are competitive on a worldwide basis. For flat-rolled steel, production costs for Brazilian producers are lower than those in Western Europe, the USA, Korea and Japan.

Gerdau is the largest 'long-product' producer in the Americas, and its dominance of this market in Brazil tends to put the company into the position of price leadership. Gerdau also has a high share of the markets in Chile and Argentina for the product lines in which it specializes. In North America the Gerdau Ameristeel operations do not have the same market dominance as in their Latin American operations, and as a consequence are 'price-takers,' as are all the other North American market participants.

As shown in Figure 9.7 the earnings before interest, taxes and depreciation (EBITDA) that Gerdau realizes in the various national and regional markets in which it operates show the advantages of operating in markets where the firm has a relatively high market share with a relatively low level of imports. About 60 per cent of sales come from Brazil, with less than 10 per cent from the rest of South America, while approximately 30 per cent of sales come from North America.

Table 9.7 Gerdau sales, EBITDA and net income, 2002

	Brazil	North America	South America**	Total
Net sales	1485.3	994.3	113.3	2592.9
EBTDA*	994.3	98.3	29.7	1122.3
Net income	113.3	31.1	9.5	153.9

* Earnings before taxes depreciation and amortization.
** Argentina, Chile, Uruguay.
Source: Gerdau, Merrill-Lynch presentation, São Paulo (25 June 2003), http://www.gerdau.com.br/port/ri/download.asp?cd_idioma = 1&categoria = 4&menu = apresentaçoes

Table 9.8 Gerdau margins, 2002

	Brazil	North America	South America**
Gross margin	40	11	30
EBTDA*	32	10	28
Net margin	12	2	10

* Earnings before taxes depreciation and amortization.
** Argentina, Chile, Uruguay.
Source: Gerdau website, Investidores, Apresentaçoes, Merrill-Lynch presentation, São Paulo (25 June 2003), http://www.gerdau.com.br/port/ri/download.asp?cd_idioma = 1&categoria = 4&menu = apresentaçoes

The margins in Brazil and the rest of South America are much higher than in North America (Figure 9.8). The lower margins in North America reflect greater global competition which affects the steel markets in that region, as well as the higher level of costs.

Promotion

The main promotional approach used by Gerdau is direct sales. The company locates mini-mills (called market mills) close to its main markets, and these are coordinated with sales offices organized under the Gerdau Comercial. In addition, Gerdau has a chain of 'cut-and-bend shops' located close to the main concentrations of customers. These installations take basic finished steel shapes and cut and bend them to the buyer specifications. The use of such facilities reduces costs and raises quality for the final buyer because the steel products are delivered to the job site ready to use in final assemblies and products without further fabrication. The emphasis on close relations with buyers has been a key factor in the company's success.

Gerdau implements essentially the same strategy in its North American operations as it does in Brazil. Its US and Canadian production and distribution operations are located East of the Mississippi river, and the concentration on operations in the Southeastern United States puts Gerdau in one of the most dynamic economic regions of the USA. The actual contact between Gerdau representatives and customers occurs both from outgoing communications and personal visits from the company, and incoming customer visits to the cut-and-bend service centres.

Gerdau has also set up an online sales facility to facilitate customer contact through electronic communication. This form of sales approach has become standard in the steel industry, although Gerdau was among the first Brazilian steel companies to implement such a system.

Distribution

Gerdau steel is delivered directly from the steel plants, through the company-controlled service centres, and through independent steel distributors. Export sales are handled by an Export Sales Department at company headquarters in Brazil. The company sells a variety of products including barbed wire, reinforcing rods and crude steel to overseas markets in South America, North America and Europe. The Gerdau-Ameristeel operations in the USA and Canada may also serve as import distributors of Gerdau products from Brazil. The Ameristeel units trade within the company in North America, but exports out of North America are very limited at the present time. The Açominas unit in Brazil is especially well-set-up for exports since the plant has a direct rail connection to an Atlantic port dedicated to steel exports. The port is jointly operated by three Brazilian steel companies, Açominas (Gerdau), Usiminas, and CST (Companhia Siderúrgica Tubarão). Table 9.9 shows that Açominas sales in 2001 were 41 per cent within Brazil, and 59 per cent to foreign markets, including 35 per cent to Asia. In the first trimester of 2003, Gerdau (including Açominas) exported 1.5 million tons of steel, representing almost 47 per cent of their total output. Based on their export success the company issued international 'Notes Based on Export Receivables', which

Table 9.9 Açominas exports, 2001

Brazil		41%
Exports:		
The Rest of South America	6%	
Mexico and Central America	3%	
North America	11%	
Sub-total Americas		20%
Europe		2%
Africa		2%
Southeast Asia	25%	
China and the Far East	10%	
Sub-total Asia		35%
Sub-total Export		59%
Total		100%[23]

Source: http://www.açominas.com.br/portug/prod/images/photo/EXPORT_atual.JPG

had a seven-year term and a coupon rate of 7.37 per cent. This financing is part of the debt restructuring of the company, and will make it possible to offer attractive payment terms to overseas customers.[22]

Conclusions

Gerdau is now a major player in the global steel industry. It has up-to-date mini-mill production facilities located close to major markets in North and South America, and also has an integrated steel mill located in one of the largest and highest-quality iron ore regions in the world with a direct export connection. The company has ample sources of low-cost, high-quality labour, which receives constant training and skill upgrading under longstanding company policy.

Gerdau has followed the strategy in Brazil of locating production units close to important regional geographic markets. The company focuses on long products and flat-rolled products, having achieved a high market share for these products. Gerdau is closely attuned to the needs of customers of all sizes. It has created a branded chain of cut-and-bend shops throughout Brazil and Eastern North America to meet customer needs, and its service centres and multiple sales offices are supplemented by a well-developed online sales facility.

Gerdau has an excellent mini-mill, Gerdau Aza, in Chile. It also has operations in Argentina and Uruguay, thereby giving it presence and experience in the southern cone countries. The company is well-positioned should regional integration through Mercosur continue.

Gerdau also seems to be well-positioned in the Eastern Canadian and US markets. It has especial strength in the southeastern region. It has presence in the Port of New York area through its plant at Perth Amboy, New Jersey. The company is also well-positioned for the continued regional integration through NAFTA.

Gerdau follows a multidomestic approach in managing its far-flung international affiliates, orientated by its core values. The company seems to be a model for the twenty-first century, stressing quality, environmental responsibility, customer orientation, employee orientation, energy conservation and an emphasis on new technology, corporate ethics and social responsibility. The global steel industry, however, is one of the most rough-and-tumble arenas in the global economy. The key is the continuing excellence of the Gerdau management, and corporate leadership. The Johannpeter brothers of the 1940s generation were remarkable in their achievements; will their sons, daughters, nephews and nieces be able to continue the excellence of this company into a fifth and sixth generation? Is Gerdau destined to become a unit in one of the super giant multinational steel companies that is emerging, or will Gerdau itself survive as one of those companies?

Notes

1. Based on slide 43, Apresentacão do Presidente da Usiminas, Rinaldo Campos Soares, durante o primeiro encontro anual com investidores e analistas, realizado em 11/04/03, http://www.usiminas.com.br/informaçoesfinanceiras/
2. Belgo-Mineira website, http://www.belgomineira.com.br/grupo/histórico.htm; and the Arcelor website, http://www.arcelor.com/index.php?page=49&lngId=1
3. http://www.japanmetalbulletin.com/top_bn/is031007.html;http://asia.news.yahoo.com/031103/5/174yp.html
4. ISPAT/LRM website, http://www.ispatinland.com/default.asp?id=corp_org_chart&menu_key=355&langid=en
5. Usiminas website, http://www.usiminas.com.br/informaçoesfinanceiras; http://usiminas.infoinvest.com.br/static/ptb/perfil_composicao.asp; Nippon Steel website, http://www0.nsc.co.jp/shinnihon_english/kankyou/
6. Gerdau website, investor relations, http://www.gerdau.com.br/port/ri/index.asp
7. POSCO website, http://www.posco.co.kr/en/index.jsp
8. Shanghai Baosteel website, http://www.baosteel.com/english_n/indexe_n.html
9. Tony Smith, 'Deal to Take Over Brazilian Steel Maker Falls Apart', *New York Times* (14 November 2002), W1; CSN website, http://csn.com; see also for Fitch's Ratings http://quickstart.clari.net/qs_se/webnews/wed/ct/Bny-fitch-ratings_csn.RiZs_DlL.html and Corus website, http://www.corusgroup.com/home/index.cfm
10. ThyssenKrupp website, http://www.thyssenkrupp.com/
11. JFE website, http://www.jfe-holdings.co.jp/en/investor/keiei/tougou.html
12. Riva website, http://www.rivagroup.com/
13. US Steel website, http://www.usx.com/corp/about.htm
14. Nucor website, http://www.nucor.com/financials.asp?finpage=newsreleases
15. International Iron and Steel Institute-IISI, 'World Steel Facts', http://www.worldsteel.org/wsif.php
16. Gerdau website, history, founders, http://www.gerdau.com.br/port/agerdau/fundadores.asp; see also http://www.belgomineira.com.br/grupo/histórico.htm
17. Gerdau, 'Gerdau Aza 50 Years', Presentation, http://www.aza.cl/index.htm
18. Gerdau, 'Nova Governança Corporativa (New Corporate Governance)' (July 2002), a presentation on the website, http://www.gerdau.com.br/port/ri/download.asp?cd_idioma=1&categoria=4&menu=apresentaçoes
19. *Ibid.*
20. 'Gerdau anuncia program de Notas de Recebiveis de Exportaçoes', Press Release (9 September 2003), http://www.gerdau.com.br/port/ri/infmercado/index.asp
21. Gerdau Ameristeel website, Investor Relations, http://www.gerdauameristeel.com/invrel/index.cfm
22. 'Gerdau anuncia program de Notas de Recebiveis de Exportaçoes', Press Release (9 September 2003), http://www.gerdau.com.br/port/ri/infmercado/index.asp

For this study, detailed information about the company was obtained from the Gerdau website, investidores, presentaçoes, http://www.gerdau.com.br.

10
China Business: A Relationship-Based Market-Entry Approach

Helena Chiu and Gerhard A. Wührer

Introduction

The visitors from Europe had had a long trip from Frankfurt, Germany, to Taichung, Taiwan. They were visiting the Mao Shun Corporation for the first time, and their first impressions were very positive. Arriving at the main entrance there was a greeting board, welcoming the guests in both Chinese and German. Inside the building there were surprisingly few signs left of the major earthquake that had shaken the area two years previously – apparently the company had been quick to recover from the damage. On their way to the Vice-President's office, the visitors passed the marketing department that was divided into small cubicles. Dozens of marketing executives were busily focused on their work, while incoming calls from all over the world brought orders for the company. Despite the hectic office life, there was a very team-oriented atmosphere with friendly smiles for the visitors.

Billy Chiu came out of his office, a tall polite man with a welcoming smile. As Vice-President for sales and marketing at Mao Shun, one of Taiwan's leading manufacturers of sealing products, Billy was responsible for market development in Europe and in the USA. He had come to realize that he liked American and German managers' ways of thinking – deal-oriented, not so complicated as their counterparts in the People's Republic of China (PRC) – while at the same time recognizing that it was Taiwan's cultural affinity with the PRC that gave Taiwanese companies a competitive edge *vis-à-vis* other countries. Like many domestic and international companies of all sizes and industries, Mao Shun had decided to set foot in the Chinese market by establishing a production site in Kunshan, PRC, in 2000.

In 2003, only three years after the official opening of the PRC subsidiary, the China business was expected to go into the black for the first time. This result exceeded Mao Shun's expectations, and Billy reflected on the reasons and circumstances that may have helped the company achieve this great result.

Industry background

Taiwan's rubber industry has grown tremendously since 1945. Since the end of the Second World War the number of rubber companies increased from almost zero to more than 600, and the production value reached US$2 billion in 2000; 60 per cent of products are expected, and the growth is expected to continue.[1]

In the 1970s the Taiwanese government shifted its economic policy to export-orientation, laying the foundations for Taiwan's current status as a leading export country. This development was absolutely necessary for the following reason: in a relatively small market with many companies producing similar types of products, market saturation and oversupply were major points of concern. In the late 1980s the rubber industry entered a transformation period which characterized by several negative factors, for example the appreciation of local currency, a labour shortage, increasing labour costs, and the exemption of tax benefits in Europe and the USA. Many companies responded to the adverse market situation by relocating their production facilities to low-cost countries such as Thailand and the PRC – a trend that is still ongoing today.

Company background

Mao Shun[2] was founded in 1976 by its current chairman Joseph Shek. Under his leadership and guidance, the company quickly developed from a small family business to become one of the country's industry leaders. In fact, with the conclusion of the initial public offering in 2002, Mao Shun was the first sealing manufacturing company to go public in Taiwanese history. In recognition of the company's outstanding performance, the Taiwanese Ministry of Economics nominated Chairman Shek the Young Entrepreneur of the Year 1990. In addition, the company won the 14th Annual National Award for Small and Medium Enterprises in 1995. Today, Mao Shun employs over 500 people in its Taiwan headquarters, and belongs to the top-four largest and most renowned manufacturers of sealing products in Taiwan. The responsibility for all operations is concentrated in the hands of the General Manager, who reports to the company's top management.

Products

The primary purpose of seals is to prevent different kinds of leakages, for example liquid leakage, air leakage, oil leakage or gas leakage. As such they find a wide array of uses in different items, from household appliances, construction equipment, all the way to automotive vehicles. The initial product range included oil seals for automotive and industrial applications, but over the years new product developments, the introduction of high-tech materials and venturing into new fields of application have led to a substantial increase of Mao Shun's product range. Today, Mao Shun products are sold under the NAK brand worldwide. At present, over 15,000 varieties of seals and rubber parts are produced, using state-of-the-art manufacturing technologies. The latest developed field of business is safety syringes developed in collaboration with the biotech industry.

International operations

Internationalization of business started in the early 1980s, when Mao Shun began exporting to the USA and Europe. The company's international operations rely primarily on an extensive network of agents and distributors, and cooperation with them helped boost Mao Shun's share of export business. In recent years, more investment-intensive forms of market entry, for example joint ventures and foreign direct investments, were chosen in order to enter strategically important countries. Mao Shun has, for instance, established its own subsidiaries in Japan and mainland China, countries geographically and culturally close to Taiwan. In more distant target markets such as the United Kingdom, Iran and Australia, it has entered into joint ventures with local business agents (see Table 10.1).

Mao Shun's international operations translate into a large network of business relations, with the different markets all over the world served either directly by the headquarters in Nantou, Taiwan, by wholly-owned subsidiaries abroad, or through above-mentioned agencies and joint ventures. Besides channel partners, the immediate network of Mao Shun also connects third parties with the business. There is a strong tie to the Taiwanese government, national science and research institutions as well as educational facilities

Table 10.1 Worldwide markets

Asia Pacific	Europe	Africa & Near East	Americas
Japan**	UK*	Egypt	USA
Korea	Ireland	Syria	Uruguay
PR China**	France	Iran*	
Thailand	Belgium	Nigeria	
Malaysia	Denmark	Zimbabwe	
Indonesia	Sweden	South Africa	
Singapore	Germany		
Philippines	Austria		
Sri Lanka	Italy		
Australia*	Spain		
	Portugal		
	Greece		

*Joint venture; **FDI.
Source: Mao Shun company internal documents.

throughout the country. Although corporate decision-making is centralized in the 'hub' Nantou, some important functions are carried out decentrally by the local subsidiaries or agents. For example, the joint venture in the UK, in which Mao Shun holds a 33 per cent share, specializing in the research, development and marketing of sealing products for racing cars.

Competition

Serving global markets, Mao Shun faces tough competition both from domestic and foreign companies. In Taiwan there are three major competitors: Tai Tsuang Co. was established in 1961 and is thus one of the oldest oil-seal manufacturers on the island, with a low-price strategy that poses a challenge to its competitors; Yuan Cherng Co., established just two years later in 1963, boasts the largest production facilities and claims market leadership for industrial rubber parts in Taiwan; Tsuang Hine Co., the third competitor, followed in 1974 and is the market player with the smallest amount of direct international engagement. The quartet of national companies share similar operation modes: all of them manufacture precision rubber parts for industrial and consumer use, they serve both original equipment manufacturers and after-markets, their business is highly export-oriented, and most of them have outsourced parts of their production process to mainland China.

The biggest rival in the global arena is the German-based Freudenberg Group, a diversified family company with activities in seals and vibration-control technology, household products, specialty lubricants and other types of products and services. Freudenberg teamed up with another major rival, Japan's NOK Corporation, to become one of the world's top-25 automotive original equipment suppliers. The Freudenberg–NOK Group now enjoys combined annual sales of more than $7.5 billion, with worldwide automotive sales topping $4 billion. Mao Shun also faces giant competitors from the USA, where Federal Mogul Co. and Chicago Rawhide Industries have been supplying automotive and industrial components to global original equipment manufacturers for many decades. Chicago Rawhide was acquired by Sweden-based SKF, the world's leading manufacturer of rolling bearings, in 1990. Although not in direct competition to Mao Shun, the SKF Group fuels the source of competition by backing Chicago Rawhide with substantial financial resources and a comprehensive range of engineering know-how.

Corporate vision and strategic implications

Mao Shun's corporate vision is to become the world's number-one manufacturer of sealing products. The key ingredients for global leadership are seen in a strong commitment to research and development, a careful expansion strategy, quality excellence, and maximum efforts in maintaining good relationships with agents and customers.

Innovation leadership

New product development and product differentiation will make Mao Shun a full-range provider of rubber products. The company has ambitious plans to enter the market of nano-technology which will open totally new perspective to product functionality and qualities. For this purpose, the company is in close touch with the Taiwanese government, which is heavily promoting activities in this field, and it cooperates with nearby universities in developing practical solutions for innovative technologies. In addition, Mao Shun has recently discovered the very promising and attractive market of medical appliances, aerospace parts and IT components. Just as in the previous cases, Mao Shun has successfully initiated cooperation with industry players in order to secure access to know-how and future markets. In 2001, R&D expenditure was 2.02 per cent of annual turnover.

Focus on international markets

In a relatively small market such as Taiwan, export business is a major pillar of the domestic economy. To Mao Shun, the most important export market by far is the European Union, where the annual demand for sealing products has grown by an average of 3.9 per cent over the past few years. While the Taiwanese average export rate of sealing products totalled 95 per cent of domestic production in recent years, Mao Shun's export rate of 87 per cent in the year 2000 was slightly lower than the national average. However, it can be stated that roughly a quarter of Taiwan's total export volume in sealing products goes to the account of Mao Shun.[3]

Reaching out to international markets also concerns resource-allocation. Facing intensifying competition at home and abroad, Mao Shun is being forced to make cost reductions one of its primary tactical goals. Already the company is coming to enjoy the financial benefits of its recently established production facility in the PRC, and in future further resource intensive business functions will gradually be moved from Taiwan to other low-cost countries, thus transforming Mao Shun into a truly global company.

Quality leadership

Ever since its inception, Mao Shun has been committed to top product quality. In addition, the company strongly relies on quality excellence as a means to distinguish itself from other competitors. A meticulous quality-control system accompanies the complete value chain, which extends from the purchase of materials, the production process, to the delivery process. Equal attention is given to service quality that is seen as the basis for customer satisfaction. As Billy Chiu notes, the time factor has become a crucial dimension, making it absolutely necessary for the company to demonstrate its ability to respond quickly to customer inquiries and adapt to customers' time schedules. He emphasizes two particularly important benchmarks: the time it takes to develop samples, and keeping to promised delivery times. Mao Shun's commitment to quality excellence resulted in the ISO 9000 and 9002 certification standards in the early 1990s, as well as the QS 9000 standard in 2000. Following ISO 9000 quality-management principles, organizational structures (business processes and their interrelations) are reconsidered and redesigned in such a way that the organization's objectives can be achieved in the most effective and most efficient way. As Mao Shun strives to make 'quality' a guiding principle of its business philosophy, its organizational structure will gradually develop from an ISO-guided organization to a constant-learning organization on a global scale.

Business relationships

An analysis of Mao Shun's client structure shows that an overwhelming part of its business, an average of 72 per cent of annual turnover in the past few years, comes from only two per cent of its customers. The business relationship with these key accounts is therefore very important. Further, nine out of the ten key accounts are foreign customers, emphasizing once more the company's high degree of international focus. Although Mao Shun is basically striving to provide the best possible service to all customers, relationship management with the large clients naturally receives special attention and is handled by selected account managers.

The PRC business

Cross-strait economic relations

Economic ties between China and Taiwan have grown considerably over the past two decades. Bilateral trade now totals more than US$25 billion annually, with average growth rates at around seven per cent per annum in the past few years. Taiwan's trade surplus has been continuous, reaching US$16 billion in 2001.[4]

China itself has also benefited considerably from business links with Taiwan. So far, more than 60,000 Taiwanese companies have invested some US$44 billion in the PRC, making Taiwan the third-largest investor in China, and China the second-largest export market for Taiwan. An estimated 300,000 Taiwanese citizens live and work in China, and more than 23 million have travelled there since the 1980s. In areas such as the southern province of Guangdong, Taiwanese businesses already account for four per cent of total export output.[5]

Cross-strait economic exchanges continue to increase, thanks to improvements in the business infrastructure. Among the most stipulated demands from business communities is the establishment of the 'Three Links', which would finally enable direct transportation, postal and direct cross-strait trade relations between China and Taiwan. The establishment of these links is seen as a small step in normalizing relations between the PRC and Taiwan, thus helping regional economic development while political problems are being solved. Despite the recent slackening in growth of the regional and global economy, China has been able to sustain an impressive growth rate of around 7 per cent, making it the world's seventh-largest economy. China's role for the Taiwanese and, in fact, the world economy will therefore become even more vital in the future.[6]

The automotive market in the PRC

A major source of demand for sealing products comes from the automotive industry, and a detailed analysis of this sector provides crucial information for market-entry decisions. In recent years, the Chinese automotive and auto parts industry[7] has witnessed tremendous growth rates due to the favourable macroeconomic environment. In the year 2003, the demand for cars in China was expected to surge to 3.3 million vehicles, with the main increase boosted by the private sector.

There are over 2,300 automotive enterprises[8] in the PRC, which include car manufacturers, car-conversion companies motorcycle companies, and auto-parts manufacturers. Roughly 1.8 million people work in the automotive industry, generating more than a quarter of total industry output. Most of the leading international car companies have moved parts of their production processes to China, and with the approval of the Chinese government, multinationals such as GM, VW, Chrysler, Honda, Citroen and Ford have been assembling cars in China for many years, bringing new business opportunities to the local auto-parts providers.[9] In fact, over 40 per cent of the parts used in the vehicles made in China come from local suppliers. In response to the large domestic demand and also in order to make use of China's favourable cost structures, many foreign automotive suppliers have established bases in China, mostly in proximity to the car manufacturers. According to statistics, one-third of all auto-parts companies in China are fully or partially foreign-invested.

PRC business development

Mao Shun's interest in China business started in the late 1980s. During that time, as there were only limited possibilities for Taiwanese companies to invest in the PRC, business existed in the form of indirect export via a trading agent in Hong Kong. In the mid-1990s, as China evolved into one of the world's premier emerging markets, detailed market research was conducted to assess the pros and cons of setting up a permanent presence in the PRC. A crucial source of information was the dialogue with the local association of Taiwanese expatriates, whose suggestions and experiences proved invaluable to newcomers such as Mao Shun. The result of market investigation indicated a sharp increase in the rate of motorization, as the Chinese exchange their bikes for motorbikes and cars. This, in turn, would lead to a high increase in the demand of automotive products – a huge market potential which, in Billy Chiu's words, Mao Shun just could not afford to miss. Besides, China was alluring with cheap resources that could be used to satisfy local demand. In addition, for a customer-oriented company like Mao Shun, it was particularly important to be in close proximity to the customer to render a better service.

The foundation-stone for a long-term engagement in the Chinese market was officially laid in 1999 when construction work for a new 16,500 square metre production facility in Kunshan in the central-eastern province of Jiangsu started. The selection of this location was the result of thorough deliberation. To Mao Shun, being close to customers was one of its primary market-entry motives. As the prospective purchasers of rubber components, namely the automotive industry and machinery manufacturers, were located in northern China and along the eastern coastline, Mao Shun had decided to establish a presence in Kunshan, a fast-growing city of 585,000, located just 50 km west of Shanghai. In recent years, Kunshan has become Taiwan's preferred industrial outpost, with some 1,000 Taiwanese companies, among which 30 are stocklisted, having invested US$10 billion into the city over the past 10 years. Pillar industries include precision machinery, IT, textile, chemicals, construction material and foods and beverages. In addition the tertiary sector is advancing rapidly. The city itself has adapted well to serve Taiwanese expatriates and their families, offering anything from Taiwan-style restaurants to the latest Taipei fashion items.

In 2001, only two and a half years after the foundation ceremony, Mao Shun's new production site went into full operation. Initial operations were headed by a highly experienced manager from the Taiwan headquarters who, equipped with management skills and technical know-how, was the most suitable person to oversee the new plant. Today, Mao Shun Kunshan employs more than 180 people, mainly in the production sector. The product range mirrors that of the headquarters in Taiwan, consisting of four main product groups:

- oil seals and o-rings;
- industrial parts (for example parts for machinery and the automotive industry);
- consumer-goods components (for example for electrical appliances and computers); and
- medicare parts (for example syringe stoppers and dialysis machine parts).

Automotive parts and consumer-goods components are expected to make up the gross of the market volume in the coming years.

Chosen strategy

Market-entry mode

There are several market-entry options for foreign firms, ranging from licensing, franchising, agency, representative offices or Chinese subsidiaries, to wholly-owned enterprises. In Mao Shun's case, the market-entry mode was chosen under consideration of primarily four goals:

1 *Market access*: to gain access to the high market potential in China.
2 *Cost reduction*: to reduce costs through use of cheap local market resources.
3 *Service quality*: to improve service quality through geographic proximity to customers.
4 *Control of operations*: the China business is to remain under the full control of Mao Shun.

Like many other Taiwanese companies, Mao Shun realizes that Taiwan is no longer a competitive base for labour- and resource-intensive mass production. Instead, Taiwan needs to bolster its capabilities in the areas of know-how-intensive manufacturing support. Thus, the best hope for Taiwan's long-term prosperity lies in competing *in* China, and not *against* China. According to this strategy, basic manufacturing processes are moved to Taiwan-invested production facilities in China, whereas high-end finishing and value-added services (for example, R&D, product design, pilot production and testing, equipment supply, logistics and engineering back-up) continue to be carried out in Taiwan. Thus this is the case with Mao Shun. In addition, it was clear that Mao Shun wanted to retain full control over the operations in China. In view of these considerations, FDI was the preferred entry mode from the beginning.

Marketing strategy

Mao Shun's marketing strategy in the PRC can be described in terms of the '7 P's':

- A **product strategy** based on offering high quality, high-tech products to (mainly) OEM customers in China.
- The **primary target market** for Mao Shun is the Kunshan–Guangzhou–Chongqing area, where the automotive industry and thus the demand for automotive parts is located. Further, a cooperation agreement signed with Shanghai's Ta-Chong automobile company will ensure a steady long-term demand in the future.
- The **pricing strategy** is in accordance with the high-quality image of the NAK brand. Although of course prices have to be competitive, the company

is determined not to enter a price war with its competitors – instead, preferring to follow the motto 'superior quality at adequate prices'.
- **Promotional activities** in the PRC market focus primarily on the participation in trade shows and different kinds of advertisements. In addition,
- **public relations** with industry associations, research institutions (schools, ministries) and customers ensure that Mao Shun is in good stead with all market players. Special attention is also given to,
- **payment management**, an important aspect in China where delayed payments or uncollectible debts are a widespread problem, putting the cash-flow situation and thus financial health of the creditor at risk.
- In general, Mao Shun's marketing strategy is based on two treasured business **principles** – a free market, and reduction of government intervention.

The role of relationships

Fundamental cultural differences between East and West have left many foreign companies struggling to come to terms with doing business in China. As Billy Chiu notes, Taiwanese companies such as Mao Shun, due to their cultural affinity with China, have a competitive edge *vis-à-vis* their European or American counterparts. Not only do they have the advantage of speaking the same language, they also understand the importance and, above all, the practice of such guiding principles as trust, face, hierarchy, harmony, long-term orientation and reciprocity. Cultural affinity between Taiwan and the PRC was a major facilitator in successful engagement with the PRC. Both countries share, for example, the same perceptions towards the role of human relationships in doing business.

Learning the hard way

As a Taiwanese, Billy Chiu knows from personal experience that establishing and fostering a good relationship is an absolute imperative in business operations with China. There are an abundance of stories about potential customers cancelling courtesy visits at the initial stage of business, because Mao Shun was regarded as having invested too little effort into nourishing the relationship. Similarly, existing customers were reported to have repeatedly refused approving quality test reports, despite excellent test results. The situation changed for the better when Mao Shun started to invite customers for a meal, for example. Relational exchange is not restricted to these areas only. In fact, as the business process moves on, relationship management is required whenever people from both sides have to interact with each other. Typically, the main exchange partners that supplier companies like Mao Shun have to deal with and to whom relationship-building activities should primarily be directed are the client's quality-control department, the R&D department, the purchasing department and the general manager.

Business networks

Equally important as dyadic relationships is the ability to access networks of relationships. From a network perspective, social and economic interaction with one exchange partner may pave the way to a related third party, which may be of relevance to one's own business endeavours. In this way, the original set of dyadic relationships is extended into other sets of relationships, transforming it into a complex network of interactions. Billy Chiu knows very well that partners of the network communicate about new members of the business 'family' in the area; he also is aware of the 'embeddedness' of his company within the various ties whether they are political, social, economical, infrastructural or other. They are sources of facilitators, provide access to resources and solutions, which may make things easier from the outset to keep the business running smoothly. The network itself therefore deserves attention and ties should be kept functioning well.

The most important network members in the market-entry stage are: PRC government officials, the local Taiwanese expatriate association, local officials, infrastructure providers, main customers and local suppliers. Certainly, the intensity and content of relationships change as the PRC engagement matures. Billy Chiu notes that as the scope of business expands, contact with local suppliers and main customers increases. Cooperation with local officials will still be required, for example in order to solve operative issues such as labour recruitment, whilst, in contrast, the role of government authorities is likely to diminish after the market-entry stage.

Business relationships in practice

The most important interface between Mao Shun and its customers are the key account managers. Basically, distribution channels are either direct channels (Mao Shun → end-user), or they involve one middleman (Mao Shun → agent → end-user) or at a maximum two middlemen (Mao Shun → agent → distributor → end-user). According to Billy Chiu, the choice of channel design (see Figure 10.1) depends less on the complexity of products, but more on the country market's requirements. In most of its European markets, for example, Mao Shun employs a two-level channel structure, for the simple reason those local agents and distributors with local market know-how are needed. In geographically and culturally closer markets such as China, Mao Shun is in a good position to handle the business directly with the customer.

Regardless of channel structure, key account managers (KAM) are an integral part of Mao Shun's relationship-focused marketing strategy. There are currently three KAMs, including Billy Chiu himself, which emphasizes the importance of this position. Each of them is responsible for a specific market region. Although their main function is to take care of agents, the KAMs also offer a channel of communication to distributors and end-users whenever

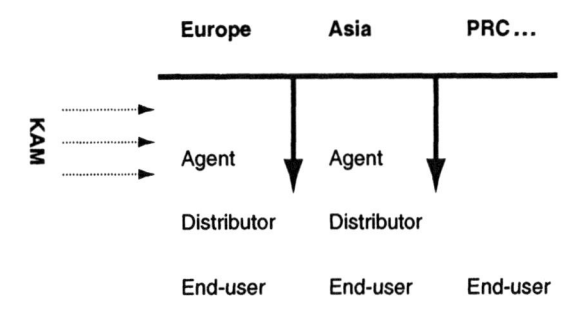

```
                    Europe      Asia       PRC...
                       |         |          |
   KAM .......>     Agent      Agent        |
       .......>       |          |          |
                      v          v          v
                   Distributor  Distributor
                      |          |          |
                      v          v          v
                   End-user   End-user   End-user
```

Figure 10.1 Channel structures
Source: Mao Shun company internal documents.

necessary. This is especially true when the end-users are industrial heavyweights such as Caterpillar or CASE Corporation. Here, upon the request and with the consent of the respective agent/distributor, the KAM will establish direct contact with the end-user in order to clarify production-related issues; for example to discuss critical applications, develop customized products, incorporate new materials, determine test series, or carry out factory audits.

After successful conclusion of a deal, the KAMs hand the business over to a central sales support team responsible for the daily operative issues. The team's duties include business correspondence, handling customer complaints, information about shipment schedules, follow-up on payment issues, and the like. As with the KAMs, each sales-support executive is responsible for specific customer accounts, ensuring a well-defined communication structure between Mao Shun and its customers.

Ethical issues

Relationship-based cultures are often branded as being corrupt. Although this perception may not always become reality, most companies[10] do practise bribery to some extent in their China business. The public sector, which is an important interface at market entry, is reported to be particularly susceptible to corruption. Small and medium-sized enterprises (SME) are usually at a disadvantage compared to their corporate counterparts: while large corporations usually start their negotiating rounds directly with the highest levels of government authorities, thus having their 'endowment' work in the right place, SMEs such as Mao Shun have to deal with lower-level public servants who do not necessarily have decision-making power. As a consequence, expenditures for relationship maintenance often fail to produce the desired results.

Implications for human-resource management (HRM)

In relationship-focused cultures, careful attention must be given to the selection and education of employees. In this respect, HRM in Kunshan works closely with that of the central HRM in Taiwan. Being primarily a manufacturing company, Mao Shun's employees naturally consist largely of skilled, blue-collar workers, and currently NAK Kunshan has a staff of 200 persons, all of them local people. The management team of five persons, however, comes from the Taiwan headquarters. Its primary task is to pass on technical and management know-how to the local staff, so that in future a local management team can take over. Mao Shun emphasizes both soft and hard skills; besides the formal qualifications necessary for a specific position, employees have to demonstrate their ability to work in a team as an important part of the company culture. Billy Chiu puts it in metaphoric terms: Mao Shun employees, including the agents and distributors, form the so-called NAK family, emphasizing the importance of employee satisfaction as a prerequisite for customer satisfaction. Nourishing the team spirit and enhancing soft skills is also an essential part of Mao Shun's personnel training scheme, which is partly outsourced to external consulting companies. Individual career talks between employees and their superiors ensure that career development is in line with employees' personal aspirations. As an interface to the customer, key account managers deserve special attention from a HRM perspective. Their performance is guided by target figures (MBO principle), with the performance indicators being jointly decided between the key account managers and top management. Further, regular training is provided in the fields of product know-how and soft skills. With respect to its reward scheme, Mao Shun grants the usual bonuses in the form of company shares and, in addition, heavily emphasizes non-monetary incentives such as job-promotion and recognition from top management. In summary, Mao Shun's HRM can be summarized as follows: a democratic leadership style, a learning organization based on TQM, an emphasis on both hard and soft skills, an achievement-based reward scheme, employee satisfaction and loyalty, and promoting the 'NAK family' mentality.

Conclusion

Following China's WTO entry in 2001, expectations are running high that WTO membership will also bring an improvement to the strained relationship between China and Taiwan. So far, the lack of direct transportation links between the two economies has cost Taiwanese businesses a substantial amount of competitive edge in the form of lost time, reduced efficiency and higher additional expenses. In the case of Mao Shun, FDI engagement in China has helped alleviate these problems to a great extent, and the output of the production site in Kunshan satisfies the domestic demand for sealing products in China. However, as Billy Chiu knows, having set up a presence in China is no sure-fire recipe for success in the challenging times that lie ahead. Companies planning or already engaged in China business need to be aware of several uncertainty factors that will influence China's future development. For instance, China's transitional economy remains burdened by persisting structural weaknesses, which will not diminish in the short term. Second, the transformation of the state sector and the unleashing of market forces could lead to economic risks and social upheavals of an unknown degree. Third, in the process of economic liberalization, China will have to eliminate tariff and non-tariff trade barriers, allowing foreign products to enter the country, fuelling competition between local manufacturers, foreign-owned local subsidiaries, and foreign companies.

In parallel, many leading car manufacturers in China are gradually adopting a global purchasing strategy in the search for more cost efficiency. The current trends in the automotive industry have already been discussed in a previous chapter and they provide just one example of the far-reaching effects WTO membership has had on China as a whole.[11] Despite the challenges that lie ahead, Billy Chiu is sure that his company is taking the right steps in the right direction. Mao Shun's internationalization strategy based on customer-orientation and quality excellence has so far served the company very well. Its guiding principle says 'We want to become the market leader for sealing products in China!'

Notes

Primary and secondary data within the NAK company are based on interviews with Mao Shun executives, 26–28 November 2002, Taichung, Taiwan, Mao Shun company internal documents.

1 See www.tria.org.tw
2 See www.nak.com.tw
3 Mao Shun company internal documents
4 *Asiaweek*, 6 July 2001, see www.asiaweek.com; Taiwan Ministry of Economic Affairs, *Cross-Strait Economic Statistics Monthly* (July 2002): 21.
5 *Asiaweek*, 6 July 2001; Taiwan Ministry of Economic Affairs, *Cross-Strait Economic Statistics Monthly*: 35.
6 See www.chinaproducts.com/eng2/content/contf1415.phtml
7 See www.caam.org.cn
8 See www.caam.org.cn
9 See www.chinaproducts.com/eng2/content/contf2009.phtml
10 http://www.transparency.org/pressrelease-archive/2002/dnld/2002.05.14.bpi.de.pdf
11 See www.chinaproducts.com/eng2/content/contf1029.phtml

11
The Attractiveness of the Azerbaijan Market: The Case of Betek

Dilek Zamantılı-Nayır and F. Zeynep Bilgin

Introduction

The developments in world trade indicate that international business operations are moving to regions where emerging markets (EMs) are located. Turkey, as a dynamic EM for investors, enjoys a unique location at the crossroads between East and West, which makes it an interesting country also because of its proximity to the newly emerging markets in Central Asia. At the same time, Turkey is a leading investor in the Caucasian and Central Asian Turkic Republics.[1]

The relationships of Turkish companies with the region have a long history and did not just arise after the dissolution of the Soviet Union, but go back a long time. Besides the physical and cultural proximity, successful uncertainty-handling stemming from the recent unpredictable and high inflationary environment of Turkey, frequent changes in economic/business policies, learned flexibility and Turks' bargaining skills, as well as similarities between bureaucracies and availability of Russian-speaking employees also helps ensure success.[2]

For this study, the activities of a Turkish company exporting to Azerbaijan are detailed. The selected firm is Betek Boya from the Turkish paint industry. The analysis provides some useful insights for firms following the same path since both countries are called EMs but are at present at different levels of economic development.

Turkey and Azerbaijan: historical ties and links today

Taking a closer look at the relations of Turkey with Azerbaijan, both countries have strong historical, cultural and linguistic bonds[3] and share the same religion. Beyond that, the links extend to the fields of economy, trade, education, agriculture, telecommunication, social security, health, science and tourism.[4] All these factors create a positive atmosphere for the improvement of international business relations. The relationships between Turkey and Azerbaijan are based on more than one hundred treaties signed between 1991 and 1999,[5] mainly aimed at increasing the level of trade and cooperation, preventing double taxation, improving mutual investments, solving business-related problems between the two countries and supporting Azerbaijan in its integration attempts with the global community.

In fact, Azerbaijan as one of the CIS-7[6] has faced particularly difficult transitions and had to cope with high levels of poverty, relatively weak institutional infrastructures and, in most cases, large external debt burdens.[7] And being part of the Black Sea Economic Cooperation (BSEC) has also provided endless opportunities to this newly emerging market to improve international business relations and reach larger export markets like Turkey. The BSEC can be a less-demanding learning ground also for smaller Turkish businesses and new entrants to global markets, and can help firms develop the skills necessary to make them strong global players and help them reach Central Asia and beyond.[8] Common membership in a regional trading bloc is assumed to increase trade threefold,[9] and over time the economies of countries within regional trading blocs are becoming more closely intertwined.[10] Supporting these views, the trade relations of Turkey and Azerbaijan have benefited from membership in the BSEC.[11]

Exports and investments attractive in Azerbaijan

Turkey is fifth in exports and the second most important import trade partner for Azerbaijan.[12] Turkish firms play an important role in the international business relations of this newly emerging market, and attempts related to the liberalization of trade have undoubtedly helped improve of relations over time. Following investment in renovations and infrastructure development, a new market has opened for exports of a variety of products from Turkey to Azerbaijan: agricultural machinery, seeds, pesticides and fertilizers and sugar, flour and margarine, soap and detergents, glassware, electrical energy, textile fibres, livestock, paints, metals, chemicals, machinery and equipment and petrol products. Starting from 1990 onwards, Turkish companies have actively taken part in the restructuring of this country and currently there are about 700 Turkish firms involved in direct investments in Azerbaijan in the chemical-petrochemical sectors, telecommunication, banking, education, publishing, construction materials, grocery, textiles, automotive/transportation and iron/steel products. The total investment volume amounts to US$1.3 billion.[13] Besides, building projects of Turkish construction companies amount to about US$0.5 billion.[14]

In fact, one of the most promising areas of investment in Azerbaijan is construction and its related industries.[15] Also, as the construction industry grows, the increased investments in that sector in Azerbaijan create a derived demand for a variety of, for example, paint products, hence there arise very many new opportunities for the paint industry to grow in that market.

Developments in the Turkish paint industry

The Turkish paint and coatings industry is the sixth biggest in Europe in terms of volumes of production. Developments in the construction, automotive and marine industries of Turkey triggered this sector to become one of the most dynamic sectors of the Turkish economy. Production increased about 10 per cent annually between 1990 and 2000, and today the production capacity is around 650,000 tons per year. Based on the yearly demand level, actual production varies between 300,000 and 400,000 tons. In Turkey, the sector has reached world quality standards. The number of firms with ISO 9000 certification is rapidly increasing as the sector adapts itself to ecological standards particularly developed in Europe.[16] Among more than 400 firms operating in the Turkish market, Marshall, DYO, Betek Boya, CBS, Polisan and Meges are the six largest.[17]

Decorative paints constitute 58 per cent of the total production capacity, out of which 55 per cent are water-based paints and 45 per cent solvent-based paints. The construction sector has a 62 per cent capacity utilization, and other sectors using paint products are furniture, automotives, leather, glass, ceramics, textiles and print.[18] Aiming towards better capacity utilization, firms focus more on export activities, and the Turkish paint sector has increased its export volume over the years. In 2000 the total value of paints and coatings exports was US$89.5 million, reaching US$112.5 million in 2002. These were mainly exported to neighbouring countries such as the Russian Federation, Azerbaijan, Romania, Israel and the Ukraine (see Table 11.1).[19]

It is also interesting to note that the prices of paint in Turkey are much lower than EU averages. For solvent-based paints, the average price in the Turkish market is US$3/kg, compared to the EU average of US$7/kg. For water-based paints, the Turkish market price is US$1.8/kg, compared to EU prices of US$4/kg.[20] Hence, especially for export markets, Turkish paint products possess a competitive price advantage.

Table 11.1 Paint exports from Turkey: the six major recipients (US$)

Countries	2000	2001	2002
Russian Federation	6,589,150	8,970,356	11,228,898
Azerbaijan	7,767,492	8,051,071	9,797,390
Romania	5,359,857	5,099,622	6,433,262
Israel	3,199,344	3,968,096	4,864,957
Ukraine	4,213,141	4,147,896	4,857,250
Georgia	5,406,038	4,096,016	4,178,091
Total	89,519,157	92,484,584	112,469,301

Source: http://www.foreigntrade.gov.tr

Betek: Turkish paint in the Azerbaijan market

Turkey, with very many investments abroad, is at the same time one of the leaders in the European market in the paint sector. Azerbaijan, with many potential investments promising growth, especially in the construction industry and its related sectors, is an interesting market. The match of these two, and their combined efforts, aids improvements in their economies, assuring a better life for both societies.

A brief look at Betek Boya

Betek Paint and Chemical Industry Corporation (Betek Boya) was established in 1988. The company name is made up of the first syllables of the words 'Beton' (concrete) and 'Teknoloji' (technology).[21] Being today one of the leading construction paint manufacturers in Turkey, Betek Boya was founded by three Turkish partners, with the major portion of shares belonging to Mr Celal Akpınar who had worked in leading firms of the Turkish economy before starting Betek. In the first four years the firm produced concrete additives, and in 1993 focused on paint manufacturing,[22] starting to cooperate technologically with Caparol one of the most prominent paint brands in Europe. In 1996, the share of Caparol became 15 per cent. Today, the ratio in this joint venture is 25 per cent to 75 per cent.[23]

Production takes place at two locations in Turkey: the 24,000 square metre production facility in Pendik, Istanbul,[24] with a second 120,000 square metre site in Gebze.[25] Eight regional offices in different parts of the country complement the Istanbul headquarters. Whereas the organization was run with 50 personnel in 1993, this number had risen to 300 in 1998, and today the number of employees has expanded to 700.[26]

Growth of the firm

Betek Boya has enjoyed growth above the sector average in recent years. While sales in the Turkish paint sector grew by an average of 10 per cent between 1996 and 2001, Betek Boya's sales growth was about 396 per cent in the same period.[27] The company was also relatively unaffected by the economic slow-down in 1998 and 1999, where the sector experienced a decline of 10–15 per cent. Even then, in 1999, the firm continued its healthy growth at 30 per cent.[28] In 2000, the Istanbul Chamber of Industry ranked Betek Boya at 222 among Turkey's 500 major industrial enterprises with total sales of US$57.4 million.[29] In 2001, when the sector shrank by 41.5 per cent, Betek Boya grew by 8 per cent and became the market leader.[30] Total production of the firm for 2001 was 90,000 tons,[31] and the total market share in the domestic market about 22 per cent.[32] According to sector websites, the Istanbul Chamber of Industry ranked Betek Boya 167th among the private and public enterprises operating in the Turkish market.[33] In 2002 the company reached a sales level of US$92.1 million.[34]

Tayfun Küçükoğlu, General Manager of Betek Boya, stated the goals of the firm as 'being innovative, focusing on high quality standards, using most recent production technologies available, and having a strong distribution network' to reach success in the sector. Besides, the management aims to become a powerful leader in foreign markets through various export initiatives over the near future.[35]

Products, segments and positioning

In its initial years, Betek Boya targeted the construction sector with the production of concrete additives, ready-made mortar and water-isolating materials. In 1992 the firm realized there was a market potential for new products in this sector,[36] and following a cooperation agreement with German Caparol in 1993, Betek Boya introduced pioneering products like silicon-based exterior paint (Amphi-Silan), Alpina Coloring Systems, water-based satin paint (Alpina-Tek), lead and aroma-free paint, and silicon-based interior paint (Alpina-Silan) between 1993 and 2001,[37] and had great market success. Currently, Betek Boya offers the widest product range in its sector, covering interior and exterior paints, coatings, primer varieties, isolation materials, sealers, repair plaster, tile adhesives, special jointures, and adhesives for synthetic and celluloid products.[38]

Using the prominent elephant logo of its German partner Caparol, Betek Boya has positioned itself as the 'Elephant Paint' among dealers, customers as well as end-users in the domestic market.[39] This choice is very effective, especially since people can more easily recall a logo once seen than remembering the brand name.

Betek Boya expects paint consumption in Turkey to rise further based on the young population, fast urbanization and changing family structure and lifestyle.[40] EMs of transition economies are especially attractive for the company since the construction sector is also growing very fast in those regions, providing a big opportunity for future sales.

International operations of the firm: the path to success

Although domestic sales constitute the major part of company turnover, exports have become increasingly important for Betek Boya, and approximately 8 per cent of total sales are generated by export activities. In 2001, Betek Boya's exports reached US$8 million, constituting 11 per cent of total sales for the firm in that year. The management of the firm aims to increase exports fivefold by 2005, to reach US$40 million.[41]

Currently, export business is done with 24 countries all over the world. Israel, Georgia, Ukraine and North Africa are the most important export destinations, but additionally, based on their geographical proximity for the management of the firm, the Balkans, Russia, the C.I.S. countries and countries around the Caspian Sea such as Azerbaijan present a serious market potential. Besides focusing on exports as a basic form of foreign market entry, Betek Boya also aims to start production abroad. Concerning Azerbaijan, the company seriously considers establishing a paint factory in the region.[42]

Organizational success factors: quality orientation and environmental concern

The main shareholder, Celal Akpınar, is also the CEO of the company. The organizational structure is relatively flat, with eight Vice-Presidents (of Sales, Marketing, PR, R&D, Purchasing, Production, F&A, HRM) who are also shareholders to varying extents.[43] With the team-motivating spirit of Mr Akpınar and his top managers (Mr Barlas, Mr Küçükoğlu and Mr Büyükcan), the vision of 'creating high customer value via introduction of the most innovative paint products in the market, quality orientation and environmental concern',[44] the firm grew in a very short period of time, in a very established sector with large experienced competitors, and assured itself of a very strong market position, also in export markets.

Betek Boya has accepted the norms set by the European Union for the protection and preservation of the environment and is a pioneer for lead and aroma-free paints that are extensively used in hospitals, laboratories and schools in Turkey.[45] People with asthma or allergy problems also prefer such products. In 1997, the firm received the ISO 9001 certificate from the Turkish Standards Institute, and aims to obtain the ISO 14000 certificate that determines standards of health and environmental protection.[46]

The firm is committed to providing its customers the best possible products by ensuring 'quality of management' instead of 'management of quality'.[47] Through its 'e- Manufacturing and Production Automation' workshop of Boğaziçi University in Istanbul,[48] Management Development Programmes for managers at all levels,[49] and similar attempts, employees are trained based on the principles of customer satisfaction and continuous development to ensure customer value-creation. Besides, customers can contact the firm through customer help-lines, email or via their user-friendly webpage that won the 2001 'Most Aesthetic Website' award for the competition for the most creative website in the paint sector.[50]

According to Mr Barlas, the demand in emerging markets would have been easy to meet with low-quality, low-price products at the beginning, but Betek Boya was not attracted to that opportunity, because such opportunist satisfaction would eventually have led to a negative image. The firm aimed to grow in export markets by offering the best products available at competitive prices right from the start. In Azerbaijan the approach was similar. As a consequence, what Turkish companies like Betek Boya do in Azerbaijan in terms of their product and service offer is considered *'geyfiyetli ve galiteli'* (Azeri expression for 'fun to work with and high quality').

Market-based strategies for Azerbaijan: the market selection process

The decisions to enter a market and the entry mode to be chosen are made relatively quickly at Betek Boya. But before the actual entry, Betek managers visit the potential country in person and collect the products and brochures of local and foreign competitors. They also obtain demographic data; information about the educational and income level of the population, the history of the country and even the characteristics of border neighbours gives an idea about the products to be offered and the overall marketing approach.[51]

The first contacts with Azerbaijan are still very vivid in the memories of Betek managers:[52] At first, the common linguistic roots between Turkey and Azerbaijan were the prime motives to enter that market. The company also took advantage of geographical closeness between the two countries and started to build links with different firms interested in good-quality construction paint materials from Turkey. The firm entered the Azeri market six years ago and increased its marketing focus immediately the year after that. The first exports took place on an irregular basis, as at that time a structured transportation and logistics system was not yet established. In those days the firm did not risk the loss of the hard-won contacts and tried to supply products to the Azerbaijan market by transporting them by cars and trucks arranged themselves. When Betek Boya started its exports to Azerbaijan as the first Turkish firm in that sector, besides the Azeri products a variety of European products were already in the market. Although Caparol and Betek Boya are partners in the local market, they became competitors in Azerbaijan. Today, Betek is the most recognized paint brand in the Azeri market.[53] The initial product range was limited to paint and paintbrushes, but today exports have expanded into the areas of chemical materials as well. Exports to Azerbaijan increased from US$0.5 million in 2000 to US$1.5 million in 2002.[54] The amount might seem modest, but reflects a significant increase in two years.

Human factors that ensure success in Azerbaijan

Mr Barlas sees the performance of the firm (and of any company, for that matter) as a combination of several appropriate factors: (1) planned growth where all elements (people, capital, production etc.) are considered simultaneously; (2) proper distribution to ensure availability; (3) and the importance of the spare wheel (the fifth P), the 'people', that is 'caring for people, assuring a positive work atmosphere, and spreading the team spirit within the firm'.

According to Mr Güzelöz, understanding the human factors and the local culture is the basis for success for a firm operating abroad. Especially when operating in EMs, it is important to note that writing detailed strategic marketing plans and developing an organizational structure to 'deal with the market in the most feasible manner' might not prove to be very successful in the way intended. Culture-bound mentalities and perception differences may dominate the scene and the way in which people want to run businesses in those markets. The firm's less-structured, 'soft' way of communicating with dealers and representatives should be interpreted as building an informal communications base to understand the local needs and expectations of the customers. It is deemed important to have a flexible mind and a sense of the invisible forces that might sometimes work as a barrier in EMs.

Betek Boya owes its dynamism to the young managerial staff running the company, in which the management has a lot of confidence. It is no wonder that trust and commitment within the management layers also leads to enhanced loyalty among staff:[55] employees are encouraged to state their views even to influence the vision and mission development of the company. This permissive management style creates a strong sense of 'belonging' among the staff, and 'socialization' within the company builds strong and close ties. The team orientation is also emphasized in relationships with customers, distributors, sales representatives and painters, and also in overseas markets. Listening to each other and understanding each other is a must for healthy relations.

Besides, when distributors or representatives from Azerbaijan or any other EMs arrive in Turkey, a very sincere hospitality beyond the formal working atmosphere is created to make these people feel at home. As opposed to business interactions common in many Western societies, the customers visiting Betek Boya are first invited to lunch or dinner before the formal business negotiations start.[56] It is very important to create a positive, friendly atmosphere while interacting with the people in the dealer network and the painters who are the main decision-makers for the end-users. In that sense 'a focus on shared values'[57] is established. Many close ties have been built over the years due to these informal relations and care for customers.

Marketing success factors for Azerbaijan

The importance of 'doing as the Romans do when one is in Rome' is the way Mr Güzelöz considers the strategies to be developed for export markets, because it is wrong to assume that the home market formula will work everywhere, even if the two cultures (Azerbaijan and Turkey) are very similar. Strategies focus rather on local understanding and are mostly tailormade.

Interestingly, Mr Büyükcan describes taste and preference differences of several geographical regions in Turkey, since Turkey borders many countries of influential cultural heritages: The west for example is located in Europe and affected by the tastes of Europe, but even more so by the Balkans: light, pastel colours prevail in the decoration of homes. In the southeast, on the other hand, the country borders Iraq and Syria, and strong colourful paints have a far higher chance of satisfying the masses than pale or light options. Again, in other regions, paint as such is not used and the population prefers wallpaper. Although Azerbaijan used to prefer petrol-based paint products of the former Soviet Republic, customer preferences soon began to shift after the market opened. Azerbaijan, bordering Russia, Georgia, Armenia and Iran, resembles both the customer choices of both Betek Boya's Black Sea region customers in Turkey, as well as those of Eastern Anatolia.

Betek Boya has a separate marketing division for activities within the country. Markets abroad are under the responsibility of the export department, with a focus on educating consumers as well as distributors in the field of environmentally-friendly paint. Every export market is treated in a unique manner. In Ukraine, for example, a local representative handles trading and marketing activities, whereas a Turkish company from Trabzon at the Turkish Black Sea coast coordinates business relations in Russia. For the Russian market, the firm has obtained a Gost-R document required for every export activity to Russia. Distribution channels also vary per country. In Russia, paint is sold side by side with bread on wooden pallets in street corners, whereas specialized paint shops are the classical outlets for paint sales in Israel. In Azerbaijan, Betek Boya establishes contact with customers through trade fairs, and an Azeri representative is responsible for the distribution of the products and all kinds of business activities. This person takes and consolidates orders, reports these to the head office, and takes care that proper distribution is assured once the goods arrive in Azerbaijan.[58] In fact the firm aims to grow with its dealer network and carry the system to export markets to grow abroad.

For strategies regarding its products, the firm puts great emphasis on what its competitors are doing. But a systematic way of collecting information is mostly lacking. Salespeople are responsible for monitoring competitors' activities in the export markets they are responsible for, by, primarily, collecting every single new competitive product they see on the shelves. These products are then analysed at the firm's laboratories for their chemical contents.[59]

Betek Boya combines prime quality with aggressive pricing to succeed in the Azeri market. That is, based on market conditions and customers' affordability levels, the prices of its products and payment conditions for dealers are adjusted. For Betek Boya, sales in Azerbaijan increased at a similar speed to their sales in Turkey, where the company grew despite a shrinking market in difficult economic conditions.[60]

According to Mr Büyükcan, concerned about the mixed images created by the brand names Betek, Caparol (in the domestic market), Alpina and the elephant logo, the company decided to first establish a concise brand image in the public mind. The first goal was to get across the message 'paint with the elephant', and all advertising efforts were centred around this theme. Nowadays Betek Boya prefers to focus on individual product categories in TV advertisements in Turkey and in the Azeri market.

Famous artists, sportsmen and even prominent journalists appear in their TV commercials and emphasize the concept of 'harmony in contradictions'.

The colours 'black and white', for example, are advertised by two journalists known for their publicly fought-out differences of opinion, or 'green and yellow' by rival top models.[61] As stated by Mr Büyükcan, in Azerbaijan, although they have their own TV channels, it is mostly possible for the public to watch Turkish TV channels, and since there are no language problems the Betek advertisements relevant for the Turkish market are also followed in the Azerbaijan market. In conjunction with the very effective advertising campaigns, they have created a push effect from the side of the painter (who is in many cases also the salesman), as well as a pull effect from the customer, who wants nothing else but 'paint with the elephant'.

Conclusion

Success is not an easy goal to achieve. Being familiar with conditions in an export market may ease operations but can never be a guarantee for long-term relations. Betek's success in export markets, particularly in Azerbaijan, is a result of the dedication of its top managers and export team. Understanding the culture by focusing on close relations contributes to success. Based on the information gathered through these close ties, managers have learned to modify their marketing strategies according to market conditions. Of course, a sound organizational system fed with well-developed corporate values and a concern for quality have helped the firm become one of the leaders in the export markets as well as in the domestic market.

Notes

Personal in-depth interviews were conducted with three top managers of the firm: Mr Hüseyin Güzelöz, Export Manager, Spring 2003; Mr Serkan Büyükcan, Assistant General Manager, Summer 2003; and Mr Demirkan Barlas, Vice-President of Betek Boya, Summer 2003.

1. www.treasury.gov.tr/english/YBSWEB/10reasons.htm (retrieved April 2002).
2. Y.T. Akis, 'Turkish Firms' Success Factors in the Former Soviet Union (FSU)', *Cross Cultural Management – An International Journal*, 6, 4 (1999): 3–10.
3. F. Gönel Doğanel, 'How Important is Intra-Industry Trade between Turkey and its Trading Partners? A Comparison between the European Union and Central Asia Turkic Republics', *Russian and East European Finance and Trade*, 37, 4 (2001): 61–76.
4. Eighth Five-Year Development Plan 2001–05 – Republic of Turkey (T.C. Sekizinci Beş Yıllık Kalkınma Planı 2001–2005), www.google.com.tr/search?q=cache:dPYCbNqz_tIJ:ekutup.dpt.gov.tr/plan/viii/plan8.pdf+%22Kalkinma+Plani%22&hl=tr&ie=UTF8 (retrieved 13 April 2002).
5. *Ibid.*
6. The CIS-7 are Armenia, Azerbaijan, Georgia, Kyrgyz Republic, Moldova, Tajikistan and Uzbekistan.
7. Press Briefing on Developments in Baltic and CIS Countries. Opening Remarks by John Odling-Smee Director, European II Department International Monetary Fund Washington DC, 28 September 2002, www.imf.org/external/np/speeches/2002/092802.htm (retrieved 27 June 2003).

8. V. Sriram and Z. Bilgin, 'Regionalism and Emerging Markets', *Marmara Journal of European Studies*, 10, 1 (2002): 154.
9. P. Ghemawat, 'Distance Still Matters. The Hard Reality of Global Expansion', *Harvard Business Review*, 79, 8 (2001): 137–47.
10. C.S. Craig and S.P. Douglas, 'Configural Advantage in Global Markets', *Journal of International Marketing*, 8, 1 (2000): 6–26.
11. The State Ministry for Relationships with Turkic Republics initiated various projects such as the establishment of the Economical Information Center, the Institution of International Investment Credit and Guarantee, and the Eurasian Insurance Union to facilitate trade between the two countries. For details see www.turkcumhuriyetleri.gov.tr (retrieved 25 April 2002).
12. The EIU, Azerbaijan Country Report May 2003, http://www.foreigntrade.gov.tr/ead/ekolar1/eko2.xls and http://www.igeme.org.tr; (26 September 2003).
13. www.dtm.gov.tr (retrieved 25 April 2002).
14. www.turkcumhuriyetleri.gov.tr (retrieved 25 April 2002).
15. County Report, www.igeme.gov.tr (retrieved 26 June 2003).
16. S. Bektaşoğlu and A. Emek, 'The Turkish Paints and Dyes Industry', Sector Report – IGEME (2003), www.igeme.gov.tr (retrived 26 June 2003)
17. Information from the Sector, based on *Dünya Gazetesi*, dated 15 September 2003, www.boyex.com/6150.asp?HaberID=1657, (retrieved 26 September 2003).
18. Sector Report, www.igeme.gov.tr
19. S. Bektaşoğlu and A. Emek, 'The Turkish Paints and Dyes Industry', *op. cit.*
20. VIII. Beş Yıllık Kalkınma Planı Kimya Sanayii Özel İhtisas Komisyonu Raporu (Boya) – VIII. Five Years Development Plan Chemistry Industry Special Expert Commission Report (Paint); www.dpt.gov.tr (retrieved 23 June 2003).
21. http://www.betek.com.tr/english/indexx.html (retrieved 15 June 2003).
22. http://www.milliyet.com.tr/2001/02/16/ekonomi/eko10.html (retrieved 25 June 2003); and http://www.betek.com.tr/english/indexx.html (retrieved 15 June 2003).
23. http://www.hürriyetim.com.tr/haber/0,,sid~4@tarih~2002-05-26-m@nvid~131448,00.asp.
24. http://www.betek.com.tr/english/indexx.html (retrieved 15 June 2003).
25. http://www.arkitera.com/haberler/2001/03/28/ (retrieved 25 June 2003).
26. Interview with Mr Serkan Büyükcan.
27. www.milliyet.com.tr/2001/02/16/ekonomi/eko10.html
28. www.betek.com.tr/english/indexx.html (retrieved 15 June 2003).
29. www.iso.org.tr/inghtml/ingsiteindex.html (retrieved 15 July 2003), the sales volume stated in TL in the source has been converted to US$ based on the year 2000 exchange rate when US$1 = 632,000 Turkish Lira based on central bank accounts. For details see http://www.tcmb.gov.tr
30. Sector News – *Dünya İnşaat Dergisi* (World Construction Magazine), dated 25 September 2002, www.boyex.com/6120.asp?HaberID = 1009 (retrieved 20 June 2003);www.hurriyetim.com.tr/haber/0,sid~4@tarih~2002-05-26-m@nvid~131448,00.asp (retrieved 20 June 2003).
31. www.boyex.com/6120.asp?haberID=479 (retrieved 23 June 2003).
32. Sector News, based on *Dünya Gazetesi*, dated 18 April 2003, http://www.boyex.com/6120.asp?HaberID=1357 (retrieved 23 June 2003).
33. Sector News – *Dünya İnşaat Dergisi* (World Construction Magazine) dated 25 September 2002.
34. Internal Company Record of Betek Boya (retrieved 8 June 2003).

35 Sectoral News – *Dünya İnşaat Dergisi* (World Construction Magazine) dated 25 September 2002.
36 www.betek.com.tr/english/indexx.html (retrieved 15 June 2003).
37 www.milliyet.com.tr/2001/02/16/ekonomi/eko10.html
38 www.betek.com.tr/english/indexx.html (retrieved 15 June 2003).
39 www.hurriyetim.com.tr/haber/0,,sid~4@tarih~2002-05-26-m@nvid~131448,00.asp (15 June 2003).
40 www.betek.com.tr/english/indexx.html (retrieved 15 June 2003).
41 www.boyex.com/6120.asp?haberID=811 (retrieved 23 June 2003).
42 Interview with Mr Hüseyin Güzelöz.
43 Interview with Mr Serkan Büyükcan.
44 Interview with Mr Hüseyin Güzelöz.
45 www.betek.com.tr/english/indexx.html (retrieved 15 June 2003).
46 www.betek.com.tr/english/indexx.html (retrieved 15 June 2003). For details about environmental concerns of Betek Boya see I. Talinli, T.T. Ertas and B. Yilmaz, 'Betek Company – Painting Industry – Environmental Impact Assessment Project (March 1997), Istanbul Technical University, Department of Environmental Engineering, Final Report.
47 www.betek.com.tr/english/indexx.html (retrieved 15 June 2003).
48 www.mathind.boun.edu.tr/Data/part_1.html
49 www.kalgem.com.tr/link5_ref.html
50 turk.internet.com/haber/yazigoster.php3?yaziid=3494
51 Interview with Mr Serkan Büyükcan.
52 Interview with Mr Hüseyin Güzelöz.
53 www.boyex.com/6120.asp?haberID=811 (retrieved 23 June 2003).
54 Betek Boya – sales in export markets, internal records 2000 and 2002.
55 Interview with Mr Serkan Büyükcan.
56 Interview with Mr Hüseyin Güzelöz.
57 www.boyex.com/6120.asp?haberID=479 (retrieved 23 June 2003).
58 Interview with Mr Serkan Büyükcan.
59 Interview with Mr Hüseyin Güzelöz.
60 *Ibid.*
61 www.aksam.com.tr/arsiv/aksam/2002/12/26/akdeniz/akdeniz3.html (retrieved 20 June 2003).

12
Expansion to International Markets by Use of Product and Trade Name Franchising: The Case of Kompen

Çağatay Ünüsan

Introduction

Exporting provides an important avenue for foreign market entry. Many domestic firms begin their forays into the international arena with direct exporting and then use their exporting experiences to move on to other types of international marketing activities. In many ways, the management of export channels involves the same issues and problems as domestic channel management. In other ways, export channel management brings with it a set of unique management issues introduces by factors such as physical and cultural distance between channel participants.[1]

In order to gain a competitive presence in either domestic or international marketplaces, a manufacturer needs an effective distribution network. Increasingly, intense competition in both domestic and global markets has encouraged many manufacturers to attempt to develop strategic advantages by establishing long-term exchange relationships in their distribution network. Manufacturers can reach consumers through two broad types of marketing channels: conventional marketing channels, and vertical or integrated marketing systems. Integrated marketing channels include systems such as pure vertical integration and vertical quasi integration (franchising, licensing, joint ventures and the like).

The shift from conventional marketing channels to vertical marketing systems has increased over the last two decades. For such vertical systems to provide a basis for developing and maintaining a competitive advantage, it is essential that channel activities are controlled and coordinated in an effective and efficient manner.

Marketing channel integration, franchising and particularly product and trade-name franchising will be examined in the following sections of this chapter. The specific objective of this study is to show the use of product and trade name franchising in the international operations of a Turkish firm, Kompen, that operates in the PVC Windows and Doors market.

Finally, necessary suggestions will be made in the light of Kompen's experience in international operations.

Marketing channel integration

The dynamic nature of business and competition slowly fostered developments in channel management and the move from conventional to integrated systems. As is well-known, conventional marketing channels are built on independently owned and managed institutions. In these channels, channel members behave according to their own objectives, and hence coordination is accomplished with other channel members through bargaining and negotiation. It is assumed that if all channel members act independently and in their own interests the outcome will be socially optimal. In addition, in these channels, systematic and preprogrammed structures do not exist. As a consequence, conventional marketing channels rely on unrestricted open market forces, via the price mechanism, causing a division of labour among channel members.[2] However, in reality, conventional marketing channels have been declining since the early 1950s in many companies because they were seen as an inefficient way of conducting business because of the conflicting interests of channel members.[3] In 1988, this type of channel sold less than 40 per cent of all retail goods and services in the USA.[4]

By contrast, vertical marketing channel systems act as unified and integrated systems that have a variety of socioeconomic characteristics. At this point, it is worth analysing the vertical marketing channel system in more detail.

In marketing science, vertical integration has been defined as 'the acquisition by a member of a distribution channel of a facility or establishment at a different level in the channel'.[5] While integration reflects the above definition, disintegration reflects a firm that sells its products through independent intermediaries. These two polar examples of integration are very similar to the transaction-cost economics market and hierarchy separation.

Vertical integration means all activities take place within the boundaries of the firm, while vertical disintegration depends on market transactions. However, between these two extremes there are a variety of forms of organizations such as franchising, contracting out and joint ventures.[6] In the literature these types of intermediate forms have been described as vertical quasi integration.[7]

Franchising as a contractual system

As with other integration methods, franchising as a contractual vertical quasi integration has several advantages and disadvantages. For example, according to Stern and El-Ansary, Brown[8] these systems allow the franchiser to increase the number of outlets with minimal capital investment and provide operating procedures and standard marketing programmes that enable franchisees to be competitive. Furthermore, franchisees are seen to be more motivated than company-owned managers because franchisees share in the profit of their business. Hence, franchise systems will ensure that the business will be operated according to required standards where monitoring of the company outlets is difficult. Also, in these systems the creation of territorial restrictions by franchiser reduces intra-brand competition. Therefore, in order to be more effective in inter-brand competition, franchisees give their attention to monitoring the quality of the good or service.

Today, as will be seen in the next sections, franchising arrangements make up a significant part of advanced market economies such as those of the UK and the United States. Also, several types of franchise systems are observed not only in advanced markets, but also in emerging markets.

Product and trade name franchising and its development in Turkey

Vertical integration is widely used in the distribution process of developed countries, but in the context of a developing country such as Turkey vertical integration or vertical marketing channel systems are little used for the distribution of goods apart from in some sectors. At this point, it can be said that there appears to be a positive correlation between economic development levels and a use of vertical integration in the whole distribution process. Franchising provides several benefits to trading partners in the system, and also to the country. For example, in manufacturer–dealer systems, manufacturers (like auto manufacturers) provide substantial training, sales, service and financial assistance to dealers because of the effects of dealer performance on the manufacturers' sales and goodwill.

These aspects of the manufacturer–dealer systems improve resource allocation and reduce the costs of retail allocation.[9] Also, these systems provide several benefits to consumers, including standardized products, after sales services, and many others. Inevitably, as in the developed countries, franchise systems provide those benefits to developing countries. The importance of marketing channels, as a concept, was not appreciated in developing countries. For example, in Turkey marketing channels and franchising were not well enough examined and researched, and there is not enough information about franchised marketing channels, their development and present situation in the country. Some studies only cover the theoretical background without its past and present situation.[10] There are no official published reports and statistics about franchising in Turkey.

In Turkey, the development of franchising followed the changing pattern of the country's economy and social environment. According to one view, franchising is reputed to have started with the development of highway transportation in Turkey, and together with petrol stations, bus companies gave the right to sell bus tickets to independent offices with some restrictions.[11]

In the 1960s, manufacturers started to appreciate the importance of manufacturer–dealer systems for the distribution of their products. For example in those years the first fridge was produced in Turkey. In the beginning, the fridge producer used conventional marketing channels and carpet sellers, electricians and drapers all around Turkey sold fridges to customers. Subsequently, the fridge producer realized that sales chaos was developing in the market because of the superficially selected distribution channels. Accordingly, the producer's sales organization reduced retail sales points from 2,400 independent retailers to 1,000 dealers.[12] In the 1970s and 1980s product and trade name franchising was used by several sectors of the economy such as automobiles, white goods, paint sellers and the construction sector. Today, firms are expanding their operations to domestic and international markets by the use of product and trade name franchising, in other words, manufacturer–dealer systems.

Use of PVC products in the Turkish construction industry

PVC, commonly known as 'vinyl', is the abbreviated form of polyvinyl chloride and is a polymer type with the chemical formula -(CH2-CH2), produced out of oil (or natural gas) and salt in petrochemical facilities. The application of PVC is widespread in many industries including construction, packaging, medical, automobiles and other sectors (toys, various sports articles, wax cloth, synthetic leather and shoes; even the production of credit cards).[13]

One of the most important markets for PVC over the past 30 years has been the use of PVC for window profiles. At the start of the millennium this sector remains strong and is still growing across Europe. In other parts of the world there are also areas, such as China, where growth rates are astonishing. Specifically in the UK, the window-profile market has given rise over the past 20 years to a parallel growth in foam profile. However, although volumes have been strong it is a different story when it comes to profitability in this sector and a number of issues need to be faced as the market in Western Europe approaches maturity. The proportion of PVC attributable to window profiles has now grown to such an extent that it now accounts for 13 per cent of the total PVC polymer market in Western Europe. The German, UK and French markets account for the vast majority of this tonnage (approximately 85 per cent). In addition there is a developing market in Central and Eastern Europe, and while usage is still relatively small, there is good growth. Currently, much of the requirement in these countries is supplied by imports, although local manufacture is relatively strong in some countries such as Poland and Russia. In addition, Turkey stands out with 110,000 tons of annual local production mainly produced by four companies.[14]

Turkey's PVC Windows and Doors market is worth approximately €1.2 billion,[15] and PVC production in Turkey grew by around 9 per cent in

1997, the fastest growth rate of all the plastics. PVC windows and doors started to be used in the 1980s and experienced a rapid growth in the 1990s. A great market emerged for PVC products that do not require any protective coating and which provide good water insulation. The increased demand caused many companies to enter the sector, and several emerged who started to manufacture by adding a suffix of 'Pen' to the end of their titles. It is reported that today there are more than 40 companies in Turkey.

Developments in this sector can be summarized as follows:[16]

- The sector, sometimes also called 'Plastic Chopping', was dominated by Istanbul initially. There were only a few companies in the 1990s, the most prominent among them being Pimaş, which initially manufactured PVC pipes. New companies entered the market in the early 1990s.
- There were still only 20 companies in 1996, but the plastic chopping field then developed quickly to become a centre of attraction for investors. During the period 1996–9, 20 new companies were incorporated due to the market's potential and high demand.
- The market is attractive for many investors due to its high-level growth. The production volume, which increased from 25,000 tons in 1996 to 100,000 tons in 1999 in an indicator of the attractiveness of the market.
- About half of the present firms also export, some to as many as 25 countries. PVC is exported to some countries in the form of profiled sections, and to others as doors and windows made from such sections. The sector has standards and Turkish manufactures conform to those standards, thereby allowing high export levels.
- Figures show that the sector is growing at an extraordinary rate in Turkey. Although a decrease in expected in the growth rate in future years, the rate is still expected to be not less than 12 per cent.
- The production of Pimaş, the oldest and leading company of the sector, was 25,000 tons in 1997, followed by Pakpen with 25,000 tons, and Fıratpen and Egepen that have a production of 10,000 tons each. Then come other companies such as Kalpen and Kompen producing about 5,000–6,000 tons. Foreign companies such as Rehan, Veka, Internon, Bruckman, Tissen, Reckendress, Sofrapen, Kömmerling and KBE are also active in Turkey.
- The capacity of the sector increased by about 30 per cent in the second half of 1997, when many new companies emerged. Turkey is the third country in the world in terms of production volume, following Germany which has a production of 250,000 tons, and England which has a production of 180,000 tons. France follows Turkey with 80,000 tons.
- A very different structure is observed in demand. The fact that there are millions of buildings in Turkey without PVC profiling affects the direction of the demand, creating a potential, but this is difficult to calculate. In many old buildings, a transition to PVC is being observed.

- Also, there is a great deal of demand from slums to modern sites, for two basic reasons. First, PVC is not harmful for human health, and second, PVC provides fuel savings. Turkish consumers, facing high fuel expenses in wintertime, recognize that PVC is not luxurious, and in addition does not require painting or similar expenses.
- Naturally, demand is higher in regions with more population, but demand is also high in some small regions where PVC has become known. Demand is also high in those regions where weather conditions are hard, due to heat savings. Coastal areas also show a high demand, because high humidity spoils wood profiles in a short time.

The case of Kompen: use of product and trade name franchising to expand international markets

A single case study was selected in order to examine the use of product trade-name franchising in the domestic and particularly international operations of a Turkish company, Kompen[17] which operates as a part of Kombassan Holding Co., established in 1989 at Konya. Kombassan Holding has made investments in many fields,[18] and established Kompen PVC windows and doors in 1996.

General information about Kompen

Kompen is located in Ladik Mevkii, 45 km from Konya, one of the fastest developing regions in Turkey. From the beginning of 1996, Kompen with its advanced production and computerized equipment, manufacturing doors windows and double-glazing, became an industry leader in this sector. Kompen's manufacturing capacity puts it in seventh place following Firatpen, Pimapen, Adopen, Pakpen, Egepen, and Esen plastìk in the PVC windows and doors sector. Kompen's PVC factory uses German and Austrian technology, and the firm has ISO 9002 quality certification and has been awarded several other standards certificates such as TSE and Laboratory Accreditation.

In the production facilities of Kompen, a total of 13,000 tons of PVC is processed with a workforce of 250 to produce profiles for use in the construction of doors and windows for office buildings, houses and mass housing units. Generally Kompen takes a 10–12 per cent share in the domestic market with the aim of achieving a 20 per cent share. Kompen profiles of matchless insulation capacity are offered to consumers through a network of specialized dealers carefully selected by the firm. Specially trained in the selection and design of profiles that are best suited to the needs of customers, the dealers are equipped with machines using the latest technology to transform the error-free Kompen profiles into doors and windows.

Kompen aims to respond to requests made by its franchisees the same day. It should also be emphasized in this respect that the company provides all the technical assistance that franchisees need. Kompen, which has obtained an outstanding position in this field due its technology and quality, does not compromise on its commitment to total quality. In addition to Turkey, it is also a leading company within Middle Eastern, Asian and European markets.

International operations of Kompen

In the beginning, there wasn't a structured and dedicated export department. In those days the supply department dealt with export and import activities. At the end of 1998, with the establishment of its Foreign Trade Department and the appointment of Mehmet Büyükserin as head of the department, foreign trade began in earnest.[19] At present, Kompen's foreign trade department divides its operations into three parts:

1 *Former Soviet and Turkic Republics of Central Asia.* Here, the company exports its products to Russia, Ukraine, Belarus, Kazakhstan, Bulgaria, Lithuania, Uzbekistan, Turkmenistan and Moldavia. In Russia and Bulgaria, Kompen's main distributors are of Turkish origin, in the other countries its main distributors are residents of those countries. In this region consumers demand PVC windows and doors of European standards of quality, but also want them cheap; the key factor of competition is price and quality.
2 *Europe.* The countries of this region are Austria, Romania, Germany, France, Macedonia and Serbia. In this region the main distributors in Macedonia and Serbia are the residents of those countries, while in the other countries they are of Turkish origin. The main problem in this region is intense competition on quality. In order to compete, Kompen produces specific PVC windows and doors, made in accordance with each country's demand. To be successful in Europe, the company's production and marketing team screens changes in consumers' requests, and adapts itself to changes in technology.
3 *Middle East.* The countries of this region are Syria, Iraq, Jordan and Yemen, and the main distributors are own residents of those countries. Because of the intense heat in these countries, products have to be modified.

In recent years Kompen has performed very well in the PVC windows and doors market, and as may be seen from Table 12.1 it was the export leader in the sector for the first six months of 2003.

Identification of the hidden success factors of Kompen in its international operations

The company has developed customer management systems emphasizing customer satisfaction, through its sales and marketing network made up of

Table 12.1 Domestic and export sales (tons) of PVC windows and doors (first six months of 2003)

Companies	Exports	Domestic sales	Total
Adopen	875	6,684	7,559
Esen Plastik	–	5,725	5,725
Ege Profil	505	6,425	6,930
Frat Plastik A.Ş.	1,590	11,073	12,663
Kompen A.Ş.	1,720	3,450	5,170
Pak Plastik A.Ş.	1,270	5,750	7,020
Pimas A.Ş.	1,611	6,205	7,816
Pilsa A.Ş.	1,185	1,785	2,970
Technoplas A.Ş	430	1,554	1,984
Total	9,186	48,651	5,783

Source: PUKAD (Turkish Association of PVC Windows and Doors Producers), 2003.

professional staff educated in their fields (graduates of well-known Turkish or German universities). Key principles of the company are: transparency, confidence, being hardworking, discipline, good timing, team work, appreciating people, being open to new ideas, being customer-focused, and with an emphasis on total quality.

Kompen's top management plays a vital role in creating and maintaining a market orientation; a business's only sustainable competitive advantage is its ability to learn faster than its competitors. A market orientation implies organizational learning, and so for maximum effectiveness in a dynamic world an organization must develop its culture as a market-oriented learning organization.

Kompen places importance on sales concepts that have been tried and tested in practice, experience in opening up new markets and a flexible approach to foreign cultures and business customs. It considers an important element in the company's increasing internationalization to be training within the company of qualified managers who think globally and operate efficiently. This is an indispensable prerequisite for its worldwide economic success in the future.

In its international operations, Kompen's strategic marketing management team (SMMT) consists of managers dealing with marketing operations and advisors who implement a screening process for collecting worldwide indicators of market potential and global customers of PVC windows and doors. The process results in a focused allocation of resources onto the markets and customers that offer the greatest opportunity for sales, profits and growth. SMMT analyses and identifies the most appropriate distribution channels, market segments, competitive pricing and market entry or expansion strategies. The process results in the positioning of the company as an effective and desirable competitor in the market. SMMT searches out, screens and qualifies, and assists in starting up master franchisers or, in other words, main distributors or dealers of preferred partner relationships. This results in an improved service to international customers, greater internal efficiencies, and an increased capacity to expand international sales.

In order to expand its operations abroad, the company uses product trade-name franchising very successfully in its international operations, exporting its products to 25 countries.[20] According to Mr San, the company's CEO, Turkish firms' experience in the PVC windows and door sector is only 25 years old, but in spite of this many Turkish firms in the sector are operating successfully in domestic and international markets. Mr San states that Kompen is expanding its international operations through the use of manufacturer–dealer franchise systems, its rewarding dealers who operate high-quality standards and after-sales services to their consumers. The company has also established very efficient monitoring mechanisms to control its dealers.[21]

Mr Küçükşehir, Marketing Manager of Kompen, also states that as a leading company in the PVC windows and doors sector, company managers attend fairs abroad, always alert for new business opportunities. Consumers' ideas and expectations are very important, and in this connection international fairs and platforms are essential for new development.

These days, Kompen's SMMT is developing new strategies in order to provide continuous operations in international markets. In fact, in order to operate in different countries, suitable marketing strategies must be developed for each country. CEO Mr San states that developing integrated marketing communications strategies is essential to be successful abroad, and the company has decided to develop and apply such strategies. To implement the strategies, one of the best Turkish media development firms, Artworks, headquartered in Istanbul, has been chosen to prepare advertising and sales promotion programmes in accordance with each country's characteristics, based on thorough pre-studies for each country. As part of its, strategic marketing plan, Kompen is investing in communications, computers to create databases, and in 2003 the company's toll-free consumer phone line was put into service.

Quality is the main reason Kompen has a strategic advantage in the global marketplace. Quality is a core competency and a focus on quality is present throughout the entire company. Employees are responsible for the quality of the products or services they provide, guided by clear and understandable quality standards, and quality will remain a major element in all business planning and goals. Continuous, measurable improvement will continue to be a normal part of every departmental function. Upper management reviews the quality system on a regular basis, and customer complaints are addressed and resolved. Manufacturing processes are documented and controlled to ensure product consistency.

The starting point of selecting a target market is that the chosen market should be as close as possible to the firm and present the minimum difficulty in doing business there. The choice of market involves careful examination, and Kompen applies a series of checks for each country. Most of the information the company needs is available from local sources such as libraries, trade statistics on foreign embassies, and typically includes: the number of users of the product, price levels, demand levels for its products, the country's stability level both politically and economically, imports of products without tariff or non-tariff barriers, the country's financial regulations allowing for payments for imports, size of the market for its products, the trend of demand for its products over the past five years and indications of demand for the next five years, and the proportion of the PVC windows and doors market that is supplied by imports and their source. In addition, information is gathered on main competitors, their market shares and their strengths and weaknesses, the costs of transport, storage and distribution, advertising methods used in the market, availability of distribution methods, and any legislation affecting the products. On this basis Kompen decides whether the target market is likely to provide the return the company is looking for. Foreign trade managers may then visit potential countries for further consideration.

Conclusion

This study shows that franchising, particularly product and trade franchising, is still very important to firms' expansion into international markets. One of the most important factors in Kompen's rapid coverage of international markets has been its efficient and effective use of franchising systems, benefiting from many advantages such as: allowing franchisees to increase the number of their outlets with minimal capital investment, and provide operating procedures and standard marketing programmes that enable them to be competitive. Franchisees are seen to be more motivated than company-owned managers because they share in the profits of their businesses. Franchise systems ensure that the businesses are operated according to required standards, where monitoring of company outlets is difficult. These benefits are core success factors for Kompen.

In fact, producers' commitments to international franchise operations must be full and long-term oriented. This study shows that the marketing-channel strategy is very important in gaining market presence in international markets. In particular, developing an efficient integrated marketing channel is important to development and also to the maintenance of the market share, both domestically and in international markets. The application of franchising in a scientific way created brand awareness for Kompen's products.

This study has also shown that in order to gain competitive presence in markets, investments in human-resource development, quality management and information technology is crucial. It is important to point out that value is delivered to consumers by both manufacturer and retailer in a manufacturer–dealer relationship in which the brand plays a key role for both sides. The creation of brand awareness and repeat sales are particularly important for success in international markets, where intense competition occurs. In order to operate long-term in a foreign country, firms should make investments in their franchise systems. The case of Kompen shows that the use of franchising in foreign markets can create very fast market coverage and sales volume for a company.

Finally, the main factors behind Kompen's success in such a short time in a highly competitive market are as follows:

- Designing the right distribution strategy through product trade-name franchising in domestic and international markets;
- Continuous screening and evaluation of current and new markets;
- Giving a high level of importance to quality, and adjusting production to each country's demands;
- Giving importance strategic marketing management to all operations of the company;
- Realizing the importance of export marketing;
- Providing efficient training support to dealers in domestic and export channels;
- Scheduled and programmed visits by the foreign trade department to each country, recognizing problems and taking corrective action on time; and
- Creation of brand awareness by use of exterior and interior showroom design, not only in the domestic but also in the international markets.

Notes

1 J.L. Johnson and V. Raven, 'Relationship Quality, Satisfaction and Performance in Export Marketing Channels', *Journal of Marketing Channels*, 5, 3/4 (1996): 19–49.
2 L.W. Stern and A.I. El-Ansary, *Marketing Channels* (Englewood Chiffs, NJ: Prentice-Hall, 1992).
3 R.F. Lusch and V.N. Lusch, *Principles of Marketing* (Boston, MA: Kent Publishing Company, 1987).
4 K.G. Hardy and A.J. Magrath, *Marketing Channel Management* (Glenview, IL: Scott, Foresman & Company, 1988).
5 M.J. Baker, *Macmillan Dictionary of Marketing and Advertising*, 2nd edn (The London: Macmillan, 1990).
6 B. Klein, R. Crawford and A. Alchian, 'Vertical Integration, Appropriate Rents, and the Competitive Contracting Process', in L. Putterman (ed.), *The Economic Nature of The Firm* (Cambridge: Cambridge University Press, 1978); O.E. Williamson, 'Transaction Cost Economics: The Governance of Contractual Relations', *Journal of*

Law and Economics, 22 (1979): 233–62; M. Wright, 'Redrawing the Boundaries of the Firm', in S. Thompson and M. Wright (eds), *Internal Organisation, Efficiency and Profit* (Atlantic Highlands, NJ: Philip Allan, 1988); M.W. Pride and O.C. Ferrel, *Marketing Concepts and Strategies* (Boston and New York: Houghton Mifflin, 2000).
7 K.J. Blois, 'Vertical Quasi-Integration', *Journal of Industrial Economics*, 21 (July 1972): 253–71; K.R. Harrigan, 'A Framework for Looking at Vertical Integration', *Academy of Management Review*, 19, 4 (1984): 638–52; A. Diamantopoulos, 'Vertical Quasi-Integration Revisited: The Role of Power', *Managerial and Decision Economics*, 8 (1987): 185–94.
8 L.W. Stern, A.I. El-Ansary and J.R. Brown, *Management in Marketing Channels*. (Englewood Cliffs, NJ: Prentice Hall, 1989).
9 T.G. Marx, 'Distribution Efficiency in Franchising', *MSU Business Topics*, 28, 1 (1980): 5–13; G.F. Mathewson and R.A. Winter, 'The Economics of Franchise Contracts', *Journal of Law and Economics*, 28 (October 1985): 503–26.
10 E.Erden, 'Pazarlama ilmi ve ilgi sahasi icerisinde "bayilik verme"' (Franchising in Marketing Science), *Hacettepe Universitesi Iktisadi ve Idari Bilimler Fakultesi Dergisi*, 3 (Nisan 1984): 107–18; D.Y. Ayhan, 'Isletmelerarasi bir birlesme bicimi: Franchising (imtiyaz) sistemi ve onemi' (Another Type of Integration Method between Firms: Franchising and its Importance), *Hacettepe Universitesi Iktisadi ve Idari Bilimler Fakultesi Dergisi*, 3 (1984): 81–93; E. Erden, 'Bayiliklerin pazarlama icerisindeki yeri ve onemi' (Place and Importance of Franchising in Marketing), *Erciyes Universitesi Iktisadi ve Idari Bilimler Fakultesi Dergisi*, 7 (Temmuz, 1985): 153–9.
11 This information is based on an interview with D.Y. Ayhan, Professor of Marketing in the Faculty of Economics and Administration, Hacettepe University (Ankara: January 1990).
12 C. Solakoglu, 'Dagitim Sistemlerinde Etkinlik ve Turkiye' (Efficiency in Distribution Systems and Turkey), *Yeni İş Dünyası*, 71 (Eylül 1985): 28–33.
13 Pakpen, www.pakpen.com.tr (2003).
14 M. Rigby and G.H. Arnold, 'The PVC-U Window Market in Europe: An Analysis of Some Key Issues Affecting Company Performance', M. Rigby (Michael Rigby Associates) and GH Arnold (Godfrey Arnold Associates), http://www.rigby-research. co.uk/marketinfo/articles/berlin (2003).
15 A. Kucukkafa, 'Türk pencere pazarı' (Turkish Windows Market), *Pencere* (Ekim-Kasım, 2002): 72–3.
16 'Invest in the most active sector', *Capital* (February 1999).
17 www.kompen.com.tr
18 *Ibid.*
19 Interview with M. Buyukserin, Head Foreign Trade Department.
20 Interview with E. Küçükşehir, Marketing Manager.
21 Interview with A. San, General Manager.

Additional data collected from public sources and in-depth interviews with Korupen executives in May 2003.

13
Best Practices in Emerging Markets: Examples from the US Hotel Industry

Michael A. Anikeeff

Introduction

Growth and change within the international hotel industry shows how companies in advanced markets can enter and succeed in emerging markets. We examine hotels in the United States since US chains dominate the industry and have a great influence in the international arena. US hotel chains have followed a classic three-step process in developing a total worldwide strategy:[1]

(1) They have developed a core strategy, the basis of competitive advantage, in the home country first.
(2) They have internationalized the core strategy through expansion of activities and adaptation.
(3) They have globalized the international strategy by integrating the strategy across countries.

The chapter begins with an overview of the industry's historic development of a core strategy. After the overview, we focus on the important success factors. An examination of the hotel industry's organization and structure, human resources and strategic behaviour shows that a hotel firm's success is a function of location, the market segment/brand, the management, and the ownership structure.[2] Fixed location is important for two reasons – market demand and the government's economic policy at the site. The market segment/brands are next in importance, determining the hotel's clients and source of business. Management is important because hotels are one of the most labour-intensive service businesses. Finally, the ownership structure determines the capital structure of the investment, which determines the investment returns and risks. The chapter ends with a case study illustrating hotel development in the emerging market of Eastern Europe's Hungary.

Overview

The organization and structure of the industry evolved over a long period. Rushmore and Baum[3] provide an historic discussion and Ingram[4] an analysis of the development of US hotel chains. Here we select from their work aspects that most influence operations in emerging markets.

Ingram[5] describes the rise of a new form of organization in the hotel industry – the hotel chain. After the Second World War, international travel increased and some large American hotel companies saw potential opportunities for expanding their development and operations into foreign countries to serve the international travel markets.[6] The operation of foreign hotels stimulated the development of management contracts, which became a popular market-entry strategy for American hotel corporations because of the low capital requirements. In addition, franchises provided chains a means for horizontal integration, and during the 1960s and 1970s more hotel companies began to expand their chains through franchising. This offered a new source of capital for hotel franchise companies.

Hotel franchisers eventually started using what was for them a new concept called market segmentation. When hotel chains began, they developed a standardized form of operation that was oriented to a single class of traveller; they developed a brand name and a loyal following among their target market. After a period, it became apparent that the markets for the core products were satisfied, and consequently the hotel chains had to find a mechanism that would let them expand, develop or franchise additional properties within their market areas. The solution was to develop a new product aimed at a different class of traveller, and therefore in order to show continuous growth the hotel companies developed a new organizational strategy. The old strategy targeted one price segment, and chain executives decided that they could create a new brand of products for other price segments. This strategy allowed chains to offer two or more affiliations in the same geographic market without directly competing against themselves. Holiday Inn, a mid-priced chain, went upscale with Crowne Plaza and downscale with Hampton Inns. This is still an expansion strategy used by hotel companies.

US firms used tactics of franchising, management service contracts and multiple brands to expand internationally. In 1978, 81 international hotel companies controlled 1,025 hotels with 270,646 rooms. According to Dunning and McQueen,[7] American companies held 22 of the 81 hotels and 56 per cent of the total inventory of international hotel rooms. The expansion of the hotel industry continued in the 1980s and 1990s. New markets emerged in Asia and Latin America, and these emerging markets provided great opportunities for international hotel development.[8]

US public companies have increasingly dominated the hotel industry since the 1990s, due in no small part to their access to world capital markets and fuelled by expectations of the capital markets for earnings growth. Market segmentation continues to provide a viable approach to achieving earnings growth, and so does the management service-contract arrangement. Public hotel companies use management service contracts because they do not like to have real estate assets (hotels) on the balance sheet for accounting reasons. The public hotel firm generally has little or no ownership interest in the hotel and is not responsible for funding any operating losses. Chains such as Marriott have created a strategy in which they develop or acquire a hotel, insert their management, and then sell the property to an individual investor or a partnership. Marriott retains operational control through the long-term contract. Due to widespread use of the management contract and franchises, chains own few hotels operating as part of their national chain.

Acquisition and mergers provide an even more efficient way to increase earnings growth, and a few multi-brand hotel companies control most of the industry's most recognized brands. Starwood Hotels and Resorts and Patriot American Hospitality (Wyndham International) are the most avid players in this arena. Starwood acquired the assets of Sheraton, Westin and HEI Hotels. Patriot American got Wyndham Hotels, Carnival Hotels & Resorts, Interstate Hotels and Grand Heritage Hotels. The pressure for earnings growth and the industry's economic structure requires globalization. According to Kogut,[9] when certain structural economies exist, industries must compete in world markets in order to survive. Three industry characteristics give global firms a sustainable advantage. First, an increase in economies of scale results from an increase in market size. Second, an increase in market scope yields an increase in product lines that can support the fixed costs of logistics, and control. Third, knowledge gained regarding market opportunities or new technologies results in relevant experience. Hotels have all three characteristics, and therefore American companies are expanding overseas, and foreign hotel companies are seeking opportunities in the USA. The major hotel chains are listed in Table 13.1, where the influence of US chains is clearly significant.

Table 13.1 International hotel chains

Hotel chain (nationality)	Countries represented 1997	Number of hotels 2002
Best Western (US)	77	4052
Six Continents (UK)	75	3200
Accor (FR)	72	3654
Starwood (US)	68	743
Marriott International (US)	53	2398
Hilton International (UK)	52	220

Sources: *Hotels*, 1998, Special Report; *Hotels*, 2002, Special Report.

Location

Strategically the hotel firm's most important concern is the facility's location.[10] Each location has its own unfamiliar institutions, technology, customers, laws and social norms. The location is important for two reasons: (1) its demand as a travel destination; and (2) the government economic policy at the site may offer incentives or disincentives. In short, a country's location may offer a comparative economic advantage or disadvantage. If the location is market-disadvantaged, then the community government incentives or the competitive elements of the firm must overcome them. In this section, we examine how firms choose their locations.[11]

Market screening and selection

A hotel location's comparative advantage is based on international regional travel patterns.[12] Jordan and Rowntree[13] find that hotel executives and analysts use regions to organize hospitality corporations' global structures, and report global hospitality performance and trends. The most common regional criteria are geographic proximity on a continent.

An examination of international travel patterns identifies potential opportunities for expansion, and travel patterns for the period 1997 to 2001 giving arrivals and revenues by region are shown in Table 13.2. The pattern was almost unchanged during the period according to Highlights 2001.[14] Europe had the highest volume, 58 per cent of the total share of international tourist arrivals and 48.6 per cent of all tourist revenues in 2000. Europe is clearly the leader in arrivals and in revenues. Yu[15] explains this pattern by the high living standards enjoyed by western and northern Europeans, their long vacations, high education level, and, most importantly, small countries that are close to each other.

Hotel demand follows tourist traffic. Table 13.2 shows that regional hotel development parallels regional travel patterns. There were 12.2 million total

Table 13.2 International travel patterns by region, revenue, arrivals and rooms

Region	Tourist revenue 2000 (%)(of $475 billion)	Tourist arrivals 2000 (%)	Total rooms 1994 (%) (of 12.2 million)
Americas	28.7	18.5	36.7
Europe	48.6	58.0	44.7
East Asia/Pacific	17.3	16.0	12.7
South Asia	2.2	.09	1.2
Middle East	2.0	2.9	1.5
Africa	2.0	4.0	3.1

Sources: Highlights 2001; Highlights 1994.

rooms in the world in Highlights 1994;[16] regionally, Europe had 5,462,000 hotel rooms in 1994 or 44.7 per cent of the world total.

Government policy

Acquiring inexpensive resources and labour attracts some hotel firms to emerging markets. In some countries, undeveloped land and labour are abundant and inexpensive, but the countries often lack capital and technology. Since hotel development is a capital-intensive business, many emerging countries are not able to build the luxury hotels that accommodate the affluent tourist, and so their governments may endeavour to attract hotel chains from affluent countries to invest in hotel operations.

Wanhill[17] says that the tourism policy of a country may have various development and investment objectives, with incentives and inducements varying based on the objectives and the role the government sees for private enterprise. Today, most governments have three objectives for their tourism development plans: employment, foreign exchange earnings and regional development – particularly in peripheral areas.

Market segments and brands

Competitive advantage

We mentioned in the overview that increased sales come from segmentation, but branding also offers advantages. Hotel firms have segmented the market to meet the needs of customers, to increase profitability and to diversify the customer base.[18] Large chains with name identities such as Marriott, or Holiday Inn, develop additional market segments with sub-brands. For example, Marriott Courtyard offers limited service, Residence Inn by Marriott provides extended stay, Holiday Inn Select has full service, and Holiday Inn Express specializes in limited service.

Building worldwide brand recognition creates a form of economy of scale, and brand recognition and brand loyalty is important in domestic and international operations. As international travel increases, the competition among brands intensifies. This is why every brand-name hotel company has a position in the strategic international travel market. They actually use international markets to compete directly with long-time domestic rivals.

Marketing mix

International hotel marketing differs from domestic marketing. Hotel brand penetration is highest in the United States and lowest in emerging markets. In the United States 60 per cent of hotels are associated with a brand. Positive brand identity is beneficial for the hotel manager and hotel owner; if the brand is effective in producing demand, management will spend less time marketing and focus on local operations and local bookings. The owners also benefit financially from increased bookings through the reservation system and potentially lower marketing costs. The existance of brand familiarity and loyalty in the US creates a barrier to entry. Since many emerging markets do not have branded hotels, this protection is lacking.

The marketing mix elements – products and services, distribution channels and promotion – require modification and adjustment. Products and services have a number of attributes that may need modification, since consumer needs vary from country to country due to cultural differences and levels of economic development. Cultural differences in particular have important implications on products and services internationally. The food service business requires greater modification to meet local needs, and the hotel architecture and interior decoration of public areas and guestrooms may also need to change.

Using channels of distribution properly can have a significant impact on sales. In the USA, hotel companies sell their products and services directly to the consumer by offering central reservation systems with toll-free telephone numbers, or by hotel sales representatives contacting business clients directly. Hotel sales through travel agents are one of the least used channels. In other countries, however, hotel services are distributed differently. Tourists tend to consult travel agents more for choosing hotels in other countries, and travel agents can influence the buying decision. Therefore developing a relationship with the retail travel network is more important.

The Global Distribution System (GDS) is used to market hotels internationally. This is the central reservation system used by travel agents to book airline seats, rental cars, hotel rooms and other services. In the past, travel agencies used major central reservations systems for booking airline and car-rental reservations electronically. Now they are increasingly dependent on GDS computers to display hotel selections and reserve rooms instantly in any geographic location worldwide. GDS allows each hotel to list all its different room types, with descriptions, rate categories, policies and special packages. The information is available to hundreds of thousands of travel agents worldwide and agents can get immediate confirmation for rooms.[19]

Management

Geller[20] says that the hotel industry is particularly vulnerable to management problems such as theft and embezzlement. This occurs for a number of reasons. First, there are many cash transactions; second, the individual hotels are small business units; third, jobs have low social status; fourth, individuals deal with items of high value (wine, steaks); and finally, many items have an appeal for personal use.

Since the 1980s, most hotel companies have reorganized themselves to meet the challenge of globalization by creating additional control mechanisms.

Yu[21] found that management controls varied, but reflected the degree of centralization, formalization and complexity desired by a particular company. In general, a number of activities including training and personnel practices, planning, coordination and financial control are centrally designed and locally implemented. International firms operate with few layers in an attempt to narrow the distance between executives/managers, employees and customers. To implement this structure, the corporate headquarters executives are responsible for strategic development, finance, global marketing programmes, legal affairs and corporate human resources. However, local hotel management makes operational, quality-control decisions based on the differences in local customs and commercial practices required. Consequently, hotels have centrally designed and customized service at the local property.

In order to have corporate policy guidelines on direct decision-making at the property level, there is a formalization of rules, policies and regulations. These formal documents provide hotel managers with sufficient guidance to operate the individual property to achieve the goals set by the corporate headquarters.

As hotel corporations grow by expanding into foreign countries, the management situation becomes more complex, and non-standard hotel operational approaches develop to meet the various needs. There is a dynamic tension in that hotel corporations have to differentiate their tasks and products sufficiently and at the same time create subdivisions that can specialize and standardize the operating procedures for efficiency.

The organizational structure of the hotel chain is large and geographically dispersed. Hotel chains rely on a cadre of trained executives for efficient control to be successful, and without them centrally-controlled formal policies, implemented in a complex environment, would not be possible. A major difference between independent hotels and hotel chains is in their reliance on professional managers. As the supply of professional managers to the hotel industry has increased, mainly through university education supported by the industry, the founding and growth rates of hotel chains increased and their success.[22] In order to control their executives, standardized training is important, but not enough. Most international hotels now require their property manager to develop a comprehensive strategic plan for operation; headquarters provide the basic framework, and regional and corporate executives review and approve the property-level plan. To monitor compliance, the manager's performance is evaluated against the plan, according to Olsen and Merna.[23]

In sum, the development of accounting and managerial information systems has permitted centralization of control, formalization of procedures, and complex organizational structures. This control technology coupled with the training of professional management has allowed the growth of chains in the industry.

Ownership structure

International hotel companies face external threats that are beyond their control – both economic and political risks – and expansion plans must take into consideration these uncontrollable factors. Appropriate ownership structures provide a mode of entry that can minimize the vulnerability of companies to political and economic risk. There are six organizational structures for market entry commonly used by hotel companies for international expansion: sole ownership, joint ventures, franchising, management contract, strategic alliances, and consortia, each of which has advantages and disadvantages in trading-off profitability and control for reduced political and financial risk. In Table 13.3, the advantages and disadvantages of each of the six entry modes are listed.[24]

Sole ownership is used to control a landmark property in a developed country. In addition, it is used to enter desirable emerging markets that lack government or private-sector investors with significant capital.

A joint venture,[25] which is a partnership between a domestic company and a foreign company, is commonly used in emerging markets. When an international hotel company is unsure about the political risk or uncertain of the business risk, often an issue in many emerging markets, it makes sense to seek a local partner to develop and operate the facility. Most rapid growth in the hotel industry occurs through franchising and management contracts.[26] These are used in high-risk environments to place business risk and real-estate risk with the local investor.[27] Some authors have found that franchising is a more prevalent choice in more developed countries. In franchise[28] agreements, a hotel company (franchiser) sells limited rights to another company or independent operator (franchisee) for the use of its brand name in selling certain standardized products or services. The franchiser receives a payment and a share of the franchisee's profits. The franchiser provides the franchisee with its business format, standard operating procedures for making products and performing services. The franchisee has to deliver a product that conforms to the franchiser's standards.

Table 13.3 Entry mode advantages and disadvantages

Entry mode	Cost of entry return	Political/financial risk/return	Quality control consistency	Brand promotion
Sole ownership	Highest	Highest	Highest	Highest
Joint venture	Moderate	Moderate	Moderate	High
Franchise	Low	Low	Varies	High
Mgmt contract	Low	Low	High	High
Alliance	Low	Low	Low	Partner's
Consortium	Low	Low	Low	Low

Source: Author and L. Yu (1999): 152.

The management contract[29] mentioned earlier is also a popular market-entry method for international expansion, particularly in emerging markets. It[30] refers to a cooperative agreement between hotel companies from two different countries, who join for mutual support and expansion of their global presence. Consortia are voluntary groups or membership affiliations of hotels.[31] They offer marketing and reservation services for independents and some chains, but differ from franchises in that they are not required to follow standardized procedures established by the franchisers. Members pay an annual fee for the marketing and reservation service; they are independent in their management and operations.

In summarizing the current organization ownership structures for market entry, certain patterns emerge. Contractor and Kundu,[32] found the distribution of hotel operations by modal type to be equity 34.6 per cent (sole ownership 15.8 per cent, joint venture 18.8 per cent) and non-equity 65.4 per cent (management service contract 37 per cent, and franchise 28.4 per cent.) The dominance of the North American firms is a result of rapid expansion using franchising and management contracts, and US brands[33] dominate both of these approaches. The five largest hotel companies worldwide have headquarters in the USA, and the North American hotels list 14 out of the top-30 and 30 of the top-50 hotel companies. Finally, there is a trend towards alliances like SAS/Radisson and more consolidation among smaller and mid-sized companies.

Hotel expansion in Central Europe

Even though much of the excitement about the opening and economic liberalization in Eastern and Central Europe has dissipated since the early 1990s, development and expansion of the hotel industry has continued.[34] Karhunen[35] examines entry-mode choice in transition economies looking at hotel companies in Russia. He builds on the work of Kostecki[36] to summarize the motivations for investment in Central and Eastern Europe, emphasizing a promising market for services and that presence helps to gain a competitive edge in the West because clients require a global service network. In addition, there are strategic concerns. Expansion in Eastern Europe is a unique opportunity. Global firms have to be present in Eastern Europe, to position themselves in terms of the market leader and other competitors. Karhunen argues that despite the non-favourable business environment of Russia for foreign tourist companies, global chains just cannot afford not to be in Russia.

There are Eastern European countries that offer a more favourable business environment than Russia, primarily the Czech Republic, the Slovak Republic, Poland and Hungary. Hungary has been particularly successful receiving over half of all foreign investment for Eastern and Central Europe in the first half of the 1990s. The number of Hungarian hotels increased from 327 to 666 from 1990 to 2000, and the number of five-star hotels doubled to 59.

We can examine the hotel success factors – location, segment/brands, management and ownership structure to understand how this emerging market growth has occurred.

Location

Travel patterns have favoured Hungary. Hungary has a long history as a tourist destination, and because of its relatively liberal pre-1989 policies it received attention from Western hotel companies even before the break up of the Soviet bloc. It was not surprising that the political changes begun in 1989 brought a number of foreign investors to Hungary.

Visitor numbers show that the travel industry has been important to Hungary. The 1989 Economist Intelligence Unit Report found that Hungary received roughly 20 per cent more visitors than the United Kingdom, although its revenues from international tourism were only about 10 per cent of the United Kingdom's because the visitors were primarily from poorer Eastern European countries.[37] Hungary, in 1992, was the most frequently visited nation in Eastern and Central Europe with 7.7 per cent of total arrivals. The total of overnight tourists was 22 million in 1992, but the total of registered hotel guests was 2.8 million. About 60 per cent of the tourists came from COMECON countries, most staying with friends or relatives or in unregistered private rooms. Officially registered rooms had a capacity of 78,000 guests nationwide, but the estimate of unregistered rooms was 558,000 – a significant share of the market.[38] In 2000, European travellers were the main source of the luxury hotel market with guests from Austria, Germany, Netherlands and the UK. At the same time, the number of guests from Eastern Europe, Scandinavia and the Far East increased.[39]

Government policy shows a commitment to economic transformation. Privatization is controlled by the government State Property Agency (SPA) that began in 1989. The goal was to transfer ownership of state-owned property to the private sector in five years. Government efforts to prevent unemployment and high inflation rates slowed privatization, and in addition the lack of an effective capital market made the valuation and sale of properties and companies difficult. SPA policy requires that bids involve more than price alone. Equally important if not more so is that takeovers or joint ventures should help the long-term economic goals of Hungary in areas such as technology, management and finance.[40] In 2001, the Hungarian government had earmarked $1 billion from the central budget to develop the national tourism industry as part of the Szechenyl Plan. The goal was to reduce the foreign account deficit.[41] The plan achieved a level of success – tourism revenue was over $2.9 billion in 2001.

Market segments and brands

The primary strategy of the major players in the initial period of Eastern Europe hotel development was to target the elite market segment. Developers moved into the capital cities to gain returns quickly by providing top accommodations at high rates and high profit margins. Urban occupancy levels in the city remained good at 70 per cent until 2000, at which point over-building began. Budapest added 1,000 hotel rooms in 1999 – an additional 365,000 room nights annually – which represented 9 per cent of the total in the city. An additional 3,200 rooms – 1.17 million room nights annually – were in the pipeline.[42]

Holiday Inn Worldwide planned to meet the demand in the two- and three-star segments by using a segmentation strategy based on multiple name-affiliated brands. Holiday Inn had identified a converging demand scenario in Eastern and Central European markets. Initial travellers were top executives that wanted five-star accommodation, but large numbers of mid-level executives with less lavish expense accounts have replaced them. Holiday Inn therefore offered mid-range Holiday Inn Express or Holiday Inn Garden Court brands – 100 to 200-room hotels in secondary locations. They thus avoided downtown locations with existing buildings, and construction times for these prefabricated hotels were only six to nine months. Besides saving time, prefabrication and standardization allowed the introduction of a consistent product. The strategy is still being worked out but there has been weak demand in the provinces over the last few years. Occupancy rates have been very low ranging from 20 per cent to mid-40s per cent. The changes were positive in the three-star and two-star categories with decreases in the one-star segment. However, small-scale family-owned hotels offering simple but modern comfort have appeared to be successful. Evidently, the market has not developed for corporate accommodations.[43]

Management

Marriott has adopted a strategy for some Eastern European properties that calls for the hiring and training of an all-new staff made up of young language-school students – preferably without prior hotel experience – and this approach has been very successful. Industry executives believe that the lack of a service orientation in Eastern Europe is not that great a problem. They have found that the Eastern European education systems produce excellent learners and employees and that comparatively good salaries can easily motivate young workers.[44]

Low wages make investment in Eastern and Central Europe attractive in spite of the relatively high risk. Initial investments have the potential of quick pay-off due to low payroll costs and comparatively high occupancy rates. Low payroll costs are important in the equation in boosting gross operating profits. This is even more noticeable for European companies since European salaries are normally considered higher than those in the USA (plus they include healthcare and longer vacation benefits).[45] Margins in Eastern and Central Europe may be 30 to 40 per cent higher than in Western Europe, with high profitability rates resulting from the hotels charging international rates and operating at local costs. This results in profitability rates of over 50 per cent compared to a 20 to 30 per cent norm in Western European countries

Setting standards and creating management controls is problematic in establishing values of properties. Conventional valuation methods for property that have become the norm in the United States and in Western Europe are virtually useless in an emerging market economy. Often true markets do not exist, transactions and historical precedents are scarce and inflation high.[46] The fact that Hungarian hotels do not follow the 'Uniform System of Accounts for Hotels' further complicates valuation.

Ownership structure

Hotel companies enter the Eastern and Central European markets using a number of methods such as franchising, management contracts, full ownership and joint ventures. Holiday Inn tried a strategy of franchising new products in secondary locations and getting management contracts for its deluxe Crowne Plaza hotels in primary locations. The problem with this strategy was that there were not enough Eastern and Central European entrepreneurs with the necessary financial capacity to make hotel franchising grow quickly. This is the reason Holiday Inn invested equity in its franchisee projects. It appears that the growing trend in Eastern and Central Europe is the joint venture agreement.

After discussing the investment situation with a number of individuals in Hungary, Lorenz and Cullen[47] summarized the investment climate. Even though hotel companies do not like having to put up 40 to 50 per cent equity for projects in Eastern and Central Europe, most believed that it is actually not that bad a deal.[48] In fact, 50 to 55 per cent equity is usually the market rate for Western Europe.[49] The local government bodies usually contribute a significant portion of the expense in the form of buildings and land, in exchange for some portion of the equity. In addition, if it can be obtained, EBRD (European Bank for Reconstruction and Development) and IFC (International Finance Corporation) financing tends to be cheaper than the loans Austrian banks offer (as the source of most Eastern and Central European financing).

Summary and conclusion

We began with an overview of the US hotel industry's historic development of a core strategy. In general, we found that expansion into international markets is an extension of the strategies and tactics developed for the domestic market. An examination of the hotel industry's organization and structure, human resources and strategic behaviour shows that a hotel firm's success is a function of its location, the market segment/brand, the management, and the ownership structure (see Table 13.4).

Table 13.4 Hotel success factors

Success factors	Location	Marketing segment brand	Management	Ownership
Organization Structure	Government policy (1) sets role of private sector, (2) creates incentives, and (3) assures security		Chains dominate	Structure a function of perceived risk
Resources		• Worldwide reservations technology • Brands & segmentation key strategy	Standardized training & procedures	Corporation access to international capital markets
Human factors Employee skills			• Executives' academic professional programme • Control low-wage service employees with MIS/accounting systems	
Strategy Selection criteria	Travellers to region			
Marketing mix	Modify product (food, architecture)	Channels include technical, personal travel agents	Corporate strategy locally customized	Need for local knowledge may influence ownership option
Entry technique		Analyse, identify segments, match existing brands to segments		Build, buy, JV, franchise, management service alliance, or consortia

A fixed location is important for two reasons – demand as a travel destination and the government economic policy at the site. The market segment and brand determine the hotel clients and source of business. Hotels use segments to identify market opportunities that they can serve with established methods, and the brand signals to the customer that a guaranteed level of service is available. Management is important because hotels are one of the most labour-intensive service businesses. The establishment of a chain structure enabled the development of the industry, and the organization of the chain requires management control systems and academically trained professional managers to implement the controls. Finally, the ownership structure determines the capital structure of the investment, which determines the investment returns and risks.

We have described a case study illustrating hotel development in Hungary. Hungary, an emerging market, will soon join the European Union, and provides an example of a country with significant advantages yet constrained by the limitations of location – in particular by government policy – which it has overcome.

Notes

1. G.S. Yip, 'Global Strategy... in a World of Nations?', *MIT Sloan Management Review* (Fall 1989).
2. Legg Mason Wood Walker, Inc., *Host Marriott Corporation Purchase Recommendation* (26 August 1999): 9.
3. S. Rushmore and E. Baum, 'Growth and Development of the Hotel–Motel Industry', *The Appraisal Journal* (April 2002): 148–62.
4. P.L. Ingram, *The Rise of Hotel Chains in the United States 1896–1980* (New York: Garland Publishing, 1996).
5. Ibid.: 3.
6. Ibid.: 17.
7. J.H. Dunning and M. McQueen, 'The Eclectic Theory of International Production: A Case Study of the Hotel Industry', *Management and Decision Economics*, 4 (1981): 197–210.
8. M.C. Burritt, 'Japanese Investment in U.S. Hotels and Resorts', *The Cornell Hotel and Restaurant Administration Quarterly* (October 1991): 60–6.
9. B. Kogut. 'Designing Global Strategies: Comparative and Competitive Value-Added Chains', *Sloan Management Review*, vol. 26 (Summer 1985): 15–28.
10. P. Buckley and N.V. Geyikdagi, 'Explaining Foreign Direct Investment in Turkey's Tourism Industry', *Transnational Corporations*, 5, 3 (December 1996).
11. L. Yu, *The International Hospitality Business: Management and Operations* (Binghamton, New York: Haworth Hospitality Press, 1999): 4–6.
12. L.E. Hudman and R.H. Jackson, *Geography of Travel and Tourism* (Albany, New York: Delmar Publishers, 1990): 7.
13. T.G. Jordan and L. Rowntree, *The Human Mosaic: A Thematic Introduction to Cultural Geography*, 5th edn (New York: Harper & Row, 1990): 7.
14. Highlights 2001, *International Tourism Review* (2001): 3.
15. L. Yu, *The International Hospitality Business: Management and Operations*, op. cit.: 33.

16 Highlights 1994, *International Tourism Review* (1996): 13.
17 S. Wanhill, 'The Economic Aspects of Location Marketing', in T. Baum and R. Mudambi (eds), *Economic and Management Methods for Tourism and Hospitality Research* (New York: John Wiley, 1999): 159–76.
18 Legg Mason Wood Walker, Inc., *op. cit.*: 12–16.
19 Hotel Clearing Corporation, 'Pegasus Systems', *HCC Corporate Fact Sheet* (October 1997): 1–2.
20 N.A. Geller. *Internal Control: A Fraud Prevention Handbook for Hotel and Restaurant Managers* (Ithaca, New York: Cornell School of Hotel Administration, 1991).
21 L. Yu, *The International Hospitality Business: Management and Operations, op. cit.*: 152.
22 P.L. Ingram, *The Rise of Hotel Chains in the United States 1896–1980, op. cit.*: 100.
23 M.D. Olsen and K.M. Merna, 'The Changing Character of the Multinational Hospitality Firm', in P. Jones and A. Pizam (eds), *The International Hospitality Industry: Organizational and Operational Issues* (New York: John Wiley, 1993): 89–103.
24 L. Yu, *The International Hospitality Business: Management and Operations, op. cit.*: 136.
25 *Ibid.*: 138–9.
26 T.D. Cruz and S. Wolchuk, 'Special Report Hotels 325', *Hotels* (July 1999).
27 F.J. Contractor and S.K. Kundu, 'Modal Choice in a World of Alliances: Analyzing Organizational Forms in the International Hotel Sector', *Journal or International Business Studies*, 29, 2 (1998): 325–58.
28 L. Yu, *The International Hospitality Business: Management and Operations, op. cit.*: 139–42.
29 *Ibid.*: 142–5.
30 *Ibid.*: 145–7.
31 *Ibid.*: 146–50.
32 F.J. Contractor and S.K. Kundu, 'Modal Choice in a World of Alliances: Analyzing Organizational Forms in the International Hotel Sector', *op. cit.*: 325–58.
33 Hotels (2002), 'Hotels 325 Corporate 300', http://www.hotelsmag.com (retrieved April 2003).
34 A.F. Lorenz and T.P. Cullen, 'Hotel Investment Opportunities in Hungary', *Cornell Hotel and Restaurant Administration Quarterly*, 35 (1994): 18–32.
35 P. Karhunen, *Entry Mode Choice in Transition Economies: Operations of International Hotel Companies in Russia*. Center for Markets in Transition (Helsinki School of Economics and Business Administration, 2003) duplicated.
36 M. Kostecki, 'Business Options in the Service Sector of the Transition Economies: A Framework for Inquiry', in M. Kostecki and A. Fehervary (eds), *Services in the Transition Economies: Business Options for Trade and Investment* (Oxford: Elsevier Sciences Ltd, 1996).
37 Economist Intelligence Unit, 'New Moves to Attract Investment for Hungary's Hotel Industry', *Travel Industry Monitor*, 45 (December 1993): 20–1.
38 World Tourism Organization, cited in Jill Hunt, 'Foreign Investment in Eastern Europe's Travel Industry', *Travel and Tourism Analyst*, 3 (1993): 67.
39 A. Takis, *Business Hungary*, 15, 10 (2001).
40 J. Hamill and G. Hunt, 'Joint Ventures in Hungary: Key Success Factors', *European Management Journal*, 11, 2 (June 1993): 241.
41 A. Takis, *Business Hungary, op. cit.*: 3.
42 T. Aoyama, *Real Estate Market in Hungary*, www.ngatlanbefektetes.hu/angol/c11.html
43 A. Solomon, 'Holiday May Take Express to Europe', *Hotel and Motel Management*, 208, 5 (22 March 1993): 6–58.
44 A.F. Lorenz and T.P. Cullen, 'Hotel Investment Opportunities in Hungary', *op. cit.*: 32.

45 *Ibid.*: 9.
46 S.G. Haggerty and K.L. Lostaglio, 'Applying Western Valuation Techniques in Emerging Hospitality Markets', *The Real Estate Finance Journal* (Winter 1994): 5.
47 A.F. Lorenz and T.P. Cullen, 'Hotel Investment Opportunities in Hungary', *op. cit.*: 32.
48 Ulrich Gevers, Managing Director, Globotels Development and Management Consulting, interviewed by A.F. Lorenz and T.P. Cullen: 16.
49 T. Myklebust, Inter-Continental Senior Vice-President, interviewed by A.F. Lorenz and T.P. Cullen: 16.

14
International Market Entry and Expansion Strategies of Anadolu Efes A. Ş.

İrem Eren-Erdoğmuş, Hale Taşdemir-Çaloğlu and Muzaffer Bodur

Introduction

Beer has been traced back to 4300 BC in Babylonian clay tablets. Commerical brewing dates back to 1200 AD in present-day Germany. Since then, worldwide, there are 20,000 brands of beer, brewed in 180 traditional styles, from ales, lagers, pilsners and stouts, to bitters. Most are national, but some have managed to go global.[1]

Anadolu Efes Biracılık ve Malt Sanayi A.Ş. (Anadolu Efes) of Turkey is one of the breweries that operate in both domestic and international markets. The company is known for its national success and is also starting to be known for its international accomplishments, becoming a national pride of Turkey in the international beer business. We will analyse the company's international operations, with particular emphasis on the emerging markets in which it directly operates. However, before this analysis, the global stance of the beer industry is presented so that the strategic actions of the company can be better understood, compared and contrasted to the general trends in the business.

Global beer industry

When the global beer business is analysed, a general framework for the global competitive situation can be drawn based on Porter's[2] five forces, namely, new entrants, market competitors, buyers, substitutes, and suppliers. This analysis is presented in Figure 14.1.

The international beer business is characterized by high entry barriers for potential entrants. Although reaching a breakeven point is not hard in beer production, severe competition inhibits companies from taking advantage of this fact. First-movers are at an advantage since they can realize

169

Potential entrants
- First-mover advantage
- Easy breakeven
- High branding and marketing expenditure
- Local regulations and policies

Buyer power
End users:
- Increasing brand loyalty
- Low price sensitivity
- Changing drinking habits

Retailers:
- Increasing power

Competitors
- Increasing Mergers and Acquisitions (a) between international and national breweries (b) among international breweries
- No market domination
- Importance of branding

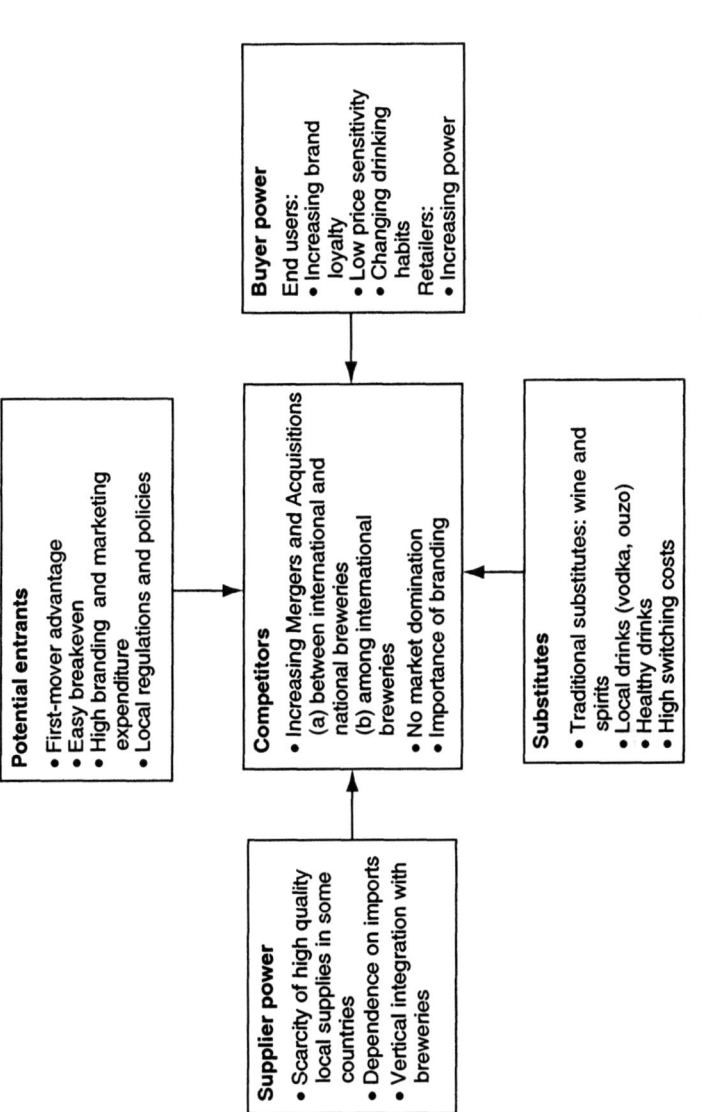

Substitutes
- Traditional substitutes: wine and spirits
- Local drinks (vodka, ouzo)
- Healthy drinks
- High switching costs

Supplier power
- Scarcity of high quality local supplies in some countries
- Dependence on imports
- Vertical integration with breweries

Figure 14.1 Analysis of the global beer business
Source: Adapted from Vrontis (1998).

a breakeven point in the first place and also take advantage of branding, becoming the dominant brands in their market. What makes one beer more successful than another in the global market is not its taste, since it can be imitated very easily, but branding and image. However, companies have to spare a big budget for branding and marketing activities.[3]

Buyers in the industry can be analysed in terms of end-users and retailers. End-users are characterized by increasing brand loyalty, low price sensitivity on the one hand and changing drinking habits in favour of non-alcoholic, healthy and local drinks on the other hand. A brand's success results from being able to sustain values and associations that create loyal customers over time with respect to competitors, who would not be coaxed away from their preferences, and are not price sensitive.[4]

Retailer power, on the other hand, is increasing in the beer market as it increases elsewhere.[5] Low market growth and the increasing power of retailers has forced companies into mergers and acquisitions to gain an overall scale of business and to retain bargaining power against retailers.[6]

The international beer trade is expected to increase significantly in the future, although slow market growth is observed. For the time being, markets are fragmented with both international and national players. The largest companies, which account for only 45.7 per cent of the market, are Anheuser Busch, Heineken, Miller, South African Breweries, Brahma, Interbrew, Carlsberg, Kirin, Group Modelo, and Danone respectively.[7] Anadolu Efes, the focus of this case, is among the 50 largest breweries worldwide.[8]

The competitive environment is characterized by increasing consolidation. Mergers and acquisitions (M&A) are common between international and national companies, as well as among international companies themselves.[9]

The substitutes of beer are many and are increasing their power against beer. Wine and spirits are traditional alcoholic substitutes for beer, but there are also various local alcoholic drinks such as raki in Turkey, ouzo in Greece or vodka in Russia and healthy soft drinks as substitutes of beer. However, the switching cost is high, since it is not very easy for people to change their habits all at once.[10]

Local supplies for the industry such as grain, water, electricity and human resources may be scarce and costly in some countries such as China.[11] In such cases, suppliers are able to raise prices or reduce quantities supplied. Large breweries mostly prefer to set up or acquire malteries to reduce the bargaining power of suppliers and to benefit from geographical proximity.

In summary, the global beer industry has a dynamic nature with ongoing mergers and acquisitions, intense competition in mature markets and opportunities in emerging markets. Although emerging markets are attractive for such companies, they are also risky and unknown. Hence, entering and making commitments in these markets is a major strategic decision.

Anadolu Efes, Turkey's most successful brewer, will be discussed in detail in the following sections. Anadolu Efes has not only contributed to the development of the beer industry in an Islamic country like Turkey, but has also been producing and selling beer in other countries. The company has been especially successful in Russia, Kazakhstan and Moldova, but is also operating in Romania and Ukraine.

Anadolu Efes and Efes Breweries International

Anadolu Efes is part of a larger group owned by two families, with principal interests in the beverages, automotive, finance and stationery products industries in Turkey. It is the largest brewer in Turkey with five breweries and two malteries. The Efes Pilsen brand is the leader in the Turkish brewing industry with a domestic market share of 76 per cent.[12] The company has been described as among the 10 evolved companies of Turkey that have helped to improve the Turkish economy, especially after it began operations in international markets.[13]

Founded in 1996, Efes Breweries International A.Ş. (EBI) is the holding company of the international beer operations. EBI is an 85 per cent-owned subsidiary of Anadolu Efes, and is based in the Netherlands.[14] The company entered Kazakhstan, Romania, Russia, Ukraine and Moldova in 1998, 1998, 1999, 2001 and 2003, respectively. EBI has seven breweries and one maltery in these countries as of 2003. In the rest of this chapter, 'Anadolu Efes' will be used when referring to the operations of EBI for simplicity.

Anadolu Efes was the tenth largest European brewer in terms of sales volume in 2002, and is set to become one of the strongest players in the region. The mission of Anadolu Efes is to become a leading low-cost producer and marketer of beverages in the region between the Adriatic and China, a region that has been experiencing high growth in beer consumption since 1992.[15] In its international markets, instead of the domestic Efes Pilsen brand, it uses the Efes Pilsener brand which it aims to develop into a leading and preferred international brand.[16] In line with this mission, Anadolu Efes has been successful in several emerging markets with a share of value greater than a share of volume. The major critical success factors of the company are: selection of the right market; selection of the right market-entry mode; local strategic planning of branding, positioning and communications; setting alternative distribution channels; and decentralized organization and cultural historical heritage.

Selection of potential markets and market-entry mode

A major critical success factor of Anadolu Efes has been its ability to select the right potential markets and the right market-entry mode for each market. Financial results and market leadership in selected market segments prove that statement. Anadolu Efes evaluates potential markets on the basis of three major criteria:[17]

- *Market potential for beer consumption.* Per capita beer consumption of the country is analysed. A low per capita consumption may indicate a high potential for market growth in most cases, if not all.
- *Competitive structure of the market.* Whether the market is dominated by a few large global players, or fragmented with numerous companies. Dominance by a few players makes the market harder to enter and obtain market share.
- *Legal and financial structure of the country.* Issues such as the inflation rate, convertibility of the local currency, repatriation of profits, legal barriers to entry or to operations of foreign direct investment are considered.

Anadolu Efes became familiar with all its potential markets through exporting before it attempted direct investments. Exporting was useful for acquiring market-specific knowledge through experience in the market.[18] Since transportation cost is a major part of total costs of exported beer, beer companies do not prefer exporting if significant market share is targeted. The profit margin on exported beer is low due to transportation costs, which are quite high, as in any product that is bulky, but cheap. Exporting may be feasible for the premium segment, however, which has a relatively high price and low sales volume in every market. Anadolu Efes currently exports its Efes Pilsener brand in the premium segment to over 35 countries.[19]

After deciding on the country to target, the company chooses the entry mode based on the country characteristics and the timing of the operation. In the countries that it has entered directly, Anadolu Efes has pursued a greenfield investment strategy, building an entirely new organization in a foreign country from scratch, or an acquisition strategy, buying the equity of a foreign company,[20] or a joint venture, creating a new company in which two or more investors share ownership and control.[21]

Anadolu Efes' first direct investment outside Turkey was attempted in Romania. When they analysed the Romanian market in 1996, it was very attractive with high growth potential and low competitive intensity. Per capita beer consumption was only 37 litres annually.[22] The Romanian government was also encouraging foreign direct investment in every way. The company chose to make a greenfield investment in Ploesti with the aim of producing a very high-quality beer with state of the art technology. However, company officials soon realized that they had not chosen the most suitable entry mode. When Anadolu Efes completed its investment in 1998, their international competitors had already dominated the market by acquiring local breweries with inferior qualities, upgrading them, and producing mediocre quality beer that was welcomed by the market. Anadolu Efes could not achieve the market share it had originally targeted. Operations in Romania could have been more profitable if the acquisition of a local brand had been preferred as the mode of entry in the first place. The Romanian beer market was the right choice as it has been growing at an average rate of 7.4 per cent between

1996 and 2001[23] since 1996, but Anadolu Efes was not able to sustain their first-mover advantage since the followers' strategies were superior. The strategic window, the limited period of time during which the 'fit' between key market requirements and the particular competencies of a firm competing in the market is optimal,[24] was closed before Anadolu Efes could act.

In 1999, Anadolu Efes restructured the company in Romania as a 50–50 per cent joint venture with Interbrew, a leading international brewery, to increase the speed of market entry. The current market share of the joint venture is 8 per cent[25] and it continues its operations successfully. The company learned from the Romania experience and was much more successful in choosing its entry mode in other markets.

In 1998, Anadolu Efes was one of the early entrants to the Russian market. The per capita consumption of beer was at a historically low level; at about 24 litres per capita,[26] and the European-based market research companies were pessimistic about the growth potential of the market. However, as Mr Güner[27] stated, the international marketing team of Anadolu Efes did not take the research results as given, and interpreted the low level of beer consumption differently – as an opportunity rather than a threat. Contrary to several global brewers, they believed that decreasing beer consumption of Russian market meant a potential of increasing consumption in the future. Russia was an ideal market for entry, with a high growth potential and low competitive consolidation. The competitive structure of the market was also favourable, and the Russian government was encouraging the inflow of foreign direct investments. Beer was legally considered almost as a soft drink and was not highly taxed like vodka or whisky, and advertising beer on TV and other media was allowed.

Anadolu Efes preferred a greenfield investment in Moscow, in partnership with the European Bank for Reconstruction and Development (EBRD) and the city government of Moscow so that they could produce the highest quality beer with state of the art technology in their own plant. Meanwhile, major international competitors were exporting premium brands to Russia and were planning acquisitions of local brands as their entry mode. Anadolu Efes could have been at a disadvantage if those multinational firms gained a quicker access to the market and were able to consolidate it before Anadolu Efes. However, as the construction of the beer-production facilities was continuing, the economic crisis in Russia started in 1998. Although most of its international competitors halted their activities and left the country, Anadolu Efes was able to use this crisis as an opportunity by continuing its activities as planned with a cash injection as paid-in capital at the day of the crisis. Production started in 1999.

The Kazakhstan experience was similar to the Russian experience in terms of the success gained, even though a totally different entry strategy was followed. Annual beer consumption in Kazakhstan was 5.2 litres per capita in 1996 when Anadolu Efes decided to enter the market. Per capita consumption grew by an average of 16 per cent per annum between 1996 and 2001,[28] and was still low at 13 litres per capita annually in 2002. FDI was supported by the local government and the level of competition was not too high. This time the mode of entry was acquiring and upgrading a local brewery in Karaganda. This way, Anadolu Efes benefited from a quick entry into the market on the one hand, and expanded its market share by improving the local brand on the other hand. In a short period, the local brand of Karagandinskoe increased its market share and became the leader of its segment. The total market share of Anadolu Efes across all segments in Kazakhstan had reached 20 per cent in 2002.[29]

In Ukraine, another fast-growing beer market, Anadolu Efes has a joint venture with Invesco Asset Management (51 and 49 per cent respectively), established in 2001. The market's average growth rate was 13 per cent between 1996 and 2001, and annual per capita beer consumption was 23 litres in 2001. Anadolu Efes improved the acquired Chernomor brand that had been in the market for 15 years with 1 per cent market share, to lift it up the quality ladder by elevating the brand to Anadolu Efes quality standards both in terms of quality and image.[30]

In 2002 Anadolu Efes decided to enter the Moldovan market, one of the fastest growing markets in Europe with favourable conditions of competition. Per capita beer consumption was as low as 9 litres as of 2001.[31] Again, Anadolu Efes chose acquisition as an entry mode since Moldova was a relatively small market; it was only feasible to acquire a local brewery with a large market share to benefit from economies of scale. Thus, Vitanta S.A. with a market share of 70 per cent was acquired through a tender offer.[32]

Local strategic planning of branding and positioning

Anadolu Efes' international product and branding history, another important critical success factor, can be described as risk-taking, proactive, innovative and clever at the same time. In all the markets that the company operates in directly, it chose to concentrate on producing local beer brands. Additionally, it exported Efes Pilsener beer brand to over 40 countries, and created and exported non-alcoholic beer brands to Muslim countries. It can be said that Anadolu Efes followed a local branding strategy along with a global branding strategy, paving the way to its international success. Anadolu Efes did not stick to only one brand, Efes Pilsener for its international expansion, but also acted through different local brands to appeal to the needs and nationalist feelings of its international consumers.

After the raising of the Iron Curtain, Russians for the first time encountered good-quality imported beer after years of drinking low-quality beer. They immediately formed a preference for imported beer. However, their acquaintance with good-quality imported beer did not last long as the 1998 economic crisis hit them hard and lifted the prices of imported goods to an unreachable level. Anadolu Efes made the right strategic move at this point and, unlike the rest of its competitors in the market, aimed right at those heartbroken Russians who were disappointed both by no longer being able to buy imported beer, and that also there was no good-quality Russian beer of their own, by creating local brand Stary Melnik and pricing it below the imported beer segment. Stary Melnik was created for the Russian people with a Russian soul to make them proud of the fact that they now had another symbol of Russia along with the Kremlin Palace.[33]

The branding process of Stary Melnik, meaning 'old miller' in English, was a carefully studied deliberate process, the result of dedicated market research. The research results indicated that this name would be associated with a specialty good such as a good quality wine, but certainly not with a regular beer. However, Cem Güner, the Chief Marketing Officer of Efes Beverage Group, and his team read between the lines of the research report to reinterpret it from their point of view, realizing that consumers attached high value to this name, and decided that 'Stary Melnik' was indeed a suitable name for their new beer brand. The brand identified its own place in the market as the local premium segment, and has defined the rules of the game for the rest of the players ever since, especially in pricing. It has maintained its position in this premium segment as the leader, with a 20 per cent market share as of 2001.[34] Soon, Stary Melnik became a regional beer brand, available in Kazakhstan and the Ukraine and exported to countries such as Israel and Greece where Russian people live in a minority.

Kazakhstan presented a similar story. There, Anadolu Efes even went a step further that constituted a revolution. Kazakh people were used to drinking their beer within days since the beer sold was non-pasteurized and did not last. Additionally, because of Kazakhstan's geography, it was not possible for a brewer to distribute the highly perishable non-pasteurized beer throughout the whole country. Seeing a niche in the market, Anadolu Efes identified a new category of beer and introduced for the first time as good-quality pasteurized local beer, Karagandinskoe, with a long shelf life, and distributed it throughout the country. Similar to the Ukrainian market, the company's strategy in Kazakhstan was to improve an acquired local brand and reposition it in the mid-priced segment. Karagandinskoe is now one of the widely recognized and preferred brands in Kazakhstan with a brand awareness of 71 per cent.[35]

In the Moldovan market, Anadolu Efes followed a different strategy and acquired the market-leader beer brands, Vitanta, Arc, Aurie, Camarad and Chisinau with 70 per cent market share. This strategy of acquiring brands rather than commodities for expansion into new markets has been commonly applied by marketers since the 1980s, since brands are valuable assets if they are managed well, and bring an unexpected but guaranteed stream of future income.[36]

Other than producing local brands in Russia, Kazakhstan, Ukraine, Romania and Moldova, Anadolu Efes also positioned the Efes Pilsener brand in these markets. This strategy can be called multiple branding,[37] which is the right strategy when intra-market heterogeneity makes it necessary to appeal to the same market with different brands. As newly-opened economies, Anadolu Efes' international markets promised different segmenting opportunities, and the company decided to position the Efes Pilsener brand in the licensed premium segment that has been recognized as rather novel and commanding an increasing proportion of sales.[38] Hence, by 2001, the Efes Pilsener brand achieved market-leader position with 29 per cent market share in the licensed premium segment of Russia. In 2002 Anadolu Efes also decided to introduce Germany's leading premium beer, Warsteiner Premium Verum, into the licensed premium segment in Russia. Additionally, the company is considering the possibility of entering into the economy segment in the Russian market.

Efes Pilsener brand is also exported to over 35 countries as a global premium beer brand. Positioning a brand in an unexplored new segment with growth opportunities increases its chances of becoming a global brand,[39] and hence, Anadolu Efes took advantage of positioning Efes Pilsener in all of its markets with cost-effective pricing. Finally, seeing the market potential for non-alcoholic beer in the Muslim countries, especially in Iraq, the United Arab Emirates and Saudi Arabia, Anadolu Efes decided to produce and export the non-alcoholic beer brands, Diamond and Festival, to these countries with the aim of becoming one of the top non-alcoholic beer exporters to Muslim countries over the following five years.[40]

Local strategic planning of communications

Another critical success factor of Anadolu Efes has been its creative communication strategy, both for its local brands and its global brand, Efes Pilsener. Anadolu Efes chose to apply a customized communications mix for its local brands, in line with the common thought that food and beverages could be particularly hard to sell globally since they are usually associated with years of tradition and entrenched preferences.[41] Stary Melnik gives the best example of how customization and creativity worked for Anadolu Efes' communication strategy. Stary Melnik was designed to suit the Russian soul, and was communicated to the public as a 'soulful beer' which had 100 per cent Russian identity. Rather than relying on the functional attributes of the beer such as its quality or price, the company followed an emotional appeal, stressing social values in its advertising message. The advertising themes and shootings were designed for the Russian market, using an international ad agency which had a Russian general manager in charge throughout the process. Thus, Anadolu Efes benefited from both international experience and systematic work, as well as the local understanding of the advertising agency. Typical advertising themes showed typical Russian people, in a respectful manner, praising them. For example, one of the most successful TV advertisements was a serial, appealing to the fatalist optimism of the

Russian.[42] Utilizing these symbolic values, Anadolu Efes tried to convey the implicit message that Stary Melnik is the beer of Russia, and that people who drink Stary Melnik belong to Russia. This is confirmed by the fact that Stary Melnik is now sold as 'the Russian beer' in countries where there are Russian communities.

Anadolu Efes used both conventional methods of communication through advertising on TV or billboards, as well as non-traditional ways of advertising using event or sports sponsorship, which is believed to be highly effective especially with young people.[43] With such activities, the brand meets its exact target audience. The parallel structure between these activities and the target audience of the brand helps to improve its positive perception.[44]

One year after the launch of the brand, Cem Güner and his team were concerned that the Stary Melnik brand might not be so appealing to young people. Accordingly, the Krylia Rock Festival was created at this point to celebrate the birthday of Stary Melnik. The festival, which turned out to be a huge success, is a 12-hour non-stop Russian rock-music marathon attended by nearly 60,000 people in Moscow. It is planned to have the festival every year. Additionally, Stary Melnik became the sponsor of the Russian national football team in the 2002 World Cup.

Anadolu Efes used a somewhat standardized global approach in communicating its Efes Pilsener brand, for which a more nationality-free advertising theme and shooting were chosen. The Turkish country of origin was avoided since Turkey does not enjoy a cultural heritage of beer; instead, an emotional appeal to physical relaxation was emphasized, and the same ad was used across Europe and Asia. Anadolu Efes was also successful in raising the profile of Efes Pilsener beer through events and sports sponsorships. The Efes Blues Festival and Efes Pilsen Basketball team have contributed significantly in this way, creating brand awareness in the international market. The Efes Festival has been taking place in Russia and Romania since 1999, and Efes Pilsen was also the main sponsor of the Turkish national football team, which along with Russia qualified to play the finals of the 2002 World Cup.

Another interesting success for Anadolu Efes has been in taking into consideration the religious beliefs of various publics in different countries, and to approach them with care. Religious beliefs present permanent barriers to certain products, one of which is alcoholic drinks. Even though there is the belief that different consumption patterns between countries might diminish in time, there are permanent factors that companies can do nothing against, and which are unlikely to disappear.[45] Seeing this, Anadolu Efes obtained both a certificate from the Turkish Grand Rabbinate, proving its beer production was according to the specifications of the Jewish religion, and also a certificate proving that its non-alcoholic beer did not contain any alcoholic content. The former was presented to Jewish consumers in the USA, and the latter to Muslim consumers in Muslim countries.[46] Anadolu Efes, by doing so, created confidence in its brands.

Setting alternative distribution channels

Since it is costly to set up new distribution systems from scratch, the company has used existing local distribution networks as have most of its global competitors. Indirect distribution, through wholesalers and retailers, was the dominant form. In Russia, the local existing network was highly complex and almost impossible to control, but despite this Anadolu Efes adapted to the existing network rather than opposing it. However, unlike its competitors, the company also started to set up its own direct distribution networks in certain markets such as Moscow, Odessa and Karaganda to establish direct linkages with retailers. These direct distribution networks serve as a control and disciplining mechanism for the local networks. Salespeople of the direct network frequently make customer calls and quote prices so that the local distributors cannot manipulate prices for their own benefit. Also, the direct network helps in gaining new customers by making customer calls to places where Anadolu Efes brands are not sold. The direct distribution network is believed to bring advantages to the company in the long run.

The Anadolu Efes beer brands are sold through all the possible retail channels that sell fast-moving consumer goods to achieve maximum penetration. For example, in the Russian market Anadolu Efes made use of both traditional and modern retail forms. These channels included both corner grocer-like shops that were transferred from the Communist era, and also the modern retail forms, the hypermarkets.[47]

Decentralized organization and cultural and historical heritage

Anadolu Efes' organizational and cultural dedication to its international markets has helped with its international success. The company did not follow a globally oriented structure, with centralization and global or regional coordination,[48] rather it acted as a local company in each of its markets. Additionally, the human resources policy of hiring local people for upper-level positions, and a preference to work with local people in outsourcing helped the company. It continuously learned from its experiences and retained its dynamic nature. In Cem Güner's words, they fell in love not only with their product, but also with their international market. Anadolu Efes felt and acted like a Russian company in the Russian market, or a Ukrainian company in the Ukrainian market. This strategy helped the company to not be seen as 'foreign', but as tailored for the local consumer.

Turkey is a country that has been experiencing all the obstacles and challenges that an emerging market can face in economical and political terms. It has survived many economical ups and downs, political turmoil and coups in the last few decades. Doing business successfully in such a volatile and risky environment, Anadolu Efes has gained a lot of knowledge and experience. This tacit knowledge is often highly personal, taken for granted, and therefore not easily articulated.[49] As Drucker[50] puts it, in these new economies this kind of knowledge becomes superior to labour, and capital – the classical factors of production. What has differentiated Anadolu Efes from its multinational competitors in these emerging markets has been this tacit knowledge. Although competitors may have been equal or better than Anadolu Efes in terms of the classical factors of production, its accumulated experience provided the company with a sustainable competitive advantage.

The cultural and historical relationships between the Ottoman Empire, the ancestor of Turkey, and the international markets of Anadolu Efes, has also helped the company's success. The Ottoman Empire ruled or had cross-border relationships with Romania, Moldova, Ukraine and Russia for centuries, and the Turkish people had become familiar with the social dynamics and ways of doing business of those countries. This was something other multinationals could not achieve; failing to recognise the ways in which the locals think, feel and act differently from Westerners.

Conclusion

Anadolu Efes, which only started international operations in 1996, has already achieved global success with its Efes Pilsener brand, and regional success with its local brands. The company is currently the tenth largest European and the 35th largest brewery worldwide.[51] It has been operating in parallel to most of the rules and trends in the global beer industry, for example in making use of acquisitions and strategic alliances to achieve strategic advantage in its international markets. However, there were times it acted against the general wisdom of the business, and a part of its success can be attributed to this 'I will do it my way' marketing strategy. In its international markets, the company acted more or less globally for its Efes Pilsener brand, but adapted its operations for local brands. In each new market Anadolu Efes invested directly, keeping to its entrepreneurial soul, and acting as if it was entering the beer business for the first time. Carefully noting the sentiments and psyche of the newly opened countries, it appealed to them as a local company that could produce quality-consistent beer like the multinationals. Originating from an emerging market, carrying the historical and cultural heritage of Turkey helped Anadolu Efes to this end. It adapted to local conditions, using local employees, local advertising themes, local media and local distribution channels. Anadolu Efes was not imported, but was in each case designed for just that country.

Notes

1 There are more than 20,000 brands of beer, http://www.didyouknow.cd/beer.htm (retrieved 15 November 2002); Beer Types and Servings Suggestions, http://www.nbwa.org/advocates/types.html (retrieved 15 November 2002).
2 M.E. Porter, *Competitive Strategy* (New York: The Free Press, 1980).

3. D. Vrontis, 'Strategic Assessment: The Importance of Branding in the European Beer Market', *British Food Journal*, 100, 2 (1998): 76–84.
4. *Ibid.*
5. S.C. Craig and S. Douglas, 'Building Global Brands in the 21st Century', *Japan and the World Economy*, 12 (2000): 273–83.
6. Deutsche Bank, *Global Brewing Report* (2001).
7. Canadean, Global Beverage Research Company, http://www.canadean.com (retrieved 15 November 2003).
8. Deutsche Bank, *Global Brewing Report* (2001).
9. Thirsting for Markets, http://www.ias.org.uk/theglbe/97issue2/alcin90s.htm (retrieved 15 November 2003).
10. D. Vrontis, 'Strategic Assessment: The Importance of Branding in the European Beer Market', *op. cit.*
11. B. Major, 'Factors Affecting Malt and Barley Selection in the Chinese Beer Market', *Proceedings of the 10th Australian Barley Technical Symposium* (2001).
12. Efes Beverage Group, *Annual Report* (2002), http://www.efespilsen.com.tr/ic.asp?target=h-faaliyet.asp
13. E. Fırat, 'DönüşenŞirketler', *Capital Aylık Ekonomi Dergisi*, April (2003): 142–6.
14. Efes Beverage Group, www.efes.bev.com (retrieved 1 May 2003).
15. İçki Sanayi Özel İhtisas Komisyon Raporu, 8. BeşYıllık Kalkınma Planı, http://ekutup.dpt.gov.tr/imalatsa/oik.543.pdf (2002) (retrieved 5 April 2003).
16. Efes Beverage Group, www.efes.bev.com (retrieved 1 May 2003).
17. Interview with Cem Güner, Chief Marketing Officer: Efes Beverage Group (4 April 2003).
18. J. Johanson and J.E. Vahlne, 'The Internationalization Theory of the Firm – A Model of Knowledge Development and Increasing Foreign Market Commitment', *Journal of International Business Studies*, 8, 1 (1977): 23–32.
19. Efes Beverage Group, *Annual Report* (2002), *op. cit.*
20. H.G. Barkema and F. Vermeulen, 'International Expansion through Start-Up or Acquisition: A Learning Perspective, *International Mergers and Acquisitions* (London: Thomson, 2002): 134–60.
21. S. Hollensen, 'Development of a Firm's International Competitiveness', in *Global Marketing A Market-Responsive Approach*, 2nd edn (Harlow: Pearson, 2001): 75–101.
22. Deutsche Bank, *Global Brewing Report* (2001).
23. Efes Beverage Group, *Annual Report* (2001), *op. cit.*
24. D.F. Abell, 'Strategic Windows', *Journal of Marketing*, 42 (1978): 21–8.
25. Efes Beverage Group, *Annual Report* (2001), *op. cit.*
26. Deutsche Bank, *Global Brewing Report* (2001).
27. Interview with C. Güner.
28. Efes Beverage Group, *Annual Report* (2001), *op. cit.*
29. *Ibid.* (2002).
30. *Ibid.* (2001).
31. Efes Beverage Group, www.efes.bev.com (retrieved 1 May 2003).
32. Efes Beverage Group, *Annual Report* (2002), *op. cit.*
33. Interview with C. Güner.
34. Efes Beverage Group, *Annual Report* (2001), *op. cit.*
35. *Ibid.*
36. J.N. Kapferer, *Strategic Brand Management*, 2nd edn (London: Kogan Page, 1997): 21–38.
37. S. Onkvisit and J.J. Shaw, 'The International Dimension of Branding: Strategic Considerations and Decisions', *International Marketing Review*, 6, 3 (1989): 22–34.

38 D. Vrontis, 'Strategic Assessment: The Importance of Branding in the European Beer Market'; Canadian, Global Beverage Research Company.
39 J.N. Kapferer, *Strategic Brand Management, op. cit.*
40 'Efes Pilsen Suudilere Alkolsüz BirayıSevdirdi', Retailing Institute Network, http://www.retailing-institute.com/network/RINetwork(27.01.2003).htm (retrieved 1 May 2003).
41 K.L. Keller, *Strategic Brand Management: Building, Measuring, and Managing Brand Equity* (New Jersey: Pearson, 2003).
42 Interview with C. Güner.
43 K.L., Keller, *Strategic Brand Management: Building, Measuring, and Managing Brand Equity, op. cit.*
44 'Sürekli Yatırım' (Continuous Investment), *Marka 03 (Brand 03) Capital*, May (2003): 98–104.
45 D.M. Sandler and D. Shani, 'Brand Globally but Advertise Locally?: An Empirical Investigation', *International Marketing Review*, 9, 4 (1992): 18–29; L. de Chernatony, C. Halliburton and R. Bernath, 'International Branding: Demand- or Supply-Driven Opportunity', *International Marketing Review*, 12, 2 (1995): 9–19.
46 'Efes Pilsen Suudilere Alkolsüz Birayı Sevdirdi', Retailing Institute Network, http://www.retailing-institute.com/network/RINetwork(27.01.2003).htm (retrieved 1 May 2003).
47 Interview with C. Güner.
48 S.C. Craig and S. Douglas, 'Building Global Brands in the 21st Century', *Japan and the World Economy*, 12 (2000): 273–83.
49 I. Nonaka, 'The Knowledge-Creating Company', *Harvard Business Review*, 69, 6 (1991): 96–105.
50 P. Drucker, 'The New Society of Organizations', *Harvard Business Review* (1992): 95–105.
51 *World Beer Report*, Plato Logic Ltd (October 2002).

Interviews were conducted with Cem Güner, Chief Marketing Officer, Kemal Gürsel, Trade and Export Director of Efes Brewery Group, and Hüseyin Öztürk, Planning Manager of Anadolu Efes, Turkey Bee Group.

15
Ashanti: Saving an African Mining Giant

Mohamed H. Warsame and Franklyn Manu

Introduction

Ashanti Goldfields Company Ltd (Ashanti) was initiated in 1890 by two Ghanaians, Joseph E. Ellis and Chief Joseph E. Biney, together with their accountant, Joseph Brown. The three acquired a 100 square mile mining concession from the then Adansi Kingdom located within the borders of the current Republic of Ghana. Since then over 25 million ounces of gold have been mined from the area and the company has become a major African multinational and a key player in the world gold mining industry.[1]

The road for Ashanti has not always been smooth. Its fortunes in the 1970s and early 1980s mirrored the economic decline of Ghana. In the late 1990s problems with its financial exposure due to transactions with derivatives led to the virtual collapse of the company. Ashanti, however, survived and remains in the top-ten of gold mining companies in the world.

This case study examines Ashanti's operations over the years and identifies factors that have made it a successful African multinational.

Ashanti's background[2]

In 1895, British adventurer Edwin Cade obtained a 99-year lease on 100 square miles of mineral-bearing land from Ellis and Biney with the help of the colonial government that developed rail tracks from the coast to Obuasi in the Adansi Kingdom. The area around Obuasi was already being mined by small-scale local miners. On 11 June 1897, Ashanti Goldfields Corporation was established and listed on the London Stock Exchange with a nominal capital of £250,000 in shares of £1 each. Over the years the company declined as a result of a lack of investment.

In 1966, the first military government in Ghana, the National Liberation Council, started seeking new investors in Ghana's gold industry and Lonrho (London and Rhodesia Mining and Land Company) acquired the company for £3 million in 1968. In return for granting an extension of 50 years on the land leases, the Ghanaian government received a 20 per cent stake with an option to purchase 20 per cent more at a fixed price of £1. After a 1972 military coup that toppled the elected government of Dr K.A. Busia, the new military government (National Redemption Council) acquired, by decree, 55 per cent of all mining companies in Ghana after which Ashanti mirrored Ghana's steady decline in the decade that followed. Production fell from 533,000 ounces in 1972 to 232,000 ounces by the end of the decade.

After Flight Lieutenant Jerry Rawlings' military regime assumed power in 1982, the process of reviving Ashanti began as part of an Economic Recovery Programme adopted under the guidance of the IMF and World Bank. Ghana pioneered the investor-friendly mining legislation subsequently adopted elsewhere in Africa, leading to the revival of Ashanti and the gold-mining industry generally in Ghana. In 1985 a loan of £159 million was granted by the International Finance Corporation, a unit of the World Bank, and other financial institutions, to finance a five-year plan to modernize operations.

Ashanti was floated on 14 March 1994, when the government sold 30 per cent of its 55 per cent stake for $454 million (about 17.9 million shares) and listed the company locally and on the London Stock Exchange. This left Lonrho, and later its successor Lonmin, with 45 per cent of the company. Even with its lower shareholding, the Ghanaian government kept a 'blocking golden share'. These events allowed Ashanti to emerge from Ghana's grim 1970s to become a continental mining giant. It became the first African company outside South Africa to be listed on the New York Stock Exchange in February 1996, and the company was also listed on the Toronto Stock Exchange, the Australian Stock Exchange and the Zimbabwe Stock Exchange. The company is the dominant force on the Accra Stock Exchange with 64 per cent of market capitalization of the stock exchange in Ghana in 1999.

In the mid-1990s Ashanti started an acquisition programme, which saw the company acquiring gold mining companies all over Africa. This was driven by the belief that acquisitions were more advantageous than exploration because of the latter's greater risk and long gestation period. Ashanti acquired a 49 per cent interest in Midras Mining Limited in 1994, and on 20 March 1996 it acquired the entire 100 per cent share capital of Cluff Resources Plc for a cash consideration of US$156,400,000. This gave Ashanti Zimbabwe's Freda-Rebecca mine and other potentially lucrative sites in other parts of Zimbabwe. These acquisitions led to the issue of a total of 20,152,964 shares diluting the holding of the Government of Ghana from 22.3 per cent to 18.6 per cent. On 3 January 1996, Ashanti acquired the Ghana Libyan Arab Mining Company Limited, a Ghanaian incorporated company that held the Bibiani gold mining concession in the southwestern part of Ghana.

In June 1996, Ashanti acquired International Gold Resources (IGR) for US$125,700,000; on 21 October 1996, Ashanti merged with Golden Shamrock Mines Limited; and in November 1998 Ashanti completed the acquisition of SAMAX Gold, Inc., a Canadian Corporation engaged in gold production and mining in Africa, for a total cost of US$140 million. This acquisition spree started worrying investors who were concerned about the managerial ability of Ashanti to wield such a diverse group into a profitable mining conglomerate. This led to a decline in Ashanti's share price and also placed a substantial burden on the company's balance sheet thus sowing the seeds of a crisis in the future.

Ashanti operations

Table 15.1 shows a summary of the acquisitions and resulting operations of the company. As a result of these activities the company's gold production steadily increased from 1.03 million in 1996 to 1.74 million ounces, even with the changes in the price of gold.[3] The company was still heavily dependent on the century-old Obuasi mine, although the curtailment of open-pit mining at Obuasi together with the tailing treatment that ended in

Table 15.1 Highlights of Ashanti mines and operations

Year	Acquired company or property	Headquarters	Value of deal (US $ millions)	Notes
1996	Cluff Resources	Australia	$156	100% of Freda-Rebecca mine in Zimbabwe
1996	Ghana Libyan Arab Mining Company and International Gold Resources	Libya and Australia	$125.7	100% of Bibiani mine in Ghana
1996 & 1998	Golden Shamrock Mines Ltd (Ghana Australian Goldfields Ltd)	Australia	$235.8	Merger; 80% of Iduapriem mine in Ghana and 85% of Siguiri mine in Guinea
1998	SAMAX Gold, Inc.	Canada	$140	100%. Prestea, Ghana mine and properties in Congo Brazzaville and Tanzania
2000	Geita Mine	Tanzania	$205	Sale of 50% of the mine to Anglogold of South Africa. Originally acquired properties from Tan Range Exploration Corp. of Canada and Resolute Ltd of Australia
2000	Pioneer Goldfields Ltd	USA	$18.8	90% of Teberebie mine in Ghana
2000	Birim Goldfields, Inc.	Canada	$1.5 plus future royalties	100% of Dunkwa mine in Ghana

Source: Ashanti, *Annual Reports*.

2002 led to Ashanti taking a $171.1 million extraordinary charge in fixed assets write-down.

Other operations are as follows:

- The Bibiani mine, which Ashanti wholly owns, is located in the western region of Ghana. It recommenced operations in the first quarter of 1998 and produces about 250,000 ounces per year.
- Ashanti has an 80 per cent interest in the Iduapriem gold mine, owned by Ghanaian-Australian Goldfields Limited (GAG), also in the western region of Ghana. In June 2000, Ashanti acquired a 90 per cent interest in the Teberebie gold mine, which is adjacent to Iduapriem. The mines currently produce close to 200,000 ounces per year.
- The Siguiri mine, located in the north-eastern part of Guinea, commenced operations in the first quarter of 1998 and produces over 260,000 ounces a year. Ashanti has an 85 per cent interest in the Siguiri mine.
- The Geita mine in Tanzania was commissioned in June 2000. Ashanti's share of Geita's production is about 290,000 ounces a year.
- The Freda-Rebecca gold mine in Zimbabwe, wholly owned by Ashanti, began operations in 1988 and produces 100,000 ounces a year.

Total reserves stood at 27.8 million ounces as of 31 December 2002. Ashanti's return on assets and return on equity over the years has generally been better than the industry average.[4] Table 15.2 shows the company's 5-year financial summary.

Table 15.2 Five-year profit and loss summary ($millions)

	2002	2001	2000	1999	1998
Turnover	552.2	554.4	582.2	582.1	600.3
Total costs before exceptional items	(466.5)	(457.6)	(493.1)	(485.8)	(500.8)
Operating profit before exceptional items	81.1	76.6	89.1	96.3	99.5
Profit before taxation and exceptional items	75.2	67.4	37.8	66.4	76.3
Exceptional items	(23.5)	0	(168.6)	(250)	(33.2)
Taxation	3.7	(9.6)	(8.8)	(2.7)	0
Profit/(loss) after taxation and exceptional items	55.4	57.8	(139.6)	(186.3)	43.1
Profit attributable to shareholders	56.2	59.9	(141.1)	(183.9)	40.7
Dividend	0	0	0	0	(10.9)
Retained profit/(loss) for the year	56.2	59.9	(141.1)	(183.9)	29.8
Earnings per share before exceptional items	0.67	0.53	0.27	0.59	0.68

Source: Ashanti, *Annual Report* (2002).

The crisis and its effects

To gold mining companies like Ashanti, a major risk factor is the impact of the price of gold on unhedged future cash flows, investment opportunities and asset values such as for mines and other specialized plants and equipment. The need for gold mining companies to hedge their risk exposure is mainly due to the fact that gold is a non-differentiable product leading to a highly competitive commodity market in which each firm is a price-taker. Therefore a firm has a choice between changing its mining strategy due to price fluctuations by mining only lower-cost ore, reducing output at higher-cost mines or even closing them each time the price of gold drops, or hedging the risk using derivatives, thereby reducing the need for production changes and their accompanying financial and social costs.

Hedging programmes are thus undertaken by commodity producers to smooth their revenues by locking in prices for future sales. Gold-producing companies utilize a variety of derivative instruments such as forwards and options contracts to protect themselves against declines in the price of gold, but also lock themselves out of gaining from any increase in the price of gold. Some of these derivative contracts require the deposit of margins whenever a derivative contract moves to the disfavour of the mining company to minimize the risk to derivative counter-parties that the company may be unable to deliver the gold.

Forward contracts involve selling a given quantity of gold for a delivery in a given future date but at a price determined in the contract. Options involve the right to buy or sell a given quantity of gold in a specified maturity period for a price determined in the contract. Other hedging techniques used by the gold-producing companies include gold loans known as spot deferred contracts. The companies take a gold loan usually from central banks, selling it in anticipation of returning the gold from their own production or even buying it from the market at a lower price. This is similar to a cash loan plus a short position in the forward gold market.

The derivatives problems of Ashanti started right after Kwame Peprah, Ghana's Finance Minister and Chairman of the Board of Directors of the company, had noted proudly at the World Bank meeting in Washington DC on 29 September 1999 that 'Ashanti shows that even if a country is not rated AAA or AA, its commodity producers can still hedge successfully.'[5] At about the same time, European central banks announced a five-year moratorium on sales of gold in their reserves sending the price of gold spirally upwards. In just four days the gold price rose by more than $75 per ounce, indicating that European central banks' sales had indeed depressed the gold market. This was especially a relief to the gold market from the decision announced by the UK treasury in May 1999 to sell 415 tons of gold from their reserves.

In a few months, Kwame Peprah resigned as Board Chairman citing pressures of the country's budget implementation process. The board also scheduled the departure of the Chief Financial Officer, Mark Keatley. The crises led to a series of shareholders lawsuits in Accra and New York. In early 2000, a New York-based law firm, Milberg Weiss Bershad Hynes & Lerach LLP, filed a class-action lawsuit charging Ashanti with violations of US securities laws. The complaint alleged that Ashanti issued a series of false and misleading statements about the company's derivatives strategy that misrepresented and concealed the hedge-book risks and its exposure to gold-price volatility. At the same time in Accra, Adryx Mining and Metal, an investment group, initiated court proceedings against the company in Ghana's high court requesting the court to order an extraordinary general meeting at which the shareholders could replace the board of directors. The dissident shareholders succeeded in obtaining a high-court order in Accra, Ghana, with a ruling that Ashanti should convene an extraordinary general meeting within 21 days to elect a new board of directors. This decision was opposed by Ashanti, with Kwame Tetteh, the company's lawyer, informing the court that 'the consequences of this decision are very drastic and might destroy the company.'[6] Michael Martinear of Adryx leading the dissenting shareholders was also quoted as saying, 'Clearly Mr. Keatley [Chief Financial Officer] must go...we have no argument with [Chief Executive Samuel] Jonah.'[7] At the same time the company was under investigation by Ghana's Serious Fraud Office in relation to its flagship Obuasi mine.

Hedging had been a crucial part of Ashanti's expansion programme, with 7.2 million ounces of gold hedged at $390 per ounce in early 1999, which represented about 60 per cent of the next five years' production. The company estimated that it had gained more than $650 million from its hedging activities since the mid-1990s. With some of these funds it was able to finance losses from three of its six mines totalling more than $70 million in 1998. Confidence in gold had been steadily declining since 1995, which resulted in short-selling by speculators, mining companies and central banks. This is the environment which led Ashanti to craft a hedging strategy against the declining price of gold.

The company aggressively protected itself against future adverse prices, and around half the company's reserves of 23 million ounces were locked into future sales. Margin limits requiring Ashanti to make cash deposits in the event of sharp adverse price fluctuations were built into the contracts to reassure the counter-parties. The sudden gold price rise increased the value of Ashanti's gold reserves in the long term, but it transformed the company's hedge book from a positive $250 million at the end of June 1999 to a negative $570 million in early October 1999, giving counter-party banks the right to call for margin deposits of $270 million, thereby leading the company into a liquidity squeeze.

In fact at the time, Ashanti had reserves of 23 million ounces in total, while its hedge book had a net 11 million ounces hedged, a disproportionately large proportion of its total reserves. The total previous year gold production stood at only 1.55 million ounces. In short, the firm had hedged more gold than it could produce during the duration of its hedge transaction. In theory, if the counter-parties to the hedge transaction stopped calling for margin deposits, Ashanti could eventually be able to meet the required quantities from its production. But the derivative contracts required Ashanti to deposit margins whenever the price of gold spiked upwards and the company was already extended in its acquisition and expansion programmes and did not have either the reserves or the borrowing capacity to meet the margins required in the derivative agreements.

Ashanti's market value was heavily hit by this liquidity crisis, sending its share price tumbling down from a high of $10.12 in September 1999 to a low of $2.44 in December 1999 as it became apparent the company could not meet the margin calls of the counter-parties. Ashanti's major counter-parties included Goldman Sachs Group ($105 million), Société Générale ($82 million), Crédit Suisse First Boston ($62 million), UBS ($61 million), AIG ($32 million) and Chase Manhattan Bank ($25 million).

Ashanti's hedging strategy came under heavy criticism especially in Ghana with one article stating that

> Ashanti's hedging strategy was not designed on managing risk. It had crossed the fine line between using derivatives as a risk management tool to using it speculatively. Prior hedging activity had provided positive returns to the firm, and it begun to see these as an alternative source of its profits. Ashanti was taking positions in the gold derivatives markets, which were much larger than actual production for the periods that these positions were open.[8]

Once the depth of the problems became apparent to the market, Samuel Jonah, Ashanti's Chief Executive, accepted that there had been some degree of speculation.

Ashanti margin limits on derivative contracts were set far lower than those for most of its peers. The Chief Financial Officer, Keatley, explained that

> the total of our margin limits with counter parties who are currently active is approximately $280 million. We know that other producers who are a similar size to ourselves or slightly bigger have margin limits which are many times higher than that, or, in some cases, have no limits at all.[9]

He went on to note that, 'our operations are entirely in Africa. Producers of a similar size and quality to us with operations in Australia or Canada are not subject to margin limits either at all or of such tightness.'[10]

Keatley disputed that Ashanti's actions were misguided:

> the total amount of hedges we have in terms of the delta – that is, the equivalent number of forward sales – is ten million ounces. For a producer with about 24 million ounces in reserves, it is not an unusually high number. And the majority of those contracts on a delta-equivalent basis are in the form of forward sales. About two-thirds are in the form of forward sales, and about one-third in the form of option contracts. So that would not generally be regarded as a risky hedging strategy.[11]

The predicament arose not from the hedge book, argued Keatley, but from other contributing factors:

> the problem was the strictness of the margin limits arising from perceptions of political risk, combined with the occurrence of an extremely unlikely event, at a time when our corporate liquidity was low. The advice we've had from independent consultants is that our systems were accurate to a high degree. Our policies were sound. The combination of the above events caused the problem. Therefore we had to find a new arrangement with our counter parties, which we have done through the issue of warrants.[12]

The sudden liquidity problems at the company sent shockwaves through Ghana, with then President Jerry Rawlings affirming the emotional symbolism of the company to Ghanaians. There were even allegations of corruption and selling-out to foreign interests made in the popular press. Once the full extent of the problems at Ashanti became public, Lonmin Plc launched a conditional bid for the company, offering 32 new Lonmin shares for every 43 Ashanti shares not owned by Lonmin. This valued Ashanti at $800 million, at a value per share of $7, equivalent to a 86 per cent premium on its closing market price. But just a few days later Lonmin Plc lowered the ratio of share exchanges, valuing the company at only $600 million. Other terms of the possible merger agreement included the irrevocable commitment of the Ghanaian government to support the merger, and the written consent of the Minister of Mines in Ghana to the merger. Lonmin Plc also required unanimous agreement of Ashanti's hedge counter-parties to a standstill covering outstanding obligations, the support of the lenders under the revolving credit facility, and appropriate shareholder approvals.

Survival strategies

Once the problems of Ashanti became known, the company started negotiating with its counter-party banks. The main objective of the company was to persuade the 15 hedge-party banks not to exercise their right to make margin calls. A temporary standstill arrangement was initiated to give the parties time to arrive at an agreement, which was finally reached on 1 November 1999, exempting the company from any requirement to post margin on any of its hedge contracts for the next three years, to 31 December 2002. During 2003, Ashanti's margin limits would be twice the existing levels, and in the following year margin limits would be one and half times existing limits.

The counter-parties required that Ashanti prepare a financial and operating plan by 2 December 1999 proving that the company had, and would continue to have, adequate financial resources for the conduct of its business. The counter-parties were also issued with unlisted warrants to subscribe for mandatory exchangeable notes that would convert into Ashanti ordinary shares at a subscription price of $4.75. If the warrants were to be exercised in full they would convert into about 19.8 million Ashanti ordinary shares (representing 15 per cent of Ashanti's share capital). Keatley had no doubts about the benefits that the agreement would bring to Ashanti: 'We think this [agreement with the counter-parties] lifts a major cloud which has been over our heads, and enables us to move forward with our project development agenda with renewed confidence.'

In order to strengthen its balance sheet and reduce debt, Ashanti sold half of the Geita mine in Tanzania for US$205 million to Anglogold, resulting in a gain of US$51.2 million. Ashanti used the proceeds to retire a bridge loan that was used to complete Geita's construction and pay down two tranches of a revolving credit. In addition to paying Ashanti $205 million in cash for a 50 per cent share of the Geita project in northern Tanzania, Anglogold provided project financing for a total of $130 million.

The company restructured 80 per cent of its hedge book to remove the sensitivity of the hedge value to further rallies in the gold price. The restructuring included converting a large part of the company's forward sale positions into synthetic put options, and the company also negotiated cancellation of the rights of hedge counter-parties to call for margins, thereby ensuring margin-free trading on its hedge book.

Thus, Ashanti survived by reaching agreements with its debtors and restructuring its financial position; it could face the future with an emphasis on operational concerns. As David Mallalieu, an analyst, put it: 'They've been doing a tremendous job with regard to operations... The Obuasi mine is generating net free cash flow, as are all their other deposits, even the Freda-Rebecca mine in Zimbabwe, which is quite a challenge.'[13]

Drivers of success

The global gold industry (Table 15.3 shows the current major players) has exhibited a number of characteristics in the past two decades, a few of which are noted here:[14]

Table 15.3 Major players in the world gold mining industry

Company	Headquarters	Annual production (million ounces, 2002)	Market capitalization (000s) (US$' 000)
Newmont Mining	USA	7.63	14,166,236
Barrick Gold	Canada	5.70	10,076,400
Anglogold	UK	5.90	8,231,911
Goldfields	South Africa	4.21	6,513,012
Placer Dome	Canada	2.82	5,402,495
Compañía De Minas Buenas	Peru	0.26	2,649,939
Goldcorp	Canada	0.61	2,501,298
Harmony Gold Mining	South Africa	2.67 (year end 30 June 2002)	2,500,272
Kinross Gold	Canada	0.89	2,300,230
Glamis Gold	USA	0.25	1,655,928
Lihir Gold	UK	0.61	1,490,314
Ashanti	Ghana	1.62	1,317,159
Meridian Gold	USA	0.44	1,169,025
Agnico-Eagle Mines	Canada	0.26	1,021,098
Lamgold	Canada	0.44	855,291
Wheaton River Minerals	Canada	0.11	819,233
Bema Gold	Canada	0.12	812,140
Randgold Resources	UK	0.42	631,927
Eldorado Gold	Canada	0.10	545,078

Sources: *Annual Reports*; Quicken Brokerage, www.quicken.com (retrieved 29 September 2003).

- Consistently falling prices since the highs of $800–1,000 per ounce in 1980 to about $250 in 1999 and about $325 presently (2003).
- Stagnation over the last five to ten years evidenced by supply increasing by only 1.5 per cent annually since 1991.
- Declining demand since 1997.
- A trend towards industry consolidation.
- The past two decades could justify a question as to whether the laws of supply and demand are truly operative or even valid. The price of gold has experienced two states during this period of time: decline and stagnation, and the former seems to occur with more frequency than the latter. Despite price conditions, gold production has more than doubled in the past two decades.

How has Ashanti, a company from a small developing country such as Ghana, been able to succeed and be ranked among the top companies in the industry? A number of factors stand out when one examines the company's history and operations.

Operations in different African countries have been managed, to a large extent, by local managers with an understanding of the technical, political and economic environments of their countries. These managers and the leadership of Ashanti, with excellent connections in different African countries and familiarity with their environments, have not fallen prey to the prejudiced perception of Western gold mining companies that bailed out of Africa for the most part. It is quite informative to look at the number of mines given up by Western companies but which are being run profitably by Ashanti. One of the keys to this success has been Ashanti's strong local training programmes that have included not only technical matters, but have also included rotation of managers through various operations in Africa. This high degree of local responsiveness has enabled Ashanti to weather the so-called risks of operating in Africa that have caused some Western companies to pull out.

The company has also emphasized efficiency in its operations. Since gold mining companies are price-takers, one of the major keys to successful operation is to reduce the costs of operating mines. This is done by reducing exploration and mining costs. Ashanti's exploration costs of $4.4 per reserve ounce and $3.3 per resource ounce is one of the lowest in the industry. Cash operating costs have also been reduced from about $250 per ounce in 1997 to $199 currently. These are a reflection of the quality of the technical capabilities of the managers as they explore new areas and manage existing operations.

Notes

1 Ashanti Goldfields Company Limited website, www.ashantigoldfields.com
2 This section summarizes material on the history of the company at www.ashantigold.com
3 Ashanti *Annual Report* (2002).
4 Quicken Brokerage, www.quicken.com (retrieved 6 June 2003).
5 'Bugs', *Economist* (US), 353, (November 1999): 74.
6 J. Kibazo and A. O'Connor, 'Ashanti Court Ruling Thwarts Refinancing Plan', *Financial Times* (10 February 2000).
7 *Ibid.*
8 R. Taylor, 'Ashanti: A Hedge Too Far', www.ghanaweb.com (retrieved 23 February 2002).
9 J. Brewis, 'Did Ashanti Break the Golden Rule?' *Corporate Finance*, 181 (December 1999).
10 *Ibid.*
11 *Ibid.*
12 *Ibid.*
13 The *Wall Street Transcript* (27 May 2002).
14 *The Intangible Asset Report* (23 January 2003).

16

From Obligation to Opportunity: A Case Study of Tasty Bite®

Ashok Vasudevan, Meera Vasudevan and Kartik Kilachand

Background

On 28 February 1990, India's Finance Minister Manmohan Singh announced to a packed parliament a series of measures liberalizing the Indian economy including opening the doors more widely to foreign investment. The country had just gone through its worst foreign exchange crisis in its history and was on the verge of defaulting on its international debt obligations. Broadcast live on national TV, a roomful of Pepsi executives watching the programme in New Delhi burst into cheers. Hundreds of companies and governments across the world applauded the move. After decades of economic ambling, India was shifting gear and looking to increased foreign direct investment (FDI) to become the new engine for economic recovery and sustained growth.

Pepsi had a special reason to celebrate; it had just received approval from the Indian government for establishing its operations in India. The industrial licence did have several strings attached though. The most important one was to generate at least 50 per cent of Pepsi's India revenues through exports. Spearheading this effort was Ashok Vasudevan, Vice-President of Exports who had joined the company after nearly a decade at Unilever. Over the next few years, Pepsi would export nearly 50 different types of products out of India (mostly profitably), and would generate nearly two-thirds of the company's revenues. One of the several projects that Pepsi India examined as part of its export operations was Tasty Bite, a range of ready-to-eat Indian foods (entrees) that were packed in a retort pouch and remained shelf-stable for up to 18 months without needing refrigeration.

The original founders of Tasty Bite Eatables Limited (TBEL) had set up manufacturing in the heart of the vegetable-growing belt near Pune in Maharashtra, India, to manufacture a range of food and vegetable products. They had done an Initial Public Offering (IPO) in the Bombay Stock Exchange before the company had even generated a rupee of revenue. Within a year of starting, however, the founders of TBEL realized that the Indian consumer was not yet ready for packaged foods, compounded by the fact that the retail price point was also very high. They needed significant management help and more capital to survive. The company had put up a state-of-the-art food manufacturing facility but lacked management depth to create a sustainable business. They had fallen into the familiar trap that most business start-ups run into, particularly in controlled economies: they had overbuilt the manufacturing facility, underestimated the cost of going to market, and overleveraged a start-up operation (4:1 debt/equity ratio) – once again, a classic symptom in developing economies where start-ups are almost 100 per cent equity funded (friends; family; private equity, and the like).

Knowing Pepsi's recent interest in promoting agricultural products exports from India, they approached the company and sought help in exporting their products to the USA. Ashok Vasudevan championed the project within Pepsi. He had long been driven by a vision of creating a global Indian brand, and in Tasty Bite he saw a glimmer of hope. However, after months of deliberation Pepsi turned down the project. Pepsi's quality-control team felt that importing food products from India posed a significant risk to the corporation.

The project died within Pepsi, but Ashok and a couple of others (Kartik Kilachand and Meera Vasudevan) were big believers that what appeared to be Pepsi's export *obligation* could be transformed into a business *opportunity*. A new initiative was born, that five years later would result in Tasty Bite becoming the number-one Indian food brand in the United States.

The Indian export quandary

Any number of attempts over the last four decades to build global Indian brands had failed since the problems faced by Indian industry were as numerous as they were complex. For starters, since the Indian market was closed to consumer-goods imports, local manufacturers could get by with whatever goods they produced – in short, a seller's market that resulted in poor-quality goods at reasonably high prices. Indian exporters, especially those that were not just 'trading' but attempting to build a sustainable value-added export business, faced additional problems that are perhaps common across several emerging markets. Specifically, these relate to poor quality, inability to meet delivery schedules, uncompetitive prices (despite low labour costs), low productivity, inadequate industrial infrastructure, and high duties and taxes) and problems in marketing and brand-building.

Preferred Brands International: A new beginning for Tasty Bite

After early years in corporate America (GE and Chemical Bank), Kartik Kilachand shifted gear to a quasi-entrepreneurial role as Chief Executive of Parle International, then India's largest beverage company (later acquired by Coke) and helped set up franchising and bottling operations in several countries in the Middle East, Africa and Europe and finally in the USA. Later, as a full time entrepreneur, he set up a joint venture with Pepsi, USA, for the global marketing of fruit drinks manufactured in India. Simultaneously, he was advising Dole Food Co. and later Tropicana on their entry strategy into India.

Meera Vasudevan is perhaps as much a specialist as Kartik is a generalist. Articulate, imaginative and organized, her early career was almost entirely in market research, more specifically qualitative research. She rose from management trainee to become a member of the management committee at MARG (India's premier market-research firm) in a record six years, before leaving to co-found Quantum, India's first qualitative research company. Having researched over 200 domestic and international brands across a host of industries she has a unique pan-cultural understanding of brands, trends, consumer behaviour and attitudes.

Ashok Vasudevan is as corporate as Kartik and Meera are entrepreneurial. A decade in Unilever followed by nearly five years with Pepsi had ensured he was a strong 'process' guy. Much of his corporate responsibilities had been in start-up situations or at any rate in 'non-mainstream' positions. For instance, he had never sold a bar of soap or NSD ('non-soapy detergent', in company parlance) during his entire stay at Unilever nor was he involved in CSD (carbonated soft drinks) at Pepsi. A good communicator and public speaker, he can be inspiring, impatient and demanding.

When AKM (as Ashok, Kartik and Meera are collectively known in the organization) co-founded Preferred Brands International (PBI), it was Ashok who brought the three together. While Meera and Kartik knew each other well, they had never worked together. Ashok, however, had worked very closely with Kartik for several years during the fruit-drink project at Pepsi. They were like two peas in a pod. So when Pepsi pulled the plug on the joint venture it seemed only natural that Ashok and Kartik would continue to work together even without a Pepsi umbrella.

AKM were aware they had to address individual concerns and potential conflicts of interests if they were to successfully work together. Meera might have felt like an outsider because she was aware of how closely Kartik and Ashok connected. 'They complete each others sentences', she would often say. For his part, Kartik would have to guard against the weight of the marriage bearing down on the partnership. It took some honest dealing, trust and open communication between Ashok, Kartik and Meera to address these issues. Even as these were being addressed and resolved over a period of several months, the company was incorporated and AKM threw themselves headlong into the venture without looking over their shoulders. It is a testimony to the relationship that since the incorporation of the company, even after several new shareholders have been inducted, the original AKM shareholders' agreement has not once been amended or even revisited.

The three founded PBI in the USA in 1995 and secured the distribution rights of Tasty Bite for the North American market. The project aborted at Pepsi was born again. When PBI decided to market Tasty Bite in the USA, one of the initial challenges was to define the market and the size of the opportunity. The simplest approach would be to distribute Tasty Bite in the South Asian grocery stores (the 'ethnic' trade) and define this as the target market. This is what all the other food brands from India had already figured – sell Indian food to the over one million Indians, Pakistanis and Bangladeshis living there and you had a captive audience and a respectable market size. Also, this seemed a logical first step considering PBI was capitalized with just $5,000 in cash, zero debt and a working capital play provided only by a 120-day credit period from the Indian exporter.

However, the company's vision was somewhat grander and AKM decided to target mainstream America and hence design their entry strategy by first understanding the overall US food market and measure the various opportunities available.

The US food industry: emerging mega trends

The United States is the world's largest importer, exporter and consumer of processed food. In 1994, the year when PBI was incorporated, Americans spent about $337 billion in retail food stores and an additional $303 billion in food-service establishments. Taken together, this appears to be greater than the GDP of all countries in the world outside the ten richest!

And, incredibly enough, the industry continues to grow, albeit modestly. The US grocery industry sales have grown by 1–2 per cent annually since 1990, and the industry appears to be a beehive of activity. For instance, in 1995 alone 17,000 new food products were introduced and US food manufacturers produced an estimated 240,000 different packaged foods.

At the retail end of the industry, drugstores, corner grocery stores and specialty stores made way for the onrush of the supermarkets. By 2002, these supermarkets were as numerous (225,000 stores across the USA) as they were varied in their offerings (grocery, nursery, bookstores, delicatessen, banking and so on) and accounted for a staggering 80 per cent of all retail sales. The 1990s also saw a wave of mergers and acquisitions in the retail industry. By 2001 the 20 largest food retailers accounted for nearly 60 per cent of the total grocery industry, up from less than 40 per cent a decade earlier.

One of the more significant trends in this mega-industry has been the emergence of natural and organic foods. The movement towards eating more natural foods began in the 1980s as a result of growing health concerns. Consumers were seeking processed foods that would retain convenience as the prime offering, but move away from the use of artificial preservatives and additives. In short, consumers were asking the industry to provide food that would combine convenience with goodness.

Despite its size, the natural food industry is fairly fragmented with fewer than 100 companies with sales in excess of $10 million. Food majors, however, are sitting up and taking note. Kraft, Nestlé, Heinz and Kellogg all appear to be exploring the natural food market's potential with acquisitions of well-known and established natural food companies.

On the retailing end, too, natural seems to be going mainstream with chains like Giants, Safeway and Kroger's beginning to add natural product aisles in their supermarkets. While several chains like Whole Foods, Wild Oats and Trader Joe's are totally dedicated natural-food retailers growing in numbers and in revenues as they expand their product offerings and move to heartland America from being just a bi-coastal phenomenon.

Industry megatrends: positioning idea for Tasty Bite

There were some very interesting mega trends influencing American eating habits and the food industry in the early 1990s – trends that would ultimately provide a positioning platform for Tasty Bite:

- Even as America was becoming more obese, Americans had embraced healthier lifestyles like never before. People quit smoking in record numbers, gyms across the country were getting fuller, beer and wine stole market share from hard liquor, and people became conscious of the need for a sustained healthy diet. Food manufacturers responded quickly to this changing environment by providing food that was both convenient and healthy. Soon, the natural foods industry grew from a fringe movement into a mainstream trend. US grocery industry sales have grown only 1–2 per cent annually since 1990, but natural foods sales continue to get stronger – burgeoning in size from $2 billion in 1993 to $15 billion in 2000. Interestingly, the natural foods segment, though less than 2 per cent of the total US food and beverage market, was growing 14 to 15 times faster than the overall food industry!
- Another big trend was that Americans were cooking less and less at home, but this, however, did not result in a corresponding growth in restaurant revenues. This anomaly was explained by a healthy increase in the convenience foods business. Also known as HMR (home meal replacement), this category includes chilled, frozen and shelf-stable dinners, salads, supermarket deli-counter sales and so on. HMR was a $60 billion market in the mid-1990s and growing at 10 per cent annually.
- The third big trend was the globalization of the American palate. The largest and fastest growing 'ethnic' segment was Mexican foods, fuelled by a wave of new immigrants. The resultant boom in Mexican restaurants piqued mainstream interest in this cuisine and triggered a growing presence of packaged foods in supermarkets (the Goya brand had an entire aisle named for it in several regional and national chains). Fast-food chains like Taco Bell had rapidly mainstreamed Mexican food and the

salsa revolution had taken hold of grocery aisles – ketchup bottles began yielding to salsa as the dip of choice, and tortilla chips and nachos were replacing potato chips. Meanwhile, Indian and Thai cuisines were quietly becoming the next new trend at restaurants. They were, however, still confined to a small segment of consumers, *viz.* those in large cities, cosmopolitan and experimentative. But, what was significant was that these restaurants had emerged out of the confines of merely attracting the diaspora – Indian or Thai – and were finding wider acceptance. They were at the stage that Mexican food was a few years earlier. Clearly, they were poised to boom.

Evolution of the marketing strategy

Aware of these trends, PBI developed the outline of its entry strategy for Tasty Bite and made some early decisions:

1 Target the brand and Indian cuisine at Americans, instead of the Indian diaspora in America. If Indian restaurants were becoming popular, then the 'usage continuum' would dictate that consumers would graduate to take-out, and then move to buying prepared meals in supermarkets and only occasionally pick up enough courage to try making it at home. The company felt this presented a unique opportunity and a first-mover advantage if it could take Tasty Bite mainstream.
2 Create excellent recipes. The idea was to replicate the good taste of an Indian restaurant experience in each pack of Tasty Bite. These were consumers whose palates had woken up to the exciting possibilities of new flavours and cuisines and the brand was, in a sense, competing with the experience of fine restaurant food.
3 Ride the Natural trend. The retort technology used to process Tasty Bite automatically ensured an all-natural product. Distribution through the natural and health-food stores would sharply position the product to the segment that cared most about some of the attributes of Tasty Bite – all-natural, Indian and convenient.
4 'Americanize' the brand. Indian cuisine is fairly complex and decidedly different from American. It can intimidate and confuse consumers. So, PBI decided to make Tasty Bite a brand that seemed more friendly than exotic; flavoursome than spicy; allowing it to become another dinner option rather than a special-occasion product.

Having decided on the entry strategy for the US market, the company turned its attention to execution. Most of the first year was spent on product-line rationalization, quality control, packaging development, building a distribution infrastructure and creating business processes for managing growth.

Execution: a few early examples

TBEL at that point had about 28 different products or stock-keeping units (SKUs) in the market, many of which were clearly not selling. The packaging comprised the retort pouch inside a printed carton. The overall graphic design of the cartons was not very modern or international, nor did it communicate easily to consumers. And to top it all, each SKU came in a 200 and 400-gram size creating a logistical and inventory-planning nightmare.

The product

The Tasty Bite range of ready-to-serve (RTS) products are fully cooked, all-natural and remain shelf-stable for up to 18 months without the need for refrigeration. Food is placed in a retort pouch, and cooked to a finish in a sterilizer. The material of construction of the pouch and the manufacturing process ensure the food is microbiologically safe even as it retains its original flavour.

The retort technology itself was not new. It actually dated back to the 1960s and was invented in the USA as part of NASA's initiative for space food. However, it did not take strong roots in supermarkets and it lost the race to frozen and chilled foods as the cold-chain infrastructure developed simultaneously in the USA and Europe. The technology did trickle into Asia over the next few decades, however, and there is today a proliferation of retorted products in Japan, Korea and the Far East and a burgeoning market in China and India.

As part of its sharp market focus, PBI made some quick changes:

- Rationalized the list of SKUs down from 28 to the top-selling eight.
- Created one standard 300gm pack offering (serves two). This immediately made it an easy sell to retailers, and also removed the logistical hurdles of maintaining an inventory of so many packs.
- Changed the names of the variants from 'authentic' ethnic names that were mostly unpronounceable to non-Indians to ones that were friendlier. So, a pack of 'Alu Chole' (potatoes with chickpeas) morphed into 'Bombay Potatoes'. 'Palak Paneer' (curried spinach with cottage cheese) became 'Kashmir Spinach'. Informal research with consumers revealed that it communicated what the product contained and also evoked an immediate association with India.
- Upgraded the pack design. PBI retained a skilled graphic designer to revamp the look of the cartons to make the brand look more modern, gourmet, natural and up-market. The designer's task was to hint Indian but create a broader appeal. 'Consumers should sense it is Indian, but don't do the Taj Mahal' was the brief. The result was a very elegant design and the packs elicited high praise from retailers, consumers and even designers.

- Outsource globally to seek efficiencies. One of the strengths that AKM had was their experience with global vendors. They immediately drew upon this network and outsourced packaging and printing to the most cost-efficient yet competent vendors in various parts of the world. The result? A whopping 30 per cent reduction in costs within the system within the first year.
- Hired a quality control specialist to the plant in India (even though PBI was only a 'distributor' at the time) to introduce quality-assurance measures and to sign off on every shipment before it was exported to the USA.

Within 12 months of the formation of the company these changes had been effected and PBI moved into secure distribution in the USA and managed to sell over a million meals the first year. The company now became TBEL's largest customer accounting for almost 70 per cent of its revenues.

The launch of Tasty Bite in the USA

The testing ground was California. The natural food trend was incubated there and AKM were convinced it was the crucible for change in America. The company moved quickly to appoint a few key distributors in northern and southern California and served them through a public warehouse in Los Angeles. The three-tier distribution system the company used resulted in an end-consumer price in the range of $2.99–3.49. Initial primary sales were low, consumer offtake sluggish, but overall distributor and broker enthusiasm was still high. Within a year Tasty Bite increased its distribution and got an all-commodity volume (ACV) of nearly 20 per cent (that is, 20 per cent of market volume) in the independent natural stores in the state. The product also trickled into the independent natural and health-food stores in Arizona, Colorado, Washington and Oregon.

The first big break came with the acceptance of the product in Trader Joe's. Trader Joe's at the time had estimated revenues of about $500 million through its 80 plus stores across California and a few neighbouring states, offering its customers a range of unique products with a great selection of cheese, wines, international foods and a wide variety of high-quality private-label products at prices that were virtually unbeatable. It combined low prices with a premium atmosphere and its customers were served by very courteous and knowledgeable 'crew members'. Unlike many other supermarkets, Trader Joe did not encourage distributors and preferred dealing directly with manufacturers. They had no need for listing fees, slotting fees, special promotions. They offered EDLP (every day low price) and virtually no product ever went on sale in the store. This contributed in no small measure to a very loyal customer base of people who are active, healthy, price-conscious, environmentally friendly and fun-loving. The exact target segment Tasty Bite was looking for. Over the next three years, Tasty Bite was listed in virtually every natural and health-food chain on the west coast, and every major distributor in the natural-foods industry had taken on the Tasty Bite line of products.

Getting authorizations in chains and enlisting high-quality distributors was one thing, but creating consumer offtake without an aggressive advertising budget in a highly competitive grocery environment was quite another challenge. PBI focused on product tastings as a single-point promotion agenda. PBI enlisted demo companies, trained personnel and conducted nearly a thousand demos over the first three years in hundreds of stores all along the west coast.

There were 'three degrees of separation', Meera would say, between consumers learning about the product to actually buying it. The first was the unfamiliarity with Indian cuisine. The second was the 'retort pouch' that US consumers were largely unfamiliar with; when one thought of prepared foods the tendency was to go the freezer shelves of supermarkets and not to expect it on ambient shelves. The third was the surprising degree of convenience the pack afforded. Most consumers when they opened the Tasty Bite pack expected 'dry' products that needed some degree of reconstitution or cooking. The demos helped focus attention on bridging these degrees of separation and the company was surprised at the trial-to-purchase ratio (TPR) these demos resulted in. On average the company found a TPR of nearly 25 per cent, that is, every fourth consumer who tried the product bought the product.

Over the next few years the company expanded its distribution to the east coast of the USA and within the first five years the product was available in nearly 50 supermarket chains across the USA. According to independent retail data bought by Tasty Bite from Spins (a leading provider of sales and consumer information to the natural products industry in the USA) in December 2001, Tasty Bite had become the largest prepared Indian food brand in the United States. What's more, the strategy of product rationalization had resulted in six of the eight original SKUs being in the top-ten in the ethnic category.

The consumer

The team started thinking hard about who exactly was buying the brand, why it seemed to do well in some cities or neighbourhoods and floundered in others despite similar marketing inputs. The brand strategy was aimed at the American consumer not just the Indian diaspora, so how much of this was really happening? Was there some way to identify which markets would always be more predisposed to Tasty Bite?

To answer these questions, PBI commissioned market research a couple of years after launch with the purpose of arriving at a geo-demographic profile of the Tasty Bite consumer. The study helped PBI identify the underlying demographic characteristics that correlated to sales performance of Tasty Bite in various neighbourhoods. It therefore not only provided an analysis of existing neighbourhoods, but also provided the tools to identify the best and worst neighbourhoods for Tasty Bite in various cities; and it provided a clear profile of the Tasty Bite consumer (Figure 16.1).

In addition, plenty of additional details such as the kind of music customers listen to, the radio stations they tune in to, that they tend to frequent Starbucks, and so forth. Some of the key demographic clusters are outlined in Figure 16.2 (based on the findings of a study conducted by the market research company hired by Tasty Bite).

So, how was PBI going to use all this data? One of the first things they resolved was that this analysis would be crucial to formulating the brand's promotional and marketing plan. Which stores to pick within a chain (best and worst neighborhoods), how to select and target programmes at specific clusters, develop new markets based on the clusters, and so on. Given the rather modest marketing budget available to PBI, they decided to use their dollars wisely – not do a scattershot approach with mass-media advertising, but to use very purposive and targeted programmes aimed precisely at their cluster segments.

This strategy not only helped PBI spend their promotional dollars wisely, but also helped in their opening pitch to new retail chain accounts. From that point on, whenever they had to present to a new chain, PBI used cluster analysis to correlate the chain's store zip codes with its own list of 'best'

PBIs customers are 3 times more likely than the population as a whole to:

- **Have a household income above $75,000**
- **Have 4+ years of higher education**
- **Hold a white collar job**
- **Be 18–24 or 45–54**
    - **18–24 – strength in college towns**
    - **45–54 – strength in upscale, suburban/urban neighborhoods**
- **Spend over $150 on grocery shopping weekly**
    - **Use whole-bean coffee**
    - **Own an espresso maker**
    - **Own a luxury car**
- **Seek the 'good life':**
    - **Travel**
    - **Books**
    - **Music**

'Tasty Target' = Customers that **all retailers** want

Figure 16.1 PBI consumer research findings
Source: Internal *Company Report* (1999).

TASTY BITE

Our Customers

Demographic Type	Description	Rank	% of Total Population
Young Literati	Young mix of professionals and students; Upper middle class; Dominant white; high Asian	1	15%
Bohemian Mix	Integrated mixture of executives, students, actors, writers; Mostly single; Middle class	2	15%
Urban Achievers	High per-capita income, single; live in densely populated areas	3	10%
Money & Brains	High per-capita income, older; live in urban areas; sophisticated consumers	4	4.5%
Blue Blood Estates	Elite super rich families; live in suburban areas; sophisticated consumers	5	3%
Winner's Circle	Wealthy executive suburban families; sophisticated consumers	6	3%
Total			50.5%

* Population Demographics within a 1.5 mile radius of the store

Household Income	Education	Age Group	Grocery Spend
>US$ 75,000 per annum	4+ years of higher education	18–24, 25–54	Over US$150 per week

Figure 16.2 Customers of Tasty Bite
Source: Langston Research Report, 1999.

zip codes for the brand. This eliminated the process of placing the brand at every store in the chain and then 'seeing what sticks'. Chain buyers appreciated this approach, as it also saved them the potential headache of delisting Tasty Bite from underperforming stores. Again not a scattershot approach, but a more targeted one that maximized volume opportunities and did not waste resources. The team understood very clearly that when you do not have big-company budgets, a laser-beam focus on details becomes crucial.

Based on this understanding of the market, PBI developed its brand positioning statement: 'A New World of Flavor in Every Tasty Bite'. The line clearly identifies the needs of the target audience, *viz.* to seek new, international eating experiences.

The organization

For a small company, Preferred Brands attracted some very high-calibre professionals. It began with the induction of Hans Taparia and Sohel Shikari into the company, both of whom had only recently graduated from the Massachusetts Institute of Technology and had set up Omni, a financial advisory firm based out of the USA and India. They were young, energetic, passionate and deeply analytical. It was Omni that had worked on the Tasty Bite acquisition for PBI. This turned out to be an extended assignment and during this period both Sohel and Hans gained an uncanny familiarity with the business and great chemistry with the principals of the firm

This subsequently resulted in an interesting restructuring exercise whereby AKM merged Omni into its holding company and the original founding team of three now grew to six with Ravi, Hans and Sohel becoming stakeholders and members of the board of the parent company.

With the senior management team firmly in place, the company moved to hire a talented group that represented a blend of education, experience and domain expertise, both in India and the USA. The culture of the company grew to becoming as informal and participative as it was analytical and demanding.

The TBEL acquisition: a turnaround story

Even as Tasty Bite was making inroads in the marketplace, PBI received word that the Indian supplier TBEL had declared bankruptcy and had been acquired by Unilever. It was not as much a strategic buy by Unilever as it was a 'tag-along' as part of a larger ice-cream acquisition.

In the 10 years the company had existed, TBEL had not had a single profitable year, Actually, revenues were less than its annual debt burdens, accumulated losses were about five times the capital base, and a 50 per cent devaluation in the Indian rupee rate vs the Japanese yen and the Deutsch Mark (the company had substantial yen and deutschemark debt as part of its asset financing) had left the company with a debt:equity ratio of nearly 5:1. The 2,000 shareholders of the company who owned 49 per cent of the equity saw the shares tumble to about a third of the purchase price and pretty much stay there for almost a decade with little hope of recovering their investment.

PBI decided to make a bid for the company and Ashok's connections within Unilever helped steer the process along smoothly. PBI felt they could turn the Indian company around since by this time it had already become TBEL's largest customer. AKM discussed the turnaround in painful detail. They had been looking at TBEL very closely, albeit from the outside; the picture was not pretty but they were convinced Tasty Bite could become a serious global Indian food brand. They were looking at the business from the market *in* rather than from the factory *out*. They felt they had the energy, the strategy and most important the *faith*. All they needed was some capital, a leader to execute the strategy, and a little luck.

The capital came in the form of private equity from CDC (Commonwealth Development Corporation) a UK private-equity firm with several offices in India who paid no premium but put up vital capital that gave them 49 per cent of a holding company, with PBI holding the balance majority with a pro rata investment that came entirely out of its balance sheet without any additional debt. The holding company acquired Unilever's entire stake (51 per cent) in TBEL and after a grateful public shed an additional 23 per cent of their holdings in an open tender offer that statutorily followed the acquisition, it now held almost 74 per cent of TBEL.

The leader came in the form of Ravi Nigam, an obvious choice for the President of TBEL but a difficult hire. He was running a successful export business for one of India's leading business groups and he was not looking for a change. For AKM, that made the decision even more attractive. Ravi had earlier worked with Ashok at Pepsi and the two had got along extremely well. He also had more than a nodding acquaintance with Kartik and Meera. AKM invited him to visit their offices in Stamford, Connecticut where they laid out their dreams and their plans. Ravi was excited at the opportunity and in the autumn of 1998 came on board as President of TBEL.

By October of that year the four of them actually conceived a turnaround strategy that resulted in the turnaround of the company in the very first year under the new management. The idea was to leverage the inherent strengths of TBEL to concentrate on the US market and the retort technology, take advantage of the demand for frozen vegetables and fruits, and use the company's blast-freezing capacity, and even company-owned land to source vegetables in-house.

1999–2003: staying the course

Over the next five years the company stayed the course of its strategy, concentrating on the US market even as it made inroads into Europe and Asia. By 2003, Tasty Bite was available in 11 other countries but the US dominated, accounting for over 80 per cent of the company's revenues. Simultaneously, the company focused on RTS products (also 80 per cent of company's revenues) for the entire period and only in 2002 widened the product portfolio to include ready-to-cook (RTC) products.

During this initial period, the company built robust systems and processes across the board, some examples of which are:

- The factory received the ISO 9002 accreditation and became one of India's earliest to receive the coveted HACCP food-safety certification. Later, in February 2002, the ISO 14000 environment certification followed, once again amongst India's earliest.
- A state-of-the-art ERP system was introduced to manage process automation and the supply chain. And this, in a factory that had no computers when it was acquired!
- A product-development department was created to design new products and constantly improve existing ones. Consequently, cycle times for new launches drastically reduced, and from five SKUs in 1998 the company now had over 30. Most importantly, managers and workers in the company genuinely felt that they made the highest quality of food manufactured in India and perhaps the highest quality of retort food anywhere in the

world. For a product that was rejected by Pepsi for fear of quality, Tasty Bite had come a long way.
- The US distribution system was extended to nearly 40 states, 35 distributors and 50 chains. ACV in the natural food supermarkets across the country exceeded 70 per cent.
- The company leveraged its distribution strength by launching a range of ready-to-serve Thai foods under the Thai Table brand name co-packed by a third-party manufacturer in Thailand.
- The company also launched a range of meat curries manufactured in the USA under the Tasty Bite brand name.
- Tastybite.com was launched in the USA, both as a profitable business and as an important test-bed for consumer research and feedback. Today, nearly 6 per cent of the company's revenues come from its website.

Competition: a need for renewal

In a bold move in mid-2002, PBI bought out the stake of CDC (the private equity investor in TBEL) and overnight doubled its stake in the Indian company. It funded this acquisition with cash generated from operations and without assuming any long-term debt. Obviously, this resulted in money shifting away from the market, and the company went on an all-out war against profligacy in every part of the business. Several discount programmes were cancelled, unexplained deductions were closely scrutinized and often rejected, and travel budgets trimmed. By mid-2002, the company had generated enough cash for the buy-out but the cut in promotional activity resulted in stagnant growth three quarters in a row, something that, surprisingly, the management had not foreseen. Even as marketing programmes were reintroduced as the cash position improved, sales were slower to recover due to a lag time that such promotions take. Just as the sales had not begun to dip for nearly two quarters after programmes were put on hold, they were taking their time climbing back after programmes were reintroduced. During this period of recovery, competitive activity increased in an unprecedented manner. Where there were two players over the last five years, five more emerged in just 12 months, mostly in India and in the ethnic markets worldwide. Already, one of them had begun presentations to major supermarket chains in the USA and it would only be a matter of time before Tasty Bite felt the pressure of the other brands, too, in its strongest market.

The board at PBI met to consider the situation as they realized that it was time to reinvent. It was time for a new long-term strategy...

Part IV
Lessons Learned

17
From Classical to Neoglobal Perspectives

F. Zeynep Bilgin, Ven Sriram and Gerhard A. Wührer

Frequently, the entire process of internationalization becomes a challenge for many firms. The problem is not that the firm or its managers are unprepared to deal with the complex issues that such an initiative entails, it is that the methods available or employed for operating abroad do not fit well with the prevailing conditions there and cannot therefore be successfully implemented by the firm and, consequently, are not of much value.

The problem of fit

So, is there then a problem with lack of fit? Perhaps this problem or feeling of unease when operating in new markets where conditions are very different from those one is used to is analogous to wearing borrowed clothes that were tailored for someone else. This problem of fit is most often observed when advanced market (AM) firms operate in emerging markets (EMs) with their tested and proven methods for strategy development. Dawar and Chattopadhyay[1] discuss the inconsistencies in the strategies used by multinational companies (MNCs) in the EMs they operated in where their marketing programmes did not seem to be properly adapted to those markets. The applications get even more complex when EM firms, with their different mindset, try to apply AM strategies in their home countries or in other EMs. The match is then rather artificially forced even though managerial perceptions of both EM countries may be similar. As a result, when the chosen strategies do not properly reflect a fit to the firm and its environment, success is often just a matter of luck, coincidence or is simply short-lived.

Coping with the problem: homogenize vs differentiate

But what then are the ways to overcome these problems of fit? There are in fact two opposing views presented in many discussions of international marketing operations, and each perceives the solution from a different perspective. On the one side is the classical view where it is said that there is a dynamic convergence process and in the end this will create such a homogeneity that all markets will begin to resemble each other after some time.[2] This would mean that strategies applicable now in AMs will also eventually become relevant and applicable in EMs and a global 'one world' will be approached.[3] The argument is based on the assumption of a slow but inexorable movement towards global convergence in consumer tastes and habits, expectations and aspirations,[4] where people are willing to sacrifice unique preferences of products they need in return for quality and affordability, and economies of scale are achieved.[5] On the other side, there is a new (neoglobal) perspective suggesting that the existing differences are not so easy to erase, and markets not so easy to homogenize, so it would be better to search for new ways and new solutions for the dynamics prevailing in the EMs, that also affect AMs.

The assumption that emerging markets are merely at an earlier stage of the same development path that advanced markets have been through, and therefore the same strategies that succeeded in AMs will eventually become applicable in EMs, is being challenged.[6] The distinctive EM environments may indeed require fresh and distinctive thinking. Whereas the first-orientation (classical) perspective has been the focus of attention for a long time, little has been done to add to the knowledge base and substantiate the validity of the second (neoglobal) perspective. Part II of this book presents three studies reflecting the classical view while at the same time discussing the transition in management thinking.

The classical approach and its transition

The classical perspective, supported by many scholars and based on empirical evidence, is certainly applicable in many markets. Convergence[7] is basically towards the Western economic model and it is expected that over time the strategies will become similar,[8] and because of advances in technology, structure and global focus, firms aim to adopt a 'one-best-way' approach to manage organizations worldwide.[9] In Chapter 4, Berács also deals with the question of when the process of transition to a Western-style market economy ends. He argues that in Central European transition economies like Hungary, Poland and Slovenia, with the acceptance of the basic standards of the EU for full membership, the focus on market orientation may well help them to homogenize to some extent with AMs, and that for a better functioning of the market a strong marketing organization and orientation is necessary. Berács also points out that great emphasis should be put on the marketing function based on the cost–benefit principle. Hence, customer focus incorporates values that can be different than the values stressed in AMs, and management thinking in transition should focus on what the marketing orientation should actually cover in EMs differently than in AMs.

Even when evidence on the progress of EMs in transition indicates that in Central and Eastern Europe, the Czech Republic, Hungary, Poland, Slovakia and Slovenia reflect similarities to their neighbouring EU countries, have made impressive progress in economic and political development and fulfil the requirements for EU membership,[10] would that mean that AM strategies would fit perfectly in these market economies? Or should we focus on the reality that markets reflect unique characteristics based on the prevailing lifestyles, and many other factors?

EMs with similar backgrounds and emphasizing the role of culture in their daily lives and business interaction are quicker learners than AM firms when they operate in other EMs. The way they develop and use their strategies reflects an understanding of the host markets. A good example of this is Bobek's study presented in Chapter 6 where he examines the jewellery exports of a Slovenian firm to the Czech Republic. Here the classical market-analysis methods to approach the export market are chosen, such as first focusing on a SWOT analysis and developing a stepwise market-research process, but Bobek does not neglect to put special emphasis on the lifestyle dimension, although the two EMs are very similar, both located in Central Europe and both being transition economies. However, it must be kept in mind that habits of daily life can also be determinants of the choice of strategy. The way the classical approach is used and presented also reflects the management thinking in transition.

Another striking example of management thinking in transition comes form Chapter 5 of this book. The variables chosen to assess leadership styles are based on the classical models developed in AMs, but nevertheless the results reflect that there are differences in the leadership styles of firms from Central and Eastern European countries compared to those of managers from Western European AMs. The self-assessments are based on variables such as dynamism and toughness, and these characteristics are far more frequently valued as good leadership qualities in non-Western cultures. So, when the managerial perceptions are different, then the way the methods are applied and used by managers can also be expected to be different.

The question to raise here is how important are these international differences. If differences in management styles primarily based on socio-cultural factors prevail, what is better? Is transfer of behaviour and techniques from country to country in a more uniform world more important than the need for more knowledge on a richer variety of management practices and techniques?[11] These and other similar questions give rise to the development of the new perspective.

The new perspective and its evolution

When a homogenous world is not seen as a realistic case, new perspectives arise. In fact, in the late 1960s Fayerweather had discussed the issue of unification versus fragmentation, and pointed out that 'differences in socio-cultural, political, and economic characteristics as well as the need for effective relations with the host country constitute fragmenting influences which necessitate adaptation to the local environment'.[12] The divergence approach basically suggests that culture should be studied because management styles are different from one country to another based on differences in value systems and behaviours, access to global resources and economic development levels.[13] But both the cultural and the historical/political focus, that is the institutional view, are found to be too deterministic and for the organizational variance the organization itself is contributive, and not just passively embedded.[14] Today the ways firms start to internationalize their operations are also different from when AMs initially evolved. Scholars like Pchounetlev[15] also point out that internationalization strategies in the modern business literature, such as the stages model, contingency models or network approach, have limited applicability to EMs in transition like Russia, where the characteristics of the market make the application of such theories developed on the evidence from AM companies, difficult.

With a unique management project, people search for a solution to these and similar problems now in Africa,[16] focusing on how to reconceptualize this continent. The aim is to understand the different interests of different parties involved in business, because from a macro perspective structural/economic 'solutions' applied to the 'African situation' have failed so far, and attempts to transpose Western approaches to management also appear to be inappropriate. Based on the levels of cultural interaction, focusing on intercontinental interactions between Western and African approaches that result in different combinations of management systems for Africa, the project further focuses on modern cross-cultural theory that is built on a concept of cross-vergence of cultures, which leads to different hybrid management systems.

So, the lessons to be learned are the following:[17]

- develop new thinking and knowledge about regional business networks,
- develop analytical methods for assessing regional drivers of success rather than globalization drivers, whereby managers should be encouraged to think regional and act local and forget the global.

This should be interpreted as perceiving the global not as a cliché but rather with a regional understanding of world markets, hence becoming a truly global firm. And what applies for the marketing mix is linked to overall strategies for internationalization, assuring a truly global outlook with tailor-made strategies.

The paths of progress

Why is such a detailed focus on differences necessary? Channon and Yaprak[18] state that the 'evolution of marketing is to be followed in different markets', and since every economy goes through different stages of development and free-market development principles do not always apply in EMs, it is way too difficult to create a framework that is fitting to every country to interpret marketing events, search for marketing opportunities, improve the marketing process and in turn add value to overall economic development. Existing frameworks can nevertheless be of some help as a guideline for firms and can be used to understand different expectations in different markets and for the development of appropriate marketing strategies.[19]

At this point it is important to highlight why the process of internationalization, and hence strategy[20] development, in EMs is not the same as in AMs. The repeated discussion[21] focuses on the 'institutional void' and how to cope with it. Being involved in international market operations has a longer history in AMs. It started with machinery and technology know-how exports following the industrial revolution, and later after the Second World War, AMs slowly improved their industries in different sectors and their firms started to go abroad, first through exporting.

And when internationalization moved from exports to international, multinational and then to a global orientation in a stepwise development, market environments presented different bases than at present. At that time, communication and transportation-related infrastructures were not yet developed at the speed of today. Now, in an era of the knowledge economy, IT-related technological advancements are enjoyed all over the world. EMs are also exposed to the most recent knowledge, and the speed of linking what is going on in the world to what individuals may need is tremendous. Via access to IT, communication channels, information and transportation infrastructures, the widespread use of these is faster than ever before. So, EM firms and consumers are enjoying a much more rapid pace of globalization, and a more holistic picture in their internationalization process. As stated by Daniels,[22] many EM firms directly start with a global focus instead of going first to geographically close countries. The owners or managers are well-educated and experienced in the field, and that makes it possible to gain a global orientation immediately and open up to a variety of markets in short periods of time. So, does this mean that the world is becoming homogenous? This does not seem to be very realistic. While EMs progress and come to one stage of their evolution, AMs may be at a different stage, even though many EMs are transitioning to a market economy and are following many of the trends they see in AMs. Core competencies for AMs and EMs will likely be different at any point in time; hence the strategies to be developed and implemented are also expected to be unique and different.

Developments follow different structures and although the goals may be the same, the path for success will be different. Hence, local sensibilities and differentiating points should be kept in mind. In the physical sciences like medicine and mathematics, the rules and methods might apply universally.

In the social sciences, theories have been developed largely based on experience gained from life. So what is applicable in one country is not necessarily applicable in another setting. Behavioural science affects strategy development for markets, which is highly culture and situation bound. And although there is a high level of 'cultural imperialism' observed coming from advanced-market MNCs with their standardized, global products, still the majority of segments served in different markets all over the world preserve many aspects of their lifestyle-based habits and needs. Lifestyles in AMs and EMs are different and there are indeed significant differences within AMs and EMs themselves. The conditions of progress and the progress itself during economic development and industrialization follow another path in EMs than that relevant during the industrialization process of the AMs. Of course some degree of homogenization may in fact be occurring as global segments emerge such as the 'global youth' and 'global élite' who may have more in common with similar people in other countries than with many in their own.

However, these are not the norm and do not reflect the entire society. A unique way of living still prevails among many consumers in AMs, and differences will exist and should be recognized. Hence it is the task of managers to find new methods to approach different countries with their

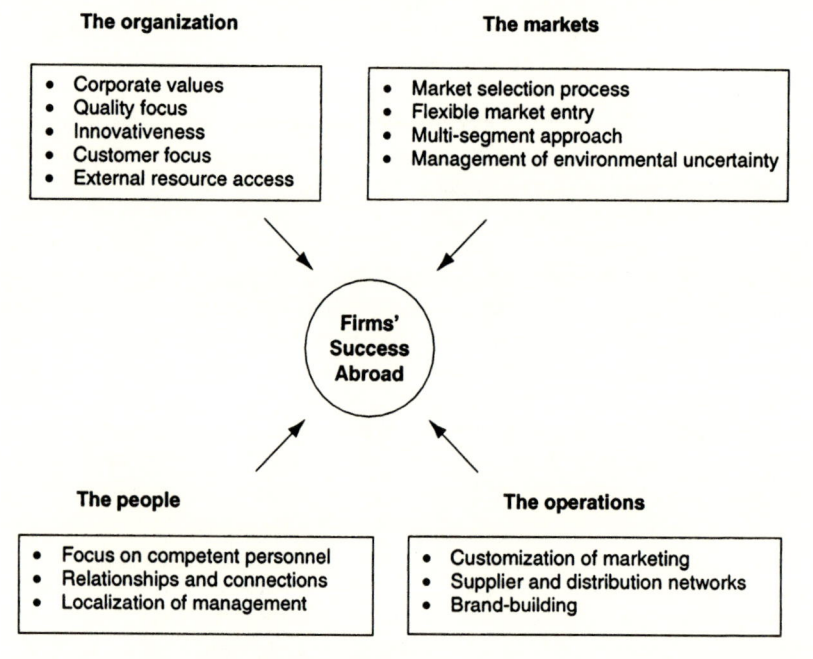

The organization
- Corporate values
- Quality focus
- Innovativeness
- Customer focus
- External resource access

The markets
- Market selection process
- Flexible market entry
- Multi-segment approach
- Management of environmental uncertainty

Firms' Success Abroad

The people
- Focus on competent personnel
- Relationships and connections
- Localization of management

The operations
- Customization of marketing
- Supplier and distribution networks
- Brand-building

Figure 17.1 Drivers of global market success

different needs and perceptions.[23] While global consumers may all strive for the same end – an improvement in their quality of life – they may take many different and often unique paths to get there.

Keeping in mind the unique characteristics of EMs, as discussed in Chapter 3, it is important to highlight how an examination of their environments and firms can contribute to an improved understanding of global business. Using the four dimensions identified in Chapter 1 as the framework for studying the key success drivers (see Figure 1.1), and based on an analysis of the studies presented in Parts II and III, Figure 17.1 summarizes the drivers of emerging market global success.

Each of these four dimensions and their components are discussed in detail in the following chapters 18–21, and conclusions are presented in Chapter 22. As will be seen, some of these success factors are consistent with the classical view of convergence in that they are common with those that drive AM companies in other AMs. Others are unique to EM firms and their environments, advancing the neoglobal perspective and thereby providing evidence in support of the notion of divergence.

Notes

1 N. Dawar and Amitava Chattopadhyay, 'Rethinking Marketing Programs for Emerging Markets', The University of Michigan Business School, William Davidson Institute, Working Paper, no. 320 (June 2000): 1–22.
2 The classical view that societies move together on a continuous basis so that over time the similarities between them will become greater than their differences in terms of social characteristics, is the basis of the 'convergence approach' and was first developed by C. Kerr and his colleagues in 1960. For details, see C. Kerr, J.T. Dunlop, F.H. Harbison and C.A. Myers, *Industrialism and Industrial Man* (Cambridge, MA: Harvard University Press, 1960).
3 Although the mainstream is from AMs to EMs, contributions to effectiveness may also be passed from EMs to AMs, before they become incorporated into the worldwide way of doing things. Pugh and Hickson discuss the contributions of a developing industry to convergence, based on examples from the industrialization process of Japan with management and quality orientations later adopted by other already industrialized nations. For details see D.S. Pugh and D.J. Hickson, 'On Organizational Convergence', in M. Warner and P. Joynt (eds), *Managing Across Cultures, Issues and Perspectives* (London: Thomson Learning, 2002): 9.
4 Global youth often aspire to similar products and tastes, see for example D.S. Pugh and D.J. Hickson (2002), *op. cit.*: 7; and W.B. Werther, 'Toward Global Convergence', *Business Horizons*, 39, 1 (1996): 3–9. There is also the trend to socialize the formation of a global vision via fashion and the use of IT facility.
5 T. Levitt, 'The Globalization of Markets', *Harvard Business Review* 61, 3 (May–June 1983): 92–102.
6 D.J. Arnold and J.A. Quelch, 'New Strategies in Emerging Markets', *Sloan Management Review*, 40,1 (1998): 7–20.
7 For a discussion of convergence–divergence–cross-vergence, see Bryan W. Husted, 'Cultural Balkanization and Hybridization in an Era of Globalization: Implications

for International Business Research', in Masaaki Kotabe and Preet S. Aulakh, *Emerging Issues in International Research* (Cheltenham: Edward Elgar, 2002): 81–95.
8 For details see M.A. Marinov and S.T. Marinova, 'Foreign Direct Investment in the Emerging Markets of Central and Eastern Europe: Motives and Marketing Strategies', in A. Yaprak and H. Tütek (eds), *Globalization, The Multinational Firm, and Emerging Economies, Advances in International Marketing*, Vol. 10, series editor S.T. Cavusgil (New York: Elsevier Science, 2001): 21–52.
9 M. Warner and P. Joynt, 'Introduction: Cross-cultural perspectives', in M. Warner and P. Joynt (eds), *Managing Across Cultures, Issues and Perspectives* (London: Thomson Learning, 2002): 3–6.
10 An interesting study here is that of J. Nowak and J. Pöschl, 'An Assessment of Progress in Transition, Economic Performance, and Market Attractiveness of CEFTA Countries', *Journal of East–West Business*, 4, 4 (1999): 27–49.
11 M. Warner and P. Joynt, 'Introduction: Cross-cultural perspectives', *op. cit.*
12 J. Fayerweather, *International Business Management: A Conceptual Framework* (New York: McGraw Hill, 1969), cited in Susan Douglas and Yoram Wind, 'The Myth of Globalization', *Columbia Journal of World Business* (Winter 1987): 19–29.
13 For details, see M. Warner and P. Joynt, 'Introduction: Cross-cultural perspectives', *op. cit.*
14 For details, see B. Wilkinson, 'Culture, Institutions, and Business in East Asia', *Organization Studies*, 17: 421–47, cited in W. Braun and M. Warner, 'The "Culture Free" versus "Culture-Specific" Management Debate', in M. Warner and P. Joynt, *Managing Across Cultures, op. cit.*: 13–25. Of course the difference can also be linked to an organization acting in high or low-context environments. For that see J. Child, 'Theorizing about Organization Cross-Nationally: Part 1 – An Introduction, in M. Warner and P. Joynt, *Managing Across Cultures, op. cit.*: 26–39.
15 V. Pchounetlev, 'Internationalization Strategies of Russian Companies' (August 2000), Aalborg University, Aalborg, Denmark.
16 For details of the project, visit http://www.africamanagement.org/project_overview.htm
17 S. Douglas and Y. Wind, 'The Myth of Globalization', *op. cit.*: 341.
18 H.M. Channon and A. Yaprak, 'Marketing and Economic Development: Implications for Emerging Economies', in A. Yaprak and H. Tütek (eds), *Globalization, The Multinational Firm, and Emerging Economies, Advances in International Marketing*, Vol. 10, series editor S.T. Cavusgil (New York: Elsevier Science, 2001): 89–110.
19 *Ibid.*
20 T. Khanna and K. Palepu, 'Why Focused Strategies May be Wrong for Emerging Markets', *Harvard Business Review*, Reprint no. 974040 (July–August 1997): 3–10.
21 See T. Khanna and K. Palepu, 'Emerging Giants: Building World-Class Companies in Emerging Markets', Harvard Business School Case Study no. 9-703-431 (15 October 2002).
22 J.D. Daniels, 'Emerging Economies and the Challenge of Globalization', in A. Yaprak and H. Tütek (eds), *Globalization, The Multinational Firm, and Emerging Economies, op. cit.*: 7–20.
23 In fact in a draft report prepared by the European Parliament on 25 September 2003, it is stated that to strengthen reciprocal knowledge and understanding

between the EU and certain non-industrialized regions in the world, the bodies involved must get acquainted with the cultural and historical characteristics of the regions concerned and pay special attention to the divergence of needs and priorities among the main regions. See details at http://www.europarl.eu.int/meetdocs/committees/afet/20031006/ 506686EN.pdf (retrieved 4 November 2003).

18
The Organization

F. Zeynep Bilgin, Ven Sriram and Gerhard A. Wührer

When firms expand into markets abroad, they would like the initial entry to be sustainable in the long term, given the effort and expense of getting accustomed to new environments. Nevertheless progress cannot be completely assessed by simply looking at outcome measures of performance[1] such as sales growth, return on investments, profitability or market share. As long as the underlying determinants of performance are not properly analysed and understood, it will be hard for any initial success to be sustainable. Of course, the drivers of organizational success are multifold.

When a certain level of control over its operations in markets abroad is not guaranteed by the internationalizing company, even a well-defined strategy may be subject to failure. Control is highly linked to the entrepreneurial perceptions nurtured in corporate values. Also, although it might appear to be an outdated way of looking at the market conditions, market-development levels have been an important topic of discussion among scholars.[2] Channon and Yaprak have highlighted looking at emerging markets (EMs) from that perspective:[3] In some EMs, where the production/product-era thinking may still prevail, cost efficiency may be an important consideration but quality still remains a focus. In the sales era, variety and convenience support innovativeness based on the competitive structure; a specialized customer orientation to detect needs is necessary for success. Even as markets evolve to a marketing era with an increased emphasis on customers, product quality continues to remain an important consideration. Given their limited incomes consumers from EMs prefer not to waste their money on cheap, but unreliable products. Besides, good links to strong bureaucratic and non-governmental institutions[4] in domestic markets are important since they help gain resource access. This chapter attempts to understand the role of the organization-related factors in driving the success of the firms described in Part III.

Figure 18.1 presents the network diagram for the five organizational factors that we believe drive success. Here, links between the individual success factors and the studies discussed in Part III are shown. For this network

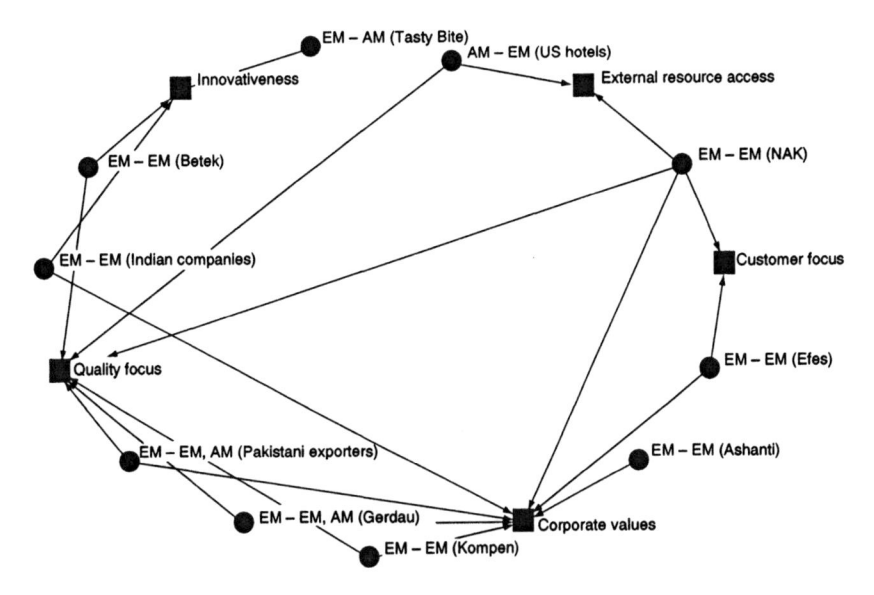

Figure 18.1 The organization network

diagram, and those of the other three success drivers (markets, people and operations) to be described in Chapters 19–21, the squares represent the second-order success factors whereas the circles represent the individual studies detailed in Part III. The first notation next to the study name indicates origin of the focal company/study and the second indicates the scope of its global business. So, for example, EM–EM, AM (Gerdau) means that this is a study of Gerdau, an EM-based company that does business in both EMs and in AMs. The details of the methodology used to develop these networks are provided in the Appendix. Multiple arrows reflect the frequency of links of different studies to individual success drivers. Accordingly, corporate values are the mostly important success factor as the most frequently cited organizational factor, followed by quality focus, innovativeness, customer focus, and external resource access. These five organizational success dimensions of firms are discussed below in the order of their importance.

Corporate values

Challenges that frustrate firms when entering EMs can be overcome when the firm develops its own systems approach and becomes competitive. Being familiar with similar conditions in their home-market settings, EM firms are more alert and interested in finding ways for solving these problems when they enter other EMs, and try to establish a certain level of managerial control in the domestic environment and abroad. This was the approach of

Indian firms. They focused on institution-building[5] where infrastructure investments were lacking, and developed their own market-research system by combining their research departments' efforts with those of outside research agencies to develop a research framework for the country. Also, the study of Pakistani exporters reveals that the most successful firms see close monitoring of export operations by management as one of the key success factors.

Managerial control is linked to close ties within the firm, but particularly to family control. In fact, as a recent study reflects, family conglomerates in EMs have local business networks, government contacts, knowledge of local markets, and even established channels in their domestic markets which Western companies do not have in EMs.[6] These links assure a certain level of control over the market operated in, and can also help for external resource access when necessary. These benefits are also enjoyed by NAK from Taiwan, and by Gerdau from Brazil, both firms with strong family involvement. Gerdau has a long history, and very early on developed a corporate culture with strong central leadership and achievement-oriented values that later led to success of the group and improved control in both home and overseas markets. Managerial responsibilities are shared and delegated to top managers for the control of operations such as IT, accounting, auditing and finance in international markets. Although not family-owned firms, Kompen and Ashanti's managerial control are remarkable as well. Ashanti succeeded through the excellent connections of their top managers in many African countries where they have their operations. Kompen developed a strategic marketing management team (SMMT) and institutionalized operations such as market research in the domestic market and abroad. Collective thinking was assured via customer management systems and organizational learning. There also, commitment via strong ties among key leaders and top managers of the firm is observed.

However, well-developed system links and managerial control by themselves are not sufficient to guarantee success. Indeed, many firms that focus on managerial control recognize the importance of controlling the financial side of their operations. Here the basic concern is cost control, particularly in the case of commodity products like steel for Gerdau, and gold in the case of Ashanti. In fact, the market sets gold prices. So being able to assure low-cost production will decrease costs in general and increase profitability. This is exactly the strategy of Ashanti. For Gerdau, steel is costly and undifferentiated, so the firm succeeds in export markets with a similar strategy: low-cost production and price-leadership through the use of low-cost, high-quality labour. Also, firms selling branded products as in the cases of NAK and Efes achieve cost reduction by moving production to low-cost manufacturing areas to provide the most affordable products in all the markets where they operate.

It should also be borne in mind that EM firms often have limited resources. Well aware of this fact, NAK applies strict financial-payment management in order to avoid delays in payments and to minimize the accounts-receivable level, because there is no room for financial slack. Efes was able to continue with its investments during the crisis in Russia with a cash injection as paid-in capital on the day of the crisis and started production in 1999. While AM multinationals often have higher margins and can therefore afford somewhat greater levels of financial risk, for many EM firms, tight financial controls and careful risk management is imperative.

Quality focus

Quality orientation is a priority for many global firms and most AM firms are familiar with excellence models, training courses for quality and quality awards well-known in Europe,[7] six-sigma programmes of the American Society of Quality (ASQ) and performance measurements and process improvement techniques of the United States,[8] but this issue is a concern for EM firms as well.[9]

In EM environments, where domestic firms are now being challenged by multinationals, and where customers have been exposed to mediocre or even low-quality products for long periods, firms nowadays can only succeed when they do not compromise on quality. Customers in EMs want to enjoy the best their money can buy. Also, quality goes hand in hand with technology improvements and R&D investments as long as the financial capacities of the firms allow. Here, two facts can be observed: the affordability problem not only pushed firms in EMs to invest in the outmoded technologies of the AM countries during the long periods of import substitution, but this also resulted in them using low-quality materials and ingredients in many cases, even for durable goods. Hence, it is a matter of pride when managers of firms like Gerdau from Brazil, Betek and Kompen from Turkey, or NAK from Taiwan talk so happily about their success with their quality awards and ISO certificates for quality excellence in production also in international markets, especially EMs. In fact, Gerdau and NAK invested early in technological improvement of their production, and started quality-control systems 'taking quality as the guide for business principles' as stated by NAK managers. Another fact for NAK is that the Chinese environment where they operate is so vulnerable to fake products that the only differentiation is on quality.

Kompen applies a total-quality orientation very successfully in export markets. For Betek it was a very important decision 'never to sell low-quality, low-price products' to meet short-term demand in transition economies, so they now experience high growth in those markets with the best available quality. No wonder that the export-award winners from Pakistan had also emphasized quality control as the most important success factor in markets abroad. It is also important to note that quality is highly important for services, where it is a particularly difficult task given the variability in the human beings that provide the service. Well-aware of the need for quality in EMs, and also well-aware of the fact that there are not many established hotel chains yet,[10] US hotels operating in Hungary first emphasized the improvement of hotel standards and hygiene factors with the quality service systems they developed. To cope with the challenges of the service characteristics, the service is divided into many components and each part is standardized as much as possible to ensure continuity in quality.

Innovativeness

Joseph Schumpeter,[11] the Austrian economist, identified innovation as the primary determinant of the cycles of technology and advancement.[12] Now, may we say that success of EM firms will depend on their contribution to marketing innovativeness? From the perspective of buyers, the desire to experience quality is highly linked to the desire to experience technologically improved, better-designed products and to enjoy innovation. Widespread telecommunication systems bring all the advancements of the world into our homes; it does not matter whether we live in an AM or an EM. As a result, firms where innovativeness is also highly valued and emphasized come closer to success in international markets. The analysis of the Indian market reflects that process innovation is an important determinant for success in competitive environments. Here, first of all, an information flow is assured as an important way to technological improvements to serve many markets with different needs, and IT investments help with developing product-mix innovations. Besides, via location of flexible production systems, manufacturing sites can be moved to the lowest-cost areas when necessary.

Firms with high levels of concern for the environment also have the potential to be future winners. Initially, and still in many cases, a dumping ground for the industrial and consumer waste of AM countries, many EM societies and their consumers are becoming more aware and concerned about issues relating to pollution and the environment. They now collaborate with organizations like Greenpeace to protect their countries. Also, for their own personal consumption the demand for healthy and environmentally friendly products is increasing. When this is recognized by exporter firms, success is not far off. An example of this is Betek where the firm created differentiation with its washable, non-toxic paint in export markets, filling a niche. Additionally, the management also focused on training the public towards a health-conscious life, and its product innovations led to increased sales as well as helping the environment.

Of course, innovativeness should not be limited to advanced thinking in technology and environmental concern. Firms focusing on ideas for creative products or for reshaping operations in a more creative way gain a competitive advantage since they can capture a niche that had long been ignored by others. This might sound a risky attempt at first glance, but can represent a huge opportunity when the hidden needs of the market are properly defined and served. When Tasty Bite entered the US market, selected dishes from Indian cuisine were introduced with new names, new package designs, and a new taste. The company was also innovative in focusing on American customers in general, and not just the ethnic segment like many of its competitors, because it read the underlying trend towards convenient, natural and ethnic foods that US consumers were seeking.

Customer focus

As more EM firms begin to enter the marketing era with its emphasis on customer satisfaction, partly as a result of competitive pressures from domestic firms, and increasingly from foreign firms as protectionist barriers come down, they can no longer take their customers for granted and have to start to think in terms of creating higher value for them. While product and process innovations and higher-quality products undoubtedly provide this value, some of this value can also come from a better understanding of customers, and being able to use techniques such as customer relationship management (CRM) to more finely tune their marketing to customer needs. Intelligent managers focus on customers not just to provide technologically advanced products high in quality, but also ones that are affordable. The variety of needs resulting from different income levels and income inequalities enforces firms to detect which product mix is relevant for which market segment within the same country.

This was also the concern of Efes when the firm entered the CIS countries and established well-known brands in those markets, primarily in Russia. Besides, operating also in countries in the Middle East where religion forbids alcohol consumption, the firm was very successful through caring about customer perceptions of beer. The lifestyle values and associations of consumers were matched with the value attached to the product to build long-term loyalty. In Russia, the Stary Melnik brand was created. Efes aimed to be a problem-solver for its customers by providing them a decent beer to drink that would fit their local emotional value-expectations. As a result, different target markets could enjoy different brands with different slogans because culture-bound perceptual differences were not ignored for the sake of creating a global product. In fact, although the product became globally successful, the adjustments and branding strategies were kept unique for each market since each market's customers are perceived to be unique.

Of course, when one operates in business-to-business markets, factors determining a firm's customer focus can be different. As NAK managers entered the Chinese market, they felt that service-quality orientation went hand in hand with customer satisfaction. Beyond that, the magic of success was their working with key-account managers and being close to their customers. Relationship-focused marketing strategies to follow the expectations of key-account customers allows a quick response to needs and the control of operations. The key-account managers are responsible for specific market regions and coordinate their efforts with the sales-support team to also detect customer complaints. In NAK, internal customer satisfaction and creation of a team spirit and socialization within the firm are important. Employees are sent from Taiwan to China to key accounts to help them to quickly learn about NAK products and target market expectations of NAK. This assures a mutual understanding and environment of trust and long-term relations with the key accounts.

External resource access

In many emerging markets, the support of third parties such as the government, universities and other institutions is often critical for success. As a result, many firms try to build their reputation and create a positive image for the firm in order to garner this support. Links[13] established with different bodies such as government institutions, research and development centres and financial institutions help to develop a network[14] that can be useful for easy access to information and knowledge, assuring a strong position in markets abroad. A firm having these networks feels more secure and can use these links to improve processing technologies and to reach new markets. For NAK and also for the US hotels operating in EMs, that focus can help in avoiding uncertainty which often hinders the flow of business. As a result, these firms can look forward in the markets where they feel comfortable, giving them the strength to go on. When the US hotel chains started to operate in the East European markets, management contracts were preferred to adjust for risk and have access to global capital. Also, links with alliances and other service providers helped to promote the hotel services, and the use of government incentives in the form of reduced taxation rates or for investments helped to cover the high fixed costs. In addition, involving the local government as a partner in the hotel venture helps to reduce some of the risks that are present in turbulent and uncertain environments. Good links with governments both in Taiwan and China helped NAK to overcome technical, bureaucratic difficulties during the start-up period of market entry, and the firm was able to fully focus on market needs and concentrate on how to provide the best solutions in the selected market. NAK also developed strong ties with infrastructure providers and national science and research institutions both in Taiwan and in China. In fact in EMs it is mostly the family-owned conglomerates that have well-developed links to government and core institutions in the domestic environments where government protection plays a big role in the growth of firms, and with their growth achieved it becomes easier for them to maintain a tight relationship with government bodies. This experience and connections with officials provides an advantage in managing business operations.[15] Hence, embedding themselves helps such firms to get close to the political power and knowledge base of the country. Our findings suggest that this resource access is important for some firms, and general anecdotal evidence supports this.

Notes

1. For a discussion of performance measurement issues, see S.T. Cavusgil and S. Zou, 'Marketing Strategy–Performance Relationship: An Investigation of the Empirical Link in Export Market Ventures', *Journal of Marketing*, 58 (1994): 1–21; and F.A. Manu, 'Innovation Orientation, Environment and Performance: A Comparison of U.S. and European Markets', *Journal of International Business Studies*, 23 (1992): 333–59.
2. Very many basic marketing books discuss this in their first chapter, like P. Kotler, *Marketing Management – International Edition*, 11th edn (New York: Pearson Education, 2003): 17–27.
3. Here detailed explanations with charts are presented in the paper by H.M. Channon and A. Yaprak, 'Marketing and Economic Development: Implications for Emerging Economies', in A. Yaprak and H. Tütek (eds), *Globalization, the Multinational Firm, and Emerging Economies: Advances in International Marketing*, Vol. 10, series editor: S.T. Cavusgil (New York: Elsevier Science, 2000).
4. S.P. Kantamneni, P. Upadhyaya and K.R. Coulson, 'Role of Local Government in Globalization', *Journal of Practical Global Business*, vol. II, 2003: 94–122.
5. See T. Khanna and K. Palepu, 'Emerging Giants: Building World-Class Companies from Emerging Markets', *Harvard Case Study* no. 9-703-431, 15 October 2002.
6. For details see D. Kim, D. Kandemir and S.T. Cavusgil, 'The Role of Family Conglomerates in Emerging Markets: What Western Companies Should Know', forthcoming in *Thunderbird International Business Review*, http://globaledge.msu.edu/KnowledgeRoom/FeaturedInsights/0005.pdf
7. See Kalder under www.kalder.org; European Foundation for Quality Management under http://www.efqm.org/; Euroqual under http://www.euroqual.org/presentation/english.htm
8. See American Society for Quality under *www.asq.org*; American Productivity and Quality Center under http://www.apqc.org/portal/apqc/site?path = root
9. See Kalder under www.kalder.org
10. Päivi Karhunen of the Centre for Markets in Transition, Helsinki School of Economics and Business Administration did a detailed study on this issue. The study is called 'Entry Mode Choice in Transition Economies – Operations of International Hotel Companies in Russia'.
11. For details see J.A. Schumpeter, *The Theory of Economic Development* (Cambridge, MA: Harvard University Press, 1934).
12. Stated in P. Marber, *From Third World to World Class – The Future of Emerging Markets in the Global Economy* (New York: Perseus Books, 1998): 26.
13. S.P. Kantamneni, P. Upadhyaya and K.R. Coulson, 'Role of Local Government in Globalization', *op. cit.*
14. See B.G. Carruthers and S.L. Babb, *Economy/Society: Markets, Meanings, and Social Structure* (Thousand Oaks, CA: Pine Forge Press, 2000): 45–69.

15 See T. Khanna and K. Palepu, 'Why Focused Strategies May be Wrong in Emerging Markets', *Harvard Business Review*, 75, 4 (1997): 41–51; C.J. Kock and M.F. Guillen, 'Strategy and Structure in Developing Countries: Business Groups as an Evolutionary Response to Opportunities for Unrelated Diversification', *Industrial and Corporate Change*, 10, 1 (2001): 77–113; cited in D. Kim, D. Kandemir and S.T. Cavusgil, 'The Role of Family Conglomerates in Emerging Markets', forthcoming, *op. cit.*

19
The Markets

F. Zeynep Bilgin, Ven Sriram and Gerhard A. Wührer

For companies that have made the decision to seek opportunities in the global market, issues relating to market choice become paramount. In addition to corporate-level issues that involve analysing and selecting potential markets for entry, this also involves the making of strategic choices relating to the timing and mode of entry,[1] business-unit-level decisions regarding segmentation and targeting, and product-level considerations involving marketing tactics. This chapter attempts to understand the role of the market-related factors in driving the success of the firms described here.

From the network diagram shown in Figure 19.1, it can be seen that four key dimensions related to the market are the common success factors that emerge from an analysis of the studies detailed in Part III. Given that much of the literature examining issues relating to internationalization has 'emphasized the activities of large firms in manufacturing sectors',[2] this emerging market (EM) perspective that examines firms of different sizes and from different industries offers a fresh viewpoint. As can be seen from the number of arrowheads in the figure, the market-selection process is the most frequently cited factor, followed by flexible market entry, the use of a multi-segment approach, and the management of environmental uncertainty.

Market-selection process

Firms look to select foreign markets[3] chiefly for two reasons: first for the opportunities they present as result of their domestic market size and growth, and second, as a location for the manufacture of products not necessarily intended for sale there. For many EM companies, the size and growth of the market in the economically developed countries is a major reason for selecting the countries in the Triad for their global push. Similarly, many advanced market (AM) companies have targeted China, India and other Big Emerging Markets (BEMs) as a result of their market potential. EMs are also often selected for their value as less-expensive manufacturing locations. Thus several paradigms[4] try to explain investment activities abroad.

228　*The Markets*

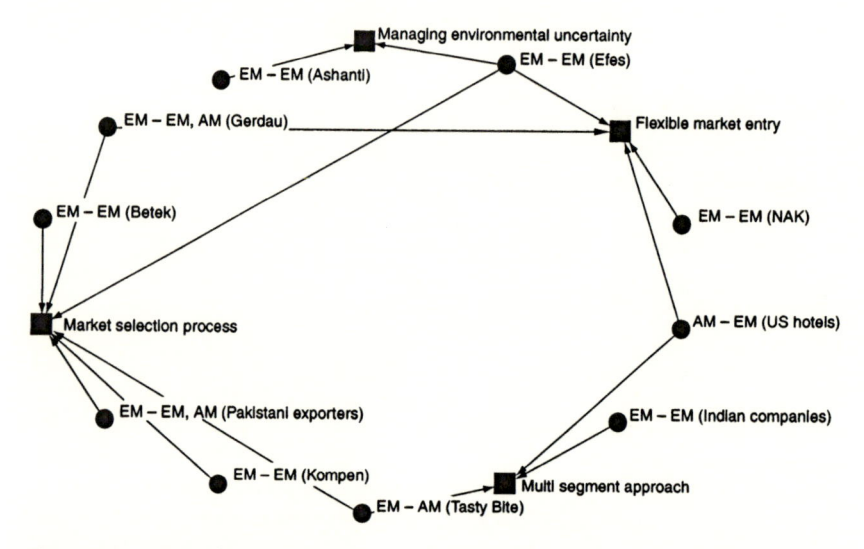

Figure 19.1 The markets network

The evidence we have provides support for both the economic and network views of globalization. To some extent, the evidence from Pakistani exporters pointing to the significance of export market selection and planning as key success factors is a general indicator of the importance of having a formal process for identifying, assessing and targeting markets for expansion. More specifically, Efes and Tasty Bite are good examples of companies that have relied, as least partially, on 'rational' quantifiable criteria in making their market selections. Before choosing target countries, Efes evaluates them on their per capita beer consumption, the competitiveness of the domestic market and examines the legal and macroeconomic environment. Countries with low consumption and less-dominant competitors are considered attractive markets since they offer opportunities for entry and expansion. Similarly, Tasty Bite decided on the USA as its initial target for global expansion based on certain characteristics that indicated a growing demand for its products. Gerdau, too, expanded into the strategically important North American market through its Canadian and US acquisitions. Given the size of these markets and the growing protectionism in the US steel industry, such market-selection decisions make sense for economic, competitive and strategic reasons.

In the use of these 'rational' selection criteria, EM companies may be no different from companies anywhere else in the world. But one clear insight that becomes apparent is that the EM companies studied here appear to rely significantly on cultural, historical, linguistic, geographic and other non-economic criteria as well in selecting foreign markets. In a manner quite consistent with the network view, Turkish Betek executives, for example, built personal linkages and contacts to create an atmosphere of trust and forge relationships with their partners in Azerbaijan. The geographic proximity of the two countries and cultural and linguistic ties also seem to have played a significant part in Betek's decision to select the Azeri market for their initial global foray. Similarly, an examination of how Kompen organized its global operations provides a useful indicator of the role of culture and geography in its market selection. Interestingly, in many of these countries, the company employs people of Turkish origin as distributors, providing further support to the network perspective of the importance of social relationships in business transactions. As mentioned earlier, while Efes uses 'rational' criteria in market selection, it is quite flexible as well. The company's international marketing team decided to enter the Russian market despite low per capita beer consumption, since they chose not to be too rigid in their reliance on statistical data. They interpreted other, less-quantitative signals such as market fragmentation and government support as positive and entered the market despite low levels of beer consumption. The lack of an institutional infrastructure, often a deterrent to market entry, is managed because these companies build their own external networks to circumvent this institutional void.

Flexible market entry

Business researchers have identified a comprehensive list of factors be examined before a company makes the decision of what mode it will use to enter foreign markets.[5] These usually include internal (such as company resources, experience, risk attitudes) and external (market environment, barriers and so on) considerations. The chain theory (or 'stage model') of internationalization[6] suggests that managerial learning dictates the pattern of internationalization followed as firms start with low-risk indirect exporting to psychically close markets, and as they gain knowledge and experience begin to expand to more distant markets using more committed forms of entry. Others have suggested that factors such as perception of risk, the need for control, desired rates of return and the resources available to the firm impact on the entry-mode decision.[7] Surprisingly, the evidence also suggests that, at least in one study of small and medium-sized companies, market selection was done in an unsystematic and *ad hoc* fashion, and in making entry-mode decisions few alternatives were considered and the decision was often 'on the basis of hunch and intuition'.[8]

Our evidence quite clearly points to the use of flexible entry modes by emerging market firms and those operating in emerging markets. The chain theory mentioned earlier is a somewhat mechanistic and rigid approach to entering foreign markets and apparently not one favoured by the EM firms studied here. There was no real evidence of this systematic and deliberate approach of 'getting ones feet wet' before committing to riskier entry modes. If anything, these firms reveal a rather bold and supple character. Efes provides a perfect illustration. In choosing to enter the Romanian market via a greenfield investment in production, the company quickly realized they had erred by not entering through the acquisition of a local brewer. They then quickly restructured the Romanian operation as a 50–50 joint venture with Interbrew. Interestingly, Efes subsequently invested in a production facility in Russia at a time when many of its global competitors were pulling out of Russia because of the looming economic crisis. In a telling demonstration of its flexibility and adaptability to local market requirements, Efes entered the Kazakh and Moldovan markets through local acquisitions while preferring a joint venture in Ukraine. NAK and Gerdau also show this kind of flexibility in choosing entry modes. In assessing the Chinese market, Taiwanese company NAK determined that given its strategic concerns (access to China, cost reduction, proximity to customers and control), FDI was the optimal entry mode. It also realized that each country had certain relative advantages: China's low-cost manufacturing and Taiwan's ability to provide high-end finishing and value-added services. Clearly issues such as risk and lack of market knowledge that an AM company, or indeed many other EM companies, may have considered in choosing a mode of entry for China were less of a concern for NAK given the short psychic and physical distance. In the case of Brazilian steel manufacturer Gerdau, global expansion has largely come through the acquisition of steel plants in Argentina, Canada, Chile and the USA. Here again, the company could have used its low production-cost advantage to simply export steel to other parts of the world, but realized that market conditions required it to consider other modes of entry. Protectionism in the USA via the imposition of tariffs against imported steel and the strategic importance of its core markets in South and North America led the company to adopt other, and what are traditionally considered riskier, entry modes.

The globalization of the hotel industry and the recent expansion of US hoteliers into Eastern Europe and other emerging markets also point to the need for flexibility – on this occasion when AM firms enter EMs. Given risk perceptions and regulations governing the industry, US hotels have used a variety of entry strategies including acquisitions, franchising, joint ventures and management contracts. They have allowed this decision to be dictated, rightly, by market conditions, strategic priorities and management capabilities.

Multi-segment approach

The need to market to several different segments of consumers, each with different and often extremely varied needs and expectations, is a fairly widely accepted concept in most AMs. When expanding into emerging markets, many AM companies initially targeted what they thought to be the 'global consumer' – people who regardless of where they lived, aspired to global quality and global brands. Very often such a segment does exist, but it usually represents a limited number of élite customers who live in large cities. These companies soon find that by restricting themselves to this market, their opportunities for growth are very limited and potential segments are overlooked. Often they discover that market-evolution patterns in EMs are very different from those found in AMs,[9] and that serving the needs of EM consumers often requires very different approaches from those used in the West.[10] Importantly, if they want to expand their businesses beyond the urban élites, they have to recognize the economic, geographic and other dual-economy characteristics that are found in EMs, and adopt a multi-segment approach. In China, for example, there are significant economic and cultural differences between the relatively affluent urban coastal populations, and those in the rural interior provinces. Sub-segments exist even within the urban population.[11] This implies that whereas single-segment concentration may be appropriate for upscale luxury products, a line of products at different price and quality levels appealing to different segments may be warranted for others.[12]

In a similar vein, several of the studies reported in Part III highlight the role of a multi-segment approach as a success driver. There are many examples from India of both Indian and non-Indian firms that serve a multitude of segments with different brands, models and channels simultaneously. Given the country's cultural diversity and significant disparities in income, it is perhaps not surprising to see that many firms have found success in India through this approach. In this respect, India, China and several of the other BEMs share these characteristics. Not surprisingly, the US hotel chains have also found the need to reach out to multiple segments as they have expanded into Hungary and other countries in Eastern Europe. Similarly, Tasty Bite reports the success it has enjoyed in the US food industry by targeting multiple segments for its Indian and Thai ready-to-eat foods. Customers are attracted to its products for a variety of reasons – convenience, globalization of the palate, healthier lifestyles and so on. Geo-demographic segmentation was first used to identify and understand the key consumer segments, particularly important since the product was targeted not at overseas Indians but at the American consumer. Interestingly, the company used this targeting very precisely by tailoring its distribution strategy based on whether a store in a particularly neighbourhood catered to the segments the company was pursuing.

Thus, if they desire to reach beyond the urban, affluent and élite customers in emerging markets, global companies need to employ at least two different approaches – one appealing to urban upmarket consumers using the traditional, sophisticated brand-building strategies employed in AMs, and the other focusing on cheaper, simpler products aimed at lower-income consumers.[13]

For example, after losing significant market share to a local, low-cost powdered detergent manufacturer in India, Unilever[14] introduced its own brand called Wheel aimed at the low-price segment, a successful marketing idea which it also implemented in a similar way in Latin America.

Managing environmental uncertainty

As discussed earlier, firms typically spend a lot of effort in selecting markets for global expansion and in choosing the most appropriate entry mode. It is important to bear in mind, however, that global market environments are dynamic and firms often have to revisit their entry and operating strategies in the light of changing external environments. This is particularly true in many emerging-market countries, as discussed in Chapter 3, where the environment is often uncertain, frequently volatile and turbulent, and also lacking in the institutions that facilitate marketing. There are often sudden changes in government accompanied by shifts in policy and legislation that can have a deep impact on businesses. As a result, companies operating in such environments not only have to decide on entry strategies, but also have to be prepared for market contraction and even market exit. In such contexts, environmental change impacts the nature of market interaction with local actors, which in turn affects, and is affected by, market knowledge and market commitment.[15]

Two of the firms described in Part III, Efes and Ashanti, appear to have found effective ways to cope with environmental uncertainty in their foreign markets, thereby contributing to their success. While their production facility in Russia was under construction, an economic crisis hit. Undeterred, Efes continued its investment with an additional cash injection, while most of its other competitors pulled out of the Russian market. To a significant degree, Efes' experience as a Turkish company and coming from an emerging market proved to be an advantage when entering other emerging markets. This knowledge provided them the ability to increase their market commitment. As a Ghanaian company with investments in many other African countries, Ashanti Goldfields also had to deal with issues relating to environmental turbulence; it had operations in countries such as Zimbabwe where political volatility forced many other companies to leave the country. Here again, as an EM company itself Ashanti had some familiarity with political and economic uncertainty. In addition to using local managers familiar with the local environment, the firm's need for low-cost operations meant that in order to be successful it had to stay committed to the countries where it had investments. In this regard, both Efes and Ashanti provide support for the argument that a long-term perspective is often necessary when operating in emerging markets and the ability to manage uncertainty can be an important success driver. Additionally, exiting the market in the face of such uncertainty and turbulence is not necessarily the best choice.

Other options include increasing commitments, assuming a sleeping position and decreasing commitments, depending on the company's market knowledge and long-term goals.[16] However, staying in the market in the face of competitors' exit can often prove to be a successful strategy.

An understanding of the global markets in which to operate requires a systematic examination of those markets. It may be argued that firms that approach overseas markets in a careful way and develop strategies based on market information can minimize the risk of entering markets where they might not be successful. However, success requires an approach that does not employ a rigid and formulaic selection process, can tolerate ambiguity and some environmental uncertainty, and permits the consideration of a variety of market-entry options. Contrary to conventional wisdom, firms that recognize and appeal to multiple segments don't seem to dilute their strengths but instead appear to broaden their prospects. Because of their familiarity with uncertain environments, EM companies are risk-takers and this familiarity helps them to see opportunities in many situations that risk-averse AM firms would probably avoid.

Notes

1. Y. Pan and D.K. Tse, 'The Hierarchical Model of Market Entry Modes', *Journal of International Business Studies*, 31, 4 (2000): 535–54.
2. N.E. Coviello and K.A-M. Martin, 'Internationalization of Service SMEs: An Integrated Perspective from the Engineering Consulting Sector', *Journal of International Marketing*, 7, 4 (2001): 42–67.
3. K.D. Brouthers, 'Institutional, Cultural and Transaction Cost Influences on Entry Mode Choices and Performance', *Journal of International Business Studies*, 33, 2 (2002): 203–21; A.J. Koch, 'Selecting Overseas Markets and Entry Modes: Two Decision Processes or One?' *Marketing Intelligence and Planning*, 19, 1 (2001): 65–75.
4. R. Vernon, 'International Investments and International Trade in the Product Life Cycle', *Quarterly Journal of Economics*, 80 (1966): 190–207; S.H. Hymer, *The International Operations of National Firms* (Cambridge, MA: The MIT Press, 1976); J.H. Dunning, 'The Eclectic Paradigm of International Production: A Restatement and Some Possible Extensions', *Journal of International Business Studies*, 19 (1988): 1–31; L. Johanson and L-G. Mattsson, 'Interorganizational Relations in Industrial Systems: A Network Approach Compared with the Transaction-Cost Approach', *International Studies of Management and Organizations*, 17,1 (1987): 34–48; D.E. Welch and L.S. Welch, 'The Internationalization Process and Networks: A Strategic Management Perspective', *Journal of International Marketing*, 3,4 (1996): 11–28.
5. See, for example, A.J. Koch, 'Factors Influencing Market and Entry Mode Selection: Developing the MEMS Model', *Marketing Intelligence and Planning*, 19, 5 (2001): 351–61.
6. J. Johanson and J.-E. Vahlne, 'The Internationalization Process of the Firm – A Model of Knowledge Development and Increasing Foreign Market Commitment', *Journal of International Business Studies*, 8 (1977): 23–32.
7. Y. Luo, 'Determinants of Entry in an Emerging Economy: A Multilevel Approach', *Journal of Management Studies*, 38, 3 (2001): 443–72.

8. P.N. O'Farrell, P.A. Wood and Jurong Zheng, 'Internationalization by Business Service SMEs: An Inter-Industry Analysis,' *International Small Business Journal*, 16, 2 (1998): 13–33.
9. D.J. Arnold and J.A. Quelch, 'New Strategies in Emerging Markets', *Sloan Management Review*, 40, 1 (1998): 7–20.
10. C.K. Prahalad and K. Lieberthal, 'The End of Corporate Imperialism', *Harvard Business Review*, 76, 4 (1998): 68–79.
11. G. Cui and Q. Liu, 'Executive Insights: Emerging Market Segments in a Transitional Economy: A Study of Urban Consumers in China', *Journal of International Marketing*, 9, 1 (2001): 84–106.
12. G. Cui and Q. Liu, 'Regional Market Segments of China: Opportunities and Barriers in a Big Emerging Market', *Journal of Consumer Marketing*, 17, 1 (2000): 55–72.
13. G.D. de Abreu Filho, N. Calicchio and F. Lunardini, 'Brand Building in Emerging Markets', *The McKinsey Quarterly*, 2 (2003).
14. *Ibid.*
15. A. Hadjikhani and J. Johanson, 'Facing Foreign Market Turbulence: Three Swedish Multinationals in Iran', *Journal of International Marketing*, 4, 4 (1996): 53–74.
16. *Ibid.*

20
The People

F. Zeynep Bilgin, Ven Sriram and Gerhard A. Wührer

Given that people[1] are the ones who develop and implement strategies, for best strategies to be created and also to be implemented in different markets abroad, firms need to hire well-educated, skilled people and also to focus on training them to become the most competent and qualified people who understand market behaviour in host countries. But being competent is not sufficient for success unless the information is shared and organizational learning takes place. It is very important to assure trustworthy relations among employees and stakeholders at all levels in a firm.

This kind of connectedness also enables a holistic vision whereby different parties linked to the firm feel a sense of ownership and belonging that creates an internal satisfaction which in turn helps not only to understand each other, but also eliminates any perception of alienation. As a result, most organizations understand the important role that people play at all managerial levels on their road to success. This chapter attempts to understand the role of these people-related factors in driving the success of the firms described in Part III of the book. Figure 20.1 again presents the network diagram. In a synoptic view, the people factor turns out to be composed of three sub-components in our overall view of important contributions to success. The most prominent are competent human resources at all management levels, followed by relationships and connections, and, finally, localization of management.

Focus on competent personnel

It has to be acknowledged that competent personnel always play an essential role in the creation and implementation[2] of successful strategies in emerging markets (EMs),[3] although there is some diversity and ambiguity in what is meant by 'competent personnel'. Sometimes[4] it may mean that top managers follow a united and cohesive vision, or that their decisions are fair, show creativity and risk-taking, or are well in tune with all employees in the firm, and whether top managers seek advice of the human-resource

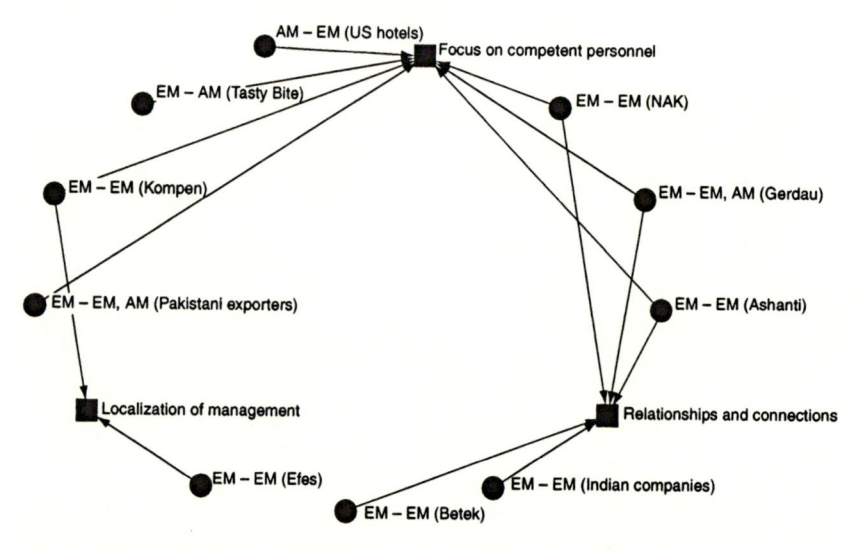

Figure 20.1 The people network

department. In another study[5] competence is measured by variables such as 'experience' of management, 'entrepreneurial profile', 'contact network', 'intelligence and planning activity', which may describe the competence of the people in an internationalizing company. But personnel competencies may also be in management, skilled and trained labour, and technical skills. As also stated at the beginning of this chapter, having well-educated, skilled, qualified and motivated people and training them on a continuous basis contributes to success, allowing the firm to slowly become a learning organization.

A typical example of the focus on competent personnel in management is the case of Kompen, where for proposes of internationalization the people in the marketing team were selected and hired from superior educational backgrounds. These personnel also carry out the guiding principles of the company, which are transparency, honesty and confidence, team orientation, and an openness to innovation. For operations abroad, providing training for these qualified managers is considered to be of great importance. As also mentioned in Chapter 18 about the organization, Kompen has a strategic marketing management team (SMMT) to carryout all the planning processes regarding market screening, selection and market entry. The competence of this team is therefore a must, and this qualified team is also responsible for developing a dealer network for the firm. Hence, the company aims to deploy qualified people at all managerial levels. A similar approach that favours and stresses the role of competent human resources is found at NAK.

The implications for human-resource management when conducting international operations in emerging markets and overseas are huge. In relationship-focused cultures, careful attention must be given to the selection and education of employees. What then are the skills that are emphasized and should be provided by competent personnel? Here soft and hard skills, that is managerial and technical skills, are crucial. NAK sent highly experienced, well-trained and skilled managers with high technical know-how to run its Chinese operations. In addition, employee satisfaction is a prerequisite for customer satisfaction. In this regard, establishing a nourishing environment of competent personnel is either provided by in-house expertise or given to external sources such as personnel-training consultants. Such a team is expected to train the local staff and improve their skills so that here again a certain level of competence is assured at all levels. Tasty Bite is another example where the people factor keeps the enterprise on the success track. It focuses on people, in addition to processes and quality, to achieve its goals. The team of professionals in key positions is equipped with accumulated experience and innovative thinking; members are committed to putting all their energy into building a team sprit, using all their skills and learning from experience focusing on systems, products, and the work ethic together. Team thinking is the basis for ongoing successful operations and the experience of the principals in the Indian and US markets and their superb working relationship is a huge source of strength for the company. The Pakistani exporters refer to qualified management when speaking about success; the quality argument is both on account of product and high-level managerial skills of both export and other staff.

In the study of Gerdau, the steel manufacturer from Brazil, the importance of 'low-cost/high-quality labour' is emphasized several times. The company hires low-cost, high-quality labour, plus the firm provides ongoing training programmes to help employees improve their skills. In a similar fashion, the US hotels need service people with skills and training. In the hotel industry the 'competent service quality[6] oriented people' factor is decisive in entering and operating in emerging markets. Where Kompen and NAK and others stress the soft and hard-skill competencies of their personnel right at the beginning when they hire people, Ashanti's success factor in personnel is its strong local training programmes. These programmes seem to give Ashanti an edge over their competitors' endeavours, many of whom bailed out of Africa as a result of the political and economic instability in their operating areas. The local training programmes and the policy of rotating managers through their various African operations give the company more familiarity with their environments, and are the basis for the excellent connections in different African countries. The firm also uses qualified engineers and local managers with high levels of know-how of the surrounding markets.

Hence, quality of staff is very important for assuring quick success in international markets. Having a pool of well-educated people, good recruitment and hiring procedures, training and qualification programmes all help. When considering EMs, it is important to keep in mind that labour costs are generally lower compared to advanced markets (AMs), so even when the best-educated and skilled people are to be hired or training is provided, these costs often provide EM companies with a competitive advantage.

Relationships and connections

There is a significant body of research from the social sciences,[7] that deals with the issue of relationships. Here, relationships and connections are seen in close connection to the competence of the human resource factor.[8] There seems to be co-occurrence of the relationship factor with a 'focus on competent people' in our studies, because the second important focus of attention for half of the firms in our analysis is 'relationships and connections', representing to a certain extent the culture of the EM. Here it is important to detect the different links for relationships and connections. On the one side there are the personal ties assuring some kind of power links that also help to overcome challenges in the markets. In the Chinese business environment, that is a common strength to be generated and applies also to NAK. Then there are certain networks different to the personal ties in that they are more institutional in nature. Here close communication and follow-up are important, like links with the local institutions as in Ashanti case, or like the fraternity-building of Indian firms. On the other side there are the informal ties, which take the form of developing a certain level of friendship, assuring hospitality, as in Betek's managers' friendly attitudes towards buyers when they visit Turkey. A closer look at these would present better insights on the issue.

NAK is a good example where, from the beginning, careful attention was given to the interface with customers and the embeddedness of business operations into the societal environment of the company in the host country. A lot[9] has been written about the negotiation style and personal relations in the Chinese business environment. A culture deeply rooted in Confucianism, with its teaching on moral development, education and learning, family and group orientation, interpersonal relationships help to meet the challenges[10] of a volatile business environment. It should be pointed out that relationships are different concepts related to the cultural environment of the manager. For relationships in China, managers understand *guanxi*, one of the most important cultural traits of Chinese people the world over. Interestingly, NAK explicitly operates with a network[11] understanding while adapting this thinking to different environments where it has business connections. Good relations with agents and customers are emphasized, so it expands the dyadic view into a polyadic version of multilateral connections.

Gerdau's managers may not speak of *guanxi* when they use relationships and connections to run their business in international environments, yet there are strong ties developed with investors and buyers. That is also the case when Ashanti's managers run their business in Africa and overseas. Their inter-links to society, industry, the business community, customers and suppliers, and connections with local institutions and agents is of a different variety, but the common trait between the numerous 'relation' concepts whether called *guanxi* or not, is the creation of trust and mutual understanding which outlasts the ups and downs in business. In addition it gives space for the evolution of a relationship, by easing frictions and reducing transaction costs during strategic or tactical operations.

'Fraternity-building' is a very special way of creating, sustaining and managing relationships and connections. For Indian firms, fraternities are consumers, trade partners, governments, social groups or vendors. Here the 'family idea' is used as a metaphor in that many Indian companies have a loose umbrella that connects their various partners via a complex web of formal and informal relationships. It is to some extent similar to the approach of Betek, where the strategic intent, structures and even processes are to some extent similar; even though it is not called fraternity-building there. Beteks's internationalization into the emerging market of Azerbaijan is a typical example of a special variant of relationship and connections. The team spirit among functional groups of employees also permeates into the relationships with customers, representatives and end-users. So the entire value-generating chain is a target for relationship understanding.

Localization of management

The discussion of localization of management may be seen as parallel to the issue of standardization vs adaptation,[12] another strand of thinking that addresses the topics in human-resource management which may be labelled global integration vs local responsiveness.[13] Regarding international companies, there seems to exist a tension between the forces that foster uniform worldwide resource deployments to ensure organizational vitality and viability. Localization pressures are environmental forces that encourage local, context-sensitive strategies and managerial practices.

Efes faced a typical emerging-market scenario when entering Russia. The company is very experienced with the operation of efficient distribution networks in Turkey, where it is also the largest supplier of dairy products in the country. For Efes, international success was also the result of a decentralized focus on the markets, on local cultural differences, and also in perceiving the need to act as a local firm in each selected market. The company relied on selected and trained local managers and employees to manage its distribution and logistic operations, and by so doing it concentrated and took into account local cultural differences, and as such acted as a local company. This strategy helped the company not to be seen as 'foreign', but rather as tailored for the local customer. The localization of management helped to form natural bonds between the company and local stakeholders. Kompen also penetrated foreign markets more quickly by using a franchise system, where the localization of management led to a regionally adapted development of marketing strategies. This approach has been backed up by a focus on competent personnel at headquarter and subsidiaries. Interestingly, in many markets Kompen uses franchisees that are of Turkish ancestry.

The motivations for such localization may well be multifold. For some EM companies in our sample, their small size and consequently small pool of qualified managers may constrain their ability to use expatriate management from home. In other cases it may be a genuine belief that their overseas markets are psychically quite distant and they may therefore be better served by using inpatriate managers with a keener understanding of local market conditions.

The evidence shown by the different studies in Part III demonstrates that the people factor is of tremendous importance to emerging-market companies. Of course one could argue that this also seems to be the case with advanced-market companies; but it speaks of something different. Emerging-market companies often operate on a low labour-cost domestic base. We can assume with certainty that, in the near future, skilled labour shortages will be overcome by formal managerial education provided by domestic top-management schools. Personnel will then determine success with their relations and connections in regions where AM managers won't willingly go. While low labour costs cannot be relied on to provide a permanent advantage at least for faster-growing EMs as other even cheaper labour markets emerge, other people-related advantages, if developed and nurtured properly, can be a longer-term source of competitive advantage for EM companies. Their ability to forge and sustain relationships, for example, can serve as a sustainable competitive advantage even in the face of competition.

Another factor to consider is to what extent expatriation is necessary. Firms are beginning to focus on inpatriation to succeed in localization of management and in developing global management strategies,[14] particularly since many of the larger EMs are beginning to develop a deep and talented pool of experienced and trained managers. Keeping in mind that firms are exposed to four basic dimensions of distance while operating internationally, namely cultural, administrative or political, geographic and economic distance, working with a large group of 'cosmopolitan' managers will help firms to overcome the problems resulting from cultural distance in particular, compared to firms where all managers are from the home country.[15] Hence, strengthened communication is a big ingredient for the success of firms dealing with EMs.

Notes

1 See the contribution in this volume by Reichl, Wührer and Sriram in Chapter 5, 'Leadership in Central and Eastern European Countries'; Chr. Brewster and R. Kabst, 'Personalpraktiken national und international tätiger Unternehmen', in J. Gutmann

and R. Kabst (eds), *Internationalisierung im Mittelstand. Chancen – Risiken – Erfolgsfaktoren* (Wiesbaden: Gabler, 2000): 291–314.
2. K.S. Law, D.K. Tse and N. Zhou, 'Does Human Resource Management Matter in a Transitional Economy? China as an Example', *Journal of International Business Studies*, 34 (2003): 255–65; A. Edström and P. Lorange, 'Matching Strategy and Human Resources in Multinational Companies', *Journal of International Business Studies*, 2, 15 (1984): 125–37.
3. H. Kantis, M. Ishida and M. Komori, 'Entrepreneurship in Emerging Economies: The Creation and Development of New Firms in Latin America and East Asia', Paper published by the Inter-American Development Bank, March 2002, http://www.iadb.org/sds/doc/IDBEnglishBookfinal.pdf (14 November 2003).
4. K.S. Law, D.K. Tse and N. Zhou (2003), *op. cit.*: 257.
5. R. Poisson, Z. Su, G. D'Amboise and Y. Gasse, 'Success Factors for Small and Medium-Sized Canadian Enterprises Doing Business in Emerging Asian Markets', Paper presented at the 'International Council for Small Business 47th World Conference', San Juan, Puerto Rico, 16–19 June 2002, http://www.sbaer.uca.edu/Research/2002/ICSB/auth_letter/pdf/020.pdf (13 November 2003).
6. C. Daesung, L. Sungjin, and S. Chung-Sub 'A Comparative Study on the Quality of Deluxe Hotel Services in Seoul – Focusing on Foreign Customers', http://myhome. hanafos.com/~madeweb/hotel.html (14 November 2003).
7. I. Wilkinson, 'A History of Network and Channels Thinking in Marketing in the 20th Century', *Australasian Journal of Marketing*, 2, 9 (2001): 23–53; Y. Luo, 'Guanxi and Performance of Foreign-Invested Enterprises in China: An Empirical Inquiry', *Management International Review*, 1, 37 (1997): 51–70.
8. Y. Luo, 'Toward a Cooperative View of MNC–Host Government Relations: Building Blocks and Performance Implications', *Journal of International Business Studies*, 3, 32 (2001): 401–19; K.S. Law, D.K. Tse and N. Zhou (2003), *op. cit.*: 255–65.
9. See for instance T. Fang, *Chinese Business Negotiating Style* (Thousand Oaks, CA.: Sage, 1999), in particular p. 118; H. Peck, A. Payne, M. Christopher and M. Clark, *Relationship Marketing. Strategy and Implementation* (Oxford: Butterworth-Heinemann, 1999).
10. T. Fang, *Chinese Business Negotiating Style*, *op. cit.*: 191.
11. J.K. Frels, T. Shervani and R.K. Srivastava, 'The Integrated Networks Model: Explaining Resource Allocations in Network Markets', *Journal of Marketing*, 1, 67 (2003): 29–45; D. McLoughlin and C. Horan, 'Markets-as-Networks: Notes on a Unique Understanding', *Journal of Business Research*, 55 (2002): 535–43.
12. P.G.P. Walters, 'International Marketing Policy: A Discussion of the Standardization Construct and its Relevance for Corporate Policy', *Journal of International Business Studies*, 2, 17 (1986): 55–69.
13. J.M. Hannon, Ing-Chung Huang and Bih-Shiaw Jaw, 'International Human Resource Strategy and its Determinants: The Case of Subsidiaries in Taiwan', *Journal of International Business Studies*, 3, 26 (1995): 531–54.
14. For details see M.G. Harvey, G. Speier and M.M. Novicevic, 'The Impact of Emerging Markets on Staffing the Global Organization: A Knowledge-based View', *Journal of International Management*, 5 (1999): 167–86.
15. T. Kit, 'Distance Still Matters', *Harvard Business Review*, 79, 8 (September 2001): 137.

21
The Operations

F. Zeynep Bilgin, Ven Sriram and Gerhard A. Wührer

The operations issues in and from emerging markets (EMs) appear at first glance to be more tactical than strategic. However, by viewing it in this way one might neglect the very core of the issue. Shouldn't we look at the quality of the market a bit more closely when dealing with the topic of operations? Since these markets are still emerging, transaction costs are high. On the other hand, the dynamics and profiles of the market structure are different in advanced markets; there is a complex web of infrastructural institutions, such as retail chains, media companies, news and advertising agencies, banks, marketing research companies and consultants that simplify marketing operations.[1] In emerging markets however, the complex web of institutions sketched out above is either absent or poorly developed, or limited to large metropolitan areas where industries and customers tend to be concentrated given the dual economy syndrome that characterizes many EMs.[2] All this highlights the fact that in many EMs, operational decisions relating to marketing and other functional areas pose a much greater challenge than in economically advanced countries.

How then is it possible to establish an adequate price/quality relationship where the marketing infrastructure functions differently? More than ever, the customization[3] of marketing and marketing policies seems to be one of the approaches to tackle the problems, a perspective which ought not to neglect the future development of emerging markets, and the marketing instruments by which companies are linked to the markets to meet their customers and competitors. This consideration is also highly linked to two other factors for exporters and customers; namely, success of operations from and in EMs relates also to generating high levels of convenience through well-established networks with suppliers and distributors. This also assures control, proper segmentation and targeting, focusing on another differentiation factor – brand-building.

The way the different studies from Part III are linked in terms of operational variables is reflected in Figure 21.1. Interestingly, these operational issues appear to be important drivers for all the companies we study, except

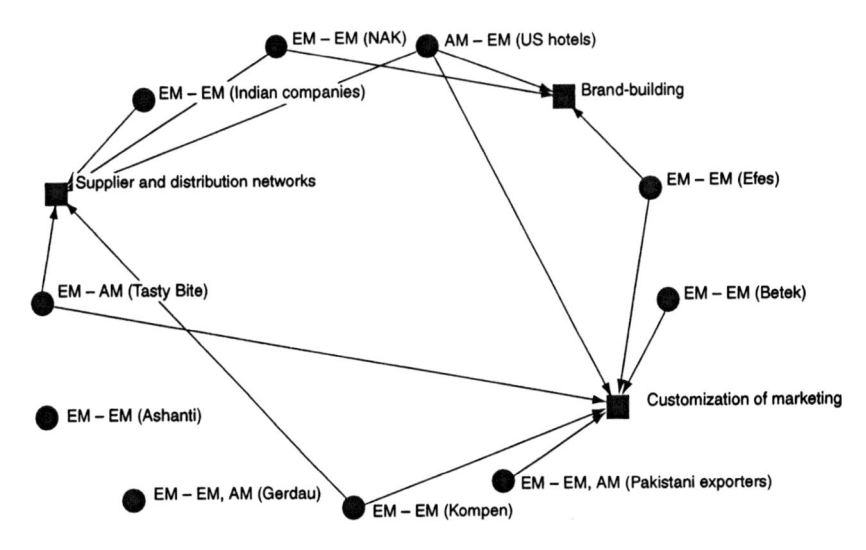

Figure 21.1 The operations network

for Ashanti and Gerdau that compete in markets where it is imperative that firms be able to produce products of international quality with a low cost structure. For them, prices are generally set by the market rather than by the company, since opportunities for product differentiation are few, and as a result operational issues relating to marketing play a less-important role.

Customization of marketing

Based on the stage of the emerging market, several options for customizing marketing to the needs and demands of the consumer seem to be possible. Different firms we studied use different strategies, with product-based customization being the most prominent, followed by the communication strategies, pricing and relevant distribution adjustments to fit to host-market needs.

Betek, when implementing its marketing strategy, followed the philosophy of 'customer value-creation'. In implementing this principle it adjusted its products and prices to the different expectations in the various markets. When servicing the Russian market it avoided the option of starting with a low-quality/low-price entry marketing strategy, although that would have been intriguing. Instead, Betek combined prime quality with aggressive pricing,[4] and the pricing strategy was also adjusted to the Azeri market according to the income levels of the people there.

For Betek the focus on product differentiation is also important. The company provides different colours in different markets matching the decoration tastes of the people in different cultures. Tasty Bite also follows the same strategy in the US market, where local taste expectations are analysed and the Indian food recipe reformulated according to the American market, and the product names chosen to reflect product contents while retaining an association with India, rather than the standard Indian names which may not describe the product to consumers unfamiliar with Indian cuisine. This was consistent with the firm's strategy of targeting the general population rather than concentrating on the Indian immigrant population in the USA.

Tasty Bite shows quite well, too, how product customization[5] accommodates the various appetites and tastes in multi-segments and leads to success in foreign markets that are culturally very heterogeneous. The 'Green Peas Pilaf', 'Bombay Potatoes', and 'Curried Vegetable Pilaf Biryani' cater to the nutrition-conscious American consumer,[6] who thinks it is 'pure' Indian or Thai food, but adjusted to the gourmet-savvy local customer. For Efes, marketing customization means focusing on product and promotion adjustments based on local conditions. As far as the product adjustments are concerned, the firm aims to serve many segments in local markets either by offering new beers such as Stary Melnik, and/or improving the quality of local brands by switching to better brewing technology such as pasteurizing beer products, catering to the tastes and demands of the local people. The brand communication is very special, emphasizing on emotional appeal. Customizing also means balanced assortment policies.[7]

Customization is also one of the major success factors of Pakistani exporters in general when doing business abroad. Here R&D plays a supportive role but successful exporters report product adaptation as being one of the five most important determinants of their superior export performance.

For Kompen, the customization of an integrated market communication is at the heart of the company's success. One of the best Turkish media development firms prepared the advertising and sales promotion programmes according to each country's cultural characteristics. The franchisor in each market benefits from this since the communication strategy is tailored to the needs of consumers in that country. Studies are conducted in each market to determine the approach that will work best.

The customized marketing approach of the US hotel industry seems quite different, probably because of the characteristics of the industry and that it reflects the strategies of AM firms in EMs. In a sector where standardization is a must for the maintenance of global quality levels, it is interesting to note that customization is also implemented. While hotels standardize their training programmes and internal procedures in order to provide acceptable international levels of quality, some degree of operational customization is needed for several sites and region-related cultural differences and reasons.

To overcome problems, Betek also took into account the different stages of the distribution system evolution and reconfigured them from those existing. This happened in the areas around the Black Sea coasts and farther abroad. In the Ukraine, a local representative is in charge of sales and marketing activities, while a Turkish company located in Trabzon services Russia. Thus, the distribution strategies applied by Betek are also consistent with their use of flexible market-entry modes, a success factor discussed in Chapter 19.

Supplier and distribution networks

For many companies, upstream relations with suppliers and downstream connections with distributors and retailers are a significant source of competitive advantage. There is compelling anecdotal evidence that companies are narrowing their supplier base and placing their input needs in the hands of a smaller number of more trusted suppliers. This has enabled them to gain economies from a reduction of inventory and also by cutting costs associated with negotiating and monitoring supplier contracts. At the other end of the distribution chain, retail access and distributor support have always been a major prerequisite of product success, particularly in consumer-goods marketing. Retail support is necessary for those products that need prime shelf space, display and merchandising, and promotional help. Distributors are vital in providing sales and service support.

Many basic marketing textbooks discuss the importance of backward and forward linkages.[8] These linkages as a basis for integrative growth strategies that may lead to success in different market settings. Consumer demand for all kinds of products may be rising in emerging markets, but for producers to get their goods to the market, the system is cumbersome, costly and slow. The question is how to deal with these externalities. One of the generic strategies[9] is to fill local-market institutional voids directly, and the majority of Indian companies carry out institution-building in various supplier networks. The markets in which institutions are developed for better functioning range from labour markets and financial markets, to production networks. These supply networks may have some redundancies, but in volatile economic conditions this is a strength as failures are fewer and better continuity in flows is achieved. Secondary effects that may occur are in the area of joint knowledge-generation and development, which may also make supplier networks unique and entry barriers for competitors.

Tasty Bite also developed a supplier system with production sites – the fields where the necessary inputs such as healthy vegetables are grown. This also ensures control. Besides this they outsourced packaging design, production and printing to global suppliers, creating a cost-reduction of an astonishing 30 per cent by doing so. A careful testing period in California with key distributors paved the way to distribution all over USA in nearly 50 well-known supermarket chains. The firm spent most of its market-entry investments in building a distribution infrastructure, where business processes guarantee growth success. In the highly competitive fast-moving consumer-goods sector in the USA, trade relations and retail access are crucial for product success. By understanding their consumer segments and working with neighbourhood-level data, Tasty Bite was able to get the product into those stores where the underlying demographics suggested that the product would sell. As a result, retailers supported the product and the company since the company did not try to gain distribution in all stores in the chain but targeted the stores carefully.

In that sense, Tasty Bite also resembles NAK, a networking company as seen by other success factors. The entire process for NAK is planned from a network perspective[10] where the network consists of a supplier and distributor network, the latter with its key-account managers. The outcomes of network-building act as inputs into the company's strategic foundation, which in turn serves as its resource base for international operations.

Of course NAK's supplier and distribution network is quite different from that of the worldwide reservation system of the US hotels operating in the East European markets. Here the technological aspect dominates the global distribution system, which it is a central reservation system used by travel agents and parallelled by the Internet where tourists and vacationers have access to booking hotels and related services. This eases access for people in EMs of transition economies where the travel and tourism infrastructure is improving, connections to travel agents are slowly becoming more important, and convenience is highly valued. As US hotels begin to expand more aggressively into Eastern Europe, mostly through franchising and other non-ownership entry modes, these centralized reservation systems become a useful tool in building a global network that binds together many properties under one central umbrella.

Kompen's approach in supplier and distribution networks is of course different, relying on the careful selection of the 'right' main distributors through whom product trade-name franchising is done.

Brand-building

Interestingly, for three of the enterprises we studied, brand-building was a success driver. For two of these, US hotels and Efes, who also emphasized customization, this may appear inconsistent. However, closer scrutiny sheds some important light on this matter. The US hotels do indeed attempt to build global brands but this seems to be part of their strategy of 'glocalization' where they standardize some elements of their marketing while customizing others. Many AM firms such as McDonald's follow this approach when going global. For Efes, the strategy is somewhat different. Their brand-building emphasizes both building local brands in addition to its flagship global brand, Efes Pilsen. For their local brands, the company uses customized marketing that fits in with local consumers, as in the case of its Russian brand, Stary Melnik, while the marketing for Efes Pilsner employs a more pan-European approach.

Brand-building aids the easy targeting of different market segments, and two approaches[11] are suggested: a step-by-step approach in which products exported from the home emerging-market country penetrate overseas markets through independent distributors serving discount channels. This gradual process permits companies to gain understanding of customer behaviour and to build brand recognition. The second approach is to buy an established brand that has perhaps fallen on hard times and then move its production either to the home country or keep it in another emerging market if benefits from lower labour costs are possible. Each of the approaches has its own advantages and returns for the internationalizing company. Efes is a good example of how a company carries out brand-building by using both models – multiple branding. While it improves locally acquired brands, in addition it creates new brands such as Stary Melnik, whose 'birthday' it celebrated in a 12-hour non-stop Russian rock-music marathon. Efes covers different segments with its Efes Pilsener and Warsteiner Premium Verum in the licensed premium segment, and Stary Melnik in the local premium segment; in this way the company will reinforce its international brand portfolio but also strengthen its market position against local and foreign competitors.

In the service sector such as the hotel industry, international branding is mostly done by the first approach, even if sometimes the acquired original hotel names remain unchanged under the new hotel chain's name, if they have strong reputations. However, building global brands in each of the category segments is a vital part of hotel marketing because brand recognition is the glue that holds the chain's identity together, since many properties are franchised, others are operated by joint venture partners and still others may be managed by contract. Because of these different entry modes, global branding is a key unifier for US hotels as they go global. NAK, whose product strategy is based on offering high-quality, high-tech products has to rely on a strong brand reputation to communicate 'superior quality at adequate prices'; the promotional activities using trade shows and different kinds of advertisements in special interest media, public relations with industry associations, research institutions and customers ensure the positioning success for the worldwide brand.

Many studies are being conducted in various markets with different levels of market development. In fact, for export success for firms' internationalization and performance in export markets it is clear that generalizibility of methods used is difficult, and hence new paradigms are needed.[12] Although it has been stated that the need to be globally competitive depends on applying global societal strategies since the world market is becoming closer due to advanced technological infrastructures,[13] adopting global marketing strategies for EMs is not always an easy task since many aspects of such strategies are culture-bound, affecting the attitudes and behaviour of managers, and the functioning of the organizations. Hence, marketing operations are also shaped accordingly. In addition, as can be seen from the examples of AM companies operating in EMs,[14] cultural differences require adaptation in product-related strategies such as display and assortment, at least in the retail business. While globally standardized strategies may be possible or even desirable for all the arguments offered in favour of standardization by large AM multinationals, given their ability to craft global promotional campaigns and design global products, our evidence suggests that this may not be an appropriate approach for EM companies. Based on the analysis of the companies presented here, customization of operations still seems to be what has made many of these companies successful. Perhaps as their brands begin to enjoy global popularity they may be tempted to go the standardization route, but for now they appear to build customer relationships by tailoring their offerings. They also emphasize cultivating relationships with their supplier and distribution networks.

In a synoptic view, the operations as a success factor build heavily on the customization of marketing, and other factors such as supplier and distribution networks as an operational approach follow. Branding should not be neglected here, but the first two seem to be more significant drivers. The lessons here are that success in operations is a function of companies leveraging their strengths in areas where they have a distinctive advantage. For the companies studied here, the evidence clearly suggests that this comes from being responsive to local market needs by adapting elements of their marketing mix and by capitalizing on their connections with suppliers and distributors. Interestingly, with the exception of a few cases, brand-building was not a central element driving operational success. This may be partly due to the fact that for companies competing in commodity markets, such as Gerdau and Ashanti, branding is not a viable option. Also, perhaps for many of these EM companies at this stage in their evolution as potential global players, they were not yet ready to take on many of their AM competitors and their global brands. As they become successful in regional markets and slowly establish a global presence, brand-building may then become a viable operational strategy.

Notes

1 T. Khanna and K. Palepu, 'Emerging Giants: Building Work-Class Companies in Emerging Markets', Harvard Case Study no. 9-703-431, in particular p. 2.
2 H.M. Cannon and A. Yaprak, 'Marketing and Economic Development: Implications for Emerging Economies', in A. Yaprak and H. Tütek (eds), *Globalization, The Multinational Firm, and Emerging Economies. Advances in International Marketing*, Vol. 10, series editor S. Cavusgil (Amsterdam: Elsevier, 2000): 89–110. S.M. Shaw and F. Wang, 'Moving Goods in China', *The McKinsey Quarterly*, 2, web exclusive, 2002.
3 See M. Bodur, G. Alpay and G. Asuğman, 'Managerial Perceptions on Performance Determinants of Multinational Companies in an Emerging Economy', in A. Yaprak and H. Tütek (eds), *Globalization, The Multinational Firm, and Emerging Economies*, op. cit.: 131–62.

4 See also M.A. Marinov and S.T. Marinova, 'Foreign Direct Investment in the Emerging Markets of Central and Eastern Europe: Motives and Marketing Strategies', in A. Yaprak and H. Tütek (eds), *Globalization, The Multinational Firm, and Emerging Economies*, op. cit.: 21–52.
5 M. Bodur, G. Alpay and G. Asuğman, 'Managerial Perceptions on Performance Determinants of Multinational Companies in an Emerging Economy', *op. cit.*
6 See http://www.tastybite.com/ (retrieved 12 October 2003). See http://www.anadolugroup.com/english/bulten10.htm (retrieved 12 October 2003).
7 See http://www.anadolugroup.com/english/bulten10.htm (retrieved 12 October 2003).
8 See P. Kotler, *Marketing Management – Analysis, Planning, Implementation, and Control*, 8th edn (NJ: Prentice Hall Int., 1994): 77–8.
9 For generic strategies see T. Khanna and K. Palepu, 'Emerging Giants: Building World-Class Companies in Emerging Markets', Harvard Business School Case Study no. 9–703–431, 15 October 2002.
10 See D.E. Welch and L.S. Welch, 'The Internationalization Process and Networks: A Strategic Management Perspective', *Journal of International Marketing*, 3, 4 (1996): 11–28.
11 P. Gao, J.R. Woetzel and Y. Wu, 'Can Chinese Brands Make It Abroad?', *McKinsey Quarterly*, 4, web exclusive 2003.
12 M. Trimeche, 'Towards an Actualization of the Factors Determining the Firm's Export Expansion: Insights from the Literature', http://copenhagen.jibs.net/LitReview/2002/2002_1_21.pdf (retrieved 17 November 2003).
13 See J. Elimimian, 'Adopting Global Marketing Strategy: Factors that will Contribute to Business Success of the Transition Economies', *Journal of Euromarketing*, 6, 3 (1997): 81–101.
14 See P. Jennifer, 'K-Mart's Eastern European Adventure', *Discount Merchandiser*, 36, 4 (April 1996): 26–32.

22
Concluding Thoughts

F. Zeynep Bilgin, Ven Sriram and Gerhard A. Wührer

One of the major challenges facing editors of books such as this is the daunting task of trying to organize and interpret the massive amount of information presented so that it can be distilled into some meaningful conclusions for readers. Our struggle was to find the right balance between maintaining the integrity of the thoughts and analyses, and indeed uniqueness, of the contributions in Parts II and III while drawing a bigger picture that enables readers to appreciate the underlying patterns and commonalities. The task is further complicated by the fact that we are trying to learn lessons from a wide range of studies – ones that not only share the rich geographic, economic and cultural diversity of emerging markets (EMs) themselves, but are based on the examination of enterprises of different sizes and from different industries, using a variety of research methodologies.[1]

This further complicates our attempt to weave these different strands into a meaningful whole. Nevertheless, given our desire, as articulated in the Preface, to provide lessons learned from the emerging-markets experience for our academic and practitioner audiences, we undertake this challenge with relish. We also believe strongly that despite this seemingly bewildering variety in the nature and content of the studies presented here, there are strong common threads that drive the successes of the companies we have analysed. We should make clear, however, that our conclusions are rooted in an analysis of the firms and industries presented in Part III, and while we believe that the discussion that follows has some meaning and significance for other emerging-market firms and those operating in EMs, our primary intention is to stimulate thought and discussion. So, based on the discussion in Chapters 17–21, there are four broad themes around which EM success can be framed: a tight–loose organizational structure, a flexible and creative approach, an emphasis on being world-class, and a relationship focus.

Tight-loose structure

Whereas the idea of having a strong set of core values ('tight') while simultaneously encouraging innovation and creativity ('loose') is not new,[2] the issue for many global companies, particularly those from EMs, is how to balance the frequently conflicting internal demands with market conditions that often require adaptability. Unlike the case of advanced market (AM) multinationals whose initial global forays are to other AMs where environments and market conditions are stable, many EM companies studied here expanded into other EMs that were often different but where they could transfer lessons learned from their domestic environments. This required a careful balancing act of maintaining consistency and coordination while being nimble and agile at the same time. It appears that one of the ways many of the firms have struck that balance is by creating a structure that has tight managerial and financial controls, but yet retains the ability to localize itself where necessary. As has been discussed in Chapter 18, for many of the EM firms that are family-owned or controlled such as Gerdau and NAK, this ownership enables close supervision over internal operations and procedures. However, even non-family-owned companies such as Kompen, Ashanti and many Pakistani exporters created structures where top management kept a very close eye over operations. For Gerdau and Ashanti who sell commodity-type products and thus have very little control over price-setting, industry and market conditions demand containment of production costs and this is where the tight control comes in. US hotels also exhibit this management approach in that they centralize strategy development and certain functions at the corporate headquarters while at the same time allowing local managers to customize service based on differences in local customs and tastes.

At the same time, these companies also felt that given the volatility in the environments in which they operate, they needed to adapt aspects of their operations as well. Also, the lack of institutions in many EMs that would allow an AM-style marketing approach has created in EM companies a self-identity and a mindset that enables them to cope extremely well with EM market conditions. NAK, Gerdau and Efes show remarkable flexibility in their choice of entry mode – ensuring that it fits the situation. Similarly, many aspects of management and marketing are localized to reflect market conditions. Kompen and Efes both reflect this looseness, the former in its selection of locals as franchisees and the latter in its reliance on local managers in virtually all its overseas operations. Both companies recognize the need to stay close to the consumer, and also to customize aspects of their marketing mix rather than attempting to standardize these strategies. Evidence from other industries[3] and contexts supports the approach of retaining some elements of central dependency while allowing necessary levels of local autonomy.

To some degree, this use of a tight–loose approach may be an outcome of several characteristics of EM companies and EM environments. The firms studied here are not that different from the large family-owned[4] companies and business groups found in many emerging markets[5] where privately-held companies are not uncommon. Additionally, in markets where liquidity and cash-flow problems abound, there are problems with customers defaulting on payments and with bad debts.[6] These conditions combine to create a situation where internal management control is not easy and financial and payment management necessary. Also, since expansion is often funded by internally generated resources as a result of limited availability of borrowing,[7] tight financial discipline becomes imperative. At the same time, many emerging-market companies have a limited pool of skilled managers to tap into in the domestic market. They frequently prefer to retain them for key positions in the headquarters and use them selectively in important foreign markets. As a result, they rely on local managers in their foreign operations and give them a considerable degree of autonomy in developing strategies for their markets.

Flexibility and creativity

For a long time, modern management theory, particularly in the West, has tended to emphasize a 'scientific' and 'rational' approach to decision-making. In most emerging markets, formal management education is a much more recent phenomenon than it is in the West, although most EMs now have top-class business schools of their own, which very often have developed education material and curricula based on US and European schools. While it is not uncommon now to find many senior managers in EM companies that have been educated in the West, and in many cases successfully implementing techniques learned there, a significant proportion of the management cadre of these companies has had the bulk of its experience in domestic markets where there are serious market and competitive data limitations. Also, they have learned to manage in turbulent environments where macroeconomic and industry forecasts are frequently unreliable. As a result, they tend to develop a much more creative management style and are less dependent on data-driven decision-making. As discussed in Chapter 5, research shows that Central and Eastern European managers are more flexible, entrepreneurial, improvizational and pragmatic in their leadership style when compared to their Western European counterparts.

Our studies show evidence of this less-rigid and more flexible approach. Significantly, in selecting markets for expansion, Efes chose to enter the Russian market even when market research data did not support the decision, because senior managers felt, based on experience and judgment, that conditions were right. Similarly they continued to operate in Russia despite market volatility because they relied on their experience from having learned to manage similar conditions in their home market in Turkey. So not only did Efes de-emphasize the data that didn't favour market entry, they decided to make further investments in Russia despite the economic crisis. Similarly, Betek did not hesitate to accept its first order from Azerbaijan although a proper distribution network was not in place at that time. This took courage and a great deal of confidence in their judgment. Many of the companies we studied also used 'softer' criteria such as geographic proximity, historic and cultural ties in selecting foreign markets. It should be emphasized that we are not suggesting ignoring conventional yardsticks in making such decisions, only that there was less rigid interpretation of these yardsticks and less fear in using qualitative factors in sizing up opportunities. In a similar fashion, Ashanti executives have acquired and profitably run gold mines given up by Western companies. Despite the obvious political turmoil in many of these countries, Ashanti probably took a subjective decision and felt able to manage the risk when the same conditions looked at objectively made Western companies conclude that the risk was too high. The familiarity with the environment and confidence in managing it, that were factors in Ashanti's and Efes' decisions, is not something that can easily be calculated or quantified when making market-selection decisions. It requires a willingness to be flexible and to think laterally. In introducing a new product such as environmentally friendly paint in Azerbaijan when there was no clear evidence that the market demanded it, Betek's managers showed a degree of creative thinking and a capacity for risk-taking.

This ability to be flexible has also been demonstrated by the use of a multi-segment approach. It took boldness and unconventional thinking for Tasty Bite to pursue the segments they did. While the immigrant Indian segment would have been an easy and safe target for the company, the company was creative enough to see that the underlying trends in US food consumption would support pursuing a larger market, something that very few of their competitors initially did.

World class

Companies from emerging markets have to battle country-of-origin perceptions that global consumers often have about products that are associated with those countries. As discussed in Chapter 3, while some brands such as Acer and Samsung have slowly begun to develop a global reputation, most emerging-market companies are still in the position of being contract manufacturers for other, better-known brands and companies. However, many are not content with simply being original equipment manufacturers (OEM), and have ambitions to develop truly global brands.[8] Companies such as Chinese white-goods manufacturer Haier[9] have already begun to make this transition. It is conceivable that as multinationals become 'rootless', some of these country-of-origin perceptions may become irrelevant,[10] but for now they represent a significant hurdle for EM multinationals interested in capturing the higher margins[11] and value-addition that result from a strong brand equity. This is particularly true for those companies that compete in markets for high-priced, technology and image-driven products targeted at upper-income consumers. Also, given these perceptions, few EM multinationals can afford to make mistakes with product quality, even as they battle consumer perceptions about low quality,[12] when they market globally because unlike AM multinationals who may be given the benefit of the doubt when they first falter, they may not get a second chance. As a result, they have to make a strong an unequivocal commitment to being world-class[13] and to overcome the institutional voids[14] that increase transaction costs and to compete with their counterparts from advanced economies.

The task is by no means an easy one since EM companies often lack distribution channels, promotional expertise and a sense of what product features will appeal to global consumers. This lack of marketing expertise, rather than manufacturing and product-quality issues, is perhaps their biggest obstacle on the global stage.[15] However, the success of Peruvian Kola Real in Central and South America shows that even small family-owned start-ups can pose a significant threat to global giants like Coca-Cola and Pepsi, despite the brand equity and distribution strength these multinationals possess.[16] Also, in many European countries consumers seem to be expressing a preference for local brands over their better-known global rivals. This may give local companies the opportunity they need if they can play up their brands' localness as being more desirable than the dulling sameness of global brands.[17] Whether EM consumers will prefer their home-grown brands is uncertain, but the initial success of Kola Real, and the launch of Ülker group's Cola Turca in Turkey, may give EM companies some hope and encouragement. The growth of Chinese TV manufacturers such as TCL International, Haier, Konka and Midea shows that they now pose a legitimate challenge to Japanese global dominance of this industry, just as the Japanese brands such as Sony and Panasonic overtook US and European companies in the past. In fact, the joint venture between TCL and France's Thomson SA is expected to displace Sony as the world's No. 1 TV manufacturer.[18] As they accumulate experience in their domestic and regional markets, EM companies such as these have the potential to become world-class competitors under their own global brands.

From our analysis, this commitment to becoming world-class can take several forms. Some, like Kompen, adhere to meeting ISO and other international quality standards, while NAK makes investments in R&D so that they can provide technologically sophisticated products. Others such as Betek form alliances in the domestic market with better-known global companies in their industry so as to reassure their customers that certain minimum global standards will be met, and to also use these ties to transfer the latest manufacturing technology to markets abroad. For Gerdau, its customers expect competitively priced steel but will not compromise quality expectations. Tasty Bite reengineered many aspects of its operations and designed its products and packaging to communicate a cutting-edge image that was perhaps necessary given its Indian roots.

A focus on skilled and competent people appears to be a key factor[19] in building world-class companies. Virtually all the enterprises we studied focus on leveraging their human capital. Emerging markets are blessed with low wage rates when compared to AMs, but they don't seem to have to compromise on the quality of their personnel. This is true across almost all the countries and industries represented in our analysis. Whether it is the steelworkers in Brazil, mining engineers in Africa, hotel employees in Hungary, staff at the Pakistani exporters, or the Taiwanese 'family' at NAK, these companies have realized the importance of having the right people in order to create an organization that can compete against the global giants.

Many emerging market companies such as Samsung feel that technological innovation is a key to global success.[20]. Chapter 7 provides many examples of the innovations many companies have made to enable them to compete against AM multinationals, largely to protect their domestic turf from the challenge posed by these new entrants with their deeper pockets, marketing muscle and global brands. These innovations are in a variety of functional areas: R&D, logistics, distribution and transportation. Clearly, as EMs open up their markets and their consumers get a taste of high-quality imports, quality expectations get ratcheted up and they expect no less from local providers.

Relationship focus

The appreciation of the importance of forging, building and strengthening relationships between business partners is certainly not new. Over the last half-century, several prominent and influential writers such as John Commons, Joseph Schumpeter and Ronald Coase[21] have recognized the role of networks. Research and anecdotal evidence has recognized that the cooperative approach is often much more effective than the traditional, and frequently adversarial, arms-length method. Our analysis of emerging-market companies reveals that while vertical connections are important and are built, many of these companies take a broader relationship focus and, consistent with the network[22] view, build trusting and collaborative links horizontally as well with agents, partners, governments, local institutions and other external constituencies. Given that regulatory bodies in particular are frequently more influential in EMs than in AMs,[23] this focus is not surprising. These companies appear to have a web of formal and informal networks, largely based on notions of interdependence and reciprocity, loosely related to the Chinese concept of *guanxi* or interpersonal connections.[24]

There are various examples of how these connections have been built and nurtured and it should be stressed that the origins of network-thinking and applications may vary from culture to culture, and market to market.[25] So, some of them are not very different from those developed by AM companies and implemented in AM contexts. The use of key-account managers by NAK is not in and of itself an unusual phenomenon. However, their use of middlemen in Europe contrasts with the greater emphasis on relationships in China, where the Vice-President Billy Chiu himself handles clients, and the cultural affinity between Taiwan and China necessitates a more personal negotiation style. In the case of a franchise operation such as Kompen, the role of the franchisees is crucial in determining the success of the company. The company therefore selects its franchisees very carefully, often using Turkish distributors in many of its foreign markets, partly in the belief that similarity in cultural background can make it easier to maintain close linkages. In a similar fashion, Betek also uses informal communication, personal ties and shared values to encourage the commitment of its Azeri partners and thereby further cement interorganizational relationships. Tasty Bite's success in the USA is partly an outcome of its ability to get the support of key supermarkets and its being able to use local market data to tailor its distribution to those locations where the underlying demographics argued in favour of its products being carried on the shelves. Here again, the company used data personalized for each store to argue why carrying their product would be a win–win situation for both Tasty Bite and the store concerned. This persuaded store buyers that the company had taken the trouble to understand the store's target customers and their needs rather than simply pushing their product. US hotel chains have used their centralized worldwide reservations systems and global brands to forge a single identity for their hotels even when the chain does not own the properties.

Other ways in which relationships are developed are more unique to emerging markets and their companies. Fraternity-building used by Indian firms to bring their partners closer is an example. Several different types of fraternities have been created but at their heart is the notion of reciprocity. While there is certainly an economic component to them, this is not necessarily either immediate or apparent. In many instances, the compelling logic to these arrangements is simply one of mutual trust and commitment, often without safeguards or other mechanisms to guard against opportunistic behaviour by either party to the arrangement. Ashanti is able to operate in environments with considerable political risk because it has built connections with local institutions that make it feel that its investments are reasonably secure even though many of its competitors exited those countries. Undoubtedly, managing relationships with governments is also a part of this relationship focus, and given the levels of corruption in many emerging markets, as discussed in Chapter 3, there are ethical issues to be considered in dealing with governments. However, in our view the companies described here appear to have made this relationship focus a key element of their strategy.

As we said earlier, our intention has been to try and draw some useful lessons for our readers by identifying the key factors that are driving global success in emerging markets and by emerging-market firms. Our lessons are drawn largely from the companies discussed in Part III although we have also looked to the literature to provide a focus and a framework for our analysis. Some of our conclusions are undoubtedly tentative and speculative and thus open to debate and alternative interpretations. However, our intention has always been to highlight the unique characteristics of emerging markets and their companies, to emphasize that there are many examples of globally successful companies from these countries, and to point out that not all their successes have been built on strategies used by companies from economically advanced nations. We hope that we have been able to draw attention to such companies and make the case that emerging-market firms are different and the factors that drive their success are in many instances unique. We are aware that there are probably as many differences within emerging markets as there are between emerging and advanced countries, and we are by no means attempting to suggest that ours is a complete analysis. It represents just a small sliver but we hope it will heighten awareness and encourage debate and motivate further analysis. If we have sowed the seeds of the idea that there is a lot that can be learned from emerging markets, and that the successes of their companies can teach us all something, we will feel satisfied that we have done what we set out to do.

Our conclusion is that the underlying pattern of success factors points to a more general pattern or principle of success in emerging markets. It is a Darwinian mutation of the 'tight–loose structure' principle, an emphasis of 'flexibility and creativity' to become 'world-class' in every competitive aspect, and to consider access to necessary resources in a network perspective via focused relationships.

Notes

1. Such as, D. Barry and M. Elmes, 'Strategy Retold: Towards a Narrative View of Strategic Discourse', *Academy of Management Review*, 2, 22 (1997): 429–52.
2. T.J. Peters and R.J. Waterman, *In Search of Excellence: Lessons From America's Best-Run Companies* (New York: Harper & Row, 1982).
3. M. Taylor and J. Lansley, 'Relating the Central and the Local: Options for Organizational Structure', *Nonprofit Management and Leadership*, 10, 24 (2000): 421–33.
4. D. Kim, D. Kandemir and S.T. Cavusgil, 'The Role of Family Conglomerates in Emerging Markets: What Western Companies should Know', *Thunderbird International Business Review*, forthcoming, http://globaledge.msu.edu/KnowledgeRoom/FeaturedInsights/0005.pdf

5. See for example, M.F. Guillen, 'Business Groups and Economic Development: A Resource Based View', in M. Kotabe and P.S. Aulakh (eds), *Emerging Issues in International Business Research* (Cheltenham: Edward Elgar, 2002): 163–98.
6. J.J. Choi, 'Global Financial Markets and Global Firms: Implications for International Business Research', in M. Kotabe and P.S. Aulakh (eds) (2000), *op. cit.*: 65–80.
7. *Ibid.*: 75.
8. G.D. De Abreu Filho, N. Calicchio and F. Lunardini, 'Brand Building in emerging markets', *The McKinsey Quarterly*, 2 (2003), premium.mckinseyquarterly.com/article_print.aspx?xar=1317&L2=16&L3=17; for an overview of the largest 200 EM companies see http://www.businessweek.com/pdfs/2002/0228-emerging.pdf
9. Y. Wu, 'China's Refrigerator Magnate', *The McKinsey Quarterly*, 3 (2003), http://www.mckinseyquarterly.com/article_page.asp?ar=1323&L2=16&srid=69
10. T. Harris, 'Commentary: Current and Future Changes in Corporate Attitudes to National Identity', *Thunderbird International Business Review*, 44, 2 (2002): 165.
11. P. Gao, J.R. Woetzel and Y. Wu, 'Can Chinese Brands Make it Abroad?', *The McKinsey Quarterly*, 4 (2003), http://www.mckinseyquarterly.com/article_abstract.asp?ar=1361&L2=16&L3=14&srid=27&gp=0
12. *Ibid.*
13. T. Khanna and K. Palepu, 'Emerging Giants: Building World-Class Companies in Emerging Markets' Harvard Business School Case Study no. 9–703–431 (15 October 2002).
14. See D. Kim, D. Kandemir and S.T. Cavusgil, 'The Role of Family Conglomerates in Emerging Markets', *op. cit.*: 35.
15. P. Gao, J.R. Woetzel and Y. Wu, 'Can Chinese Brands Make it Abroad?', *op. cit.*
16. D. Luhnow and C. Terhune, 'A Low-Budget Cola Shakes Up Markets South of the Border', *The Wall Street Journal*, CCXLII, no. 83 (27 October 2003).
17. D. MacKenzie, 'Brands Have to Meet Consumers' "Local" Demands,' *Marketing* (30 August 2001): 18.
18. 'Chinese TV Makers Rival Sony', *The Baltimore Sun* (11 November 2003): 2D.
19. For the theoretical underpinnings see T. Grebel, A. Pyka and H. Hanusch, 'An Evolutionary Approach to the Theory of Entrepreneurship', http://www.wiwi.uni-jena.de/Mikro/pdf/Vortrag-Grebel-131201.pdf; Chia Siow Yue, 'Critical Elements in Competitiveness Strategies in East Asia', Paper presented at the Third Asia Development Forum. Asia's Future Economy, http://www.sustainability.com/developing-value/matrix.asp and Rizwanul Islam, 'Economic Development in Asia and the Pacific in the 21st Century: Issues and Challenges', Paper presented at the ILO Workshop on Employers' Organizations in Asia-Pacific in the Twenty-First Century Turin, Italy, 5–13 May 1997, http://www.ilo.org/public/english/dialogue/actemp/papers/1998/riecodev.htm#c54
20. H. Sender, 'Back from the Brink', *Wall Street Journal* (22 September 2003): R5.
21. I. Wilkinson, 'A History of Network and Channels Thinking in Marketing in the 20th Century', *Australasian Journal of Marketing*, 9, 2 (2001): 23–53.
22. See D. McLoughlin and C. Horan, 'Markets-As-Networks: Notes on a Unique Understanding', *Journal of Business Research*, 55 (2002): 535–43; J.K. Frels, T. Shervani and R.K. Srivastava, 'The Integrated Networks Model: Explaining Resource Allocations in Network Markets', *Journal of Marketing*, 67 (January 2003): 29–45.
23. D.J. Arnold and J.A. Quelch, 'New Strategies in Emerging Markets', *Sloan Management Review*, 40, 1 (1998): 7–20.

24 See T. Gold, D. Guthrie and D. Wank, *Social Connections in China: Institutions, Culture, and the Changing Nature of Guanxi* (New York: Cambridge University Press, 2002).
25 See for instance M.E.M. Akoorie, 'Organizational Clusters in a Resource Based Industry: Empirical Evidence from New Zealand', in M.B. Green and R.B. McNaughton (eds), *Industrial Networks and Proximity* (Aldershot: Ashgate, 2000): 133–64.

Appendix: Methodology for Networks – a Meta-Analysis

Introduction

The collected contributions differ not only in their topics, but also in their methodology. Some studies are written entirely in an academic style, some of them use the qualitative approach, while others are more descriptive. The challenge is to present an overall picture of the results provided by the various qualitative and quantitative studies and to synthesize the research and insights offered by the different authors, so that it is meaningful for the reader. One of the approaches could be to leave the synthesis open to readers themselves. Many academic books often follow this approach,[1] and doing so may have its own value. Others provide a synthesis or integration of the findings and offer conclusions based on the contributions. Although it may well be a more demanding task from an intellectual point of view to proceed this way, we wanted to do it in the hope that it might generate more critical reflection as readers may draw their own conclusions that might differ from the ones proposed by the editors.

Research synthesis about providing the evidence

Until recently, social science methodologists paid little attention to how investigators ought to find, evaluate and integrate past research. This omission in methods became especially apparent when huge increases in the amount of social research put the lack of synthesis in bold relief.[2] The question is, which approaches might be suitable to proceed with that task? Several possibilities seem to be available and they are linked to the approaches outlined above. However, it is not our intent to discuss or make a contribution to the 'positivism vs constructivism'[3] debate that is ongoing and documented elsewhere.[4]

The research integration procedure used here relies on several steps that mainly follow an adapted approach, which is used in mapping management knowledge[5] – so the process of providing the evidence of the contributions in an integrated form follows the general steps suggested by Huff and Jenkins:[6]

1 The strategic issues and theoretical resources are provided in Part I, where we report about the nature of emerging markets and the success factors applicable there.
2 The knowledge and mapping questions addressed look for the commonalities of the mental models of the different contributions in Parts II and III; in particular they consist of the studies in Part III, Management in Practice.
3 The data source/level of analysis proceeded as pattern-coding[7] in several activities.[8]

   a According to the main concepts or first-order concepts introduced in Part I as success drivers, namely organizations, markets, people and operations, each of the editors separately read through the studies provided in Part III and looked for corresponding text 'third-level indicators' identifying patterns of the main concepts.
   b After this step, each of the editors provided their list of third-level indicators that were then purified during several group discussions. The outcome of this discussion

process was a list of 'second-order' concepts or sub-codes, which were used as a codebook for further coding. This process resulted in the identification of 15 success factors across the four first-order concepts. The list of sub-codes consisted of:

- *Organizations* (5 sub-codes): corporate values, quality focus, innovativeness, customer focus, external resource access.
- *Markets* (4): market-selection process, managing environmental uncertainty, flexible market entry, multi-segment approach.
- *People* (3): focus on competent personnel, relationships and connections, localization of management.
- *Operations* (3): customization of marketing, supplier and distribution networks, brand-building.

c Following that, the three editors separately coded each of the papers supplied by the different contributors according to this list of sub-codes. This process was repeated twice, with a group presentation and discussion of the preliminary results in between.[9] After a third meeting, the final outcome of the coding process resulted in a rectangular matrix where column entries contained the editors' codes and the individual studies were the row entries. The inter-rater reliability of the coding process is described in Table A1. Three reliability coefficients were computed[10] and are provided here. Lombard, Snyder-Duch and Campanella Bracken[11] suggest '... select an appropriate minimum acceptable level of reliability' and mention 'coefficients of 0.90 or greater are nearly always acceptable, 0.80 or greater is acceptable in most situations, and 0.70 may be appropriate in some exploratory studies for some indices'.

We accepted a lower limit of 0.80, considering the different nature and scopes of the studies that create additional variance in interpretation. All coefficients except Lin concordance for 'people' are 0.80 or above, which show a considerable degree of inter-coder reliability. As readers go through the studies on their own, they may interpret some of the studies in a different way, which as mentioned earlier may stimulate thought and discussion.

4 The visualization of coded information is the final step, as the synthesizing interpretation of the studies bases its findings on the visualization[12] of the coded studies. For this purpose the final coded matrix was transformed[13] into a study-by-sub-code matrix; the studies are the row entries, the sub-codes serve as column entries. That basic matrix was the starting point for visualization by means of maps.

Table A1 Reliability of coding process

Concepts	Per cent agreement	Lin concordance	Holsti's coefficient of reliability	Number of sub-codes
Markets	0.80	0.81	0.86	4
Organizations	0.82	0.82	0.82	5
People	0.80	0.68	0.80	3
Operations	0.86	0.83	0.86	3

By certain mathematical operations[14] it can be either transformed into a study-by-study matrix, or into a sub-code-by-sub-code matrix, where the sub-codes are interlinked by the studies. The image of the overall sub-code-by-sub-code matrix is presented in FigureA1.

The network of concepts shows that 'corporate values' has the densest interlinkages and the most connections with the other sub-codes, and is therefore the most frequently cited success driver among all the studies. It is mentioned much more frequently than any of the other concepts. 'Focus on competent people' is the next most important characteristic in the success factors and their linkages. After them comes 'quality focus', 'customization of marketing', and 'market-selection process'. 'Supplier and distribution networks', and an emphasis on 'flexible market entry' follow these. 'Relationships and connections' and 'brand-building' are positioned in-between the others; they are the 'average' of connectedness in the studies. The importance of the key success drivers as seen visually in Figure A1 is shown quantitatively in Table A.2. Less prominently observed in a relative sense across all studies are 'multi-segment approach', 'customer focus', 'external resource access', 'localization of management', 'managing environmental uncertainty' and 'innovativeness'.

For ease of interpretation, in Part IV the study-by-sub-code matrices are used for each of the second-order concepts and mapped. So the reader has to deal with four maps, one for each first first-order concept, that are used as facilitating[15] images. This makes it easier to consider the implications of 'standing' at different points on the map, where we have the studies and the sub-codes as indicators.

In these maps presented in Chapters 18–21, one for each of the four first-order success drivers, the squares represent the second-order success factors and the circles represent the studies detailed in Part III, with the study names in parentheses. The first notation next to the study name indicates the origin of the focal company/study

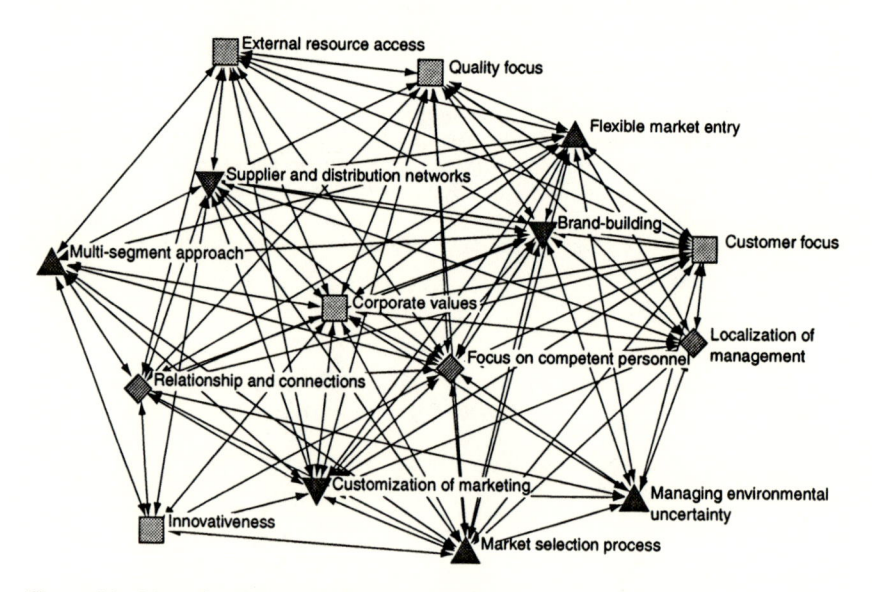

Figure A1 Map of interlinked sub-codes network
Notes: Triangle up = markets; square = organizations; diamond = people; triangle down = operations.

Table A2 Interlinkages of concepts

Sub-codes	Degree of interlinkage	Main concept is...
Corporate values	41	Organizations
Focus on competent personnel	38	People
Quality focus	34	Organizations
Customization of marketing	33	Operations
Market-selection process	31	Markets
Supplier and distribution networks	30	Operations
Flexible market entry	27	Markets
Relationships and connections	24	People
Brand-building	22	Operations
Multi-segment approach	16	Markets
Customer focus	15	Organizations
External resource access	15	Organizations
Localization of management	13	Personnel
Managing environmental uncertainty	10	Markets
Innovativeness	9	Organizations
Average degree	23.9	

and the second indicates the scope of its global business. So for example, EM–EM, AM (Gerdau) means that this is a study of Gerdau, an EM-based company that does business in both EMs and in AMs.

Notes

1. See C.C.J.M Millar, R.M. Grant and C.J. Choi (eds), *International Business – Emerging Issues and Emerging Markets* (London: Macmillan – now Palgrave, 2000); M.C. Frazer and M. Chatterji (eds), *Management Education in Countries in Transition* (London: Macmillan – now Palgrave, 1999); M. Kotabe and P.S. Aulakh (eds), *Emerging Issues in International Business Research* (Northhampton, MA, USA: Edward Elgar, 2002); or A. Yaprak and H. Tütek (eds), *Globalization, the Multinational Firm, and Emerging Economies* (New York: Elsevier, 2000).
2. H. Cooper, *Synthesizing Research. A Guide for Literature Reviews*, 3rd edn (Thousand Oaks, CA: Sage, 1998).
3. See J. Jackson, *Explore the Strengths and Weakness of Classical Content Analysis*, http://www.spinworks.demon.co.uk/pub/content2.htm; see D.R. Harvey, 'The Nature of a Possible Social Science Synthesis', http://www.staff.ncl.ac.uk/david.harvey/AEF801/Why/Synthesis.html (21 September 2003).
4. See A. Tashakkori and C. Teddlie (eds), *Handbook of Mixed Methods in Social and Behavioral Research* (Thousand Oaks, CA: Sage, 2003).
5. A.S. Huff and M. Jenkins (eds), *Mapping Strategic Knowledge*, (Thousand Oaks, CA: Sage, 2002).
6. A.S. Huff and M. Jenkins, 'Introduction' in A.S. Huff and M. Jenkins (eds) (2002), *op. cit.*: 9–13.
7. M.B. Miles and A.M. Huberman, *Qualitative Data Analysis: An Expanded Source Book*, 2nd edn (Thousand Oaks, CA: Sage, 1994): 69–72.
8. This work took place at Marmara University in Istanbul during 7–15 August 2003.

9. It was '...an intellectually pleasurable process. Those codes that survive the onslaught of several phases at the case and several attempts to disqualify them often turn out to be the conceptual hooks on which the analysts hang the meatiest part of the analysis', Miles and Huberman, *op. cit.*: 72.
10. The software used is available at http://academic.csuohio.edu/kneuendorf/content/reliable/rel.htm
11. M. Lombard, J. Snyder-Duch and Ch. C. Bracken, *Practical Resources for Assessing and Reporting Intercoder Reliability in Content Analysis Research Projects*, http://www.temple.edu/mmc/reliability (28 September 2003).
12. M.B. Miles and A.M. Huberman, *Qualitative Data Analysis: An Expanded Source Book*, 2nd edn, *op. cit.*: 71.
13. For details see *Ibid.*: 172–206.
14. For graph-theoretical concepts and matrix operations, see D. Iacobucci, 'Graphs and Matrices', in S. Wasserman and K. Faust (eds), *Social Network Analysis. Methods and Applications* (Cambridge: Cambridge University Press, 1994): 92–166.
15. A.S. Huff and M. Jenkins, 'Introduction' in A.S. Huff and M. Jenkins (eds) (2002), *op. cit.*: 6.

Bibliography

Selected books with focus on emerging markets

Alon, I. and D. Welsh (eds) (2001) *International Franchising in Emerging Markets: Central and Eastern Europe and Latin America* (Washington DC: CCH Publishing).

Batra, R. (ed.) (1999) *Marketing Issues in Transitional Economies* (Boston, MA: Kluwer Academic Publishers).

Caslione, J.A. and A.R. Thomas (2002) *Global Manifest Destiny: Growing Your Business in a Borderless Economy* (Chicago, IL: Dearborn Trade Publishing).

Cavusgil, S.T., P.N. Ghauri and M.R. Agarwal (2002) *Doing Business in Emerging Markets: Entry and Negotiation Strategies* (Thousand Oaks, CA: Sage).

Chua, A. (2003) *World on Fire: How Exporting Free Market Democracy Breeds Ethnic hatred and Global Instability* (New York: Doubleday).

Frazer, M.C. and M. Chatterji (1999) *Management Education in Countries of Transition* (London: Macmillan – Palgrave).

Friedman, T.L. (2000) *The Lexus and the Olive Tree* (New York: Anchor Books).

Gras, G.L. (2002) *The New, New World. The Re-Emerging Markets of South America* (Reuters).

Garten, J.E. (1997) *The Big Ten: The Big Emerging Markets and How They Will Change Our Lives* (New York: Basic Books).

Greider, W. (1997) *One World, Ready or Not: The Manic Logic of Global Capitalism* (New York: A Touchstone Book published by Simon & Schuster).

Hertz, N. (2001) *Silent Takeover: Global Capitalism and the Death of Democracy* (New York: The Free Press).

Hampden-Turner, C. and F. Trompenaars (1998) *Riding the Waves of Culture: Understanding Diversity in Global Business* (New York: McGraw-Hill).

International Forum on Globalization (2002) *Alternatives to Economic Globalization: A Better World is Possible* (San Francisco, CA: Berrett-Koehler).

Jading, L. (2002) *Multinational Enterprises in Emerging Markets* (Denmark: Copenhagen Business School Press).

Kanter, R.M. (1995) *World Class: Thriving Locally in the Global Economy* (New York: Simon & Schuster).

Kirkbride, P. (ed.) (2001) *Globalization: The External Pressures* (Chichester: John Wiley & Sons).

Luo, Y. (2002) *Multinational Enterprises in Emerging Markets* (Denmark: Copenhagen Business School Press).

Marber, P. (1998) *From Third World to World Class – The Future of Emerging Markets in the Global Economy* (Reading, MA: Perseus Books).

Millar, C.C.J.M., R.M. Grant and C.J. Choi (eds) (2000) *International Business: Emerging Issues and Emerging Markets* (London: Macmillan – now Palgrave).

Miller, R.R. (2000) *Doing Business in Newly Privatized Markets: Global Opportunities and Challenges* (Westport, CT: Quorum Books).

Miller, R.R. (1998) *Selling to Newly Emerging Markets* (Westport, CT: Quorum Books).

Morrison, I. (1996) *The Second Curve: Managing Velocity of Change* (New York: Ballantine).

Rugman, A.M. (2001) *The End of Globalization: Why Global Strategy is a Myth and How to Profit From the Realities of Regional Markets* (New York: AMACOM).

Soros, G. (2002) *On Globalization* (Oxford: Public Affairs Ltd.).
Stiglitz, J.E. (2002) *Globalization and Its Discontents* (New York: W.W. Norton).
Tatoglu, E. and K.W. Glaister (2000) *Dimensions of Western Foreign Direct Investment in Turkey* (Westport, CT: Quorum Books).
Warner, M. and P. Joynt (eds) (2002). *Managing Across Cultures: Issues and Perspectives* (London: Thomson Learning).
Yaprak, A. and H. Tütek (eds) (2000) *Globalization, the Multinational Firm and Emerging Economies* (New York: JAI Press/Elsevier).

Index

Note: f=figure; n=note; t=table; bold=extended discussion or heading in main text.

Aaby, N.E. 85
ABN LaSalle Bank 108
academics ix, 76
Accor (French hotel chain) 154t
accounting 107, 158, 220
Accra 187
Accra Stock Exchange 183
Acer 35, 253
Aceralia (Spain) 99
Acesita 105t
Aço-Norte 106t
Açominas 104t, 106, 106t, 107, 108
 exports (2001) 111, 111t
 sales (2001) 111
 steel production (2002) 105t
Aços Villares 105t
acquisitions 179, 183, 228, 230
 market-entry mode 174
 strategy 172
Adansi Kingdom 182
adaptability 251
adaptation 239, 244, 248
Adopen 145, 147t
Adryx Mining and Metal (investment group) 187
advanced markets (AMs)/ developed countries 3, 14, 15–16, 17–18, 85, 86, 88, 90t, 91, 92, 93, 95, 98, 142, 142, 148, 159, 209–15, 215(n3), 221, 230, 238, 242, 255, 257, 258(n22)
 economic growth comparatively slow 29
 market-evolution patterns 231
 share of world exports 34
 see also multinational companies
advertising 15, 31, 64, 68, 79, 80, 136–7, 148, 149, 173, 242, 244, 247
 local themes 176, 177, 179, 223
 targeted at cluster segments 202–3
 see also promotion
affordability 210, 223
Africa 10, 13, 111t, 183, 184, 188, 192, 194, 212, 216(n16), 232, 239, 255
 Mao Shun markets 116t
 tourism 155t

after-sales service 47t, 89
Agarwal, M.R. 5, 26
age groups 74
agents 116, 117, 120, 124, 125f, 126, 238, 239, 255
Agnico-Eagle Mines 191t
agricultural sector 108
AIG 188
Akpınar, C. 131, 133
Albania 28, 29t
all-commodity volume (ACV) 200, 206
alliances (corporate) 159t, 160, 164t, 179, 254
Allure (chain store) 64
Alpina 136
Alstom 73
AM to EM analysis 4, 215(n3), 244, 248
 markets network 228f
 operations network 243f
 organization network 219f
 people network 236f
 US hotels 219f
 see also multinational companies
American Express 73
American Society of Quality (ASQ) 221
American Tourister 77
Americas 116t, 155t
Amerisafe 101, 104t, 106
 Gerdau Ameristeel Corporation 106t, 107, 108, 109, 111
Amir, I. xi
Amul (cooperative) 78
Anadolu Efes Biracılık ve Malt Sanayi A.Ş. (Anadolu Efes)
 brand-building 246–7
 competitive structure of market 172
 corporate values 220, 221
 critical success factors 171, 174
 customer focus 223
 customization of marketing 244
 decentralized organization and cultural and historical heritage 178–9
 flexibility and creativity 252–3
 flexible market entry 230

Anadolu Efes Biracılık ve Malt Sanayi A.Ş. (Anadolu Efes) (*Continued*)
  international market entry and expansion strategies 168–81
  legal and financial structure of country 172
  local strategic planning of branding and positioning 174–6
  local strategic planning of communications 176–7
  localization of management 239
  managing environmental uncertainty 232
  market potential for beer consumption 172
  market selection process 228, 229
  markets network 228f
  operations network 243f
  organization network 219f
  people network 236f
  sales volume 171
  selection of potential markets and market-entry mode 171–4
  setting alternative distribution channels 176
  see also Efes Pilsen brand
Anchor Health 76t
Anglo American (company) 35t
Anglogold 184t, 190, 191t
Anheuser Busch 170
Anikeeff, M.A. xi
Anshan 99t
Aracaria (Pernambuco state) 103
Arbed (Luxembourg) 99
Arc (beer brand) 175
Arcelor Group 99t, 99–100, 105t, 108
Argentina 12, 28, 29t, 32, 99t, 101, 103, 106, 107, 109, 112, 230
  Gerdau Group expansion 104t
  location of Gerdau steel production 106t
  share of world exports and imports (1995–2001) 33t, 34t
Ariel 77
Arif, F. xi
Arizona 200
Armenia 136, 137(n6)
Artworks (Turkish media development firm) 148
Ashanti
  background 182–5, 192(n2)
  brand-building 'not a viable option' 248
  competent personnel 237
  corporate values 220
  counter-parties 187, 188, 189, 190
  derivatives crisis 186–9
  drivers of success 190–2
  emotional symbolism to Ghanaians 189
  flexibility and creativity 253
  gold reserves 187–8, 189
  liquidity crisis 188, 189
  managing environmental uncertainty 232
  margin limits 189, 190
  market capitalization 183
  markets network 228f
  non-family-owned 251
  operations 184–5
  operations network 243f
  organization network 219f
  people network 236f
  production 188
  profit and loss (1998–2002) 185
  relationships and connections 238–9, 256–7
  return on assets 185
  return on equity 185
  saving an African mining giant 182–92
  share price 184
  survival strategies 189–90
Ashanti Goldfields Company Limited (1890–) 182
Ashanti Goldfields Corporation (1897–) 182
Asia 10, 11, 13, 111, 111t, 125f, 146, 153, 177, 205
Asia–Pacific 116t
Asia–Pacific Economic Cooperation (APEC) 14
Asian Paints 78
Athens 42
auditing 107, 220
Aurie (beer brand) 175
Australia 14, 99t, 116, 184t, 188
Austria 99t, 146, 161
authoritarianism 9, 10, 11–13
Ayhan, D.Y. 151(n11)
Ayur (cosmetics) 83
Aza (Chilean steel-producer) 104t, 105, 106t, 107
  Gerdau Aza 112
Azerbaijan 128–39, 229, 239, 243, 253, 256

backward and forward linkages 245, 249(n8)
backward integration 105
bad debts 252
Bahia (state) 103

Bajaj Scooters 36, 78
Balkans 132, 135
Baltic States 28
Bamesa Aceros 36
Banco Gerdau 107
Bangladesh 10, 88
Bank of America 108
banking 12, 31, 35, 76, 81
bankruptcy 204
banks 81, 108, 163, 242
Barão de Cocais 103, 104t, 106t
bargaining skills (Turkish) 128
Barlas, D. 133, 134, 137n
Barra Mansa 105t
Barrick Gold 191t
barriers to entry 157, 168, 172
Baskin Robbins 77, 80
Baum, E. 153
beer 168–81, 197, 229
  brands 168, 179(n1)
  break-even point 168, 170
  consumption per capita 173–4, 228, 229
  global industry 168–71, 179
  global premium brands 176
  non-alcoholic (Muslim countries) 174, 176, 177
  non-pasteurized and pasteurized 175
beer substitutes 168, 169f
Belarus 28, 29t, 146
Belgium/Belgians 18, 42
Belgo-Mineira 99, 105t, 108
Bema Gold 191t
BEMs see big emerging markets
Benxi (steel production, 2002) 99t
Berács, J. xi–xii, 47n, 210
best practices (US hotel industry) 152–67
Best Western (US hotel chain) 154t
Betek (*Beton Teknoloji*, concrete technology) 131
Betek Paint and Chemical Industry Corporation (Betek Boya, 1988–)
  attractiveness of Azerbaijan market 128–39
  background 131
  commitment to becoming world class 254
  customization of marketing 243, 244–5
  exports 132
  flexibility and creativity 253
  growth 131–2
  human factors that ensure success in Azerbaijan 134–5
  innovativeness 222
  international operations (path to success) 132–3
  market selection process 229
  market-based strategies for Azerbaijan 134
  market-selection process 134
  marketing success factors for Azerbaijan 135–7
  markets network 228f
  meaning of 'Betek' acronym 131
  operations network 243f
  organization network 219f
  organization success factors 133
  people network 236f
  products, segments, positioning 132
  quality focus 221
  quality orientation and environmental concern 133, 135–6, 139(n46)
  relationships and connections 238, 239, 256
Bethlehem Steel 98t, 99, 100
beverages 121
Bharti 76
BHP (steel production, 2002) 99t
Bibiani gold-mining concession 183, 184t, 185
big emerging markets (BEMs) 28, 29t, 29, 30t, 30, 32, 33, 227, 231
  share of world exports and imports (1995–2001) 33, 33t, 34t, 34
Bilgin, Z. xii
Bilkey, W.J. 85
Biney, Chief J.E. 182
Biotique 83
Birim Goldfields, Inc. 184t
Black Sea Economic Cooperation (BSEC) 129
Bobek, V. xii, 18, 24(n44), 211
Bodur, M. xii
Bôlsa de Valores de São Paulo (BOVESPA) 109
Bombay Stock Exchange 193
Borusan Group 36
Bosnia and Herzegovina 61
Bracken, Ch. C. 264(n11)
Brahma 170
brand awareness/recognition 149, 150, 175, 247
brand investment 78–9
brand loyalty 156–7, 169f
brand promotion 159t
brand strategy 201

brand-building 214f, 242, 243f, 246–8, 262
  interlinkages of concepts 263t
  map of interlinked sub-codes network 262f
  'second-order concept' (sub-code) 261
branding 50, 67, 156, 169f, 170, 174–6, 248
brands/brand names 35, 61, 62, 63, 65, 66, 75–7, 79, 81, 82, 136, 142, 159, 178, 195, 198, 206, 220, 223
  elites 161–2
  Gerdau 108–9, 112
  global 16, 19, 83, 176, 231, 247, 248, 253, 254, 255, 256
  global Indian 194, 204
  hotels 154, 156–7, 161–2, 163, 164t, 165
  Indian food in USA 194
  local 172, 174, 175, 179, 244, 246, 254
  localization 78
  multiple 153
  paint 134
  'shock and awe' strategy 80
  sub-brands 156
  target audience 177
  US 160
Brazil 20, 28, 29t, 32, 33, 34, 35t, 103, 220, 221, 237, 255
  direct costs of steel production (2001) 98t
  E7 group 27
  foreign debt 103
  'lost decade' (1980s) 103
  share of world exports and imports (1995–2001) 33t, 34t
  steel 97–113
  steel production companies (2002) 99t
Brazilian government 101
Bretton Woods system 16
bribery 125
Britain *see* United Kingdom
British Steel 100
broadcasting 12
Brown, J. 182
Brown, J.R. 141
Bruckman (company) 144
Brunei 28, 29t
BSNL (company) 76
Budapest 41, 162
Budapest: Akadémiai Kiadó 22(n3)
Buddhists 74
Bulgaria 28, 29t, 44, 146

bureaucracy 67f
Burton, F.N. 85
Busia, Dr K.A. 183
business
  global 215
  international 18–19
business background 5
business groups 252, 258(n5)
business knowledge 11
business methods 17
business networks 124, 220
business schools 252
business start-ups 194, 195
business strategies 46, 47t
buyers 168, 169f, 170
buying agents 91
Büyükcan, S. 133, 135, 136, 137, 137n
Büyükserin, M. 146

Cadbury 76t
Cade, E. 182
California 200, 245
Camarad (beer brand) 175
Cambridge (Canada) 106t
Canada 14, 105, 110, 111, 112, 184t, 188, 228, 230
  Gerdau Group expansion 104t
  gold-mining companies 191t
  locations of Gerdau steel production 106t
  steel production companies (2002) 99t
Caparol (paint brand) 131, 132, 134, 136
capital 22, 102, 153, 156, 173, 179, 194, 196, 204, 221
  international movements 16–17
capital cities 162
capital markets 153–4, 161, 164t
capitalism 2, 9, 11
Caribbean 10, 13
Carlsberg 170
Carnival Hotels & Resorts 154
Carrefour 66, 67
cars/automobiles 1, 2, 35, 36, 76, 77, 78, 80, 81, 83, 122, 143
  automotive parts 121
  manufacturers 120, 127, 142
  PRC 120
Cartersville 106t
case studies 95
Caslione, J.A. 20, 24–5(n62)
Caspian Sea 132
Catch (brand) 79
CavinKare 76t
Cavusgil, S.T. 5, 26, 85, 225(n1)

Index 271

CBS (paint company) 130
Ceara (state) 103
Cearense 104t, 106
CEFTA 67f
cement 36, 82
Central America 10, 254
Central Asia 128, 129, 137(n6), 146
central banks 138(n29), 186, 187
Central and Eastern Europe (CEE) 4, 14, 43, 61, 62, 143, 210
  leadership 54–60, 211, 252
Central Europe 45, 46, 211
  hotel expansion 160–3
central planning 11, 31, 54
centralization 158, 178, 251
chain stores 64, 66, 68
Channon, H.M. 212–13, 218, 225(n3)
Charlotte 106t
Chase Manhattan Bank 188
Chatterji, M. 58, 60(n17)
Chattopadhyay, A. 209
chefs of private caterers (fraternity) 79
Chemical Bank 194
chemical materials 134
chemicals 121, 136
Chernomor (beer brand) 174
Chhibba, R. xiii
Chia Siow Yue 258(n19)
Chicago Rawhide Industries 117
chief executives 86
ChiK Shampoo 77
Child, J. 216(n14)
child labour 75
Chile 33, 105, 107, 109, 230
  Gerdau Group expansion 104t
  location of Gerdau steel production 106t
China (People's Republic; PRC) 2, 9, 11, 12, 28, 29t, 32, 33, 34, 35t, 73, 88, 97, 111t, 143, 170, 171, 199, 227, 230, 237, 238, 256
  automobile market 1, 120
  business development 120–1
  cross-strait economic relations 119–20
  direct costs of steel production (2001) 98t
  dual economy syndrome 31, 231
  E7 group 27
  motorization 121
  negotiation style and personal relations 238, 241(n9)
  relationship-based market-entry 114–27, 223–4
  'seventh-largest economy' 120
  share of world exports and imports (1995–2001) 33t, 34t
  steel production companies (2002) 99t
  Taiwanese investment 119
  WTO entry (2001) 126, 127
China Steel 98t, 99t
Chinese Economic Area (Garten) 28, 29t
Chinese (PRC) government 120
Chisinau (beer brand) 175
Chiu, B. 114, 118, 121, 123, 124, 126, 127, 256
Chiu, H. xiii–xiv
Chongqing 122
Christians 74
Christopher, M. 241(n9)
Chrysler 120
CIBC 108
CIS countries 132, 223
CIS-7 129, 137(n6)
CIT 108
cities 20, 31, 64, 198, 201, 231
Citroën 120
Clark, M. 241(n9)
Clinton administration 29
Cluff Resources Plc 183, 184t
cluster analysis 202–3
Co-Steel (Canada) 104t, 107
Coase, R. 255
Coca-Cola/Coke 83, 194, 254
Cola Turca 254
cold chain (logistics institution) 80
Cold War 9
Colgate 76, 79
Colgate Palmolive 73
colonialism 9, 10, 12
Colorado 200
COMECON countries 161
Comerica Bank 108
commitment 135, 256
Commons, J. 255
Commonwealth 13–14
Commonwealth Development Corporation (CDC) 204, 206
communication 31, 35, 78, 111, 213, 238, 240, 244, 256
communication channels 31
communication skills 58
communism 9, 10, 11, 12, 31, 57, 65, 178
  collapse 11, 54, 174
Companhia Siderúrgica de Guanabara (Cosigua) 100, 102, 106t
Companhia Siderúrgica Nacional (CSN) 98t, 98–9, 99t, 100, 102, 104, 105t

272 Index

Companhia Siderúrgica Tubarão (CST) 99t, 102, 105t
Companhia Vale do Rio Doce 100
Compañía de Minas Buenas 191t
companies 45, 141, 144, 193, 209, 210, 213, 215, 224, 250
  advanced market 227, 230, 231, 233, 240, 246, 256
  AM multinationals 255
  bus 142
  cash-flow problems 252
  CEE 58, 59
  core issues 42
  domestic 63
  emerging market 222, 228, 229, 230, 233, 240, 248, 251–2, 254, 255, 257
  emerging market (global impact) 34–6
  European 59, 254
  evolutionary theory 42
  family-owned/controlled 97, 112, 224, 251, 252, 257(n4)
  foreign 48, 144
  Ghanaian 232
  global 160, 251, 254
  Hungarian (strategic priorities, 1992–2000) 48t
  internationalizing 236
  Indian 238, 239
  Indian and non-Indian 231
  Indian (FMCG sector) 76t, 76
  Japanese 1
  large corporations 125
  large manufacturing 227
  local 179, 254
  'local' 178
  market positioning 61
  mining/gold-mining 182, 183, 187, 191t, 192,
  multidimensional theory needed 42
  North American 160
  Pakistani (award-winning export success) 85–96
  price-takers 186, 192
  responsiveness 44
  sector, size, ownership 48
  size 240
  smaller 93
  South Korean 35
  Taiwanese 119, 120, 121, 122
  Turkish 36, 128, 129, 148, 232, 245
  US 1, 254
  Western 253
  world class 253–5
  see also Fortune 500
company-owned sales subsidiary (market-entry strategy) 66–7, 69
comparative advantage 155
competition 20, 62, 67f, 94, 110, 127, 146, 168, 170, 174, 240
  global ix
  Mao Shun Corporation 117
  neoclassical theory 50
competition orientation 44, 46
competitive advantage 78, 79, 80, 140, 147, 179, 222, 238, 240, 245
  cultural affinity 123
  hotels 156–7
  Turkish paints 130
competitiveness 27, 49, 57, 58, 73, 142, 228
competitors 123, 133, 134, 136, 147, 149, 160, 172, 175, 178, 228, 230, 232, 233, 237, 242, 253, 256
  beer industry 168, 169f
  international 173
  multinational 179
  understanding strategies pursued by x
computers 35, 148, 157
conceptual mapping technique 6, 260–4
concrete additives 131, 132
conflict of interest 195
Confucianism 241(n9)
Congo-Brazzaville 184t
Congo-Kinshasa (Democratic Republic of Congo) 10
consortia 159t, 160, 164t
construction 102, 108, 129, 130, 132, 143–5
construction materials 121
constructivism 260
consultants/consulting companies 76, 126, 189
consumer
  advantage 81, 82
  boom 27, 29
  consciousness 16
  demand 245
  durables 221
  electronics 2, 35
  goods 121, 194
  needs 157
  protection 16
  value 77, 78, 81–2, 83
'consumer of promotions' 80
consumers 33, 63, 78, 136, 140, 142, 145, 146, 148, 150, 198,

199, 201, 213, 214, 218, 222,
    244, 251, 254, 255
  global 215, 231, 253
  global convergence thesis 210
  Indian 193
  local 178
  middle-class segment 22
  neoglobal thesis 210
  purchasing power 27
  sophisticated 94
  variability 30
consuming class 74
consumption 22, 30–1
contacts 229, 220
contract manufacturers 35, 253
contracting out 141
Contractor, F.J. 160
control 218, 229
control of operations 122
convergence approach 210,
    215(n2–3, n7)
coordination 44, 46, 178
copper 10
core competencies 57, 79, 80, 148, 213
corporate culture 17, 101, 126,
    147, 220
corporate theory 50
corporate values 214f, 218, 219f,
    219–21, 262
  core 251
  interlinkages of concepts 263t
  map of interlinked sub-codes
    network 262f
  'second-order concept' (sub-
    code) 261
corruption 31–3, 67f, 125, 189, 256
Corruption Perception Index (CPI) 32
Corus 99t, 100
Cosigua (Companhia Siderúrgica de
    Guanabara) 100, 102, 106t
COSIPA (steel production, 2002) 99t,
    105t
cosmetics 83
Cosmopolitan 64
cost reduction/saving 34, 80, 81, 122,
    127, 218
cost-benefit principle 210
cost-sharing 78
costs 36, 45, 81, 109, 110, 118, 120,
    126, 149, 220, 224, 245
  exploration and mining 192
  local 163
counterfeiting 31
courtesy visits 124
Courtice Steel Company (Canada) 103,
    104t, 107

creativity 176, 251, 252–3
credit 190
Crédit Suisse First Boston 188
Croatia 61
Cronbach's alpha 46
cross shareholdings 105
cross-cultural studies 95
cross-vergence 18, 212, 215(n7)
Crowne Plaza (up-market) 153, 163
crude steel 108, 108t
CSN *see* Companhia Siderúrgica
    Nacional
CST (Companhia Siderúrgica
    Tubarao) 99t, 102, 105t
Cuba 12
Cullen, T.P. 163
cultural affinity 128, 137, 228–9,
    253, 256
cultural Balkanization 18–19
cultural distance 123, 157, 240, 248
'cultural imperialism' 214
culture 3, 15, 56, 74, 85,
    137, 178–9, 212, 214,
    216(n14), 217, 247, 256
  affinity (Taiwan-PRC) 114, 123
  challenge to globalization 17–19
  cross-vergence 18, 212
  Czech Republic 63
  impact on management and
    leadership styles 59
  local 134, 239
  low and high context 17, 23(n34)
  relationship-focused 237
currency 103, 115, 172, 204
customer complaints 125, 148
customer focus 214f, 218, 219f, 219,
    223–4, 262
  interlinkages of concepts 263t
  map of interlinked sub-codes
    network 262f
  'second-order concept'
    (sub-code) 261
customer management systems
    146, 220
customer needs 5, 43, 65
customer orientation 44, 46, 48,
    112, 218
customer relations/relationships
    43, 135
customer relationship management
    (CRM) 223
customer satisfaction 46, 47t, 118–19,
    223, 224
customer service 65, 66, 67,
    68, 122
customer value 46, 47t, 133, 243

customers 5, 56, 76, 91, 112, 121, 123, 124, 132, 135, 136, 137, 143, 145, 147, 156, 158, 200, 221, 231, 238, 239, 242, 247, 254
  international 148
  more discerning 67
  new 178
  target segments 61
customization of marketing 176, 214f, 242, 243f, 243–5, 248, 251, 262
  interlinkages of concepts 263t
  map of interlinked sub-codes network 262f
  'second-order concept' (sub-code) 261
CVRD (Brazilian iron-ore producer) 100, 101
Czech Assay Office 64
Czech Republic 11, 28, 29t, 54, 160, 210
  country risk and opportunity analysis 62–6
  duties and taxes 62
  environment (trade, cultural, social) 62–3
  market entry (Slovenian jewellery producer) 61–70, 211
  market segmentation (seven-step approach) 64–6
  target positioning 66
Czechoslovakia (former) 15

D'Amboise, G. 241(n5)
Dabur Vatika Hair Oil 82
Daewoo 2
dairying 78, 82, 239
Daniels, J.D. 213
Danis, W.M. 60(n8)
Danone 170
data 260
  award-winning Pakistani firms 86
  Czech jewellery market 64
  inaccurate, outdated, lacking 32
  limitations 252
  macroeconomic 49
  'problem of fit' 32
data collection 95
databases 148
Dawar, N. 2, 36, 209
dealers 66, 69, 132, 135, 143, 148
debt maturities 107–8
decision-making 117, 125, 135, 158
  political base 57
  'scientific, rational' approach 252
Delhi/New Delhi 82, 193
  Hyatt Regency Hotel 78

demand 68, 144, 145, 165, 245
  hotels 155t, 155–6
  steel/steel products 98, 108
democracy 18, 19
demographics/population 21, 29, 30, 134, 145, 202, 202f, 246, 256
Deng, S. 95(n4)
derivatives 182, 186–90
  forward contracts 186, 189, 190
  gold loans 186
  options contracts 186, 189
  spot deferred contracts 186
Desc, S.A. 21
design/designers 62, 65, 67f, 67, 199
Desphande, R. 43
Dettol 76
Deutsche Mark 204
'developing countries' 26, 27t
Dhara Vegetable Oil & Foods 76t
Diamond (non-alcoholic beer) 176
differentiation 209–10
discounting 77, 247
distribution 67, 78, 91, 136, 142, 149, 200, 201, 231, 255, 256
  Gerdau Steel 111–12
distribution channels 143, 157, 179, 254
  Anadolu Efes 178
distribution infrastructure 198
distribution networks 140, 239, 253
distribution strategies 150, 245
distribution systems 31, 81, 206, 244
distributors 29, 116, 124, 125f, 126, 135, 136, 146, 229, 242, 245, 248
  independent 247
  Turkish 256
divergence approach 212
diversification 156
Divinopolis 106t
Dnes (professional magazine) 68
Dofasco (steel production, 2002) 99t
Dole Food Co. 195
domain expertise 204
doors 140, 143–4, 145, 146, 147, 148, 149
double taxation 129
Drucker, P. 178–9
dual economy syndrome 30–1, 231
Dunkwa mine (Ghana) 184t
Dunlop, J.T. 215(n2)
Dunning, J.H. 153
durability 65
Dutch 18
DYO (company) 130

E7 group 27, 37(n8)
East Asia 155t
East Timor 15
Eastern Anatolia 136
Eastern Europe 9, 11, 21, 100, 224, 230, 246
economic development 10, 142, 157, 212, 213, 214
economic efficiency 18
economic growth 49, 74, 120
economic liberalization 160
Economic Recovery Programme (Ghana) 183
Economical Information Centre 138(n11)
economics/economic science 50
  evolutionary 42
  traditional 41
economies (savings) 245
economies of scale 13, 98, 154, 156, 174, 210
Economist Intelligence Unit 161
Eczacibaşi Vitra 36
education ix, 79, 80, 109, 116–17, 155, 162, 204
  managerial 240
  university 158
Efes Blues Festival 177
Efes Breweries International A.Ş. (EBI, 1996–) 171
  'referred to as Anadolu Efes for simplicity' 171
Efes Pilsen Basketball 177
Efes Pilsen brand 171, 172, 174–7, 179
efficiency 20, 45, 58, 126, 158, 192
Ege Profil 147t
Egepen 144, 145
El-Ansary, A.I. 141
Eldorado Gold 191t
Electrolux 1
electronic mail 133
elephant logo (Caparol) 132, 136, 137
elites 161–2, 214, 231
Elle 64
Ellis, J.E. 182
EM to AM analysis 4, 215(n3)
  operations network 243f
  organization network 219f
  people network 236f
  Tasty Bite 219f
EM to EM analysis 4
  Ashanti 219f
  Betek 219f
  Efes 219f
  Indian companies 219f
  Kompen 219f

markets network 228f
NAK 219f
operations network 243f
organization network 219f
people network 236f
EM to EM and AM analysis 263
  Gerdau 219f, 219, 263
  markets network 228f
  operations network 243f
  organization network 219f
  Pakistani exporters 219f
  people network 236f
emerging market (EM) companies 1, 3, 4
  cultural and business backgrounds ix
  defence of home turf against MNCs 2
  factors that might hamper success (CEE countries) 58
  global impact 34–6
  'optimism factor' (Hungary) 48–9
  strategies and global vision ix
  success drivers 4f, 4–6
emerging markets (EMs) x, 1–6, 7–38
  attractiveness of Azerbaijan (Betek) 128–39
  'battleground for sales and profit' 36
  best practices (examples from US hotel industry) 152–67
  characteristics 29–33
  classification 30t
  corruption and shadow economy 31–3
  definition 27
  distinctiveness 210
  dual economy syndrome 30–1
  evaluation 32
  evolution of concept 26–33
  export success (lessons from Pakistani firms) 85–96
  'FILIP' marketing strategy 73–84
  general 26–38, 215, 232
  Gerdau (multinational steel giant from Brazil) 97–113
  global impact 34–6
  global trade and investment 33–4
  history 9–13
  importance 33–6
  institutional frameworks 79
  integration and disintegration attempts 13–15
  interlinkages of concepts 263t
  international business operations ix
  leadership in CEE countries 54–60, 211, 252
  main concepts 263t

emerging markets (EM) (*continued*)
  management thinking in transition (Part II) x, 3, 4, 5, 39–70, 250, 260
  management in practice (Part III) x, 3, 4, 5, 6, 71–206, 250, 257, 260, 262
  map of interlinked sub-codes network 262f
  market orientation (Hungarian perspective) 41–53, 210–11
  market-entry and expansion strategies (Anadolu Efes A.Ş.) 168–81
  market-entry strategy (Slovenian jewellery producer) 61–70, 211
  market-evolution patterns 231
  methodology 260–4
  necessity of local strategy 3
  from obligation to opportunity (Tasty Bite) 193–206
  paradigm shift 27t
  philosophy, goals, objectives of book 3
  plan/organization of book x, 3–6
  'problem of fit' (data comparison) 32
  product and trade name franchising (Kompen) 140–51
  qualitative and quantitative studies 260
  regionalism 13–15
  relationship-based market-entry (China) 114–27, 223–4
  reliability of coding process 261t
  research synthesis about providing the evidence 260–3
  saving an African mining giant (Ashanti) 182–92
  share of world exports (1995, 2001) 33t
  share of world imports (1995, 2001) 34t
  strategic issues and theoretical resources 260
  sub-codes 263t
  success drivers 4f, 4–6
  target readership ix–x
  terminology 26
  top companies 35t
  types 28–9
  world trade trends x, 9–25
  see also BEMs; SEMs; TEs
emerging markets: lessons learned (Part IV) x, 3, 4, 5, 207–59, 262
  from classical to neo-global perspectives 209–17
  concluding thoughts 250–9

  flexible and creative approach 250, 252–3, 259
  four broad themes 250
  markets 227–34
  operations 242–9
  organization 218–26
  people 235–41
  relationship focus 250, 255–7, 259
  'think regional, act local, forget global' 212
  tight–loose structure 250, 251–2, 259
  unique characteristics 257
  world class (emphasis on being) 250, 253–5, 259
empirical evidence 58, 85, 210
employee orientation 112
employee satisfaction 126, 237
employee skills 164t
employees 44, 47t, 48, 86–7, 88, 89t, 91, 102, 126, 135, 148, 158, 162, 179, 224, 235, 239
  reward schemes 126
employment 15, 20, 156
  job opportunities 31
end-users 124, 125f, 125, 132, 135, 169f, 170, 239
energy conservation 112
engineers 237, 255
England 144
Enron 75
entrepreneurs/entrepreneurship 11, 41, 61, 68, 163, 179
environment (business) ix, 17, 18, 56, 58, 75, 192, 215, 219, 227, 237, 238, 241(n9), 251, 256
  African 253
  competitive 222
  emerging market 252
  high or low-context 216(n14)
  legal and macroeconomic 228
  local 212
environment (natural) 20, 103, 109, 112, 222
  Betek Boya's concern 133, 135–6, 139(n46)
  regulations 94
equal opportunities 75
equipment 10, 145
equity 160
Erdemir Group (steel production, 2002) 99t
Erem, T. x
Eren-Erdoğmuş, İ. † xiv
Ericsson 2
Eritrea 15
ERP system 205

Ertas, T.T. 139(n46)
Esen Plastik 145, 147t
ethical issues 125, 256
Ethiopia 15
Eurasian Insurance Union 138(n11)
Euro (professional magazine) 68
Euro-oven 1
Europe 2, 97, 101, 111, 111t, 114, 115, 116, 125f, 135, 143, 146, 177, 194, 199, 205, 252, 254, 256
Mao Shun markets 116t
tourism 155, 155t, 156
European Bank for Reconstruction and Development (EBRD) 163, 173
European Parliament 216(n23)
European Single Market 1
European Union (including forerunners) 9, 11, 12, 13, 14, 15, 41, 42, 50, 63, 118, 130, 133, 210–11, 216(n10), 217
internal differences 18
every day low price (EDLP) 200
evolutionary company theory 48
exchange of goods 49
exchange rates 138(n29)
excise tax 62
executives 76, 127n, 153, 155
expatriation 240
experience 67f, 154, 176, 178, 179, 204, 214, 229, 237, 252–3, 254
exploration 183
export competence 89
export experience 87
export initiatives 132
export performance 86, 94, 244
export promotion 90, 94
export success (Pakistan) 85–96
exporters 86, 194, 242
guidelines 93–4
exporting 140, 172, 194, 213
Taiwan 115, 118
exports 10, 62, **129**, 134, 136, 144, 193
steel 100, 104
external resource access 214f, 218, 219f, 219, **224–5**, 259, 262
interlinkages of concepts 263t
map of interlinked sub-codes network 262f
'second-order concept' (sub-code) 261

face (Chinese concept) 123
family 74, 102, 194
family businesses 30, 115
family control 220
'family idea' 239

family structure 132
Fang, T. 241(n9)
Far East 50, 161
fashion 65, 77, 121, 215(n4)
fast-moving consumer goods (FMCG) 75–6, 76t, 78, 82, 178, 245
Fayerweather, J. 211–12
Federal Mogul Company (USA) 117
Federation of Pakistan Chambers of Commerce and Industry (FPCCI) 86
Festival (non-alcoholic beer) 176
Fiat 77
'FILIP' model **73–84**
acronym
Fraternity-building 77, **78–9**, 83, 238, 239, 256
Institution-building 77, 78, **79–80**, 83
Logically modular investment 77, 78, **80–1**, 83
Indigenous innovation 77, 78, **81–2**, 83
Portfolio of market segments 77, 78, **82–3**
general
defining marketing success 76–7
failure to give a 'FILIP' 83
findings 77–83
lessons 83
proactive initiatives and de-risking strategies 78
the study 75–6
financial institutions 224
financial markets 245
Finland 42, 99t
Firatpen 144, 145
first-mover advantage 173
first-movers 168, 169f
first order concepts 260
flexibility 251, **252–3**
flexible market entry 214f, 227, 228f, 229–30, 233(n5), 262
interlinkages of concepts 263t
map of interlinked sub-codes network 262f
'second-order concept' (sub-code) 261
focus on competent personnel 214f, **235–8**, 255, 258(n19), 262
interlinkages of concepts 263t
map of interlinked sub-codes network 262f
'second-order concept' (sub-code) 261

Folli Follie 64
food 121, 157
  frozen and chilled 199
  Indian 196, 198, 231, 244
  Mexican 197–8
  natural 196, 197, 198, 200, 201
  organic 196
  packaged 193, 197
  snack 76, 77
  Thai 198, 206, 231, 244
Food Service (Nirulas) 77
Ford 120
foreign direct investment (FDI) 1, 12, 13, 34, 44, 116, 116t, 122, 126, 172, 173, 174, 193, 216(n8), 230
foreign exchange earnings 15, 156
formalization 158
Fortune 500 largest companies 35
  see also Indian companies
France 2, 42, 55, 98t, 99t, 143, 144, 146, 254
franchisees 142, 148, 240, 251, 256
franchising 153, 154, 159, 159t, 160, 163, 164t, 230, 240, 246, 256
  advantages 149
  contractual system 141–3
  development in Turkey 142–3
  Kompen 140–51
Frankfurt 114
Frat Plastik A.Ş. 147t
fraternities 77, 78–9, 83, 238, 239, 256
  real-estate 81
  sources of staff 81
  suppliers 80
  vendors 81
Freda-Rebecca mine (Zimbabwe) 183, 184t, 185, 190
free market 9, 11, 19, 29, 33, 54, 123
Free Trade Area of Americas (FTAA) 14, 20
Freudenberg Group (German-based) 117
Freudenberg-NOK Group 117
Friedman, T. 31
Frost, T. 2, 36
Funabashi Steel 103
Fundaçao Gerdau (1963–) 102

Gallatin 106t
Garten, J.E. 28, 37(n15)
Gasse, Y. 241(n5)
Gazprom 35t
GDP 12, 27, 29, 196
GE 73, 194
GE Capital 108
Gebze 131

Geita Mine (Tanzania) 184t, 185, 190
Geller, N.A. 157
General Agreement of Tariffs and Trade (GATT) *see* World Trade Organization
geography 175, 228
Georgia 130t, 132, 136, 137(n6)
Gerdau American Depository Receipts 109
Gerdau 'brand' 108–9
Gerdau Commercial Division (1971–) 102, 110
Gerdau family
  fourth generation 107
  Gerdau, J. 101
  Helda (grand-daughter of J. Gerdau) 101
  Johannpeter brothers 112
  Johannpeter, C. 101
  Johannpeter, A.G. 107
  Johannpeter, C.G. 107
  Johannpeter, F.G. 107
  Johannpeter, J.G. 101, 107
Gerdau Group 101, 103, 105
Gerdau International 107
Gerdau Steel (Brazil) 97–113, 219f, 263
  affiliates 106t, 112
  Ameristeel Unit 101
  brand-building 'not a viable option' 248
  commitment to becoming world class 254–5
  competent personnel 237
  corporate values 220
  'cut-and-bend shops' 110, 111, 112
  debt 111–12
  distribution 111–12
  EBITDA 109, 110t
  expansion (1980–2003) 104t
  flexible market entry 230
  geographical locations of production 106t
  historical development 101–8
  market selection process 228
  market strategy 108–12
  markets network 228f
  operations network 243f
  organization network 219f
  people network 236f
  price 109–10
  profit margins 110t, 110
  promotion (of products) 110–11
  quality focus 221
  relationships and connections 238
  steel production (2002) 99t, 105t

Germany 20, 42, 55, 88, 101, 117, 143, 144, 146, 161, 176
  brewing 168
  steel production companies (2002) 99t
geyfiyetli ve galiteli 133
Ghana 10, 184t
  high court 187
  saving an African mining giant (Ashanti) 182–92
Ghana: National Liberation Council 182
Ghana: National Redemption Council 183
Ghana Libyan Arab Mining Company Limited 183, 184t
Ghanaian–Australian Goldfields Limited (GAG) 184t, 185
Ghanaian government 183, 189
Ghauri, P.N. 5, 26
Giants (retailing chain in USA) 197
Glamis Gold 191t
Global Distribution System (GDS) 157
'global manifest destiny' (Caslione and Thomas) 20
global resources, access to 212
globalization 1, 2, 15–17, 26, 30, 36, 59, 63, 109, 157, 197, 213
  alternatives 16
  benefits 16
  challenge (power of culture) 17–19
  critics 19–21
  economic view 228
  hotel industry 230
  network view 228, 229
  palate 197, 231
  steel industry 97
Globus 66, 67
'glocalization' 246
GM 120
GNP growth 26
Godrej Hi-Care 76t, 81
gold 220
  global industry 190
  industry consolidation trend 191
  major players 191t
  market capitalization 191t
  production (2002) 191t
  saving an African mining giant (Ashanti) 182–92
  Western companies (prejudiced perception) 192
gold mines 253
gold price 184, 186, 187, 190, 191, 220
gold reserves (UK sale, 1999) 186
Goldcorp 191t

Golden Shamrock Mines Limited 183, 184t
golden share 183
Goldman Sachs Group 188
Gost-R document 136
government controls 32
government economic policy 165
government intervention (reduction) 123
government policy 161, 164t
  tourism 156
government support 90, 92, 229
governments 78, 98, 193, 224, 255, 256
  steel industry 97
Govindarajan, V. 25(n62)
Goya brand 197
grain 170
Grand Heritage Hotels 154
graph-theoretical concepts 264(n14)
Grebel, T. 258(n19)
Greece 20, 170, 175
Greenfield investment 100, 172, 173, 230
Greenpeace 222
Group Modelo 170
Guáira (Paraná state) 103, 104t, 106t
Guangdong 119
Guangzhou 122
guanxi 238, 239, 255, 259(n24)
Guillen, M.F. 258(n5)
Guinea 184t, 185
Gujarat Amboja (cement brand) 82
Güner, C. 173, 175, 177, 178, 180(n17, n27)
Gupta, A. 25(n62)
Güzelöz, H. 134, 135, 137n

HACCP food-safety certification 205
Hadeed (steel production, 2002) 99t
Haier (Chinese manufacturer) 253, 254, 258(n9)
Haldiram (company) 76t, 77
Hall, E.T. 23(n34)
halwais (sweet-shop owners) 79
Hampden-Turner, C. 17, 23(n36)
Hampton Inns 153
Hanusch, H. 258(n19)
Harbison, F.H. 215(n2)
harmony 123
'harmony in contradictions' 136
Harmony Gold Mining 191t
HDFC Bank 76, 77, 81
headquarters/head office 136, 158
health/healthcare 79, 80, 102, 145, 162
hedging 186–90
Heineken 170

Heinz 197
HEI Hotels 154
Heritage Foundation 12
Hero Motors 78
Hewlett Packard xv
Hickson, D.J. 215(n3–4)
hierarchy 123
Highlights 155–6
Hilton International (hotel chain) 154t
Hime 103
Hindus 74
Hindustan Lever 78, 79
HMT 77
Hodgetts, R. 2
Hofstede, G. 17
Holiday Inn 153, 156, 163
  Holiday Inn Express 156, 162
  Holiday Inn Garden Court 162
  Holiday Inn Select 156
  Holiday Inn Worldwide 162
Holsti's coefficient of
  reliability 261t
home meal replacement (HMR) 197
homogenization 209–10, 214
Honda 36, 120
Hong Kong 13, 28, 29t, 88, 120
Hoogovens 100
Hooley, G. 45
hospitals 133
hotel chains 152, 158, 164t
  see also US hotel companies
hotels 68, 244
  employees 255
  family-owned 162
  independent 158
  luxury/five-star 160, 161, 162
  occupancy rates 162
HSBC 73
Huberman, A.M. 264(n9, 12–13)
Huff, A.S. 260
human capital 51, 255
human factors 134–5, 164t
human resource management
  (HRM) 54, 73, 125–6, 239
human resources 59, 107, 150, 158,
  163, 170, 178, 235–6
human rights 19
Hungary 11, 22(n3), 28, 29t, 45, 55,
  152, 210, 222, 231, 255
  EU membership 42
  hotel expansion 160–5
  hotels 160
  market orientation 41–53, 210–11
  theoretical hypotheses and practical
    measurements 42–9
  tourism revenue 161

transformation of economy 42
urban hotel occupancy 162
Hungary: State Property Agency
  (SPA) 161
Hunt, S.D. 49–50
Hylsamex (steel production, 2002) 99t
hypermarkets 66, 67, 69, 178
Hypernova 66, 67
Hyundai 2, 35

Iacobucci, D. 264(n14)
ICICI (bank) 76, 81
identity
  cultural 13
  ethnic 19
  local 19, 20, 176
  national 18, 20
  Russian 175, 176–7
Iduapriem mine (Ghana), 184t, 185
IKEA 2
image 170, 174, 224, 254, 255
imperialism 14
import tariffs (absence) 89t, 91
import-substitution 12, 221
imports 15, 109, 149, 194, 255
incentive systems 57, 93
incentives 164t
income (low level) 30
income distribution 19
income inequalities 22
Indah Kiat Pulp and Paper 36
Index of Economic Freedom (Heritage
  Foundation) 12–13
India 2, 10, 15, 21, 24–5(n62),
  28, 29t, 29, 32, 33, 35t, 97, 100,
  227, 232, 237, 244
  consumer profile 74t
  democratic institutions 75
  direct costs of steel production
    (2001) 98t
  diversity 74
  E7 group 27
  economic liberalization 193
  export quandary 194
  fastest-growing FMCG
    companies 76t
  'FILIP' marketing strategy 73–84
  global exposure 74–5
  growth potential 74
  'microcosm of global
    marketplace' 73–5
  multi-segment approach 231
  private enterprise 75
  share of world exports and imports
    (1995–2001) 33t, 34t
  size 73

Index 281

socialist principles 12
wealth profile 74
Indian Census (2001) 74
Indian companies
 corporate values 219-20
 markets network 228f
 operations network 243f
 organization network 219f
 people network 236f
 relationship focus 256
 supplier and distribution
  networks 245
 see also multinational companies
Indian diaspora 75, 196, 201, 244, 253
Indian government 193
Indian Oil 35t
Indo Nissin Foods 80
Indonesia 15, 27, 29t, 32, 33,
 33t, 34t, 36
industrial revolution 213
industrialization 102, 214, 215(n3)
inequality (income and wealth) 32, 63
inflation 103, 128, 161, 163, 172
information 16, 120, 136, 149, 213,
 222, 224
 computerized systems 102
 generation 46, 47t
information technology 2, 57, 107,
 121, 150, 213, 215(n4), 220, 222
 components 117
 investments 80
Infosys 2
infrastructure ix, 30, 31, 32, 59, 91, 94,
 194, 220, 246, 247
 business 119-20
 communications 213
 information 213
 institutional 229
 institutional (Azerbaijan) 129
 transportation 213
Ingram, P.L. 153
INI Steel (production, 2002) 99t
initial public offering (IPO) 101, 115,
 193
Inland Steel Company (USA) 100
innovation 82, 237, 251
 indigenous, to deliver consumer
  value 77, 78, 81-2, 83
 technological 255
innovativeness 214f, 218, 219f, 219,
 222-3, 262
 interlinkages of concepts 263t
 map of interlinked sub-codes
  network 262f
 'second-order concept'
  (sub-code) 261

inpatriation 240
inputs 94, 246
Institution of International Investment
 Credit and Guarantee 138(n11)
institution-building 77, 78, 79-80,
 83, 220
institutions 242, 251
 democratic 75
 local 239, 255
 voids 254
integrated steel mills 104t, 112
integrated steel-makers 105
Interbrew 170, 173, 230
international business 16, 17
 paradigm shift 27t
 trends 4
International Finance Corporation
 (IFC) 163, 183
International Forum on
 Globalization 16
International Gold Resources
 (IGR) 183, 184t
International Labour Organization 75
International Monetary Fund (IMF)
 16-17, 19, 183
internationalization 209, 212, 213,
 236, 239, 247
 chain theory/stage model 229
 Mao Shun Corporation 116-17
 motivations 5
internet 64, 111, 112, 133, 246
Internon 144
Interstate Hotels 154
interviews 48, 54, 59, 76, 77, 95, 127n,
 137n, 151(n11), 180(n17)
Invesco Asset Management 174
investment 11, 15, 31, 65, 78, 79, 83,
 102, 129, 141, 162, 182, 224, 227
 back-end 81
 cross-border 34
 logically modular and phased 77, 78,
  80-1, 83
 long-term plans 94
 motivations 160
 see also foreign direct investment
investment opportunities 186
investment returns 35t, 165,
 218, 229
investor confidence 34
investor relations (Gerdau) 107-8
investors 128, 144, 161, 184, 238
Iran 99t, 116, 136
Iraq 135, 146, 176
iron ore 102, 105, 112
ISG 100
Islam/Muslims 74, 171, 174, 176, 177

ISO certification 108–9, 221, 254
  ISO 9000 119, 130
  ISO 9001 62, 133
  ISO 9002 119, 145, 205
  ISO 14000 133, 205
Ispat-LNM 100
Israel 130, 130t, 136
Istanbul 2, 148
Istanbul: Pendik 131
Istanbul Chamber of Commerce 131
Italy 1–2, 19, 20, 99t, 100
Ivory Coast 10

Jackson (place-name) 106t
Jacksonville 106t
Japan 21, 62, 88, 98, 100, 101, 109, 116, 199, 254
  direct costs of steel production (2001) 98t
  steel production companies (2002) 99t
  industrialization process 215(n3)
Jaworski, B.J. 43, 46, 52(n18)
Jenkins, M. 260
jewellery 61–70, 211
Jewish religion 177
Jiangsu Province (PRC) 121
Johannpeter, C. *see* Gerdau family
joint ventures 35, 100, 101, 102, 105, 116, 116t, 117, 131, 140, 141, 159, 159t, 160, 161, 163, 164t, 172, 173, 174, 194, 195, 230, 247
  TCL-Thomson SA 254
Jonah, S. 187, 188
Jordan 146
Jordan, T.G. 155
Journal of Marketing 42, 43
JP Morgan Chase Bank 108
jute 10

Kalpen 144
KAM *see* key account managers
Kanpur Detergents 76t
Kapás, J. 42
Karaganda 174, 178
Karagandinskoe (beer brand) 174, 175
Karhunen, P. 160, 225(n10)
Karlovy Vary 64
Katsikeas, C., *et al.* (1997) 85, 86, 95(n4)
  Deng, S. 95(n4)
  Wortzel, L. 95(n4)
Katsikeas, C.S. 85, 95(n5)
Kawasaki 99t, 100
Kazakhstan 97, 146, 171, 173–4, 175, 230

Kazakhstan government 174
KBE (company) 144
Keatley, M. 187, 188–9, 190
Keegan, W.L. 23(n34)
Kellogg 197
Kerr, C. 215(n2)
Keszey, T. 47n
key account managers (KAM) 119, 124, 125f, 125, 126, 224, 246, 256
KFC 77
Khanna, T. 27, 249(n9)
Kia 2, 35
Kilachand, K. 194, 195, 205
  'AKM' (Ashok, Kartik, Meera) 195, 196, 200, 204, 205
Kingfisher 2
Kinross Gold 191t
kirana (grocery stores) 82
Kirin 170
Klein, N. 19
Klenoty Aurum 64
knowledge 16, 154, 224, 229
  cognitive 58
  market-specific 172
  tacit 178, 179
knowledge economy 213
Knoxville 106t
Kobe Steel (steel production, 2002) 99t
Koch, A.J. 233(n5)
Kogut, B. 154
Kohli, A.K. 43, 46, 52(n18)
Kola Real 254
Kombassan Holding Co. 145
Kömmerling (company) 144
Kompen A.Ş. (1989–): product and trade name franchising 140–51
  commitment to becoming world class 254
  competent personnel 236, 237, 240
  corporate values 220
  customization of marketing 244
  expansion in international markets 145–6
  general information 145–6
  international operations 146
  localization of management 239–40
  market selection process 229
  markets network 228f
  non-family-owned 251
  operations network 243f
  organization network 219f
  people network 236f
  quality focus 221
  relationship focus 256
  sales (2003) 147t

success factors 146–9, 150
supplier and distribution
  networks 246
Konka (Chinese television
  manufacturer) 254
Konya 145
Korea Electric Power 35t
Kostecki, M. 160, 166(n36)
Kotler, P. 51(n3), 225(n2), 249(n8)
Kraft 197
Krivorozstal (steel production, 2002) 99t
Kroger's 197
Krylia Rock Festival 177
KSA Technopak (consulting firm) 82
Küçükoğlu, T 132, 133
Küçükşehir, Mr 148
Kundu, S.K. 160
Kunshan (Jiangsu Province, PRC) 114, 121, 122, 125–6
Kyrgyz Republic 137(n6)

labelling 43, 63
laboratories 133, 136
Laboratory Accreditation 145
labour 34, 81, 156, 179, 220, 245
  cheap 1, 30
  low-cost 240
  low-cost/high quality 112, 237
  shortage 115
  skill shortages 240
  skilled 62, 236
labour costs 115, 238, 247
  payroll costs 162
labour laws 75
labour markets 79–80
labour recruitment 124
labour regulations 32
Ladik Mevkii 145
Lages, L.F. 85
Lahore: Imperial College xi
Laisa (Uruguayan steel-maker) 103, 104t, 106t, 107
Lamgold 191t
language 18, 74, 123, 128, 137, 162, 228, 229
  Azeri 133
  Chinese 114
  dialects 74
  German 114
  English 68
Latin America 11, 14, 20, 21, 153, 232
Lavigne, M. 41
leadership in CEE countries 54–60, 211, 252
  characterization 56t, 56
  main findings 55–8
  management style (assessment/ perception) 55f, 56t, 57
  sample and methodology 54–5
  strengths and weakness 56t, 56
learning organization 126, 147, 236
  organizational learning 220, 235
LG Electronics 2, 35, 35t, 82
Libya 184t
licensing 35, 140
lifestyle 15, 31, 132, 197, 211, 214, 223, 231
Lihir Gold 191t
Lijjat Papad 78
Lin concordance 261, 261t
literature 257
  Anglo-Saxon (loose terminology) 43
  business 212
  EM groupings 28
  export success 85, 88, 89, 93, 95
  government support for export
    activities 94
  international business operations
    (Western perspective) 16
  internationalization issues 227
  leadership studies 56
  marketing 41, 225(n2)
  marketing textbooks (basic) 245, 249(n8)
  multinational companies, 4
  role of EMs in world trade 4
  vertical quasi integration 141
Lithuania 146
living conditions 20
living standards 22, 62, 155
LNM Group 99t
localization of management 214f, 262
  driver of global business success 235, 236f, 239–40
  interlinkages of concepts 263t
  map of interlinked sub-codes
    network 262f
  'second-order concept'
    (sub-code) 261
location
  hotels 155–6, 161, 163, 164t, 165
  manufacture of products 227
logistics 107, 134, 154, 239, 255
  multi-modal 82
Lombard, M. 264(n11)
London and Rhodesia Mining and Land
  Company (Lonrho) 182, 183
London Stock Exchange 182, 183
Lonmin Plc 183, 189
Lorenz, A.F. 163
Los Angeles 200

loyalty programmes 80
LTV Company 100
Lucie Hubacova (company) 64
Lux (brand) 76, 79
luxury products 231

Macedonia 146
machinery 10, 91, 121, 213
McQueen, M. 153
macroeconomic
  environment 120
  perspective 93
  processes 50–1
macroeconomics 68
Madrid Stock Exchange 109
Madsen, T.K. 85
magazines 64, 68
Magnitogorsk (steel production, 2002) 99t
Maharashtra (India) 193
Mahindra & Mahindra (company) 76
Mahindra Scorpio 81
mail surveys 86, 94
Malaysia 2, 10, 28, 29t, 33
Mallalieu, D. 190
management 126, 132, 135, 194, 205, 206, 222, 236, 251
  competence 89
  expatriate 240
  hotels 156, 157–8, 160, 161, 162–3, 164t, 165
  information systems 158
  monitoring of export operations 220
  qualified 237
  quality 89, 133
  theory and practice ix
management capabilities 230
management consulting 54
management contracts 153, 154, 159t, 160, 163, 224, 230
management control systems 165
management controls 158
management development 58, 133
management of environmental uncertainty 214f, 227, 228f, 232–3, 262
  interlinkages of concepts 263t
  map of interlinked sub-codes network 262f
  'second-order concept' (sub-code) 261
management knowledge (mapping) 260

management in practice (Part III) x, 3, 4, 5, 6, 71–206, 250, 257, 260, 262
  attractiveness of Azerbaijan (Betek) 128–39
  best practices in emerging markets (examples from US hotel industry) 152–67
  export success (lessons from Pakistani firms) 85–96
  'FILIP' marketing strategy 73–84
  Gerdau (multinational steel giant from Brazil) 97–113
  market-entry and expansion strategies (Anadolu Efes A.Ş.) 168–81
  from obligation to opportunity (Tasty Bite) 193–206
  product and trade name franchising (Kompen) 140–51
  relationship-based market-entry (China) 114–27, 223–4
  saving an African mining giant (Ashanti) 182–92
management qualifications 58
management skills 35, 121
management style 18, 30, 211–12
management thinking in transition (Part II) x, 3, 4, 5, 39–70, 250, 260
  'classical view' 210
  leadership in CEE countries 54–60, 211, 252
  market orientation (Hungarian perspective) 41–53, 210–11
  market-entry strategy (Slovenian jewellery producer) 61–70, 211
management training 58
managerial control 220
managerial learning 229
managerial staff, young 135
managers ix, 41, 44, 46, 47t, 50, 61, 68, 83, 114, 142, 147, 149, 158, 165, 205, 209, 213, 214, 221, 223, 238, 247
  CEE 54–60, 211, 252
  challenges of EU accession underestimated 59
  competence (CEE countries) 54
  cosmopolitan 240
  EU 54–60, 211, 252
  expectations 48
  local 192, 232, 237, 251, 252
  personal attributes 58
  'practitioners' x
  recruitment 58
  rotation 192
  senior 252
  training programmes 58

Manitoba 105
Manrai, A.K. 13
Manrai, L.A. 13
Manu, F. xiv
Manu, F.A. 225(n1)
manufactured goods 10
manufacturer-dealer systems 142, 143, 148
manufacturers 29, 140, 144, 145, 150, 200
manufacturing 33, 75, 78, 80, 93, 122, 126, 127, 227, 254
 food 194, 197
 low-cost 230
manufacturing processes 148
manufacturing sites 222
Mao Shun Corporation (Taiwan, 1976–)
 awards 115
 background 115–19
 business relationships 119
 channel design 124, 125f
 competition 117
 corporate vision and strategic implications 117–19
 expansion into PRC 119–21
 human-resource management 125–6
 innovation leadership 118
 international markets (focus on) 118
 international operations 116–17
 market-entry mode 122
 marketing strategy 122–3
 product strategy 122
 products 115–16, 121
 quality leadership 118–19
 relationship-based market-entry (PRC) 114–27, 223–4
 role of relationships 123–5
 strategy 122–6
 subsidiaries 116, 117
 subsidiary in PRC 114, 116, 121
 worldwide markets 116t
 see also NAK
Mao Shun Kunshan 121
Marber, P. 29
MARG (India) 195
Marico Industries 76t
Marinov, M.A. 216(n8)
Marinova, S.T. 216(n8)
Mariupol Ilyich (steel production, 2002) 99t
market
 access 11, 20, 89t, 91, 94, 122
 analysis 61
 capitalism 11–12
 capitalization 191t
 competition 50

 conditions 218, 230
 coverage 150
 data 31
 economy 41, 42, 49, 50, 210, 211
 forces 57, 127, 141
 fragmentation 229
 information 43, 44, 51
 knowledge 46, 47t, 220, 230, 232, 233
 leaders/leadership 160, 171, 174, 175
 opportunities 154, 165
 planning 89
 position 133, 174–6
market orientation 45, 62, 147
 academic research (limited scope) 50–1
 definition (Narver and Slater) 44, 51
 elements (Kohli and Jaworski) 43–4
 factor analysis 47t
 factors 43
 Hungarian perspective 41–53, 210–11
 measurement 43–4
 measurement (Narver and Slater scales) 44–8
 serving economic growth 49–50
 short-term and long-term objectives 48
 socialism 11
 strategic priorities (changes in 1990s) 48–9
 terminology 43
market research 63, 64, 68, 79, 120, 195, 201, 202f, 211, 220, 242, 252
market screening and selection (hotel sector) 155–6
market segmentation/segments 67, 80, 147, 153, 154, 164t, 171, 174, 175, 200–2, 223, 227, 242, 246, 247
 Betek Boya 132
 elites 161–2
 hotels 156–7, 161–2, 163, 164t, 165
 new 176
 portfolio served from day one 77, 78, 82–3
 seven-step approach 64–6, 211
market share 1, 2, 35, 76, 77, 82, 83, 109, 112, 131, 149, 171, 172, 173, 174, 175, 218
 Gerdau (in Brazil, 1980–2001), 108, 108t
 global, 36
market-entry 224
 exporting 140
 international hotel companies 159–60

market-entry (*continued*)
  product and trade name
    franchising 140–51
  speed 173
  sustainable 218
market-entry mode 164t, 195, 251
  Anadolu Efes 171–4
  flexible 245
  Mao Shun Corporation 122
  relationship-based (China) 114–27, 223–4
  Slovenian jewellery producer 61–70, 211
market-selection process 134, 214f, 227–9, 262
  Anadolu Efes 171–4
  interlinkages of concepts 263t
  map of interlinked sub-codes network 262f
  non-economic criteria 228–9
  'rational' criteria 228, 229
  'second-order concept' (sub-code) 261
marketing 2, 22(n3), 30, 31, 35, 41, 42, 43, 63, 102, 105, 114, 117, 136, 142, 146, 160, 169f, 170, 194, 195, 206, 218, 223, 232, 240, 242, 251
  contribution to profitability 50
  cost–benefit principles 50
  cross-border 83
  customer-goods 245
  definition of success 76–7
  evolution 212–13
  'FILIP' strategy 73–84
  four Ps 64, 77, 78, 83
  generic strategies 245, 249(n9)
  global 73, 83, 247
  international 140
  to serve economic growth 49–50
  strategic plans 134–5
marketing channels 141, 142, 143, 149
marketing costs 68
marketing customization 244
marketing expertise 254
marketing experts 51
marketing mix 61, 212, 248, 251
  hotels 156–7, 164t
  strategies 67
marketing organization 210
marketing programmes 209
marketing research 48
Marketing Science Institute 43
marketing strategy 45
  'FILIP' 73–84
  seven Ps (Mao Shun Corporation) 122–3
marketing success 76–7, 81

marketing team 236
marketization 49
markets (general) 31, 143, 144, 147, 247, 256
  continuous screening 150
  definition 196
  developed 83
  domestic 20, 140, 143, 145, 148, 150, 163, 168, 218, 220, 227, 252–4
  evolving 77
  export 92, 133, 136, 137, 220
  foreign 88, 90t, 150, 256
  global 57, 129, 140, 233
  international 69, 118, 143, 148, 149, 150, 163, 168, 171, 178, 179, 220, 221, 222
  Indian 194, 222
  new 16, 18, 22, 61, 179, 209, 224
  overseas 247
  primary target (Mao Shun Corporation) 122
  psychically-close 229
  regional 254
  size 196
  target 91, 149
  unique characteristics 211
  world 22, 49
markets (one of four principal 'success drivers') 4, 4f, 5, 214f, 227–34
  first-order concept 261, 261t
  flexible market entry 227, 228f, 229–30
  managing environmental uncertainty 227, 228f, 232–3
  multi-segment approach 227, 228f, 230–2, 233
  selection process 227–9
  sub-codes 261, 261t
Marriott Courtyard (sub-brand) 156
Marriott International (US hotel chain) 154, 154t, 156, 162
Marshall (company) 130
Martinear, M. 187
Maruti Suzuki cars 78
Marxism 11
Massachusetts Institute of Technology 203
Maytag 2
MBA students 82
MBO principle 126
McCarthy, J.E. 65
McDonald's 2, 19, 42, 80, 246
MDH (spice brand) 79
media/press 31, 36, 51, 64, 74, 78, 79, 80, 148, 173, 179, 189, 242, 244, 247
medical appliances 118
medicare parts 121

Meges (company) 130
mentality 3, 135
Mercosur 103, 112
mergers and acquisitions (M&A) 154, 169f, 170, 183–4, 196
Meridian Gold 191t
Merna, K.M. 158
Metalúrgica Gerdau 107
methodologies 48, 54–5, 86–7, 219f, 219, 250, 260–4
Mexico 21, 24(n62), 28, 29t, 32, 34, 36
E7 group 27
share of world exports and imports (1995–2001) 33t, 34t
steel producer (2002) 99t
Michell, P. 85
microeconomy 50, 54, 68
middle class 31, 33, 63
Middle East 10, 11, 14, 146, 155t, 194, 223
'Arab countries' 12
middlemen 256
Midea (Chinese television manufacturer) 254
Midras Mining Limited 183
Milberg Weiss Bershad Hynes & Lerach LLP (New York-based law-firm) 187
Miles, M.B. 264(n9, 12–13)
milk 78, 82
Miller (company) 170
Minas Gerais (state) 102, 103
mini-mills (steel), 100–1, 103, 104t, 105, 106, 107, 112
'market mills' 110
mixed economy 12
Moldavia 146
Moldova 137(n6), 171, 174, 175, 179, 230
Moore, R.M. xiv–xv
Moorman, C. 43, 46
Morgan R.M. 50
Moscow 173, 177, 178
Mother Dairy 78, 82
motivation 59, 149, 162, 236
motor scooters 36
motorcycles 78, 121
MRM 104t, 105, 106t, 107
multi-segment approach 214f, 227, 228f, 230–2, 233, 244, 253, 262
interlinkages of concepts 263t
map of interlinked sub-codes network 262f
'second-order concept' (sub-code) 261

multinational companies (MNCs) 15–16, 19, 21, 35, 36, 63, 83, 173, 179, 209, 214, 221, 248, 251
advantages and disadvantages 1
African 182
become 'rootless' 253
emerging market 254
entry into emerging markets 20
impact in emerging markets 31
imperialist mind-set 36
'not always successful in EMs in long run' 18
operations in emerging markets ix
strategies 2
see also SMEs
multiple branding 176, 247
multiple channel strategy 83
municipalities 48
Myers, C.A. 215(n2)

NAK 220, 255
brand-building 246, 247
commitment to becoming world class 254
competent personnel 236–7
corporate values 220–1
customer focus 223–4
external resource access 224
family-owned 251
flexible market entry 230
markets network 228f
operations network 243f
organization network 219f
people network 236f
quality focus 221
relationships and connections 238, 256
supplier and distribution networks 246
NAK brand (Mao Shun) 116, 122–3, 127n
NAK family (so-called) 126
NAK Kunshan 126
nano-technology 118
Nantou (Taiwan) 116, 117
Narver, J.C. 44
Narver and Slater scales (market orientation) **44–8**
NASA 199
National Steel (USA) 100
natural gas 143
Nayır, D.Z. xv
neighbourhoods 201, 202
neocolonialism 14
neoglobal thesis 210, 215, 215(n7)
Nescafé 2

Nestlé 197
Netherlands 42, 55, 99t, 161, 171
network perspective 259
network view 255
networks 224, 238, 242
　external 229
　markets 228f
　methodology 219, 260–4
　operations 243f
　organization 219f
　people 236f
　role 255–6, 258(n22)
'new economic mechanism' 43
New York 112, 187
New York Stock Exchange 109, 183
New Zealand 14, 42
Newmont Mining 191t
Newport Jeans 77
Nigam, R. 204, 205
Nippon Steel 98t, 99t, 100, 103, 105t
Nirlep (non-stick cookware) 79
Nirma 81
Nirulas (company) 77
NISCO (steel production, 2002) 99t
NKK 99t, 100
NOK Corporation (Japan) 117
Nokia 2
non-governmental institutions 80, 218
non-industrialized regions 217
non-tariff barriers 127, 149
noodles 80
Nortel Networks 2
North Africa 132
North America 21, 97, 109, 110t, 110, 111, 111t, 112, 230
North American Free Trade Agreement (NAFTA) 9, 100, 104, 107, 112
North Korea 12
'Notes Based on Export Receivables' (Gerdau) 111–12
Novolipetsk (steel production, 2002) 99t
Nowak, J. 211
Nucor 99t, 100–1, 107

Obuasi 182
Obuasi mine 184–5, 187, 190
Odessa 178
Ohmae, K. 21
oil/petroleum 10, 35, 143
Olsen, M.D. 158
Omni 203
operations (one of four principal 'success drivers') 4, 4f, 5, 214f, 242–9
　brand-building 242, 243f, 246–8
　customization of marketing 242, 243f, 243–5

　first-order concept 261, 261t
　sub-codes 261, 261t
　supplier and distribution networks 242, 243f, 245–6, 248
opportunism 256
Oregon 200
organization (one of four principal 'success drivers') 4–5, 4f, 218–26
　corporate values 218, 219f, 219–21
　customer focus 218, 219f, 219, 223–4
　decentralized 178–9
　external resource access, 218, 219f, 219, 224–5
　first-order concept 261, 261t
　five second-order success factors 218, 219f
　innovativeness 218, 219f, 219, 222–3
　network 219f
　quality focus 218, 219f, 219, 221–2
　sub-codes 261, 261t
　see also markets; people; operations
Organisation for Economic Co-operation and Development (OECD) 29
organization success factors 133
organizational structure 119
original equipment manufacturers (OEMs) 117, 122, 253
Ottoman Empire 179
outsourcing 1, 178, 200
ouzo (alcoholic drink) 170
ownership structure 163, 164t

P&O 2
Pacific/Pacific Rim 21, 155t
packaging 81, 143, 198, 245, 255
　retort pouch inside printed carton 199, 201, 205
Page, S. 14
Pains 104t
paint 143, 222, 253
　Betek Boya (attractiveness of Azerbaijan market) 128–39
Pak Plastik A.Ş. 147t
Pakistani exporters 85–96, 255
　additional factors 88–9
　bilateral trade agreements 89t, 91
　categories for comparison 88
　close monitoring of export operations by management 87, 87t, 89
　company size 86, 88, 89t, 90t, 91, 92, 93
　competent personnel 237
　corporate values 220
　export direction 88, 89t, 90t, 91

Index 289

export direction (consistent and inconsistent performers) 88, 90t, 92
export direction (EM→AM) 86
export direction (market and company dimensions) 90t, 92–3
export experience 86, 88, 90t, 92, 93
external factors 85, 93
findings 87–8
firm-specific factors 85
frequency of awards 86, 90t
governmental support 90, 92, 93
guidelines for export promotion agencies 94
guidelines for exporters 93–4
import tariffs (absence) 89t, 91
key determinants 85–6
limitations and directions for future research 94–5
literature 85
market coverage 86, 88, 89t, 90t, 91, 92, 93
market selection process 228
marketing policy elements 85
markets network 228f
methodology 86–7
non-family-owned 251
operations network 243f
organization network 219f
people network 236f
physical distribution 91
quality (emphasis on) 89–90, 93
quality control 87, 87t
quality focus 221
quality of staff 87, 87t, 89t, 89, 91
success factors (ranking) 87t
success factors across market and company dimensions 89t, 81
validity of export success factors 88–9
Pakpen 144, 145
Palepu, K. 27, 249(n9)
Panasonic 254
Panzihua (steel production, 2002) 99t
papad (Indian snack) 78
paper 36
Parachute Oil 82
Paraguay 103
Parakh Foods 76t
Paraná (state) 103
Paris 19
Paris Pointed Nail Factory (*Fábrica de Pregas Pontas de Paris*) 101
Parle International (India) 194
Parsons, T. 23(n36)
Patel, Mr 81

Patriot American Hospitality 154
payment management (Mao Shun Corporation) 123
Payne, A. 241(n9)
Pchounetlev, V. 212, 215(n15)
Peck, H. 241(n9)
pensions 102
people (one of four principal 'success drivers') 4, 4f, 5, 214f, 235–41
first-order concept 261, 261t
focus on competent personnel 235–8
localization of management 235, 236f, 239–40
relationships and connections 235, 236f, 238–9
sub-codes 261, 261t
Peprah, K. 186–7
Pepsi 76, 193, 194, 195, 205, 206, 254
perception 135, 215, 230
consumer 254
country-of-origin 253–4
managerial 209
Perfetti India 76t
performance measurement 57, 218, 225(n1)
Pernambuco 102, 103
Perreault, W.D. 65
personnel 158
perspectives
classical 209–10, 215, 215(n2)
classical approach and its transition 210–11
classical to neoglobal 209–17
homogenization versus differentiation 209–10
macro 212
new perspective and its evolution 211–12
'one-best-way' approach 210
paths of progress 212–15
problem of fit 209
'think regional, act local, forget global' 212
Perth Amboy (New Jersey) 106t, 112
Peru 191t, 254
Petrobras 35t
Petrochina 35t
petrol stations 142
Petry, C. 107
Philippines 28, 29t
Piaggio 77
Piercy, N.F. 85
Pilsa A.Ş. 147t
Pimapen 145
Pimas A.Ş. 144, 147t
Pioneer Goldfields Ltd 184t

Piratini 104t, 106, 106t
place (one of the four Ps of
   marketing) 67–8, 77
Placer Dome 191t
plastic chopping 144
plastics 144
Ploesti 172
Poisson, R. 241(n5)
Poland 11, 28, 29t, 32, 44, 45, 54, 99t,
   143, 160, 210
Polisan (company) 130
political turmoil 253
political upheaval 26
pollution 222
Polski Huti St (steel production, 2002) 99t
polymers 143
polyvinyl chloride (PVC)
   products 143–5
Porter, M.E. 168
Pôrto Alegre 101, 103, 107
Pöschl, J. 211
POSCO 98t, 99t, 100
positivism 260
postal links (PRC-Taiwan) 120
poverty 19, 31, 74, 80, 129
power (political) 18, 19, 31
Prague 62, 64, 66, 67f, 69
Prague Business Journal 68
Prague Post 68
Preferred Brands International LLC (PBI,
   Stamford, Connecticut, 1995–) xiv,
   xvi, xvii, 194–206
   acquisition of TBEL 204–5
   competition: need for renewal 206
   consumers 201–3
   execution 199–200
   launch 200–4
   marketing strategy 198
   new beginning for Tasty Bite 194–6
   organization 203–4
   positioning idea (US market) 197–8,
      223
   product 199–200
   staying the course (1999–2003) 205–6
   time for new strategy 206
presents 65, 66
Prestea 184t
price 65, 67f, 67–8, 146, 231,
   242, 243, 254
   Gerdau steel 109–10
   retail 193–4
   steel 98–9
   Turkish paint 130
   world market 109
price mechanism 141
price segments 153

pricing 136, 176, 243
   competitive 147
   Mao Shun Corporation 122–3
   one of the four Ps of marketing 77, 81
Primossa 64
private enterprise 75
private ownership 12
private sector 120, 161, 164t
privatization 11, 12, 35, 44, 49, 104,
   105, 161
problem of fit 209
process innovation 222, 223
processes 81, 82
Procter & Gamble 2
product
   customization 244
   development 43
   differentiation 243
   markets 66
   names 244
   strengths 5
product-mix innovation 222
production 54, 57, 81, 130, 144, 145,
   146, 221
   cost advantage 230
   factors of 179
   gold 186
   local 143
   low-cost 220
production costs 251
production networks 245
production orientation 44
production sites 245
productivity 15, 62, 194
products 10, 36, 67–8, 74, 129, 136,
   143, 148, 157, 159, 178, 193,
   215(n4), 243, 245, 255
   agricultural 194
   Betek Boya 132
   cheaper, simpler 231–2
   commodity-type 251
   four Ps of marketing 77, 81
   industrial versus consumer 93
   mature categories 76
   retorted 199, 201, 205
   standardized 142, 214
professionals 65, 68
profit goals 83
profit margins 110t, 110, 162, 172, 254
profitability 2, 77, 107, 108, 143, 156,
   159, 162–3, 192, 218, 220
profits 35t, 36, 69, 83, 101, 147, 149,
   159, 162, 188
   corporate 19
   earnings growth 154
   repatriation 172

project financing 190
promotion 67, 68, 78, 79, 157
  Gerdau steel 110–11
  Mao Shun Corporation 123
  one of the four Ps of marketing 77
  see also advertising
promotional expertise 254
protectionism 1, 12, 103, 104, 109, 223, 224–5, 228, 230
Proton 2
public relations 123, 247
public sector 35, 125
Pugh, D.S. 215(n3–4)
Pune 193
purchasing 123, 127
purchasing power parity (PPP) 27, 37(n10)
PVC pipes 144
PVC products 143–5, 146, 147, 148, 149
Pyka, A. 258(n19)

QS 9000 standard 119
quality 89, 137, 146, 148, 150, 174, 179, 210, 215(n3), 218, 223, 231, 237, 242, 243, 244, 254
  emphasis on 89–90, 93
  expectations 255
  Gerdau 103, 108–9, 112
  Mao Shun Corporation 117, **118–19**
  test reports 123
  world class (success factor) 77, 83
quality control 91, 94, 123, 159t, 194, 198, 200
quality focus 214f, 218, 219f, 219, 221–2, 262
  interlinkages of concepts 263t
  map of interlinked sub-codes network 262f
  'second-order concept' (sub-code) 261
quality of life 215
quality orientation 62, **133**
quality standards 132, 144, 254
Quantum (India) 195
questionnaires 55, 59(n5), 86, 94–5, 96(n20)

racing cars 117
railways 182
Rajanigandha (chewing tobacco) 81
raki (alcoholic drink) 170
Ranbaxy Pharmaceuticals 21
Randgold Resources 191t
Ratarukki (steel production, 2002) 99t
raw materials 34, 91, 94

Rawlings, J. 183, 189
Raymonds (men's formal wear) 82
ready-to-cook (RTC) products 205
ready-to-serve (RTS) products 199, 205
real estate 154, 159t
Reckendress 144
red tape 94
reforestation 103, 107, 109
regional development 156
regionalism 13–15
Rehan 144
Reichl, M. xv, 240(n1)
relationship-based market-entry 114–27, 223–4
  business networks 124
  ethical issues 125
  learning the hard way 123
  in practice 124–5
  role (in market-entry) 123–5
relationships and connections 214f, 255–7, 262
  driver of global business success 235, 236f, **238–9**
  interlinkages of concepts 263t
  map of interlinked sub-codes network 262f
  'second-order concept' (sub-code) 261
Reliance Industries 76, 79
religion 18, 74, 128, 177, 223
repeat business/sales 77, 150
reputation 224, 253
research and development 81, 123, 221, 224, 244, 254, 255
  sealing products 117
research institutions 116
reservation/booking systems 156–7, 160, 164t, 246, 256
Residence Inn 156
Resolute Ltd (Australia) 184t
'resource' (economic term) 49
resource allocation 118, 142, 147
responsiveness (strategic) 46, 47t, 48
restaurants 68, 121, 197, 198
retail
  chains 80, 242
  goods and services 141
  investors 79
  travel networks 157
retailers/retailing 143, 150, 169f, 170, 178, 199, 245, 246, 248
  food 196–7
Rio Grande do Sul 101, 103, 106
Rio de Janeiro 100, 102, 103, 105
Riograndense 106t

risk 27, 31, 127, 159, 159t, 162, 164t, 165, 174, 178, 188, 189, 221, 224, 229, 230, 233, 253, 256
  de-risking strategies 78, 80, 83
  see also hedging
Riva 99t, 100
Rizwanul Islam 258(n19)
Roland Berger Strategy Consultants (Vienna) xv, 54, 59(n5)
rolling mills (steel) 104t
Romania 28, 29t, 55, 130, 130t, 146, 171, 172, 173, 175, 177, 179, 230
Rome 19
Rowntree, L. 155
rubber/rubber products 10, 115, 117, 118, 121
Ruggiero, R. 14
Rugman, A. 2
rupee 204
rural areas 31
Rushmore, S. 153
Russia/Russian Federation 11, 15, 28, 29t, 30, 35t, 36, 97, 136, 143, 146, 170, 171, 177, 178, 179, 212, 223, 230, 232, 239, 243, 252
  E7 group 27
  economic crisis (1998) 173, 174, 221, 230, 232
  entry-mode choice (hotel companies) 160
  export market for Turkish paints 130, 130t, 132
  licensed premium segment (beer) 176
  steel production companies (2002) 99t
Russian government 173
Rust, R.T. 43, 46

Sabanci çimsa 36
Safeway 197
SAIL 98t, 99t
Sajtos, L. 47n
salaries 68, 82, 162
sales 35t, 77, 83, 86, 114, 125, 136, 142, 147, 148, 156, 176, 218, 244
  Betek Boya 131
  direct 110
sales concepts 147
sales force 68
sales growth 218
sales networks 64, 146–7
sales promotion 44, 148, 244
sales representatives 135
sales turnover/volume 76, 150
Salzgitter 99t

SAMAX Gold, Inc. 183–4, 184t
Samsung 2, 35, 35t, 82, 83, 253, 255
San, Mr 148
São Paulo 103, 105
São Paulo: São Judas Tadeu steel plant 102
Sarajevo 61
SAS/Radisson alliance 160
Saudi Arabia 99t, 176
Sayreville 106t
SBI 76
scales 44, 86
Scandinavia 161
Schirmer, O. 107
Schlegelmilch, B.B. 85
scholarship (Western bias) 17
Schumpeter, J.A. 222, 225(n11), 255
sciences
  behavioural 214
  physical 213–14
  social 214
sealing products 114, 115–16, 117, 120, 121, 126, 127
Second World War 9
  post-war era (1945–) 13, 16, 115, 153, 213
SEIVA (1971–) 103, 109
self-employment 75
Serbia 146
Serious Fraud Office (Ghana) 187
service orientation 162
services 74, 93, 121, 148, 157, 159, 221–2, 230, 247
Severstal (steel production, 2002) 99t
shadow economy 18, 31–3
Shanghai 31, 121, 122
Shanghai Baosteel 99t, 100
Shapiro, B. 43
shared values 135, 256
shareholders 57, 76, 187, 189, 195, 204
Shek, J. 115
Sheraton Hotels 154
Shikari, S. 203–4
Shopper's Stop 80–1
short-selling 187
Shougang Bethlehem (steel production, 2002) 99t
Siderúrgica Aço-Norte 102
Siderúrgica Riograndense 101, 102
SIDOR (steel production, 2002) 99t
Siguiri mine (Guinea) 184t, 185
Sikhs 74
Singapore 11, 12, 28, 29t, 75
Singh, M. 193
SINOPEC 35t
Sipar 104t, 106, 106t, 107

Sipsa   104t, 106
Six Continents (UK hotel chain)   154t
SKF Group (Sweden-based)   117
skills   42, 112, 236
   hard and soft   126
   managerial   93
   operational   58
   organizational   58
   soft and hard/managerial and
      technical   237
   strategic   58
Slater, S.F.   44, 85
Slovak Republic/Slovakia   28, 29t, 54,
   64, 160, 210
Slovenia   44, 45, 210
   jewellery producer   61–70, 211
Slow Cities movement   19–20
Slow Food movement   19–20
small and medium-sized companies
   (SMEs)   3, 16, 125, 160, 229
   see also subsidiary companies
SMMT (strategic marketing management
   team)   147–8, 220, 236
Snyder–Duch, J.   264(n11)
social
   class   61, 65, 66, 67f
   development   79
   groups   78
   responsibility   102–3, 112
   sciences   238
   status   157
   structure   69
socialism   11, 12, 75
socialization   135, 224
Société Générale   188
Sofrapen   144
soft drinks   170, 173
software   264(n10)
sole ownership   159, 159t, 160
Sony   80, 254
South Africa   28, 29t, 32, 33t, 34t, 183,
   184t, 191t
South African Breweries   170
South America   10, 97, 109, 110t, 110,
   111, 111t, 112, 230, 254
South Asia   155t
South Korea   2, 28, 29t, 32, 33,
   35, 35t, 97, 100, 109, 199
   direct costs of steel production
      (2001)   98t
   E7 group   27
   share of world exports and imports
      (1995–2001)   33t, 34t
   steel production companies
      (2002)   99t
South-East Asia   111t

Soviet bloc   161
Soviet Union/USSR   11, 15, 100
   collapse/dissolution   9, 128
   former   28, 29t, 54, 136
Spain   15, 36, 55
special occasions   65
specialty seekers   66
specialty steel   106, 107, 108
speculation/speculators   187, 188
Spins   201
sponsorship   177
Sri Lanka   15
Sriram, V.   x, xv–xvi, 240(n1)
Stamford (Connecticut)   205
Stan, S.   85
Stanchart   73
standardization   16, 142, 159, 162,
   214, 222, 239, 248
Starbucks   202
starting emerging markets (SEMs)
   28, 29t, 30t, 30
Starwood Hotels and Resorts
   154, 154t
Stary Melnik ('old miller' beer
   brand)   175–7, 223, 244, 246–7
state, the   11
state of economy (foreign target
   market)   90t, 92
state-owned enterprises   12, 48, 105,
   127, 161
status   63, 65
Status Quo (magazine)   64, 68
steel   12, 36, 80, **97–113**, 220,
   230, 237, 255
   continuous casting   102
   direct costs of production (2001)   98t
   global trends   97–101
   largest world producers (2002)   99t
   long products   97, 102, 103, 107,
      108, 108t, 112
   restructuring   97, 99, 107
   rolled products   102
Steel Dynamics   98t
Steel Manufacturing Association ('North
   America')   107
Stelco (steel production, 2002)   99t
Stern, L.W.   141
Stiglitz, J.   17
stock exchanges   75, 109
stock-keeping units (SKUs)   199,
   201, 205
strategic marketing management team
   (SMMT)   147–8, 220, 236
strategic priorities   230
Su, Z.   241(n5)
sub-markets   65

subsidiary companies   114, 116, 117, 127
  see also US hotel companies
subsidies   14–15, 90, 94, 97
'success diamond'   4f, 4–5
success factors / drivers of business success   3, 4f, 4–6, 214, 250–9
  coding process   261, 261t, 264(n9)
  common denominators   6
  'fifteen success factors'   261, 262, 262f, 263t
  first-order concepts   260, 261, 262, 262f, 263t
  map of interlinked sub-codes network   262f
  markets   4, 4f, 5, 214f, 227–34, 260, 261, 261t, 262f, 263t
  matrix   261, 262, 264(n14)
  methodology   219f, 219, 260–4
  operations   4, 4f, 5, 214f, 242–9, 260, 261, 261t, 262f, 263t
  organization   4f, 4–5, 214f, 218–26, 260, 261, 261t, 262f, 263t
  people   4, 4f, 5, 214f, 235–41, 260, 261, 261t, 262f, 263t
  reliability coefficients   261, 261t, 264(n10)
  second-order concepts (sub-codes)   261, 262, 262f, 263t
  third-level indicators   260
  visualization of coded information   261, 262f
Sumitomo (steel production, 2002)   99t
superior technology   35
supermarkets   196, 198, 199, 200, 201, 206, 245, 256
supplier contracts   245
supplier and distribution networks   214f, 242, 243f, 245–6, 248, 262
  interlinkages of concepts   263t
  map of interlinked sub-codes network   262f
  'second-order concept' (sub-code)   261
suppliers   120, 124, 239, 242, 248
  beer industry   168, 169f
  global   245
supply   68, 107
  gold   191
  steel   98
sustainable advantage   154
Switzerland   20, 55, 75
SWOT (strength, weakness, opportunities, threats) analysis   66, 67f, 211

Syria   135, 146
Szechenyl Plan (Hungary)   161

t-test analysis   87, 88, 89t, 90t
Ta-Chong automobile company (Shanghai)   122
Taco Bell (fast-food chain)   197–8
Tai Tsuang Company (Taiwan)   117
Taichung (Taiwan)   114, 127n
'tailoring'   178, 256
Taiwan   28, 29t, 33, 220, 221, 223–4, 256
  'competing *in* China, not *against* China'   122
  competitors of Mao Shun   117
  cross-strait economic relations   119–20
  export-orientation (1970s-)   115
  rubber industry   115
  trade surplus   119
  see also Mao Shun Corporation
Taiwanese expatriates   120–1
Taiwanese government   116, 118
Tajikistan   137(n6)
Talinli, I.   139(n46)
Tan Range Exploration Corporation (Canada), 184t
Tang   77
Tanzania   184t, 185, 190
Taparia, H.   203–4
tariffs   127, 149, 230
Taşdemir-Çaloğlu, H.   xiii
taste   135, 210, 215(n4)
Tasty Bite[(R)] Eatables Limited (TBEL, India)   xiv, xvii
  background   193–4
  bankruptcy; acquisition by Unilever   204
  commitment to becoming world class   255
  competent personnel   237
  competition: need for renewal   206
  customers   203f
  customization of marketing   243–4
  flexibility and creativity   253
  innovativeness   222, 223
  launch in USA   200–4
  market selection process   228
  markets network   228f
  multi-segment approach   231, 253
  from obligation to opportunity   193–206
  operations network   243f
  organization network   219f
  people network   236f

Index

positioning idea (US market) 197–8, 223
relationship focus 256
staying the course (1999–2003) 205–6
supplier and distribution networks 245–6
see also Preferred Brands International
Tastybite.com 206
Tata 76, 79–80
Tata Indica 77, 80, 81, 83
Tata Salt 79
Tata Steel 80, 99–100
tax evasion 18
tax benefits/incentives 90t, 90, 92, 115
taxation 32, 194, 224
taxis/taxi-drivers 79, 83
TCL International (Chinese television manufacturer) 254
team spirit 126, 133, 224, 237
Teberebie mine (Ghana) 184t, 185
Techint (steel production, 2002) 99t
technology 30, 36, 59, 81, 101, 112, 146, 156, 161, 210, 213, 221, 254
  German and Austrian 145
  new 154
technology cycles (Schumpeter) 222
technology transfer 254
Technoplas A.Ş. 147t
telecommunications 76, 222
Televisa 36
television 136, 137, 173, 176, 177
television manufacturers 254
television sets 2–3, 36
terms of trade 13
Tesco 66, 67
Tetteh, K. 187
textiles 10, 79, 121
Thai Table (brand name) 206
Thailand 28, 29t, 33, 75, 115, 206
Thomas, A.R. 20, 24–5(n62)
Thomson SA 254
Three Links (PRC-Taiwan) 120
Thums Up 83
Thyssen 102
Thyssen-Krupp 99t, 100
tight–loose structure 250, **251–2**
time 17, 63, 126, 129, 170, 210, 213
Timex 73, 80
Tissen 144
Titan Watches 80
top/senior management 5, 47t, 86, 115, 126, 137, 147, 148, 204, 220, 235, 251
Toronto Dominium (bank) 108
Toronto Stock Exchange 109, 183

tourism 10, 156, 161, 246
  revenues (Hungary versus UK) 161
  see also hotels
tourists 63, 64, 65, 67f, 68, 75, 246
TQM 126
Trabzon 136
trade, *see* world trade
trade unions 12
Trader Joe's 197, 200
training ix, 112, 126, 142, 147, 158, 162, 164t, 192, 222, 236, 237, 238, 244
transaction costs 141, 239, 242
transition economies (TEs) 18, 28, 30, 44, 48, 49, 59, 62, 132, 211, 212, 213, 221, 246
  entry-mode choice 160
  PRC 127
  terminal point 41–2, 210–11, 216(n10)
Transparency International 32
transport 149
transportation 12, 31, 134, 172, 213, 255
  PRC–Taiwan 120, 126
travel 155, 155t
travel agents 157, 164t
treaties (Turkey–Azerbaijan) 129
Triad concept (Ohmae) 21, 26, 35, 227
trial-to-purchase ratio (TPR) 201
Trompenaars, F. 17, 23(n36)
Tropicana 195
trust 123, 135, 229, 239, 245, 255, 256
TSE 145
Tsuang Hine Company (Taiwan) 117
Turkey 2, 12, 15, 28, 29t, 32, 33, 221, 238, 239, 253, 254
  Anadolu Efes A.Ş. (international market entry) **168–81**
  Betek Boya (attractiveness of Azerbaijan market) **128–39**
  five hundred major industrial enterprises 131, 138(n29)
  paint consumption 132
  paint exports (2000–02) 130t
  paint industry 130
  product and trade name franchising (Kompen) **140–51**
  share of world exports and imports (1995–2001) 33t, 34t
  use of PVC products in construction industry 143–5
Turkey: State Ministry for Relationships with Turkic Republics 138(n11)
Turkish Grand Rabbinate 177

Turkish Standards Institute 133
Turkmenistan 146

UBS 188
Ukraine 28, 29t, 30, 97, 136, 146, 171, 174, 175, 178, 179, 230, 244
   export market for Turkish paints 130, 130t, 132
   steel production companies (2002) 99t
Ulker group 254
uncertainty 54, 126, 128, 224, 227, 232-3
   see also management of environmental uncertainty; volatility
UNCTAD 33, 33t, 34t
unemployment 12, 161
'Uniform System of Accounts for Hotels' 163
Unilever 2, 73, 78, 79, 193, 195, 204, 205, 232
United Arab Emirates 88, 176
United Kingdom 13, 42, 44, 55, 88, 116, 117, 142, 143
   fewer visitors than Hungary 161
   gold-mining companies 191t
   steel production companies (2002) 99t
United States 14, 20, 42, 49, 50, 62, 74, 88, 94, 97-101, 109-12, 114-17, 141, 142, 156, 157, 160, 162, 163, 177, 184t, 194, 221, 223, 237, 244, 245, 252, 256
   direct costs of steel production (2001) 98t
   food industry (mega trends) 196-7
   Gerdau Group expansion 104t
   gold-mining companies 191t
   Indian, Pakistani, Bangladeshi expatriates 196
   locations of Gerdau steel production 106t
   positioning idea for Tasty Bite 197-8
   protectionism 103, 104, 228, 230
   securities laws 187
   steel production companies (2002) 99t
   see also hotel industry (USA); Preferred Brands International (PBI)
universities
   Baltimore University x, xv
   Budapest University of Economic Sciences and Public Administration xi
   'external resource' 224
   German 147
   Graz: Technical University xv
   Hacettepe University 151(n11)
   Harvard University 43
   Hofstra University (USA) xiv
   Istanbul: Boğaziçi University xii, xiii, xiv, 133
   Istanbul: Marmara University x, xii, xv, 263(n8)
   Johns Hopkins University xi
   Konya: Selcuk University xvi
   Lahore University of Management Sciences (LUMS) xi
   Linz: Johannes Kepler University x, xiii
   Maribor University (Slovenia) xii, xvii
   Morgan State University (USA) xiv, xvii
   National Kaohsiung First University of Science and Technology (Taiwan) xiii
   Taiwanese 118
   Turkish 147
Ünüsan, Ç. xvi
urban areas/urbanization 30-1, 132
Uruguay 101, 103, 104t, 106t, 107, 112
US Department of Commerce 28
US hotel companies
   best practices (USA) 152-67
   brand-building 246, 247
   competent personnel 237
   competitive advantage 156
   entry modes 159t, 164t
   expansion in Central Europe 160-3
   external resource access 224
   flexible market entry 230
   government policy 156
   Hungary 160-5
   industry characteristics 154
   international travel patterns 155t
   international chains 154t
   location 155-6, 161, 163, 164t, 165
   management 157-8, 162-3, 164t
   market screening and selection 155-6
   market segments and brands 156-7, 161-2, 163, 164t, 165
   marketing mix 156-7
   markets network 228f
   multiple segment approach 231
   operations network 243f
   organization network 219f
   organization and structure 163, 164t
   overview 153-4
   ownership structure 159-60, 163, 164t

people network 236f
quality focus 222
relationship focus 256
resources 164t
strategy 164t
success factors 167, 164t
supplier and distribution
 networks 246
tight–loose structure 251
see also companies
US Steel (USX) 98t, 98t, 99, 100–1
US–Canada Free Trade Area 104
Usiba 103, 104t, 106t
Usiminas 99t, 100, 102, 104, 105, 111
Usinor (France) 98t, 99
USS Košice (Slovakia) 100
utilities 94
Uzbekistan 137(n6), 146

V & N do Brasil (steel production, 2002) 105t
vacation benefits 162
value chain 57, 118
value systems 13, 212
value-added tax 62
value-addition 122, 194, 230, 254
Vasconcellos, P. 107
Vasudevan, A. xvi, 193, 194, 195, 204, 205
Vasudevan, M. xvi–xvii, 194, 195, 201, 205
 'AKM' (Ashok, Kartik, Meera) 195, 196, 200, 204, 205
vegetables 193, 205, 245
Veka 144
vendors 76, 78
Venezuela 99t
vertical connections 255
vertical integration 142
vertical quasi integration 141
Vestel 2–3, 36
Vietnam 9, 28, 29t
villages 78, 80
Vilnius 41
'vinyl' (PVC products): use in Turkish construction industry 143–5
Vitanta S.A. 174, 175
vodka 170, 173
volatility 29, 245, 251, 252
VW 120

wages 20, 62, 255
Wanhill, S. 156
warrants 189, 190
Warsame, M. xvii

Warsteiner Premium Verum (beer) 176, 247
Warwick Business School x
Washington (state) 200
Washington DC 186
websites 82, 131, 133, 192(n2), 206, 216(n16)
Werther, W.B. 215(n4)
West, the 252
Western Europe 21, 45, 94, 109, 143, 162, 163
Westin Hotels 154
Westside 80–1
Wheaton River Minerals 191t
Wheel (Unilever brand) 232
Whirlpool 2, 73, 82
whisky 173
Whitby (Canada) 106t
white goods 2, 81, 143, 253
Whole Foods 197
wholesale sector/wholesalers 48, 64, 178
Wild Oats 197
Wilkinson, B. 216(n14)
windows 140, 143–4, 145, 146, 147, 148, 149
wine 175, 197
wine and spirits 170
Wipro 2
women 75, 78
work ethic 237
workers
 blue-collar 126
 white-collar 63
workforce 145
working capital 78
working conditions 20
World Bank (WB) 16–17, 29, 183, 186
world class (emphasis on being) 250, 253–5, 259
world trade 20, 26, 128
 'counter-trade agreements' 90
 'free trade' 13–14, 19
 'preferential agreements' 14
 'trade' 21, 28, 30, 129, 138(n11)
 'trade agreements' 89t, 90, 91, 94
 'trade fairs' 136
 'trade liberalization' 12, 129
World Trade Organization (WTO) 13, 14, 19
 General Agreement of Tariffs and Trade (GATT) 14
 'non-trade-distorting' subsidies 15
 PRC entry (2001) 126, 127

world trade trends 9–25
 EM perspective 9
 'first curve' and 'second curve'
  countries 22
 global shift 21–2
 globalization and
  anti-globalization 15–21
 history 9–13
 integration and disintegration
  attempts 13–15
 'key emerging second-curve
  countries' 28, 29t
 regionalism 13–15
Wortzel, L. 95(n4)
Wuhan (steel production,
 2002) 99t
Wührer, G.A. xvii, 240(n1)
Wyndham International (hotels) 154

Yaprak, A. 212–13, 218, 225(n3)
Yemen 146
yen 204
Yilmaz, B. 139(n46)
youth/young people 177,
 214, 215(n4)
Yu, L. 155, 158, 166(n28)

Yuan Cherng Company
 (Taiwan) 117
Yugoslavia (former) 15, 28, 29t,
 61, 62, 69

Zagreb 61
Zaparozstahl (steel production,
 2002) 99t
Zimbabwe 183, 184t, 185, 190
Zimbabwe Stock Exchange 183
zip codes 202–3
Zivko, T. 18, 24(n44)
Zlatarna Celje (Slovene jeweller,
  1844–) 61–70, 211
 background 62
 Czech jewellery market research 64
 market-entry strategy 66–7
 marketing-mix strategy 67
 product, price, place 67–8
 promotion 68
 strategic goals 62
 SWOT analysis 67f
 target position in Czech market 63, 66
zlatnitvi (small jewellery shops) 64
Zou, S. 85, 225(n1)
Zver, M. 18, 24(n44)